ADVANCED HUNTING

TIPS & TECHNIQUES

ADVANCED HUNTING
TIPS & TECHNIQUES

Robert Elman

WINCHESTER PRESS
An Imprint of
NEW CENTURY PUBLISHERS, INC.

Library of Congress Cataloging in Publication Data
Elman, Robert.
   1001 hunting tips.
   Includes index.
   1. Hunting. I. Title. II. Title: One thousand one
hunting tips. III. Title: One thousand and one
hunting tips.
SK33.E47 1983 799.2 83-6920
ISBN 0-8329-0347-7

To Danny

Contents

SMALL GAME

Squirrels

Where squirrels are plentiful and the hunting pressure hasn't been very heavy, I usually hunt bannertails with a shotgun rather than a rifle because running or leaping targets make better sport. I also prefer a shotgun where the woods are so thick that I may seldom get more than a flickering sight of a moving, partially obscured target. As a rule, I use my 20-gauge Magnum, which is chambered for 3-inch shells. In tall, thick woods I like short or long Magnums loaded, respectively, with 1⅛ or 1¼ ounces of No. 6 shot. Where Magnums aren't needed, I use standard high-velocity loads with an ounce of No. 6's.

Any bore size from 12 to 28 will do nicely—I just happen to like my fast-swinging 20-gauge double—but whatever gauge you use, the charges ought to be heavy for clean kills in the squirrel woods, and No. 6 pellets give you an ideal combination of dense enough pattern with sufficient energy per pellet.

When hunting squirrels in an area where I can walk a few fields and edge cover for rabbits and ringnecks, I often use a 12-gauge pump gun with a variable choke device. For most shots at squirrels, the average hunter will do best with a modified choke.

Where squirreling with a rifle is both permissible and practical, a rimfire is the obvious choice. I generally use standard-velocity Long Rifle cartridges with solid bullets, though I sometimes switch to high-velocity cartridges where the shots are apt to be long or when the hunting has been good enough that I restrict myself to head shots. I don't use hollow-points. They aren't needed and they can waste good meat. On occasion, however, I've used a .22 Magnum where there was a chance I'd get shots at chucks or other game in the same neighborhood on the same day. (Yes, there are states where the squirrel season is open during the warm months generally associated with chuck hunting.)

My squirrel rifle is equipped with a 3–6X variable scope. I most often have it set at its lowest power. (Depending on whether most shots are short or long in a given neighborhood, 2½X to 4X is considered the best magnification.) I keep it sighted in at 100 yards because I'm familiar enough with the rifle to score at half that distance by holding it a hair low and at more than 100 yards by holding it a bit high. I've used the same rifle on crows and rabbits. But in many regions, a 2½X scope zeroed at 50 yards would be a better choice.

Using a rifle and restricting yourself to head shots can make squirreling a very challenging sport, but I think the most challenging approach of all is handgunning. I've killed squirrels at short range with an iron-sighted pistol, but I recommend using a scope. You don't want much magnification; 2X is plenty, and I prefer 1.3X. Like most people, I can't make consistent hits on small targets from more

For hunting squirrels in thick woods, the author prefers a shotgun to a rifle because shots often have to be made quickly at moving, partly obscured targets like the squirrel in this photo.

A .22 rimfire rifle loaded with standard-velocity LR cartridges is excellent for squirreling. The most popular scope magnification is 2½X, but in sparse cover like this many hunters prefer 4X.

than about 35 yards with a handgun, even when I cushion my hands against a good steady rest such as a tree stump. Greater magnification doesn't help; in fact, a higher-power scope just exaggerates the apparent wobbling of the sight picture. As for the handgun to use, any reliable, accurate .22 revolver or auto will serve nicely.

Squirrel dogs have long been out of fashion in my part of the country, but they're still used by a few scattergunners in some regions, and I feel they add to the sport. Any small, quiet, close-working dog with a good nose can be trained to hunt squirrels. A pup that shows enthusiasm won't need much training. Mongrels are often used. Those with some terrier blood are likely to combine good size and working style.

A fairly drab-colored dog is best, because squirrels can see bright splotches quite far off, and their reaction is to hide in a tree before the dog has scented them or you have sighted them.

Squirreling with a dog is best early in the season, when the squirrels are spending much of their time on the ground, scampering about and burying nuts. The dog will usually scent game and will tree the squirrel before you can see it. Sometimes the squirrel will then scurry or leap through the branches, presenting a sporty shot-gunning target. Just about as often it will flatten itself against the trunk or a branch and look down inquisitively at the dog. You can then approach quietly from the opposite side and get into shooting position while the squirrel's attention is riveted on the dog.

With a dog, fox squirrels are easier game than grays because they spend more time on the ground, generally inhabit more open woods, and aren't quite as fast or acrobatic in the trees. When a fox squirrel is spooked on the ground, it's apt to head for a den tree rather than the nearest tree and—if the dog doesn't overtake it before it can get aloft—it will probably stay put in that same tree. Personally, I feel the sport is more challenging with dogs where gray squirrels prevail.

Without a dog, I like to arrive in the woods early—the earlier the better—and just sit quietly against the base of a tree, watching and listening, until about half an hour after first light. If I haven't heard or seen anything by then, I begin walking as slowly and quietly as possible, with lots of pauses. It's really the same technique as still-hunting for woodland deer.

For good visibility, I prefer the sun at my back. I scan everything from the ground to the treetops for a movement, a patch of gray fur, a bump that looks too soft to be part of a tree, a tail twitching or being ruffled by a breeze. And I listen for chatter and for the light, scratchy sounds of running or climbing. This technique is recommended whether you use a shotgun or a rifled arm. If it doesn't produce, sit quietly again for a little while just before dusk. Squirrels are most active at first and last light.

Sometimes, when stealthy walking produces nothing but fatigue, it makes sense to blunder your way into a stand of feeding trees and nesting or den trees, making no attempt to be quiet. But once in there, sit down and be silent for 15 minutes or so. This seems to give squirrels the impression that danger has come and gone. Soon they venture out to feed, play, or bask in the sun on the higher branches.

This handgunner has just connected. A close look at the photo will reveal a falling squirrel. Garbed in camouflage, the hunter arrived in the woods very early in the morning and played a waiting-watching-listening game—one good way to limit out.

Nutting time is great for squirreling. Loose, recently fallen leaves on the forest floor may almost conceal a bannertail gleaning acorns but the animal's rustling sounds reveal its location. Squirrels foraging in mast tend to be nervous but you can get running shots as they go up and through the trees.

I like to canoe for squirrels, drifting along a creek while watching the brush, vines, and trees on the shoreline. Another good way to hunt silently is to walk a dry, sandy creek bed.

When I'm hunting with a partner, we generally keep about 40 yards between us. That way, each of us may push squirrels toward the other hunter. I prefer to hunt only with partners I know well, however. It's comforting to be sure the other hunter will be as careful as I am about where a load of shot goes.

Just as a squirrel in a turning-wheel cage can walk endlessly without getting anywhere, a hunter can follow a squirrel around and around a shielding tree trunk without much hope of a payoff. A ploy that is more likely to get the game back into view is to toss a stone or small branch to the far side of the trunk. It will often send the startled squirrel scampering around toward you.

This is a fox squirrel—a species that grows larger than the gray squirrel. It usually inhabits slightly more open woods than the gray and, when spooked on the ground, is apt to scamper for a den tree rather than the nearest tree.

I used to hunt with a man who could click, cluck, squeak, and chatter like a squirrel. I've never mastered the language, though I can manage a passable squeak by sucking the back of my hand. And sometimes squirrels will answer or inquisitively approach the sound of two stones rapidly clicked together, or a coin rapped sharply on a gun butt.

For my money, a bellows-type commercial squirrel call is much better. Cup a hand over the open end of the call, rap the bulb end rapidly against your other hand, and you'll produce squirrel chatter. Don't overdo it. If your call is answered, repeat it briefly and then be still. I've used this method when rifle-hunting as well as scattergunning. In some open woods not long ago, I was answered by a scolding quite high and far away, and I spotted a gray squirrel on a limb about 50 yards off. Only the head and a curve of twitching tail showed, but I had a scoped .22 with me that day and I got lucky.

When snow is on the ground, I watch for squirrel tracks. Otherwise, the only signs that seem to pay off for me are nests, den trees, and signs of "nutting"—that is, diggings or gnawed acorns, hickories, and the like.

Nutting time, by the way, is also a good time to look for squirrels around fruit trees.

Here are four types of commercial squirrel calls. The one at far left is worked by striking wood on wood. The others can be rapped against almost any object. The author's favorite is the bellows type. He get his best results by holding the tubular end, slightly cupping his hand over it, and rapidly hitting the accordion end against his other hand or his leg.

I should mention that I look for nests only as an indication that squirrels are around. I've done my share of stupid things, but I haven't yet been unsportsmanlike enough to shoot into a nest, hoping to kill an unseen target. A squirrel shot in its nest will rarely tumble out, and any nest-shooter who climbs a tree and reaches into a nest in the hope of retrieving a squirrel richly deserves any bites and scratches he gets.

Rabbits
and Hares

The two shotguns I use for rabbits are a 12-gauge and a 20, though a 16 would be just as good, and a really adept scattergunner can collect cottontails with a 28-gauge. My 20 is a double, choked improved and modified, a good combination for hunting amid the slash piles, greenbrier tangles, brush, shrubs, and high weeds of typical cottontail country. My 12 is a pump with a variable choke, and it's a good choice for open fields where I sometimes walk up pheasants as well as cottontails, and for a lot of open jack-rabbit terrain in the West. I've used it in Texas to alternate between jacks, cottontails, and blue quail—and I left the choke set at full because I couldn't seem to get within 40 yards of anything I shot at.

I also favor my 12-gauge with the choke at the modified setting for snowshoe hares (or varying hares, or snowshoe rabbits, or whatever you choose to call them) in the North. I'm sure the 20 would do about as well, but I suspect I'd be using the tighter of its barrels more often than not.

When I go beagling for cottontails, I use low-brass No. 6's. When I hunt without dogs, I generally stay with No. 6 shot, but I favor the heavier charges with a few more pellets per load—the same sort of thing I recommend for squirrels. High-velocity shells are also recommended for jacks and snowshoes, and you may prefer 4's or 5's if the hares in your region are big and the shots tend to be long. (Jack rabbits, by the way, are not true rabbits but hares. They were originally called "jackass rabbits" by settlers who marveled at their long ears. Snowshoe hares are also hares, despite the regional name "snowshoe rabbit." America's only native rabbits are the many varieties of cottontails and their close relatives, such as the swamp rabbits and marsh rabbits, which belong to the same genus.)

Here's a bonus tip for dogless hunters: Cottontails, like most prey species, have bulging eyes set far to the sides of the skull so that they can see enemies approaching from the rear, and they also have extremely keen hearing. Yet you can stalk as close as this in high grass or brushy ground cover because the rabbit will freeze before it runs—hoping to escape detection. Move in slowly and obliquely, not straight at the animal, in order to preserve its illusion that it hasn't been seen. This one was an easy target for a camera in one hand and a rimfire pistol in the other.

For jacks, which are not only bigger but tougher than other hares and rabbits, many riflemen use hollow-points, some use .22 Magnums, and some even use .22 centerfire rifles or pistols of the sort generally associated with long-range chuck shooting. For cottontails and even for snowshoe hares, however, a standard-velocity .22 Long Rifle cartridge with a solid bullet is generally all you need.

I prefer a 2½X scope for most rabbit hunting with a rifle. But in parts of the West and Midwest where the terrain is open, I would choose a 4X model or a variable.

Some hunters enjoy tracking rabbits on snow, and even a snowshoe hare that has turned winter-white may be spotted by its dark eyes and ear tips, though its body is well camouflaged and it may be sitting in screening cover. Having spotted a snowshoe hare, or any hare or rabbit, it's often possible to stalk within handgunning distance. A .22 rimfire revolver or auto is fine for this.

Here's another bonus tip for dogless hunters: Early-season hunting for snowshoe hares is sometimes most productive because the animals may not have turned completely winter-white. Their patchy color is perfect camouflage in some cover but it can make them all the more visible after an early snow.

Some hunters use scoped handguns, especially if jack rabbits are the game. I usually don't because shots often have to be made very fast. But long-range spotting and shooting at jacks with a scoped .22 Magnum can be rewarding sport.

With cottontails especially, scattergunning misses are often caused by swinging ahead of the target and overshooting as the bouncing, zigzagging rabbit abruptly switches its course and vanishes. A smooth swing and good understanding of lead are of little avail in this situation, so a majority of experienced rabbit gunners—whether they realize it or not—are snap-shooters. They knock over rabbits the way many of us knock down grouse or woodcock, by getting on target fast and snapping off a shot the instant the muzzle passes it.

A successful shotgunner carries home a snowshoe hare. High-velocity loads of No. 6 shot are recommended. Look for trails where the hares find winter browse—the bark, twigs, and tender tips of such plants as pine, spruce, fir, white cedar, aspen, willow, and birch. Also comb fir and cedar swamps.

Another method that works for some hunters is to swing with a running rabbit, put the bead on it as it bounds, judge where it will land, pull ahead to that spot, and fire. It has to be done in one smooth, quick action. Fast reflexes help.

This rifleman holds a pair of jacks. Jack rabbits are big, tough hares. The author recommends high-velocity .22 LR hollow-points or .22 Magnums.

For me, the finest rabbit hunting is beagling, and three or four beagles are that many times better than one. I'm of the school that won't dress a rabbit in the field, much less reward a dog with a bite of raw meat, because there's a hazard to dogs in this practice. Watery cysts called "bladder worms" are sometimes found in a rabbit's body cavity. They're larval tapeworms of a kind that can't mature in a rabbit and are harmless to man, but are very dangerous to dogs.

Another rabbit parasite—fortunately, one that is no longer common—is the *Bacterium tularense*, the producer of tularemia, or "rabbit fever." It's carried from rabbit to rabbit by ticks, fleas, and other biting insects. The meat of an infected rabbit is perfectly safe to eat if thoroughly cooked, but it is possible for a human to contract this disease through a cut or abrasion. For this reason, some hunters wear rubber gloves when dressing or skinning a rabbit. Such precautions are no longer needed, at least in the Northern states, unless your newspaper or state game department announces signs of an outbreak. The insect carriers hibernate after the first heavy frosts, and any infected rabbits will die within a week. Thus, where the hunting season opens after the frosts have arrived, there can be no danger.

Cottontails provide splendid sport for a handgun hunter. Any reliable, accurate rimfire revolver or auto will do nicely. Since these rabbits aren't as big or tough as jacks, standard-velocity .22 LR cartridges with solid bullets are all you ever need.

When hunting with beagles, there's a strong temptation to follow the dogs every time they start to chase a cottontail. This is precisely the wrong tactic unless your dogs are too pushy—in which case the rabbit will dive for a hole and whatever you do probably won't matter. If your dogs press along with merry, bugling determination but no terrifying rush, a cottontail will most often move in a rough circle of no more than a few hundred yards. It is traveling through its home grounds, confident that it can elude its present pursuers just as it has eluded predators. You won't keep up with the dogs or the

Don't try to follow the beagles when they push a cottontail out. The rabbit will move in rough circles, coming around to a point near where it was started if the dogs don't push too hard. Just wait, as this hunter did, near that spot and where the ground visibility is good.

rabbit anyhow, so just wait in a fairly open spot or on the nearest little rise, preferably close to where the hounds first got hot. The rabbit will probably come bounding back, presenting a shot.

The small, dark marsh rabbit and big, pale swamp rabbit, both close relatives of the cottontail, range from Virginia to Florida and westward into Texas. Their common names are a clue to likely hunting areas. These hunters are preparing to go beagling for marsh rabbits on a North Carolina island.

A young snowshoe hare will often behave like a cottontail when pursued by dogs. An older, more experienced one will often move over a much greater radius. Its first circle may cover a mile and never bring the game within your view. Find a fair vantage point commanding possible crossings. Try to stand where you'll be inconspicuous, if not hidden, and be patient. Subsequent circles will shrink. The chase may be quick or it may last for hours.

An exception to the rule occurs if the hounds soon move out of your hearing and seem to have taken a fairly straight course. Sometimes an old, experienced snowshoe hare runs straight out for quite a distance before circling. If this seems to be the case, you'll be well advised to follow for a while and then take a stand where the hound music again grows loud.

For cottontails, many of us prefer small dogs that can squirm through low tangles without any real effort. The so-called "13-inch beagles" are great for this. But hounds for snowshoe hares should have more leg, more stamina, and strong voices. Bear in mind that they may have to plow through snow drifts and make long chases. Foxhounds, 15-inch beagles, and beagle-foxhound crossbreeds are excellent.

When hunting cottontails with friends other than dogs, you can stage a rabbit drive. Unlike a pheasant drive, this doesn't require standers to intercept the game, because a rabbit's first defense is to freeze at the approach of danger, hoping to escape detection. It moves when it senses that the hope is gone, and by then, you'll generally be quite close. Just form a line, spacing the hunters at wide intervals, and walk through fields, brushy meadows, and other promising patches of low cover. While jumping rabbits this way, you may also walk up pheasants or other game.

As a rule, jack rabbits are easily spotted without dogs. Besides, they can outrun dogs and they don't usually circle, so dogs can be more hindrance than help. I just go out and look for them wherever cover and food are adequate. If I'm hunting with a handgun or rifle and I flush one instead of seeing it at a distance, I just stop where I am. Jacks have a habit of running no more than about 40 yards and

Jack rabbits can outrun dogs, and they don't usually circle, but in their open habitat you don't need dogs because you can spot the game easily, and often within shotgun range. Here the author holds one of the blacktailed jacks he took with a 12 gauge on the desert flats in Texas.

then stopping to look back, the way a mule deer does when it feels it's out of danger. I'm ready to shoot when it stops.

Good spots to look for rabbits are overgrown fencerows, brush or weed patches, run-down orchards, windbreaks, shrubs, slash piles—wherever there is food, a measure of concealment, and some protection from wind.

A warming trend after a cold spell makes for good hunting, regardless of which kind of rabbit you're after, and good places to look then are grassy, weedy, or brushy stretches along creeks and ditches.

When cottontails are the game, be sure to check any strips of sumac, particularly if the strips have heavy ground cover. Sumac bark has a high fat content and cottontails love it as a winter food.

In very cold weather—below about 12°—cottontails hole up in woodchuck burrows, badger dens, and the like. I generally hole up, too, in that kind of weather, but snowshoe hares don't. If you can take the cold, try combing the dense conifer swamps for snowshoes in midwinter. Jacks, too, usually stay out in cold weather. They may be warming themselves in brushy depressions, moving about searching for food, or sunning themselves on the warmer sides of hills.

When hunting alone for rabbits, as for most small game, it pays to pause now and then and switch directions slightly. This can unnerve and flush a rabbit from hiding just as it can flush a grouse, woodcock, or ringneck.

Chucks

I've read dozens—no, scores—of magazine articles touting one cartridge or another for hunting woodchucks and rockchucks. There's no such thing as a best caliber for chucks, though there's often a best caliber for an individual chuck hunter. The choice depends on a number of factors other than the generalization that chucks are rather small targets frequently shot at long range. When I was a boy I stalked my woodchucks and got close enough to kill them with an open-sighted .22 because that was the only rifle I could lay my hands on. I still enjoy hunting chucks with a rimfire, a scoped bolt-action .22 Magnum, though I switch to a centerfire for more "serious," long-range sessions. There are super-velocity buffs who swear by the .17 Remington cartridge, despite the fact that its light, wind-sensitive bullet loses a lot of speed by the time it travels 300 yards, at which range it has less velocity than the .22–250 and a comparable trajectory. Your choice of caliber ought to depend, in part, on whether you hunt chucks for the sake of hunting chucks or primarily as practice for medium to big game and, in part, on how long most of the shots are in your hunting area and how much noise the local residents will tolerate.

The aged .22 Hornet with a 45-grain bullet is still fine for 100- to 125-yard shooting, with the advantage of minimal noise. Out to 250 yards, the .222 with a 50-grain bullet and the .222 Magnum or .223 with a 55-grain bullet are excellent, and in thickly settled farm country, they have the advantage of being less noisy than the long-range numbers. Out to 350 yards, outstanding cartridges are the .22–250 with a 55-grain bullet, the .224 Weatherby with a 50- or 55-grain bullet, and the .225 Winchester with a 55-grain bullet. Then there are the medium-game calibers such as the .243 Winchester and 6mm Remington, which are accurate enough even at 400 yards or so if properly scoped and handled by an accomplished rifleman.

After caliber, the question that perplexes chuck hunters concerns the most desirable scope power. This, too, depends on several factors, though the primary consideration is range. Up to 200 yards or so, a 6X or 8X scope provides all the magnification needed. Up to

Your choice of chuck rifle and scope should depend in part on your style of hunting. This man is using a fairly heavy rifle and powerful scope, but nothing cumbersome enough to stop him from walking the Eastern farm fields where woodchucks abound.

300 yards, 8X to 10X is more than sufficient. If the ranges where you hunt are widely variable, a variable scope may be best for you—say, 3–9X or 2–10X. But for very long ranges, a 12X will serve you better once you've mastered it. The higher-power scopes developed for target shooting are optical wonders but are relatively long, heavy, and expensive. Until recently, they were also more difficult—or delicate—to operate and were sometimes fragile. Now, however, their advantages are being incorporated into solidly bridge-mounted hunting-type scopes, or "varmint" scopes, with magnifications of 15X and more. They are not at all fragile.

The focus is more critical than in lower-power scopes, but if you set it to suit your eyes at 200 yards, it will be sharp from 100 yards out, which should suffice for any chuck-shooting situation. The eye relief is shorter and the field of vision narrower with high-power scopes, but shooting practice alleviates these difficulties.

High magnification also intensifies the apparent wavering of the sight picture—not only the wobble caused by any unsteadiness of hold, but even the tremor produced by your heartbeat. Again, practice reduces the difficulty. Since you can't hit what you can't see, a sensible rule is to use as much magnification as you can handle.

But your style of hunting and type of rifle also affect scope selection. The majority of those who hunt on foot carry relatively light "sporter" rifles mounted with 6X to 10X scopes or, if the same arms are to be used for bigger game, variable power scopes set at their highest magnification. Often such a scope features a range-estimating scale on its reticle. Those who prowl the countryside in an automobile or recreational vehicle and then spend hours in one place—with a rifle stand and spotting scope—tend to favor heavy-barreled target or varmint rifles with big, powerful scopes.

There are three distinct but closely related species of marmot, more commonly called chucks, and 31 subspecies. The nine subspecies of woodchuck (*Marmota monax*) are most plentiful in the eastern half of the United States but range into the West and all the way across Canada. The rockchucks include 12 subspecies of yellow-bellied, or yellow-footed, marmot (*M. flaviventris*) and 10 subspecies of hoary marmot (*M. caligata*). The yellow-bellied mar-

Some woodchuck hunters do most of their scouting by vehicle and then remain for long periods in one spot overlooking chuck-dotted fields or pastures. These sedentary hunters take great pride in their long-range shooting. They generally use heavy-barreled varmint rifles and big, powerful scopes. This man, using a portable shooting rest, is aiming through a high-power target scope. Less delicate but equally powerful "varminting" scopes are beginning to replace target models.

mots range chiefly through South Dakota's Black Hills, the Rockies from Colorado northward, and the slopes of the Far West from California to central British Columbia. The hoary marmots range from Alaska and the Yukon down into Washington, Idaho, and western Montana.

Labels can be misleading. The woodchuck is certainly no forest animal. Its name is derived from an old Algonquian word that was, itself, neither descriptive nor accurate. Woodchucks like to dig their hibernation burrows in woodland edges, but during the warm months, they dig their burrows and do their foraging—"gorging" might be a better term—in pastures, meadows, and fields. They particularly love clover, alfalfa, and bluegrass, but also have a hardy appetite for other grasses, soybeans, garden crops, and a wide assortment of wild fruits and greens. They're the "flatlander" marmots, most successfully sought in gently rolling farm country. Yellow-bellied marmots, in the southern part of their range, can be hunted on the same kind of agricultural land. They feed heavily on alfalfa, pasture grasses, beans, and truck crops. In the northern part of their range, they share much of the habitat and many of the foods of the hoary marmots, which are truly rockchucks. They subsist on wild grasses and forbs, roots, berries, flowers, and shrubs. Mountain meadows adjacent to jumbled, rocky retreats—outcroppings, rock slides, and such—near or above the timberline are the classic places to look for rockchucks.

This Eastern woodchuck is shown in classic farmland habitat. Though chucks will gorge on a wide variety of greens, their favorite foods are clover, alfalfa, and bluegrass.

It pays to approach a mountain meadow quietly, but even so, it may appear deserted if it has been hunted recently. Such meadows are seldom "shot out," so when you see mounded chuck holes but no chucks, there's no reason to assume you're looking at a rockchucks' ghost town. The animals have probably heard you, possibly scented you, and they're down below waiting for the danger to pass. Use this time to get into a solid shooting position and then just wait quietly. After a few minutes, chuck heads will probably begin to pop up.

Whether you're hunting rockchucks or woodchucks, you should have a sturdy, easily adjustable binocular with you at all times. Opinions differ regarding the best power for field glasses. I like mine fairly compact, but also fairly powerful, and I also insist on a wide field of view—a combination that calls for a degree of compromise. For many years, the most popular binoculars for all-around hunting use were 6X35, meaning a power of 6X and an objective-lens diameter of 35mm. Improvements in optical design and construction shifted the choice to 7X35, and that's still my favorite. Now, however, further improvements have caused many outdoorsmen to favor 8X35 or even 9X35, and either of these specifications would certainly be a good choice if the same binoculars are to be used for hunting bigger mountain game such as sheep.

I've noticed that many people miss a lot of details (including game) when peering through field glasses, and also have trouble finding small objects that are dimly visible with the naked eye, especially when using a high power. The trick is to steady the instrument by pressing your thumbs or fingers against your face, and practice making very slow, steady sweeps of the terrain you're glassing. At the same time, of course, you must practice making quick and sharp focusing adjustments.

If you enjoy the sedentary style of chuck hunting, sitting in one spot while glassing wide, long vistas of farm country, a spotting scope is also a great help. My own preference is a 20X scope. Spotting scopes are available with higher and lower powers or interchangeable eyepieces, and you can also buy a zoom-type scope with variable power, but 20X suits me well enough for chuck shooting, target shooting, and on occasion, judging big-game trophies on the hoof. Like the binocular, a spotting scope is an essential piece of equipment for hunting trophy sheep and the like. Chucks provide good practice with it. The weight and power of the instrument, incidentally, demand the use of a tripod or other solid support, or it won't be steady enough for chuck-spotting.

The hoary marmot is truly a rockchuck. This photo shows one in typical habitat. Rockchucks often sit up just as woodchucks do, thus offering picturebook targets.

The spotting scope is not the only piece of equipment that needs support. For long-range shooting, you'll want an extremely steady rifle rest. Easily portable (and in many cases collapsible) unipods, bipods, and tripods are available commercially, and some shooters fashion their own.

When glassing for woodchucks or rockchucks, I try to be alert for three different sights: chucks sitting up on their haunches in the classic pose as they look, listen, and sniff for danger; chucks down on their bellies nibbling; and the mounds of dirt and patches of bare earth marking burrows. I'm willing to wait for quite some time in the hope that a chuck will emerge from a burrow. I'm also willing to wait for a chuck to interrupt its feeding and sit up. It's bound to do that before too much time elapses. At long range, a chuck with its belly

The yellow-bellied marmot is also called a rockchuck. In the southerly part of its range it can be found in agricultural fields and pastures but in the Northwest it inhabits the same kind of high, rough terrain as the hoary marmot.

on the ground can be an almost impossible target, especially if the grass or other forage is fairly high, whereas a chuck sitting up presents a perfect target.

Chucks can make a variety of small squeaking and grunting sounds plus one more audible noise, a short, shrill whistle like the sound a man makes by whistling with two fingers between his teeth. It's an alarm call. When a chuck whistles, other chucks in the neighborhood sit up to see where the danger is. By imitating this whistle, a hunter can sometimes make a chuck sit up and offer a clear target. Frankly, this has never yet worked for me with Eastern woodchucks, but a friend of mine has used the trick successfully. And I did once whistle up a rockchuck, so I guess it's worth trying. Since rockchucks have a much louder call than woodchucks, perhaps they're more inclined to take notice of a distant whistle. Or perhaps they're just more naive because they aren't as heavily hunted.

It pays to approach a mountain chuck meadow quietly and then, like this Western hunter, get into a good shooting position and wait alertly even if no rockchucks are in sight. If the meadow has any mounded chuck holes, the animals are probably in good supply and will soon emerge.

Here's a tip that pertains more often to rockchucks than woodchucks, and it also pertains to the hunting of bigger mountain game. When making a long shot at a steep angle, there's an almost inescapable tendency to shoot too high, whether the angle is uphill or downhill. You'll make fewer misses if you understand the gravitational principle involved, so try this experiment. Draw an equilateral triangle and then draw a line down its center from apex to base. The line from the base to the point where the slanting sides meet is obviously shorter than the sides themselves. Turn the triangle until this perpendicular centerline is horizontal. It represents level ground, while the angled sides represent shots uphill and downhill. Since the uphill and downhill sides are longer than the horizontal plane—level ground—it seems reasonable to hold high as a compensation for the extra distance. But this is a misconception. The force of gravity is exerted only for the distance of the horizontal plane—from your rifle to a point directly above or below the uphill or downhill target.

To put it another way, gravity pulls down on the bullet only for the distance from your rifle to where the target would be if the ground were level. I don't understand the physics involved, but it's been proved. Since the "gravity distance" is shorter than your line of sight, the bullet will have dropped less than you'd think when it reaches the target. Naturally, you still have to hold high for a very long shot, but not quite as high as you would on level terrain. So if you've been missing shots like that, try a little less hold-over.

I dislike the old-fashioned term "varmint," because it carries the connotation that an animal is a worthless pest, and I can't think of any huntable species that can be so described. Chucks are not only game animals (by my definition and, in some states, legally) but particularly delicious game animals. They metabolize all that succulent green fodder into tasty meat, just as beef cattle and rabbits do. Anyone who leaves chucks to rot in the fields or hangs them over fences suffers from gastronomic ignorance, is maltreating the landowner as well as the game, is offending the eyes of passersby (including me), and is supplying antihunters with persuasive propaganda pictures. Whether it is fried, braised, roasted, stewed, or pied, chuck is actually better than cottontail. For a magnificent treat, modify any standard hassenpfeffer recipe by adding 12 ounces of beer to the marinade; nothing beats chuck in a beer hasenpfeffer.

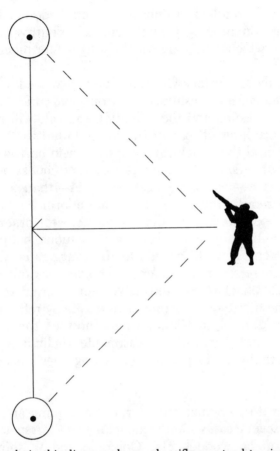

The triangle in this diagram shows why riflemen tend to aim too high at distant targets situated steeply uphill or downhill. The horizontal arrow reveals how much shorter the range would be if the target—a rockchuck, for instance—stood on level ground. The downward (gravitational) pull on the bullet is related only to the length of this horizontal plane, not to the greater distance between the shooter and the higher or lower target, represented by bull's-eyes in the diagram. The bullet therefore drops only as much as it would at the shorter, level distance. Some holdover is needed for long shots regardless of angle, but less than is needed for level shots at equal range. Another diagram, in the chapter on sheep, illustrates how this principle operates at an angle of 45° and a range of 250 yards.

Chucks that are shot in springtime—even as late as June—occasionally have patchy or balding coats. Nothing serious is wrong with them, and they're perfectly safe to eat. Although mites can transmit mange to chucks as well as to many other animals, the patchiness usually results from normal spring shedding. The baldness can result from rubbing when the chuck was burrowing or from the position in which it slept during the long winter hibernation.

I'm one of those hunters who have long advocated a regulated chuck-shooting season, lasting only from mid-June (when the chucklings are weaned and the killing of a female will no longer doom her entire litter of four or five young) until the shortening autumn days prod the chucks to leave their field burrows and dig hibernation burrows. Studies have proved that chucks do less agricultural damage—except in localized cases—than is generally supposed. Moreover, they turn and aerate enormous amounts of soil, and they provide escape and shelter dens for other wildlife. Regulated hunting could control chuck infestations, but most state game departments tend to accede to the exaggerated worries of farmers and, therefore, refuse to grant the marmot game status. In some areas, the chuck populations have been devastated. You can help assure the future of the game in your area by refraining from shooting chucks until mid-June, when most of the young are weaned. You might also impose a reasonable bag limit on yourself. Bear in mind that a chuck per acre or two signifies a healthy local population.

Some states do recognize the marmot as a game animal—but grudgingly in several cases. Connecticut and New Jersey have established a season on woodchucks, Colorado and Washington on rockchucks. However, the season opens in all of those states before the chuck litters have been weaned. Illinois has a better arrangement, closing the season in April and May. Two states have adopted truly adequate regulations. Iowa's open season runs from mid-June through October, and Pennsylvania (which has one of the country's finest game departments as well as plenty of chucks and chuck hunters) closes the season from late November until mid-June. Game-department policies are often reviewed and changed so, wherever you live, check your state's laws before setting out to hunt the various chuck species.

On a windless day or when the breeze is blowing toward them, chucks can hear a boot crackling leaves 200 yards away and can spot movement at 700 yards, so it pays to get into position quietly and then move about as little as possible.

Not only do chucks hibernate in winter; they also aestivate on very hot summer days. This doesn't apply to rockchucks of the Northern high country, but to rockchucks in the southern part of the range and, of course, to woodchucks. On uncomfortably hot, bright days, they drowse in the coolness of their burrows, and a hunter might as well emulate the instinctive wisdom of the chuck by finding his own cool drowsing spot.

Another good time not to hunt chucks is when the hay is so high you can't see them. Learn the harvesting cycle in your region,

A detachable or (in this case) collapsible shooting rest is an excellent accessory for a heavy-barreled chuck rifle. A height-adjustable bipod is shown here. There are also tripods and unipods.

because the chucking is best during the first couple of weeks after a field is cut.

Despite their keen senses, chucks are not quickly spooked by rifle fire. They don't associate it with danger, at least where hunting pressure has been light. Often a chuck will ignore the crack of a rifle, even if a bullet plows up dirt a foot away or kills another animal a few yards off. There's no reason to leave a good shooting site after a miss—or after a kill, if other chucks are within range. Even if they go for their burrows, it pays to wait.

Because all marmots are extremely resistant to shock, a high-powered, fast-expanding bullet will not invariably stop a body-hit chuck from reaching its burrow, where it will die slowly. A chuck has a virtually neckless, apple-sized head. I'm not one of those expert marksmen who can hit the head almost every time, but I try for head shots all the same, for humane reasons.

Prairie Dogs

A lot of old-time prairie-dog hunters (and chuck hunters, as well) are still handloading the .220 Swift. But the Swift, like the .22 Hornet, is overshadowed by the hot modern chamberings. The same .22 centerfire cartridges I recommend for medium-range chuck shooting are the ones for prairie dogs.

Regardless of which caliber I chose, I would either mount a variable-power scope on the rifle or use a 6X or 8X scope, and I'd generally sight it in at 200 yards—although I'd hope to creep within 150 yards of a dog town if it hadn't been heavily hunted.

In many regions, prairie dogs are now protected, having been almost extirpated after more than a century of poisoning by stockmen and government "control" agents whose goal was extermination. An overpopulation of prairie dogs can ruin grazing land for livestock, since 250 of the little rodents can eat as much grass in a day as a 1,000-pound cow. But a realistically managed population—controlled by natural predators, sport hunting, and modern habitat manipulation—can actually benefit rangeland. Where the prairie dog was eliminated, so was the black-footed ferret, a mink-sized weasel that relies chiefly on this prey for its subsistence. Never very plentiful, this ferret is now rare. We are all impoverished by the extinction of any wild creature, and I heartily support the full protection of prairie-dog towns where such protection has been deemed necessary.

On the other hand, there are still areas where prairie dogs can be hunted—and should be, to prevent overpopulation. For that matter, there are privately owned rangelands where these big, chubby ground squirrels (and ground squirrels they are, though bigger than other species) are managed on a sustained-yield basis. Some of the ranchers who once tried to eradicate them now maintain a profitable supply for fee-paying hunters who prevent the population from getting out of hand. In parts of the West and Midwest—Colorado and South Dakota, for example—there is no closed season, and

Like chucks, prairie dogs often sit up. You then have three target zones—the head, chest, and paunch—which are the size, respectively, of a small apple, medium apple, and large apple. With one of the recommended .22 centerfires, a hit in any of these zones should result in an instant kill.

100-acre dog towns still pock the plains with mounded burrows that look like miniature volcanoes. Check with the state game department to find out if they may be hunted and then ask local residents, particularly landowners, where to scout for these "picket-pin" targets.

In recent years, long-range handgunning for small game—including prairie dogs—has gained increased popularity. The pistols most often used are the Thompson/Center Contender in any of the hot .22 centerfire "varmint" calibers, the Merrill Sportsman in some of those same calibers, and the Remington XP-100 chambered for the .221 Fireball cartridge. There are also a few fortunate handgunners who own the discontinued Ruger Hawkeye, chambered for the .256 Winchester Magnum. All of these are accurate single-shot pistols, and all should be scoped for this kind of hunting. Handgunning has achieved less popularity among chuck hunters, but it's great sport with chucks as well as prairie dogs. I'd choose a 2½X scope.

I won't try to persuade anyone that prairie-dog meat is as good as chuck or rabbit, but the Indians and early settlers feasted on it, and it is quite palatable. Any squirrel recipe will work well with prairie dog, and so will any rabbit recipe scaled down to accommodate a slightly smaller animal. Come to think of it, you may not have to scale it down. An adult prairie dog weighs about 1½ pounds in the spring, but it is twice as heavy by fall.

Prairie dogs are noted for their yelping, but their barks of alarm will not send all of a dog town's residents scurrying for their holes and thus end a hunting session. Which dogs disappear and which ones stay above ground may depend on your approach, for these animals respond differently to different kinds of danger. When a bird of prey circles, all the dogs plunge for safety, but the approach of a coyote sends only the nearest ones under, while the others sit up and yap. On the open flats colonized by prairie dogs, there isn't enough cover to permit stalking, and many hunters laugh at the notion of crawling into range. They walk upright, then assume a solid sitting or prone position and wait for the animals within range to emerge again. But a crawling hunter can get closer. Perhaps he appears to prairie dogs as a coyote with severe glandular trouble.

Prairie dogs are colonial animals, living in large "dog towns" and never venturing very far from their holes. If a rifleman misses because he misjudges the range or size of the target, he can often mark where the bullet strikes the mounded earth around a burrow. After scoring a first kill, he'll know where to hold for other prairie dogs standing close to the first one.

Regardless of approach, animals 200 yards away may take alarm if the town has been heavily hunted. If it hasn't, you may be able to cut that distance in half—or get even closer by crawling. I'd count on the prairie dogs within 100 yards submerging. In a typical dog town, that still leaves a lot of targets.

Prairie-dog country is usually open and often flat. The lower you stay to the ground, the closer you can get to a dog town without sending the animals diving down their holes. And you can generally shoot from the prone position, the steadiest field position a rifleman can take.

When scouting for new dog towns, bear in mind that these animals always dig where the vegetation is low enough that they can watch for enemies. Also bear in mind their favorite kinds of pasturage: wheat grasses, blue grama, buffalo grass, fescue grass, foxtail, bromegrass, dandelion, young Russian thistle, and sand dropseed.

Most animals don't seem to associate vehicles with the enemy. Sometimes the best shooting can be done by driving a car right up to a dog town and easing out on the far side. If the animals do plunge out of sight (having learned about cars from recent experience) just stay still and wait a few minutes.

A mature prairie dog has a body about 14 inches long, not counting a three-inch tail. When it's down on all fours, the top of its back is only about five inches from the ground, and that's not much of a target, but when it sits up on its haunches, it stands about 10 inches high and presents three overlapping bull's-eyes—a head about 1½ inches across, a chest about 2½ inches across, and a bulging paunch about 3½ inches across. Knowing the dimensions can help you estimate the range and adjust your hold accordingly. Since these animals are not nearly as resistant to shock as chucks are, a bullet centered in any of these bull's-eyes should give you an instant kill.

When you've potted a prairie dog, visualize its size as it appeared in your scope. Another prairie dog that appears to be about the same

Long-range handgunning for prairie dogs and other small game has been gaining increased popularity. Good calibers include the .221 Fireball and .256 Winchester Magnum. Here the late Larry Koller, a notable hunting writer, is shown zeroing a scoped .221. He's using a 1.5X scope, but many pistol shooters are now mounting slightly more powerful models for small targets at long range.

size when viewed through the reticle should be at about the same range. "Pups" are sometimes only a third as large as adults, but the burrows—and the animals themselves—are generally close enough together for comparison. Thus you can tell if one that seems small is a pup or is an adult at longer range, and you can aim accordingly: high, low, or dead on.

Judging wind drift is harder than judging range and can be especially difficult when making long shots in open country. I sometimes wonder why "Kentucky windage" isn't called "South Dakota windage." The strength and direction of the wind may not be at all the same where you are and out where the targets are. Watch the grass or any other vegetation out there and note how it bends. Often, you'll just have to rely on guesswork for the first shot, but you can mark where that shot strikes and hold accordingly. And you may get off six or eight shots before having to rest the town.

Raccoons

Coon hunting comes in two categories—hunting with dogs and hunting with a call. Either way, shots are usually made at very short range. Since hunting with hounds is generally a nighttime revel, with headlamps or other lanterns supplying the only light, anything more than very short range would be out of the question. Whether you call in your raccoons or follow the calls of the hounds, all you need in the way of armament is a .22 rimfire rifle or pistol loaded with Long Rifle cartridges. Predator-calling has added the raccoon to the list of game taken with the bow and arrow, but an archer must be well camouflaged and must be adept at both the call and the bow to bring such small game within range and hit it consistently.

For hunting with hounds, I prefer an open-sighted rifle or pistol. When calling, however, a low-power scope can be a help because now and then a shot may present itself at moderately long range. A 2½X scope is recommended with a rifle, 1.3X with a handgun.

In autumn, when coon hunting is best, raccoons are feeding heavily in order to put on the fat that will help them get through the winter. Particularly in states where the weather turns cold and food is hard to come by in winter, a mature specimen may accumulate considerable fat in the abdominal cavity, plus another inch of it between skin and body. Fat can sometimes account for nearly half the animal's weight. It can ruin a pelt unless the hide is scraped thoroughly, and it can also ruin the flavor of the meat. Removing all of it is a tedious but necessary job. With the fat trimmed away, a coon roast or barbecue is a delight.

Raccoons are not true hibernators, but they become lethargic and

One good place to start hounds is a denning area. Here, the hounds are baying at a raccoon that has holed up in an old maple den tree. Dens are also found in several other large hardwoods listed in the text.

den up when the temperature remains fairly steadily below 28° or so. Being short-legged, they're also inclined to quit foraging and den up if more than a little snow is on the ground. Some states have fairly short seasons, others have long ones, and in some there is no closed season. Coons can be hunted all winter long in parts of the South. However, the hunting is best in late fall, when the animals are most active. This is true whether you use a call or follow·the hounds. In February—or about a month earlier in the warmest latitudes, a month later in the coldest—the males wander from den to den looking for mates. Where the season is open at this time, the hunting can become fairly good again, but fall is still best.

If you're hunting in winter, a denning area is a good bet. Typical denning hollows are found in large basswoods, elms, beeches, oaks, maples, and sycamores. Coons also den beneath rocky overhangs, in caves or rock crevices, unused tile drains, empty mines, grass tussocks in marshes, and even in chuck burrows.

In late fall, many nights are damp and relatively warm. The scent is heavy then, and hounds work best on such nights.

Some states allow coon hunting in late summer. This is almost as good as the autumnal "hungry time" for calling, if you're willing to settle for fairly small, young coons. The young of the previous spring have not yet learned to be as suspicious as their elders, and since they're feeding heavily, they tend to come to a call readily.

Young, small raccoons set out on their nocturnal foraging expeditions earlier than their elders, and these small ones are the coons most often treed. In some areas where coon hunting is a very popular traditional sport, the local hunters spare the young ones unless the farms in the vicinity have been suffering heavy coon seizures. The species has a lifespan of eight or ten years. By letting the younger specimens go, the hunters assure themselves of more good-sized raccoons in future years.

Like foxes and crows, raccoons feast on such carrion as animals killed by automobiles. Therefore, many hunters begin an evening's sport by driving slowly along back roads while a hound runs ahead to check ditches and brush, hoping to strike a scent trail.

In most localities, a good place to start the dogs is near or at a stream. The opportunistic diet of the raccoon includes tadpoles, clams, small fish, turtles and turtle eggs, worms, frogs, insects, crawfish, and other stream denizens. Moreover, on Atlantic shad rivers and Pacific salmon rivers, raccoons come in search of dead fish during the spawning runs.

Another good place to start coon hounds is at or near a stream. Raccoons feed on tadpoles, small fish, and numerous other kinds of aquatic prey.

Still another excellent spot to start the hounds is at the edge of a cornfield, particularly an edge adjacent to brush or woods. Hungry raccoons can inflict great damage on a corn crop, and farmers generally hunt raccoons or welcome others who do.

Additional good hunting areas are the sources of vegetable foods avidly sought by raccoons in autumn: wild or cultivated grapes, pecans, hickory nuts, acorns, beechnuts, and hazelnuts. In the South, a persimmon tree is also likely to be another excellent starting point.

These Tennessee hounds have put a coon up near a cornfield—still another excellent place to cast dogs. Because raccoons can severely damage a corn crop, farmers tend to be coon hunters and usually welcome other hunters.

Wherever you've seen coons or coon sign in the past, you're probably not far from game. A typical raccoon passes most of the year on no more, and often less, than about a square mile of land.

There are two basic types of coon hounds—the more or less silent dogs and the open trailers. The majority of coon hunters love the music of a vociferous hound pack, but quiet dogs can be very efficient if the object of the hunt is pest-control or meat. Coons have keen hearing and night-vision, but in heavy cover, they often fail to see the hounds at a distance and, when engaged in an autumnal feeding orgy, they often ignore quiet dogs until the pack is so close that the chase will be brief. Among the silent hounds, no particular breed dominates. Desirable characteristics, apart from silence while trailing, are stamina, speed, intelligence, eagerness, and, of course, a keen nose.

A *classic* coon hunt requires full-voiced hounds. Top breeds are the treeing Walker, black-and-tan, redbone, and bluetick, though there are other regional or local favorites. Noisy hounds may not tree quite as many coons, or do it quite as fast, but on the other hand, they probably lose fewer than do the quiet dogs. A treed coon, after all, doesn't always stay treed. The far-carrying sound of open trailers lets the hunters follow part or all of the chase. And then, when the dogs bark "treed!" the hunters can race for the sound. The very fact that the chase tends to be longer can also be cited as an advantage of musically inclined hounds. For many hunters, the enjoyment lies in the music itself and in a long, tricky but successful pursuit.

A single good hound can lead you to raccoons, but there are great advantages to releasing at least two or three dogs, preferably more if they work well together. The more dogs you have, the better the chance of striking a hot trail. Several dogs can make louder music than one. Several dogs will have a better chance of staying with a resourceful raccoon or picking up the trail again after it has been broken by a coon that walked a fence rail, doubled back, crossed water, or climbed a tree and dropped down again from a long limb or a neighboring tree. Raccoons can be almost as sly as foxes. Finally, if a raccoon is overtaken on the ground or in the water, it can be too tough an opponent for a single dog.

If you wrap the dogs' collars with reflective tape, they'll show up better in the beams of headlamps.

The headlamps worn by spelunkers and miners have largely replaced other types of lanterns for nighttime coon hunting, whether with dogs or a call. They leave both hands free; they're bright, sturdy, and reliable; and they can be tilted to a desired angle.

When calling in raccoons at night, tilt your headlamp so that just the edge of the beam touches the ground in front of your cover. You'll have sufficient illumination to see the reflected eye shine of an incoming raccoon or other animal, but the beam won't be aimed so low that its harsh, moving light spooks the game.

Nighttime coon callers now have something even better than a conventional headlamp. It's a red-lensed headlamp, intended specifically for coon hunting, and is available at some sporting-goods stores. You can fashion your own by taping transparent red plastic or glass over your lamp's ordinary lens. This dims the beam somewhat but gives you sufficient illumination. The theory is that most mammals, being color-blind, perceive almost no difference between red and black; hence, they can't see the red light. Whether or not the theory is correct, field tests have proved tht red light doesn't spook the animals.

Some states prohibit hunting with a light. Fortunately, raccoons will respond to realistic calling even on the brightest moonlit nights, and you can bring them in close enough to shoot without artificial illumination if your hiding place faces an area with sharp contrast—such as dead grass, or a sandbar—so that you can spot a silhouetted animal approaching. Ordinarily I don't like shotguns for raccoon hunting because I'd rather not put all those pellet holes in the skin. But for night hunting without a lamp, a scattergun and loads of No. 4's are the logical combination.

Just as a stream or pond is a good starting place for hounds, it is also a good place to find a natural blind or rig one and start calling. Raccoons expect to find prey as well as edible vegetation near water, even when the pickings are slim elsewhere.

It's possible—though more difficult and far less consistently successful—to call in raccoons during daylight hours. The best times, of course, are at first and last light. Camouflage clothing is a

In some locales, nighttime predator calling can bring coons in so close that archers can take the ringtails. Note the headlamp worn by one of the bowhunters. Red-lensed lamps are favored because they give sufficient illumination without alarming the game. In some areas, night hunting with lights is prohibited, so check your state laws.

big help for this, and it should include a face net or mask unless you thoroughly smudge your face. The kind of outfit worn by bow-hunters on deer stands is what you want. Be sure to do your calling from a natural hide or rigged blind where the breeze won't drench the avenue of approach with your scent.

This is the print of a raccoon's forefoot. Coon tracks are easily recognized. If you find them you can generally count on good hunting in the vicinity. These animals don't travel much except when pursued.

In many states, phonographic devices are legal for calling raccoons (as well as crows and those mammals normally classified as predators). Battery-powered machines and expert calling records and tape cassettes are commercially available. Some of them come with instructional booklets that can teach you a great deal about calling a given kind of animal. Many hunters prefer a mouth-operated call. They feel that electronic gadgetry gives them an unfair advantage over the game and that it's aesthetically offensive in the woods—about like a neon sign erected to mark a scenic view. Frankly, I would heartily agree if only I could become masterful with a mouth call, and sooner or later perhaps I will. Meanwhile, I must plead guilty to having used a phonograph both to help me practice and to help me take game. I certainly see no harm in its use where overabundant raccoons are a problem to farmers.

The best-known sound for luring small predators is the dying-rabbit squeal. This sound will sometimes attract a raccoon as readily as a coyote, and it's the noise emitted by some of the calling records and tapes as well as conventional mouth-operated predator calls. However, a raccoon will respond more eagerly—sometimes almost heedless of possible danger—to the trill or shriek of a bird in distress. Some hunters have learned to mimic this sound convincingly by trilling their tongues while blowing standard dying-rabbit calls. But there are also mouth-operated dying-bird calls designed for raccoon hunting, and there are records and tapes featuring these same cries. Whether mouth- or battery-powered, this is the most effective sound for coon callers.

Opossums

Nothing more accurate or powerful than an open-sighted rimfire rifle or pistol is needed to kill opossums. Probably nine out of ten possums killed are treed during coon hunts. Whether this strange little species—North America's only marsupial—is taken in this incidental manner or hunted for its own sake, the range is invariably so short that any serviceable .22 will do the job.

Possums were originally Southeastern animals. Late in the 19th century they began to expand their range steadily northward, and later they were introduced along the West Coast—in California, Oregon, and Washington. In the East they have now expanded their range all the way into Ontario, and in the West they have spread down to Baja and up into British Columbia. They're so poorly adapted to cold weather that they often lose bits of their naked tails and ears to frostbite, so perhaps their present range represents the final limit.

I don't know of any Northern hunters who take their dogs out specifically to hunt possum, but at one time possum hunts were a common Southern means of merrymaking, if not precisely a sport in the usual sense. And there are still a few Southerners who love to go out at night—the darkest nights are best—and crash through tangles and brush until their hounds end a brief chase by putting a possum up some spindly tree. A possum is too slow to elude pursuers for long, as a coon can, so the hunt is usually short if the dogs pick up the scent early. On the other hand, they may not strike a trail for hours, or they may strike several in a night and thus prolong the revelry.

Most coon hunters profess to be purists, and they become—or perhaps pretend to become—annoyed when their dogs tree a pos-

Photographed in summer, this female opossum still has her young clinging to her. As with raccoons, hunting is generally best in the fall, when the young ones are dispersing and both old and young are feeding very actively.

sum. But stewed possum or possum baked with sweet potatoes can be very good. I used to like it baked, yet I must confess I had difficulty finishing the last one I prepared that way. The meat is sometimes tough and stringy, and there may not be much of it after the fat is removed—and the fat must be removed if the dish is to be palatable. My favorite way of preparing it now is to simmer it slowly in a stew pot or an electric slow-cooking crock until there's no question about its tenderness.

With most game animals, food sources provide good hunting areas. Over much of its range, however, the possum is an exception because it's so omnivorous. Until a few favored food plants ripen in the fall, the chief dietary components are probably insects, small rodents, carrion, worms, frogs, newts, lizards, birds' eggs and hatchlings, grain, and assorted greens. But a hunter should be aware that possums are very fond of mulberries, corn, grapes, and acorns. They are even fonder of ripe persimmon fruits, and Southern hunters often cast their dogs at a persimmon tree or near the edge of a crop field. Any hound with a keen nose and a strong treeing voice can become a good possum hunter.

Possums den in hollow trees and logs, woodpiles, culverts, rock clefts, abandoned chuck burrows (and occupied burrows when the chucks are hibernating), and even under buildings. A known denning area is another good place to start the hounds.

As with raccoons, the hunting is best in the fall, not only because the possums are engaged in a prewinter feeding orgy and their favorite foods are ripe, but also because the young ones are dispersing to unoccupied territories. These combined factors keep the animals very active.

Ordinarily, there's no point in hunting possums without a dog because encountering one will be a matter of sheer luck. After a snow, however, their distinctive tracks—which look like tiny, widespread handprints—make trailing easy. A mature possum's home territory is no more than 15 acres. A hunter who follows the tracks through farm country will probably find the end of the trail no more than a couple of fields away. But any such tracking ought to be done

Most-possums are treed at night during coon hunts. Coon hunters often express annoyance when their hounds waste time on a possum, though this animal can provide an amusing change of pace. The specimen pictured is opening its mouth to display its 50 teeth—a bluffing reflex action often seen when possums feel cornered.

very early or late in the day because a possum will be denned when the sun is up.

Hunters who are unfamiliar with this species may be disappointed when a treed or cornered possum refuses to "play possum." Several

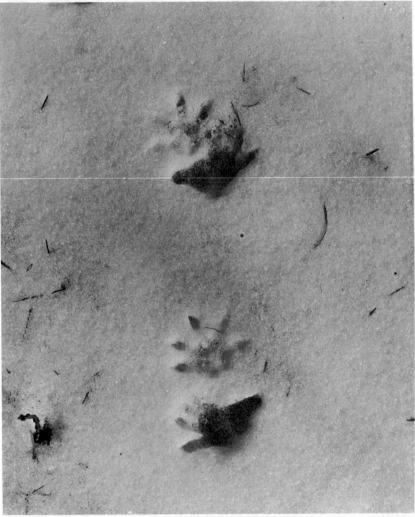

As a rule, finding a possum without a dog would be sheer luck. After a snow, however, their little "handprints" leave easy trails. Follow one and you might just find its maker because possums have small home territories.

other creatures, including some snakes, feign death when cornered, and this defense ought to work especially well for the possum because many carnivores dislike possum meat and will leave off attacking a possum (which they do for "sport") if the victim appears to be dead. All the same, possums don't very often live up to their reputation for playing dead.

Occasionally, one will fall on its side, open its mouth, and go limp as it's supposed to do. This is an involuntary defense mechanism comparable to a state of shock. The animal retains at least a degree of consciousness, and when the enemy loses interest and leaves, the possum quickly recovers and scampers away. But a cornered possum more often faces the enemy, hissing, salivating, and opening its mouth wide to display all 50 teeth. Although this show of ferocity is mostly bluff, it would be foolish to put a hand too close to that mouth, or close to any cornered animal.

Javelinas

I killed my first javelina at about 230 yards with one shot from a .264 Winchester Magnum bolt-action rifle under a 4X scope. My second was only a few yards away when I put a hollow-point bullet from a .22 Magnum revolver into its shoulder, and its reaction convinced me that the use of a rimfire even at such a short range was a stupid mistake. Actually, my first revolver shot had been at slightly longer range, and it had gone high, only creasing the animal's back. The javelina came at me, its back hair up and its short tusks clicking. As a rule, any stories about the aggressiveness of this species are exaggerated. On the rare occasions when a javelina comes toward a hunter, it's probably not charging but only trying—in its nearsighted and not very intelligent way—to escape. This time, however, the animal had scented me, heard me, was close enough to see me, and there was no doubt about its intention. A third shot from the .22 spun the javelina around, and it started over a hillock at a fast run. By then the animal was close to death, but honesty compels me to admit that if my hunting partner hadn't made an anchoring shot with a .44 Magnum, I'd have had to follow the blood trail and pick my way through patches of Spanish bayonet and prickly pear to find my trophy. More important, I'd failed to kill it in the quickest, most humane way.

Javelinas have been called miniature big game. They have thick, tough hides and thicker, tougher muscles. In my opinion, a rimfire Magnum is not powerful enough for this game even when the bullet strikes the chest cavity. Some pistol hunters use "varmint" calibers such as the .221 Remington or .256 Winchester Magnum. At short range, a .38 Special hollow-point is quite sufficient, and some handgunners carry a .357 Magnum revolver loaded with .38's. Others prefer the power of .357 loads (as I do at somewhat longer ranges), and still others carry a .41 Magnum.

This typical adult javelina has a massive head and shoulders but a small body. If you're hunting peccary in conjunction with other Southwestern game such as deer, then a flat-shooting deer rifle with a scope (2½X, 4X, or a variable model) is the arm to use. If you're out exclusively for a javelina, a .22 centerfire is all you need.

Among riflemen, many favor the .22 centerfires. My own javelina hunts have been an adjunct to deer-hunting trips, and I think it's sensible to carry a deer rifle. The flat-shooting .243 Winchester, 6 mm Remington, and .25-06 are fine choices. For that matter, so are the bigger deer calibers, from .270 Winchester to .30-06.

In areas of rough, hilly terrain where vegetation is not too sparse and where javelinas are abundant and haven't recently been subjected to heavy hunting pressure, it's sometimes possible—in fact, easy—to stalk within close range. Under these circumstances they can be taken with an open-sighted handgun. But in most areas the terrain is open and the range long. A handgun scope with a magnification as high as 2½X may be desirable in some regions. I wouldn't think of using an unscoped rifle. In my own experience—chiefly in the Big Bend country of southwestern Texas—javelina shots varied from 50 yards or less all the way out to 300 or so. I was comfortable with a 4X scope, though a 2½X or a variable scope would have served equally as well.

The javelina, or collared peccary, is related to domestic hogs and wild boars but belongs to a separate family, distinguished by fewer teeth, straight tusks, a single dewclaw instead of two on each hind foot, and several other anatomical features, including a musk gland on the back just forward of the rump.

When a peccary raises his back hair in alarm or anger, a small amount of musk discharges. It isn't a pleasant odor, but neither is it so strong that the animal has to be treated with the caution a skunk demands. This odor, like the javelina's ferocity, falls far short of its reputation. At least one famous (and otherwise authoritative) hunting book states that no one has ever concocted an appetizing dish from the meat of an adult peccary because "no matter how carefully the flesh is prepared, it holds its odor" and "when you put it on the stove you will not want to remain in the kitchen." *This information is simply not true.*

The musk gland, which looks like a navel, should be cut out promptly after the game is killed, and care should be taken to get no musk on your hands or clothing or on the meat. If this is done, the meat holds no unpleasant odor. It's light and dry, rather like pork, and can be cooked in any of the ways appropriate to pork. The meat of an old boar can be tough, but that of a young, medium-sized javelina is delicious.

The North American species of peccary once ranged as far north as Arkansas. Unfortunately, settlers killed the animals indiscriminately for meat and to alleviate crop damage (which was probably exaggerated). Many more javelinas were later killed to supply cheap "pigskin." Today the animals range from Mexico up into parts of Texas, Arizona, and New Mexico.

In Texas, where the javelina population is greatest, most of the hunting lands are privately owned and ranchers offer hunting privileges for a fee. A package hunt, including a guide and transportation, usually costs about $100. Some ranches provide meals and lodging at extra cost. The hunting is mostly done by cruising ranch trails in a four-wheel-drive vehicle and by glassing and walking. A few ranchers conduct hunts with dogs. Either way,

A shot at a javelina may be at almost any range—from less than 50 yards to more than 300. It's essential to practice range estimation, because judging distance is very difficult in flat, open desert country without trees or other familiar objects to use as size references. Here, the author fires at a javelina about 200 yards away; the camera lens was long, yet the peccary looks like a tiny blob.

Texas hunter and guide Biddy Martin examines the flattened snout and straight, thick tusks of a javelina killed by the author. The animal is well adapted to rooting in hard, rocky soil and devouring such formidable vegetation as prickly pear cactus. Other plants common to the habitat include thorn bush and Spanish bayonet.

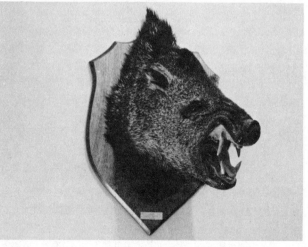

The author killed this javelina with a .22 Magnum revolver, but he recommends centerfire handguns. Though the ferocious look of this mounted head typifies good taxidermy, and the animals do look like miniature wild boars, javelinas are not dangerous game. (However, any animal can be dangerous when wounded or cornered.)

the success ratio is high. The two best areas in the state are the Big Bend region west of the Pecos River and the brush country south and west of San Antonio. In most of the javelina counties, the season runs from early October through December.

There is also good hunting in Arizona, which was the first state to grant the javelina game status and protective management. The state holds an annual drawing for several thousand javelina permits, and there is a short season, usually in February or March. The best Arizona areas for javelina hunting are in the small southeastern mountain ranges—the Santa Teresas, Galiuros, Grahams, Santa Ritas, and Chiricahuas. Also good are the Superstition Mountains near Phoenix and the deserts between Phoenix and Tuscon.

New Mexico's season is generally about the same as Arizona's. As a rule it's for residents only. The best hunting is in Hidalgo County's Animas and Peloncillo mountains.

If you plan to have a javelina head mounted, you'll definitely want to place your shot in the rib cage. This isn't really very difficult to do, even at more than 200 yards, if the target is in open country. I think some misses result from incorrect range estimation when hunters who aren't familiar with the species overestimate its size. This peccary is a chunky, short-legged animal, usually weighing from 30 to 50 pounds at maturity (a 60-pounder is exceptionally large) and standing about 18 to 22 inches high. I try to keep that height in mind, because I find range estimation very difficult in arid country where these animals are to be found and where there are no familiar species of trees to serve as a visual reference.

Once in a while, you may encounter an old javelina that has become a loner, but the animals usually forage in bands ranging from scores to half a dozen or less. Thus, all the javelinas on a mountain or a stretch of desert may be concentrated in one or two areas, so it pays to watch for sign. On low mountain slopes in Arizona and New Mexico, the little musk hogs eat quantities of scrub-oak acorns, but on the desert flats, their primary food is prickly pear. They consume the cactus pads, thorns and all. Where you see patches of prickly pear ripped up, javelinas have been feeding. The gouged, bitten, or tooth-marked pads are mostly those one to two feet above the ground. Also look for the spiny, fleshy-leaved agave plants known as lechuguilla, another favorite food. The droves of javelinas tear it up on the hillsides. Other foods include tubers and roots, berries, and mesquite beans and pods. You may see rooted-up patches of ground, like the rootings of pigs. And you may see wallows, particularly near waterholes. And usually you'll see the small, blunt, two-lobed tracks. An area with plenty of sign is an area that merits careful glassing.

The author points out the small, blunt, two-lobed tracks of a javelina near a waterhole. In typically arid habitat, mud dries so quickly that it's very easy to tell whether tracks are fresh.

Glass for javelinas slowly, and be alert for movement in the low brush that blankets many draws. Javelinas are often out in the open and easy to spot, but when they're in brush they can be difficult to see because they're so low to the ground.

Sometimes, when you're near a drove of javelinas, you'll smell their musk. They use it not only as an alarm signal but to maintain contact with one another. Getting a whiff of it doesn't necessarily mean they're spooked, but only that they're somewhere near.

Where ground cover is dense but crosshatched with ranch trails, a popular method is to take a stand on a ridge and watch the openings and trails on either side for crossing bands of javelinas. A stand overlooking a waterhole is also good.

In some ways, peccaries behave like deer. Early and late in the day are the best times to find them on the move, but cool, overcast weather may keep them wandering and foraging throughout the day. As a rule, they escape the midday heat by going up among the rimrock crevices and caves or down into the brushy shade near waterholes or in deep washes. You may be able to flush them out by merely walking these areas.

Though javelinas have a sharp sense of smell, their hearing is only fair and their eyesight is weak. This makes them relatively easy to stalk. Just approach into the wind and move slowly, quietly. If they catch your scent, they may click their teeth and raise their bristly hair. In that event, stop moving and remain motionless for a few seconds, then continue to stalk until you can get into a steady position where you're sure of your shot.

I've never personally tried this method, but my friend Byron Dalrymple, a justly famous outdoor writer, says that javelinas will sometimes respond to a predator call—the same squealing-rabbit call that brings coyotes. This may draw one out of thick brush. Byron doesn't claim to know why it works, and neither do I, but peccaries are not strict vegetarians. They eat toads, lizards, eggs, the young of ground-nesting birds, worms, and any mice caught in the nests they root up. So perhaps they respond to the predator call in the hope of finding a young rabbit too badly injured to escape.

In arid country, tracks dry so quickly that you can generally tell if trails around a gully or waterhole are fresh. If they are, javelinas are probably within a quarter of a mile of you.

PREDATORS

Bobcats

There are only two basic ways to hunt bobcats—using a predator call or hounds—but there are several minor variations on these themes. The recommended arms and loads depend on your manner of hunting. For calling bobcats in comparatively thick, brushy cover where shots are likely to be close, a shotgun has obvious advantages. It also has advantages for a hunter who goes on stand where his dogs may push a cat out of brushy cover at considerable speed. I'd use a full-choked 12-gauge Magnum gun with 3-inch shells carrying 1⅛ ounces of No. 2 or No. 4 shot, although some cat hunters prefer Magnum BB loads.

In most situations I'd rather be carrying a rifle or handgun since I'd want to avoid producing a pellet-riddled pelt. I don't try to demand that all hunters share my attitude, but I don't kill anything I won't use. It's an attitude prompted, in part, by continuing habitat reduction and the resulting decrease in wildlife populations. I feel a strong aversion to wasting wildlife, and wildlife includes predators as well as those species normally designated as game. If I'm not going to use the meat, I must prize the pelt all the more or I won't shoot the animal. I have yet to eat bobcat meat, but I'd be willing to try it. I'm told it tastes a little like veal. And whether or not bobcat *en brochette* has a place in my cuisine, I want as perfect a skin as possible from any cat I take, so the shotgun isn't my favorite arm for this kind of hunting. For that matter, there are a few hound fanciers who carry no gun at all. They spare any treed cat, for they've had their sport in the running of the dogs and they want to guarantee a cat population for future runs.

A hunter who follows his hounds to a bobcat in a tree or at bay on a rock ledge can bring the cat down with a hollow-point from an open-sighted .22 rimfire rifle or pistol. Back in 1951, a 69-pound bobcat was taken in Colorado, but the average is 15 to 30 pounds, and a Long Rifle cartridge is more than sufficient for such quarry at very short range.

A treed bobcat is a close, easy target and can be killed cleanly with a .22. Most of these cats weigh between 15 and 30 pounds. The Arizona cat pictured here was a rogue that had killed more than 30 lambs. However, bobcats seldom pose a threat to domestic stock, and many states now classify them as game animals, protecting their population through stipulated seasons and limits.

For calling, some hunters use a .22 centerfire rifle or pistol—one of the "varmint" calibers. There's nothing wrong with this, but among rifle chamberings for both bobcats and coyotes, I think a .243, 6mm, or .25-06 is the optimum. I happen to have a Mannlicher-stocked .243 carbine that I like very much (and it's also fine for deer hunting in some parts of the country). It has all the power needed for fairly large predators, it's accurate enough for fairly long shots, and moreover it's fast-swinging enough for sudden, close shots.

On two occasions, in open Southwestern terrain, I've seen a predator caller make a remarkably long shot, but in both instances the animal was a coyote. Few cats are shot at long range. A 2½X rifle scope is powerful enough and, for closer shots, it's easier and faster to use than a high-power scope. On a pistol, I think a 1.3X scope is sufficient. Some handgun hunters use open sights when calling, just as they do when following the hounds.

At one time, many a farmer waged a lifelong vendetta against bobcats, because an abundance of cats could mean occasional losses of poultry and even small livestock. However, most bobcats are reluctant to approach a human habitation closely enough to take domestic prey unless their wild prey is scarce. Rabbits and hares, a mainstay of their diet, are sufficiently plentiful so that bobcats are no threat to the game population. In fact, in the Northern states, bobcat numbers fluctuate in accordance with the population cycles of the snowshoe hare.

Bobcats have been known to kill fawns and, on rare occasions, even full-grown deer, and they also take some grouse, quail, and other game birds—but, again, not enough to warrant the bounties and poisoning campaigns that were formerly directed against predators. Because they kill a great many rats and other rodents, they're more beneficial than harmful, except in isolated instances. Unfortunately, the value of their fur has risen enormously since a ban was enacted on the importation of exotic spotted-cat pelts. Prior to that ban, the antipredator campaigns had taken a great toll, and since then, the fur trade has had a serious effect.

All the same, in a recent survey by the National Wildlife Federation, 25 states reported stable bobcat populations and two (Kansas and South Carolina) reported an increase. In some other states, particularly in the Far West, the Midwest, and along the mid-Atlantic Seaboard, this cat is declining, and four states regard it as endangered or extinct. Very few still classify the bobcat as a predator, granting it little or no protection from overharvesting. Some states regulate the trapping of this species, and 15 list it as a game animal and grant it protection through stipulated seasons and bag limits. In many states, therefore, the law no longer lets you hunt bobcats whenever you please or take as many as you can. Check your state's regulations before you hunt. It's safe to assume that where the law allows you to take these cats, they're to be found in sufficient supply so that regulated sport hunting won't deplete the population.

Since bobcats are nocturnal prowlers, night-hunting with a predator call and a red-lensed headlamp can be productive. Where such hunting isn't legal, the best times for calling are very early in the morning and at dusk.

The right kind of spot for calling is a brush clump, a jumble of rocks, or an elevation—a natural blind with a wide view. Some hunters carry camouflage material in case the natural blind can stand improvement. Wear camouflage clothing—as a rule, the conventional spotted type that blends with foliage, though white coveralls are worn when snow blankets the ground. If you don't wear a camouflage head net and don't like greasepaint, it's a good idea to smudge your face. In picking your spot, pay attention to the prevailing breeze; you not only want to hide yourself from vision, but conceal your scent as well. Although bobcats stalk chiefly by sight and sound, they have keen noses, and they'll abandon an approach to your call if they smell you. Besides, other predators such as coyotes may be in the vicinity, and your scent may warn them off even sooner than it will spook a bobcat.

Bobcats are more reluctant than other predators to eat carrion but, like other predators, they frequently hunt back roads, abandoned roads, and trails. They're not interested in road kills or food left by humans (as a coyote or fox is) but are looking for the rabbits, birds, and small rodents that populate the edge habitat. For the same reason they also prowl about waterholes and brushy or rocky areas. These are good sites for calling.

With a predator call, it's a mistake (unless there's no choice) to hunt the same place time after time. Predators are intelligent and they won't be fooled repeatedly. In fact, they soon learn to associate danger instead of food with the sound of a call. If you have access to only a few good hunting spots, you can sometimes offset this disadvantage by switching calls. The dying-rabbit squeal is the standard—and most productive—type, but the bird-in-distress call, primarily designed to lure raccoons, will often bring bobcats, too.

Scout your general hunting area and pick several good calling spots at least half a mile apart. The sound of a call will carry farther than that unless blocked by terrain or thick foliage, or unless the wind pushes it in the wrong direction.

Whereas a coyote tends to respond quickly and more or less directly to a call, a bobcat makes a slow, cautious, circuitous stalk. Don't give up too soon. Repeat the call at short intervals, but don't overdo it and don't make any other sounds. Give any cats in the area a half-hour opportunity to show up before you move on.

Where phonographic devices are legal, many hunters use them, but a mouth-operated call is just as productive when used expertly, and the most adept predator hunters generally take pride in doing the calling themselves. The problem is, how to become sufficiently expert. Unless you have a friend who's a fine caller, the phonographs are the best teachers. The sounds of real animals as well as experienced callers have been recorded, and the instructional records and tapes can guide you in improving your mimicry.

Calls differ in tone and volume. In cottontail or snowshoe country, especially where the cover is relatively dense and predators may be quite near, a rather high-pitched, piercing scream is effective. In jack-rabbit country and for long-range calling, a deeper tone is better and it can be obtained by using a call with a bigger reed. You can also vary the pitch somewhat by your manner of blowing the call and cupping your hands. If a predator responds but doesn't quite present the target you need, a high squeal may be the final bit of coaxing that brings it into full view.

Bobcats and other predatory species are sometimes tolled in by hunters using either mouth-operated or electronic predator calls. This hunter, carrying a scoped .221 pistol, will lure them by playing taped dying-rabbit squeals. After trying one area unsuccessfully for half an hour, he's moving on to find a natural blind in a different location.

With hounds, bobcat hunting is at its best after a light, fresh snow that holds only last night's tracks and won't impede your progress. If you become fatigued with scouting, the dogs can help, but ordinarily, the pack is cast only on a fresh trail. The hunters do the preliminary work of scouting trails, back roads, rocky slopes, canyons, brushy passes, and the like.

When there's no snow to help with the search for tracks, many hunters release a single hound—invariably a sharp-nosed member of the pack that has proved its ability as a "strike dog"—and when that one bellows "hot trail," the others are turned loose.

Mongrels sometimes make fine trail dogs for cat hunting, but foxhounds are the favorites in the East. In the West, where the same pack may hunt a 20-pound bobcat or a 140-pound cougar, foxhound-bloodhound crosses are outstanding. They must have excellent scenting ability, plenty of stamina, pugnacity, and an instinct for teamwork that makes you think of a wolf pack. The combination of teamwork and pugnacity is sometimes needed to keep a big, enraged cat at bay until the hunters catch up.

Bobcats bed during the day under blowdowns, in thickets, in clefts between rocks, and similar hiding places. In desert country, they escape the heat by sheltering in caves or crevices and in hollows shaded by overhangs. During the night, a cat may prowl only a short distance or may patrol for several miles, seldom hunting the same spots it hunted the night before, but often revisiting favorite vantage points such as boulders, ledges, or low tree crotches. At such spots, the hounds may find a strong, seemingly hot scent, even though the cat hasn't been there for a day or two. Thus they may track a cat all day. Or they may jump one from its bed and corner or tree it within a few hundred yards. Or they may lose a trail and then find another. Meanwhile, the hunters try their best to judge the pack's distance and direction by its collective voice. And when they hear the dogs holler "treed" they try to catch up as fast as possible, hoping that the cat will still be there and that none of the dogs has become foolhardy and sustained an injury. For this sport, a hunter may need the kind of stamina he demands of his dogs.

The type of hunt just described is popular in many parts of the country, where the hunters follow (or try to follow) the hounds on foot or on horseback. But in the timber of the Northeast and densely brushy areas in parts of the South, the hunters often take stands at openings, ready to shoot fast if a cat crosses with the dogs in pursuit. Habitat influences the behavior of wildlife, and habitat of this kind influences a bobcat to run rather like a fox, in a rough, wide circle. A hunter who knows the country well can take a stand at a strategic point.

In the Northern woods and in the relatively open country of the West, many fine hunting packs consist of only two or three hounds. But big packs are favored in some parts of the South. One experienced Southern hunter told me that he enjoys using at least half a dozen dogs, preferably more, because "the bigger the pack is, the likelier it is to keep a cat treed." I can understand his logic, but I suspect that there are two other, equally important reasons for the bigger packs. First, in some of that thick Southern cover, the extra dogs are a big help in cutting off or hemming in a running bobcat. Second, big packs that make loud music are a rollicking Southern tradition.

Coyotes

Most coyote hunters use predator calls. Some extremely skillful hunters—most of them old-timers practicing a difficult and fading art—take coyotes consistently without calls, merely by scouting, tracking, and glassing the animals, or by ambushing them. And a very few hunters use dogs, relying chiefly on sight hounds rather than trailers. I'll explain the method in due course, but first let's examine the choice of arms and the logic underlying the choice.

Many ranchers and farmers are beginning to treat coyotes more or less as game animals, having belatedly discovered that occasional losses of lambs, kids, calves, or poultry are offset to some degree by the control of jack rabbits and undesirable rodents. Most states are extremely reluctant to grant game status to this species but, for humane reasons, I believe the state game departments should at least prohibit the use of rimfires in coyote hunting. A typical adult coyote weighs between 20 and 30 pounds, and once in a while a very big one weighs more than 40. A rimfire bullet just doesn't have sufficient power and expansion for clean kills, nor does it have the speed and accuracy for long shots.

Even among the predator callers, a good many shots are made at 150 yards or more, and longer shots are common among those who hunt by cruising and glassing or waiting on stand. A high-velocity, reasonably heavy bullet from one of the .22 centerfires—the 55-grain .22–250, for instance—is a good choice for coyotes. Even better, in my estimation, are the flat-shooting medium-game calibers such as the .243 Winchester, 6mm Remington, .25–06, and .257 Roberts. Many Western hunters use the same rifles for coyotes as for deer or pronghorns.

Coyotes can also be taken with handguns, though self-restraint should be exercised in passing up overly long shots. (Both riflemen and handgunners should also pass up the very tempting shots at skylined coyotes in country where a stray bullet can travel far enough to be a hazard.) A good handgun choice would be one of the long-range single-shots chambered for the .221 Remington Fireball, .256 Winchester Magnum, .222, or a hot semi-wildcat like the .30 Herrett.

A predator call can draw coyotes very close. This handsome specimen was photographed on the flats in southeastern Colorado. The best calling periods are generally the first and last two hours of light, when the wind is down and coyotes are actively looking for prey.

A predator caller can use a shotgun, of course, if he waits until he's lured his quarry to within 40 yards. I'd recommend 2¾- or 3-inch Magnum loads of No. 2's or No. 4's in a full-choked 12-gauge gun.

The few hunters who run hounds for coyotes can use the same smoothbore loads or one of the aforementioned rifles or pistols. For that matter, they can use any reasonably powerful handgun, including an open-sighted .38 Special.

On snow in open country, a hunter is just too conspicuous unless he camouflages himself thoroughly. This hunter is wearing oversized dairyman's coveralls, with insulated clothing underneath, plus a white ski mask and cap. His scope, rifle, and shooting mittens are covered with two-inch white adhesive tape. If the tape is removed carefully afterward, it won't harm a rifle's stock finish. Take a tip from the pictured hunter, who is using one other very helpful accessory: a white, rubber-backed crib sheet, bought at a baby-furniture store, to keep himself dry while sitting or kneeling on snow. White camouflage is a great aid for hunting foxes as well as coyotes in winter.

A good handgun choice for coyotes is one of the long-range single-shot pistols. Shown here are the .221 Remington XP-100 (top) and the Ruger Hawkeye. The Hawkeye has been discontinued, but a used one sometimes becomes available. It's chambered for the .256 Winchester Magnum, a cartridge favored by many predator hunters.

For called coyotes, a handgun should be scoped because occasional shots are apt to be long. The same scopes recommended for chucks or bobcats will do nicely. The right scope for a rifle depends in large degree on your style of hunting. If you call most of your animals in pretty close, you may want no more power than 2½X. I have a notion that a better choice for most hunters might be a 2–7X variable or a 4X scope sighted in at 150 or 200 yards.

Coyotes keep turning up in new regions. Even in states that aren't traditional coyote havens, you may want to ask landowners and the game department about the hunting possibilities. A number of authorities—ranging from naturalist-photographer Leonard Lee Rue to Joe Martin, an outstanding old Texas outdoorsman who once guided me on a deer and turkey hunt—claim that the coyote is

America's most intelligent and adaptable wild animal. I agree. Certainly no other carnivore has tripled its range in spite of man's most strenuous efforts to curtail it. Because the little "prarie wolf" was unable to compete with the larger timber wolf, it formerly ranged only through the deserts, prairies, and plateaus west of the Mississippi from lower Canada down into Mexico. But the species spread northward and southward, following the livestock of settlers, and then it spread in other directions to occupy the lands vacated by the wolf. Coyotes have extended their distribution into lower Central America, and after the Klondike Gold Rush, they became established in Alaska. They have also spread through western and southeastern Canada and have now arrived in most of the states east of the Mississippi.

The hunting method I want to discuss first is "coursing" with hounds because it's the least common and I have the least to say about it. In fact, what I can tell you regarding this method is based on hearsay, not my personal experience, but my sources are reliable. I'm told that scent hounds are seldom used because few such dogs can overtake a coyote. Now and then they're employed in a limited way—just to find fresh tracks and start the sight hounds within coursing distance of the quarry. The job is then taken over by such speedy types as greyhounds, whippets, wolfhounds, Scottish deerhounds, and appropriate crossbreeds. Even these fast sight hounds are often defeated when a coyote disappears into thick, brushy scrub or a jumbled maze of rocks. The hunters try their best to follow on horseback or in a four-wheel-drive vehicle. A successful chase generally ends after a mile or two, when the coyote tires or gives up the attempt to outdistance the pack on a more or less straight course. The coyote may then try to hide but, with the dogs closing in, is apt to run in tight circles. The pack may finish the coyote in a bloody fight if a hunter doesn't arrive fast. He has to shoot quickly, while taking care not to endanger a hound.

Although whelping time varies somewhat with latitude, most coyote litters are born in April. The den is usually a wide-mouthed tunnel, a foot or two in diameter. Likely den sites are well-drained slopes, riverbanks, and the sides of canyons or gullies. Sometimes a den can be located by the tracks radiating from the mound of earth at the entrance. If the site is disturbed, the litter is usually moved to a new den. A hunter who finds a den and refrains from approaching it will probably have good fall or winter hunting in the vicinity. By then the den will be deserted, but the coyote family—even after it disperses—will continue to forage in the same general area.

Coyotes sometimes dig for water in a dry wash, but more often they seek water holes, for there they frequently find prey as well as drink. When a scouting hunter spots an elevation overlooking a water hole, he's found a good site for calling or just lying in wait. The heads and mouths of draws, washes, gullies, and canyons are also good hunting spots.

Not many hunters seem to be aware that both coyotes and foxes are more inclined than most predators to eat vegetation. They're particularly fond of fruits. Sometimes the most productive places for a cruising coyote hunter are those that furnish both fruit and small prey—patches of prickly pear, juniper, hawthorn, mesquite, or chokecherry, for example, and even the edges of orchards. Coyotes also seek gophers, prairie dogs, or marmots in meadows and prairie grasses, and they hunt for small rodents, rabbits, and birds near or in crop fields. My friend Joe Martin once surprised an especially big coyote right out in the open in the middle of a field, where the animal was probably mousing.

Like wolves, coyotes habitually hunt along "runways" that meander over their home range. Such routes and their periphery can often be recognized by tracks, den sites, scent posts, droppings, and bones or other debris that have been buried and then dug up for another meal. Foraging coyotes periodically move off to the sides of a runway and then return—but not always to the same part of the trail—so the entire patrolling area should be scouted.

A combination of scouting, resting at promising spots, and calling may well be the most productive hunting method. Whether a hunter moves on foot or by horse or vehicle, he should be carrying the same sort of binoculars I recommended for chuck hunting, and he should use it often. Coyotes, like human hunters, often spot their quarry by scanning the terrain from ridges or hilltops. They can spot enemies, too, from these elevations. Be alert not only for signs but for distant coyotes, often on ridges or knolls or just below their rims.

Coyote calling is best on windless or almost windless days, because any species with a keen enough sense of smell to sniff out a mouse certainly has no trouble winding a hunter.

A lot of prime coyote habitat is virtually devoid of trees, but if there's a tree crotch or wide limb at a promising site, it makes an excellent stand, placing the hunter above the coyote's line of sight and scent while giving him a good, wide view. Brushy slopes and bluffs are also good, but don't sit on a rim where you're silhouetted.

Calling coyotes, either with a phonograph (where legal) or a mouth-operated call that mimics the squeal of a dying rabbit, is easier than using a crow call or a duck call convincingly, yet the best predator callers now and then experience several unproductive days in a row. The only solution is to try again, in a new spot, making sure that you get into position silently, remain silent except for the calling, are well camouflaged or hidden, and are calling realistically.

I've already mentioned the use of instructional predator calling records. You can also obtain a very helpful free booklet entitled *How to Call Coyotes* by Bob Henderson, Extension Specialist of Wildlife Damage Control at Kansas State University. To get it, write to Wildlife Damage Control, Kansas State University, Manhattan, Kansas 66502. I'll go into greater detail regarding calling techniques in the section on foxes, because foxes are so widespread and abundant, because many of the same principles apply, because they're even more wary than coyotes in areas where they've been heavily hunted—and frankly, because I've had more experience with them.

Coyotes can be called at any time of day or night, but the best periods are generally the first and last two hours of light. These are relatively windless times and peak hours of coyote activity.

The best months for calling (or, in my opinion, for any kind of coyote hunting) are September, October, and February. The early autumn months are good because coyote families are dispersing, the coyote population is high, and the animals are extremely active. February rivals these months in productivity because the animals are again very active—they're in the rut—and in many regions, the ground is covered with snow that quickly reveals tracks and sign. Moreover, the pelts are prime in February.

Until snow covers the ground, camouflage isn't much of a problem. Just follow the same advice I gave concerning bobcats. But when snow blankets open coyote country, a hunter can have great difficulty making himself less conspicuous than a camel on a glacier. At this time of year, many adept coyote and fox hunters go to

In February, coyote pelts are prime, and the hunting is good for two reasons—because the animals are breeding and therefore very active, and because tracks and sign show clearly on snow.

extremes that pay off, covering their rifles and scopes with white tape and covering themselves with white knit caps, white ski masks, dairymen's coveralls, and even white mittens with a hole for the trigger finger.

Call into the wind. A coyote can hear at long distances and can smell you at almost comparable distances if the wind is wrong. If you

In recent years, coyotes have proliferated in the East. This big specimen was taken in New Jersey.

work with a partner, station yourself about 30 yards away from him and have just one man do the calling. A coyote that grows suspicious during the final approach may still present a shot to one hunter or the other.

Coyotes don't scout around and stalk as bobcats do when they hear a toothsome rabbit announce their dinner and its own demise. They come headlong at it. Often they'll arrive from far off within five minutes, though sometimes they can take three times that long. Whereas it pays to wait in one spot as long as half an hour for bobcats, there's no reason to wait more than 15 or 20 minutes in the hope that a coyote will show up. After that, move to another likely spot. Calling sites should be at least a mile apart, so unless you plan to scout on foot between calling sessions, you'll do well to travel by vehicle.

Foxes

For hunting foxes with hounds—and for hunting without them in dense cover, especially before the snow comes—a shotgun is a very efficient arm. This is true whether or not you call them in, though it pertains more strongly to gray foxes than to red foxes because the grays tend to favor slightly thicker cover. In 12 gauge I like 2¾-inch Magnums loaded with No. 2's or 4's—preferably 4's—and in 20-gauge I use shot of the same size, but I'm glad my 20 is chambered for 3-inch Magnums. If you use a repeater, it will perform on foxes most reliably if it has a full choke or an adjustable choke set at full. If you use a double, the best choke combination is modified and full.

Of course, there are occasions even in thick brush or tangled woods when a rifle will serve better than a smoothbore, or when you just don't need a scattergun and would prefer to avoid putting pellet holes in a fox skin when a single bullet hole will do. This is why some hunters like combination rifle-shotguns for fox hunting. The three-barreled European drillings or the two-barreled over-under combinations made both in Europe and the United States let you choose instantly between a smoothbore and a rifle barrel. Whether scoped or not, they seem a trifle more difficult than a conventional shotgun for most hunters to swing smoothly, quickly, and accurately, but they do take a lot of game. For foxes (and for turkeys in some regions, as well) I think the best combination is a .222 rifle barrel over a 20-gauge Magnum or under a 12-gauge smoothbore.

Among conventional rifles, any of the popular .22 cartridges will do nicely. The average fox, red or gray, weighs no more than a house cat. Since it's smaller and easier to kill than a bobcat or coyote, some hunters use rimfire Magnums. These are all right, but only for close-in calling.

A bedded fox doesn't sleep soundly but only catnaps, raising its head occasionally to watch for danger. The animal usually curls up facing its backtrail and with its rear to the wind.

The same basic observations apply to handguns. Again, a rimfire Magnum is adequate if you can call foxes in close, but I prefer to think of the .22 Remington Jet as minimum, and I'd rather use one of the hotter .22 centerfires recommended for other predators.

From what I've already said, it's obvious that under some circumstances you might want to hunt foxes with an iron-sighted rifle or pistol. Generally speaking, however, your most reliable rifle sight would be a 2½X or 4X scope, and your zero should be at 100 yards. Many handgunners rely on a 1.3X scope, but in relatively open terrain, a lot of them prefer slightly higher magnification.

Many a gray fox has a heavy suffusion of red in its coat, and many a red fox has a great deal of salt-and-pepper gray mixed in with its coppery fur. There's one sure way to tell the two species apart. The gray's bushy tail, or brush, usually has a manelike black stripe from rump to tip, and it always has a black tip. A red fox—even one in the dark "silver" phase—always has a white brush tip.

The most commonly hunted fox species are, of course, the red and the gray. At one time, popular accounts described the red fox as a European animal, unknown in America until it was imported by fox-hunting enthusiasts among the English colonists. This is not true. There are about a dozen subspecies of red fox in North America alone, and others in Europe and Asia. American red foxes originally inhabited parts of Alaska and all of Canada from that country's lower border almost to the Arctic regions. During the

This is a young Southern gray fox. Sometimes the species is coppery—and many a red fox is grayish—but the tail of the gray species always has a black tip which provides definite identification.

1700's, European red foxes were released in at least five of the colonies, from New York southward. They were a subspecies, or race, of the same species as the American red fox. Gradually, the native race extended its range southward while the imported variety

A successful hunter and his hound trudge home with a red fox (white tail tip) and a gray fox (black tail tip). For the American style of hunting, relatively slow-moving dogs are more efficient than the classic English foxhounds, and in the Northern states hunters often use just one or two rather than a pack.

extended its range in all directions. Inevitably, the two strains inter-bred and became impossible to tell apart. Red foxes now inhabit all 48 contiguous states. They're least abundant (and therefore the hunting for them is poor) in the lower Southeast, much of the Southwest, and the Rocky Mountain states. Probably the best red-fox hunting is in the Midwest and from New England down to the mid-South.

The gray fox was originally native to the southern two-thirds of the United States and parts of Mexico. Gradually, it has extended its range far northward, though it remains absent or scarce in most of the Rocky Mountain states and the neighboring high plains. Along the Pacific Coast, it's fairly abundant from lower Washington down to Baja, and it's plentiful from the eastern fringes of the Dakotas to the Atlantic Seaboard.

The gray fox and, to a slighter extent, the red fox share part of their range with two smaller foxes. In the arid Southwest you'll find the desert fox, or kit fox, smallest and fastest of the American varieties but incapable of sustaining its speed for long distances. A lean, buff-yellow and gray creature with a black-tipped tail, it gener-ally weighs between three and six pounds at maturity, whereas a red or gray fox usually weighs from seven to twelve, or sometimes a bit more. This desert fox is probably a subspecies of the other small variety, known as the swift fox. The swift is just a trifle larger. It's buff-yellow with a black-tipped tail and blackish patches on the snout. It ranges from the Southwest up through the Dakotas and the Rockies. Both the desert fox and the swift fox are less wary than other varieties, and both have been devastated by ranching opera-tions and the now-discredited predator-poisoning campaigns. They've become so scarce that they're protected in many areas. Regardless of where they're seen, they should not be shot. This presents no real problem to the hunter, because it's easy to distin-guish one of these miniatures from a gray or red fox.

Another American species, the arctic fox, inhabits Alaska, north-ern Canada, Greenland, and several arctic islands. Few out-doorsmen realize that this animal is not a true fox, though it is closely related. Brownish-gray in summer, most arctic foxes turn winter-white except for the black nose, eyes, claws, and a few tail hairs. Some, however, exhibit a "blue phase"—turning smoky blue-gray or blackish-gray in winter. Because arctic foxes occupy such a remote range, the majority of them haven't learned to fear man. The species doesn't present enough challenge to be called huntable, but it deserves mention here because it's occasionally shot by a hungry traveler in regions where game is scarce, and its meat, though edible, can be dangerous. It should be thoroughly cooked to avoid trichinosis, and its liver should never be eaten because, like the livers of some other arctic animals, it has an extremely high vitamin A content that can be toxic.

The true foxes—both the red and the gray—are edible if you're hungry enough, but very few modern sportsmen are inclined to emulate the Indians, who at one time dined on fox as well as coyote. The typical hunter seeks foxes chiefly for the joy of the hunt. A second reason is the value of the pelt. A third is that hunting and trapping keep the fox population sufficiently in check that these predators are no serious threat to poultry or wildlife.

There are fox-hunting purists (or perhaps I should call them snobs) who insist that only the red fox is wily enough to be worth seeking. The truth is, the gray is just as wary, just as elusive. It's inferior only when pursued by hounds. It is slightly shorter-legged than the red, and because it has smaller lungs, it has less stamina. Therefore a chase sometimes lasts only a few minutes with a gray fox, and seldom more than an hour. This species is the only American canine with real tree-climbing ability. When pressed, it usually holes up or else finds a low-branched or leaning tree trunk and scrambles aloft. But it can run short distances at speeds of more than 20 miles an hour, and it sometimes escapes the hounds and the hunter by diving and weaving through dense tangles. One moment it's there, and the next it seems to have melted into the woods.

In some states the fox season is open only in fall and winter. This is fine because it's when the hunting is best and the pelts are prime. The more active an animal is—that is, the more it moves about through a hunting area—the better chance a hunter has. Most animals are especially active when seeking mates. As early as mid-fall, a few of the gray-fox males become restless, though mating activity doesn't reach its peak until February. Red foxes begin to feel the mating urge somewhat later, at least in the regions I'm familiar with, but the peak of their rut occurs at about the same time or even a little earlier—in January and February.

Another good reason to hunt foxes in the winter is that their tracks show up well on fresh snow. To me, the prints look more like a cat's than a dog's. The fore prints are slightly larger than the hind prints, and the trail is narrow—almost a single dotted line. A fox with a very bulky brush will often leave a drag mark in the snow. The fore print of a gray fox is apt to be about 1½ inches long, though it may be a trifle shorter or it may be almost two inches long. That of a red fox is apt to be at least two inches long, though the toes usually look smaller and the whole print may have a blurred appearance. This is because the red evolved in a more northerly climate and has more fur around the toes and the pad.

In the northern latitudes there's still another reason for good winter hunting. Some of the small prey species hibernate, so a fox has to accelerate its activity, going abroad for more hours per day to find food. But even in winter, if I'm hunting without hounds I limit myself to the most productive times. The best calling times are brief—from daybreak until about half an hour after sunup and (even better) from an hour before sunset until last light.

If I'm tracking or scouting, however, I quit by midafternoon. I might get a shot at a bedded fox after that, but if I jump one without getting a shot, it won't soon bed down again as it would have earlier in the day. Instead, it will probably keep moving and hunting right into the night.

Red foxes dig their dens in the spring, generally in March. A red-fox den is a nursery, and it may be abandoned before summer is over, for the young can soon fend for themselves, and family groups begin to disperse by late August. In winter, reds den again only for short periods in extremely cold weather. Normally they sleep in the open, whereas gray foxes use winter dens for warmth, shelter, and safety.

Most commonly, red-fox dens are enlarged chuck or badger holes on hummocks or slight rises in open terrains such as fields. A red fox likes to have a view of all approaches. Other sites are stream banks, rock piles, slopes, and sometimes hollow trees or logs. When it's out in the open, the main entrance is easy to spot. It's a hole surrounded by a mound or fan of packed earth, often marked by bones, feathers, bits of fur, and the like. A gray-fox den is usually harder to locate. Grays do no digging if they can find a ready-made burrow in the woods or among rocks. They like hollow trees—particularly oaks—and they also use logs, slash piles, small caves, crevices, and hollows in talus slopes.

If you spot a red-fox den, you know that foxes have been and probably still are frequenting the area. Spotting gray-fox dens can be helpful in a more direct way, because grays often hole up before the hunter gets a shot. In some regions, there are hunters who don't use hounds but take a small fox terrier along. They walk the rocky ridges until they find a den that looks as if it's in use. In goes the terrier and—if the hunter is lucky—out comes a fox. Some hunters who use hounds also carry a little terrier along. When the hounds run a fox into a den, the terrier is again put into the hole to flush it out. Of course, dens have more than one opening, and the fox doesn't always emerge where expected. It may escape and renew the chase. Wherever the fox comes out, it comes out fast. This kind of hunt requires a shotgun, and the gunner has to be alert.

For the very formal, ritualized mounted hunts of the elite, scarlet-jacketed clubs that emulate the equestrian chases of the Old World, the finest dogs are foxhounds of English bloodlines. They're more tractable and single-minded than the American strains. They perform very well on gray foxes, but they're not the best choice for the typical American-style hunting of red foxes. In the North, a hunter or several hunters will go on stand, ready to intercept the fox at strategic points where they think the dogs will push it. In parts of the South, a traditional nighttime "jug hunt" involves passing a jug around a hilltop fire while following the hounds by their sound. Sometimes the fox leads the dogs so far away that the hilltop is abandoned while the hunters patrol the back roads by car, listening for the pack. Or, if they're confident that their hounds will eventually bring the fox around, they may stay by the fire for many more hours, swapping jokes, gossip, and tall stories. Later, if at all, they may leave to pick up their dogs or intercept the fox. A few of these hunts have been known to last for three days, with the hounds finally picked up 45 miles from the starting point. If the dogs catch their quarry, they usually kill it, but a typical "hilltopper" is perfectly happy when a fox escapes after a good chase. On the big jug hunts there's usually a good deal of friendly bantering over whose dogs are the best.

Both for the hilltop socials and the more sedate style of running dogs while hunting on foot, English foxhounds are outperformed by such famous American breeds as the black-and-tan, bluetick, Arkansas traveler, Trumbo, July, redbone, Walker, and Trigg. These dogs have plenty of foxhound in them, but they're modified strains. The Walker and Trigg are probably the most widely admired. Such hounds are superb at ranging wide and then bringing a fox around or staying with it over a long course. And they have exceptionally keen noses, great stamina, bugling voices—and fox sense. In the North, hunters very often use only one or two dogs. For such hunting, it's all the more important for a hound to be a full-voiced, determined trailer and not easily put off the scent.

The American hunter wants a relatively slow-moving dog, not a racer. When pressed by hounds and horses in the English manner, a fox often runs very far into unfamiliar territory. A red fox is not only longer-winded than a gray, but much speedier. Still, if hunted in the American style, not pressed too hard, even a wily and strong red fox is likely to stay within a couple of square miles, circling like a rabbit though on an enormously wider radius over a home range. And that's how the hunter wants his fox moved.

Foxes, like deer, habitually travel favorite routes. They repeatedly use the same trails, back roads, woodland edges, fences, gates, stream crossings, and so on. After a hunter has worked a given area several times, he begins to know the usual escape routes. He also knows that when a fox escapes, it remembers the route or trick that succeeded and will repeat it. The hunter stations himself accordingly. Of course, if he's hunting an unfamiliar area, he has little choice but to judge the direction and distance of his dog or dogs by sound, then take a stand on high ground above a likely crossing area. The chance of taking the fox is considerably improved if the hunter has at least a partner or two who can rush to additional likely points of interception.

Once on stand, a hunter must be silent and stay still. Dogs seldom panic a red fox. Even while being pursued, the fox will watch and listen for new enemies. On past occasions, it has probably slipped past many human beings within shooting distance. It won't hole up

Foxes habitually travel favorite routes. When the hounds are running a fox, the shotgunners can take stands on bluffs, outcroppings, and saddles that give them an open view of trails and crossings.

or tree as a gray will, but it often avoids being run to ground. It may cross other fox trails to produce what might be called a confusion of scent. It may slip through hollow logs and culverts, trot through a stream to break its scent, walk the top of a stone fence for a while, and then jump down and double back before switching directions again—and it may know numerous other tricks. The hunter who uses hounds in unfamiliar territory must be alert, canny, fast with a shotgun, and optimistic.

Gray foxes keep to the woods and brush more diligently than reds, and they like rocky, somewhat mountainous, or at least rough, terrain. In areas where they're known to be abundant, a caller can pick a promising stand by finding the right kind of cover and topography and then looking for tracks, sign, and denning spots. Bear in mind that these animals like oak and beech stands and that grapes and cherries are probably their favorite wild fruits. (All foxes eat fruit as well as meat.) Rocky ridges and draws are promising, as are patches of heavy second growth. In the West, mesquite or chaparral thickets are good. In all regions, foxes patrol man-made trails, looking for rodents, birds, and rabbits in the trailside brush, and they patrol back roads for the same reason, as well as to pick up road kills.

Search an area for signs of use—tracks, scat, scent posts, and caches. Foxes often bury part of a kill or a bit of carrion, and they don't conceal the burial, nor do they conceal the hole when they later dig up such treasures. A spot that looks as if something had been buried there recently is apt to be a cache. It can sometimes be verified by tracks or scat—especially on snow.

If you find natural cavities along wooded edges or on a rocky slope, you may be in a denning area, and it's all the more promising if it overlooks some bottomland. It's more promising still if you see cache spots, dug-up holes, or discarded bits of bone and other debris. Try to do your calling from a nearby stand with good concealment and a good view.

Much of the same advice applies to calling red foxes, but reds prefer patchy or even open terrain for their foraging expeditions, so good calling spots are lightly wooded hilltops or ridges and the fringes of brush and woods. Advantageous features include some elevation and a downwind place of concealment with a wide view.

The same type of camouflage recommended for calling coyotes is advisable for calling foxes. This includes "winter whites"—and not only for calling but for tracking and stalking red foxes, which are commonly taken in wide-open fields where a hunter can be seen at a great distance. Winter hunts sometimes combine calling and tracking sessions. Whichever method a hunter happens to be using, he should remember that all canine species, including foxes, can recognize human beings. Some other wild animals fail to do so when a man stands or sits perfectly still. They seem to perceive a stationary hunter as an inanimate object. But a fox perceives a stationary hunter as a stationary hunter.

Calling foxes involves the same general principles as calling coyotes, but a few minor variations and refinements are worth remembering. Naturally, you'll want a wide view from your hiding spot, but the downwind direction is one you can ignore. In typical fox-hunting country—farmlands and the woods near farmlands—foxes have been hunted for many generations. For that matter, there are heavily hunted areas where calling is the least productive, rather than the most productive, way to hunt foxes. They have an acute sense of smell and tend to be more cautious than coyotes, though whether they're equally intelligent is questionable. In any event, their approach isn't the coyote's headlong charge, but a stealthier investigation, intermediate between the coyote's style and the bobcat's. If a hungry fox hears your call and doesn't become suspicious, it will probably appear within 15 minutes, sometimes much sooner. But it will seldom come within close range from a direction that allows you to be scented. This tip is especially important in states like New Jersey, where the law limits you to using a shotgun. In regions where you can use a rifle, you can often find a natural blind with a long view of open spaces or patchy cover. While you won't often catch a gray fox out in the open, the reds like such terrain, and you can't be sure where you'll see a distant target. But even so, you want the wind in your favor.

In some states, it's legal to hunt by calling at night and using a red-lensed headlamp. In some, it's also legal to use phonograph records or tapes. These approaches work, but so does mouth-calling

Many shotgunners abide by old fox-hunting traditions. This man is using a horn to call his hounds in after a good run.

during the still hours of half-light. The dying-rabbit squeal brings foxes, sometimes the bird-in-distress call brings foxes, and quite often a loud mouse squeak is just as effective, except that it doesn't carry as far. With a bit of practice, you can produce an inviting squeak by merely sucking the back of your hand.

Where foxes are frequently hunted, a call must not only be realistic but so inviting that a fox has difficulty resisting it. Start with the shriek of a suddenly injured rabbit and gradually change the series of squeals to the kind of whimpers a rabbit might make with its last gasps. Then be quiet for a while before repeating the series. And remember that even with this kind of coaxing, a fox that has had experience with humans may violate the usual rules and take almost half an hour before coming close.

Tracking is one of the most enjoyable ways to hunt foxes. Grays are supposed to be much harder to track than reds because they weave through such dense cover and bed in less open areas—or in a den if the weather is cold enough. Nonetheless, we take a lot of gray foxes in my part of the country, and I vividly remember an occasion when I almost stepped on one in a jungle of honeysuckle that formed a border between a woodlot and a soybean field. With either kind of fox, you have a headstart if you know how to find reasonably open places that have some special attractions for the animals. I've already mentioned cover, roads, and trails, and the attraction of grapes and cherries. In addition, Northeastern hunters have learned that it pays to investigate apple orchards in the early morning and at twilight. In overcast weather, I must add, the time of day doesn't matter much. In the South, the edges of peanut fields are good starting points for a tracking expedition or a hunt with hounds. Nor is the fox's taste for fruits and vegetables restricted to those choice morsels. Foxes (as well as coyotes, come to think of it) are sometimes surprised while raiding melon fields. Like raccoons, they also raid corn. They enjoy plums and peaches, too. And Southern foxes like persimmons as much as Northern foxes like apples. Wild fruits that attract them include strawberries, blueberries, gooseberries, crowberries, serviceberries, and blackberries.

Whether walking the rolling farmlands looking for red foxes or cruising the back roads in a car, carry binoculars—7X35 is a good size—just as you would for coyotes or chucks. This is especially productive when snow is on the ground. Early in the morning, a fox generally meanders about looking for mice, and a little later finds a slightly elevated spot from which to watch its back trail. There it beds—not sleeping soundly but catnapping, raising its head now and then to watch for danger. Sometimes a fox climbs a higher elevation to bed. It may use a mound, slash pile, or even a haystack. Glass all such places. Against white snow, the coppery coat of a fox can be seen at a great distance, and with a scoped rifle, you may not have to stalk closer than the point from which you first see your fox.

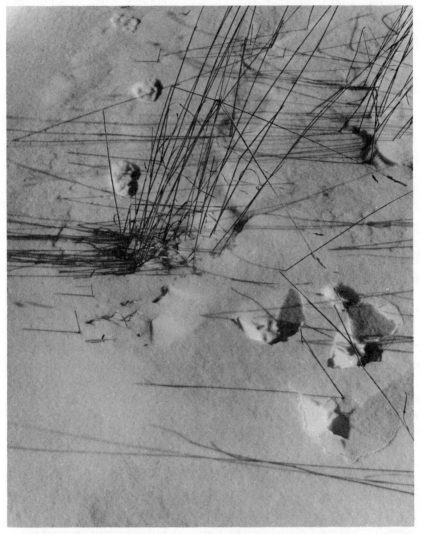

With snow on the ground, you can often trail a fox to its bed. Here, the tracks of a red fox lead to and away from a scent post. The small dark dots sprinkled at the bases of the stalks are urine crystals.

If you do have to stalk closer, crouch, go slowly, use every available bit of cover, and approach from downwind. Stop dead-still whenever the fox raises its head.

Without snow on the ground, you can seldom follow the trail of a fox. With a shallow blanket of fresh snow, it's relatively simple, but I don't bother to go out if the snow is still falling at dawn. Foxes, like most predators, do little if any foraging while it's storming. Besides, the falling snow blurs or obliterates tracks. But after a prolonged snowfall, predators are hungry enough to be out everywhere, and if the blanket isn't too deep, the tracking is easy and so is the walking.

A snaking maze of fox tracks indicates mousing. I've read that such tracks can be followed. Maybe they can by the tracking wizard who wrote that, but not by me and not by most people. If I can't find a trail heading away from the maze, I just go on scouting. When the fox has finished mousing, it heads for another area—usually for a bedding spot—leaving a straighter trail. As it remains alert for both prey and danger, it generally heads into the prevailing wind. Don't follow the trail precisely, but stay off to one side or crisscross it as you move along. For one thing, the fox may detour at short intervals to do some more mousing. For another, it will eventually leave its roughly straight course and begin zigzagging as it looks for a safe bedding spot. Before finally bedding down, it always circles, and it again walks into the wind as it approaches the spot where it will bed. Then it will curl up with its rear to the wind. That way, it's more or less facing its backtrail to watch for danger, and it can still smell anything coming from the opposite direction.

Sometimes, when lone tracking produces nothing, a group drive will. Several standers are stationed at the downwind end of a woodlot. A couple of drivers start walking toward them from the other end, keeping to opposite sides of the lot. Two or more additional drivers soon follow, walking through the woods. This is best done with shotguns rather than rifles. The hunters can then be far enough apart for safety, but close enough together to reduce the likelihood that a fox will slip through unseen. The drive has to be a quiet one, or a spooked fox will manage to slip back between the drivers, even if they're closely spaced.

I wonder if hunters in other parts of the country are familiar with the driving variation known as "belling the fox." I was introduced to it in New Jersey. One hunter follows a fox track through brush or woods, now and then ringing a cow bell. A couple of partners keep slightly ahead of him and out to each side, within sight if possible, but at least 100 yards away. A fox is a very inquisitive animal. Started from its bed but not yet fully alarmed by the noise, it will cautiously move back toward the bell and then cut away to one side, past one flanker or the other. This doesn't work every time, but quite often—certainly often enough to be worth a try when nothing else has produced any action.

MEDIUM GAME

Cougars

The cougar—also known as mountain lion, puma, panther, and catamount—is a fairly big, tough animal, yet one that doesn't require a very high-powered or big-bored rifle. A mature male generally measures at least six feet long from his nose to the tip of his 2½-foot tail, and he's apt to weigh about 140 pounds. A female is often a third lighter, which is still a lot of animal. Why, then, do most lion hunters seem almost careless in the choice of rifle or handgun caliber? The answer lies in the hunting method, which almost always involves the use of hounds. A cougar simply doesn't expose itself to long shots, so there's no need for long-range accuracy and power.

When treed, or bayed in a maze of rimrock, a big lion can be killed cleanly with a light deer rifle such as a .270, .25–06, or .243. Even smaller calibers will suffice, though the favorites are those in the .30 class. Many lion hunters use a .30–30 lever-action. They rely on open sights since the target will be big and close and, as a matter of fact, they'll move in as close as possible. What they want is something fast-handling, particularly in case a follow-up shot is needed to prevent a cat from tangling with the dogs.

A good many lion hunters use handguns. One well-known lion hunter always wore a .38 Special. The usual choices are .357 Magnum, .41 Magnum, .44 Magnum, or .45, but some experienced hunters use rimfire handguns. A .22 Long Rifle hollow-point is all that's needed when you walk right up to a treed cougar. A single-action will do as well as a double-action or auto if the shooter is quick and accurate with it.

There are two schools of thought regarding bullet placement. Some guides recommend head shots, on the theory that such

Mountain lions like brushy habitat but they also like high, dry, rough rim-rock. If there are canyons that provide both, or if there's rocky terrain close above the brush, an area is all the more promising. When pressed by hounds, these cats instinctively head upward into the rocks, so be prepared for a rigorous chase before you catch up to the pack.

placement will result in an almost instant kill and prevent the cat from killing any dogs. But others point out that a head shot can spoil a trophy skull, and that a lion hit there may actually come out of a tree fighting and inflict considerable damage before he dies. They recommend a lung shot—behind the shoulder and a little more than halfway down from the spine. A lion hit there is likely to cling to the tree for a moment but dies quickly and will be dead when it falls to the ground. If the shot isn't so perfectly placed that this happens, it will jump down and run. This rarely presents any danger because it will die very quickly—before the dogs can catch it.

Although the foregoing advice may help to safeguard the hounds, they should be tied securely before any shooting is done. A wounded cougar can kill a dog, and a follow-up shot can be almost impossible with the pack in the way.

Biologically, the mountain lion is of course a predatory species, but it is now generally classified as a game animal and accorded more protection than those classified as predators—which is why I've included it in this section rather than in the chapter devoted to the other, smaller American predators.

The word "predator" is still tainted with the connotation of "varmint," but the time of the lion bounties is gone, and none too soon. Though it's true that an occasional cougar becomes a livestock-killing rogue and must be eliminated, raids on domestic animals are infrequent and cougars are generally beneficial to their wild prey. Their diet includes all manner of small game, rodents, and birds. However, they prefer deer—especially mule deer. Since a healthy cougar kills about one deer per week where the prey is sufficiently plentiful, an overabundance of lions would certainly be undesirable. But these predators are far from overabundant. A six-year study in an Idaho primitive area where they're relatively plentiful indicated that cougars tend to kill the easiest prey among deer and elk: the defective young, the old, and the weak. They deter the spread of disease by removing sick animals, and they alleviate overbrowsing in winter habitat.

Although, at this writing, there's no closed season in British Columbia and Arizona, the cougar has been granted the status of game in most of the West and is fully protected in the scant Eastern regions where it survives. Five Western states—Colorado, Idaho, Montana, Nevada, and Utah—open the cougar season at various dates in autumn and keep it open until March or April. Oregon has a short season—December only. New Mexico's season lasts from early August until mid-January, Washington's from the beginning of August until the end of March. Be sure to check state regulations—which may include a permit-purchasing requirement.

One reason why the open season is set at such widely varying times of year in some localities is that cougars have no set breeding season. In some areas of mild climate on the West Coast, most females give birth in winter, whereas in Idaho, most births occur in spring or early summer. Thus, the season in a given region is likely to be set when there's least chance of orphaning young cubs.

For anyone who doesn't live in prime lion country, the only way to plan a hunt is to contact one of the licensed guide-outfitters who advertise cougar hunts. Such advertisements appear in a number of outdoor magazines. In addition, the state game departments and guides' associations will furnish lists of lion-hunting guides. It's wise—vital, in fact—to check an outfitter's credentials with the state game department and to check the references he provides from previous clients.

A competent, properly equipped guide is needed for two reasons. First, he knows where and how to find the game. Second, he provides a number of crucial assets, which may include horses and will certainly include hounds. A successful lion hunt without a good dog pack is rare indeed, even though cougars are killed now and then in chance encounters when hunters are out for deer or other game.

The most popular lion dogs are foxhounds, foxhound-bloodhound crosses, and occasionally purebred bloodhounds.

The cougar's favorite food is deer—especially mule deer. This cat is dining on a deer it killed. After eating its fill, it will cache the deer by loosely heaping leaves and branches. Then it will "lie up" to rest nearby. It will keep returning—probably for several days, until the meat becomes "ripe"—so a fresh cache indicates that a lion may be in the immediate vicinity.

Walker, Plott, redbone, blue-tick, and black-and-tan hounds are also used. Now and then, a big, keen-nosed mongrel turns out to be a good trail dog, too. I've read of an Airedale-collie cross that was outstanding as a cougar dog. It takes years to develop a good pack of lion hounds. They must be adept at trailing, they must be tireless, and they must be so thoroughly trained that they won't run deer, coyotes, or other animals. Not even hot bobcat scent should distract a truly fine cougar hound from its work. The dogs must also be persistent enough to keep a cat treed or bayed, perhaps for hours, while the hunters catch up.

As a rule, the hunters follow the hounds on horseback or afoot. (In some regions walking is more common than riding, especially in winter, when a cougar may lead pursuers over terrain impassable for a horse.) Since the pursuit can sometimes be long and grueling, a hunter should get himself into condition before setting out on a lion trip, and should practice his horsemanship if it's to be a mounted hunt. He should also plan to travel light, which is why some hunters strongly prefer sidearms.

However, lion-hunting stories have tended to exaggerate the stamina of the average cougar. A number of factors, including the individual cougar, determine the duration of a successful hunt. To begin with, the dogs may strike a warm trail almost immediately or not for days. If the cougar is hiding somewhere close when they find the fresh spoor, they may give chase at top speed and the run will be brief because—legend to the contrary notwithstanding—the cougar is a rather short-winded animal. And if he has fed recently and heavily, he may tree or scramble up a rimrock and come to bay within a few hundred yards. More often, though, the chase will last for something closer to a mile when a cougar is pushed hard. And when circumstances are somewhat more in favor of the lion, six or eight miles may be closer to the average. Once a lion is treed, horseback hunters almost always have to dismount and walk up because the cat will seek the roughest possible terrain before treeing.

An 8-mile walk or ride in typically rugged cougar terrain can be very demanding. Moreover, it may be preceded by a long, tough search for a reasonably fresh trail. A lion's home range may cover up to 30 miles, a lot of territory. And, finally, if a trail is cold or merely warm—not really hot—the pursuit itself may go on for several days.

This is not because of the lion's exaggerated stamina or speed but because there's nothing exaggerated about the stories of a lion's elusive cunning. The animal will backtrack, weave through and across canyons, make its way through and over broken rimrock (where a horse can seldom follow, by the way), cut back into thick woods, move out over dry, flat rock that holds scent poorly, and cross streams on logs or rocks when possible or swim them when necessary.

It helps to know that, more often than not, a cougar instinctively heads upward when a pack gets fairly close. Sometimes the hunters can judge where the chase will end and use a shortcut to get there.

More than one noted cougar hunter has preferred to use a single exceptional dog, but most hound packs number from a pair to half a dozen or so. Probably the easiest hunting method is to scout in a four-wheel-drive after snow has fallen. When a track is found, the hunters move out with a couple of hounds on leash and then turn them loose when the cat is jumped.

Truly fine, experienced hounds need no snow. They can follow a two-day-old lion trail even on bare ground. Therefore, a sportier hunting method is to camp out in known lion country and start early in the morning, by horseback, with up to half a dozen hounds. A couple of them should be outstanding "strike" dogs. The pair of strike dogs will do the hunting for a trail, while the others are kept on leads, following the horses. When the strike dogs pick up scent, even if it's cold, the others are released and the actual pursuit begins.

Many experienced lion hunters bell their dogs. This is not to keep track of them but to keep lions from attacking them. When a trail becomes hard to follow, even a very open trailer sometimes works silently. Any dog that barks loudly enough can tree a full-sized cougar, yet the lions have little fear of a silent dog. On occasion, cougars have turned back on silent dogs, ambushed, and killed them. The bell prevents this.

Although trailing a cougar without hounds is futile, it pays to know lion tracks and sign so that you'll recognize likely places to cast the dogs. The tracks are generally spaced about two feet apart in a rather direct line, and in snow the tail may leave drag traces between the prints. The forefoot print is likely to be three to four inches in length and width, slightly larger in soft snow, and quite round, with the indentations of four toes in a curved row in front of the heel pad. The fifth toe is too high to leave an indentation. The hind print is similar but slightly smaller. It's seldom placed precisely in the front print, as with some other species, but it may overlap. The claws, normally retracted, leave no mark.

Some hunters scout on snow until they find tracks. Then they follow the trail with the hounds on leash, turning them loose when the cat is jumped. These tracks measure a bit over three inches long.

Good lion country is usually rather brushy, with such foliage as scrub oak, juniper, cedar, pine, manzanita, and the like, and with high, dry, rough rimrock where a cougar can "lie up" when not hunting. Such country may have tracts of good deer browse— promising areas for a lion hunt. A cougar hunter who knows where the local mule deer browse has a definite advantage.

While patrolling its home range, seeking prey, a cougar occasionally rises on its hind legs and sharpens its front claws by raking a tree trunk. Along the way, it also scrapes up small mounds of snow or twigs, leaves, and dirt, on which it urinates. It may deposit scat as well as urine. If this scent post is fresh, another cougar happening upon it will add to it and then leave the vicinity. It's a mechanism to facilitate mutual avoidance—a way of staking out hunting territories. The scratching posts and sign heaps mark good starting places for hounds.

Another important kind of sign is a lion's cached kill. After pulling down a deer, a cougar generally drags the carcass to the nearest cover, such as a deadfall or a patch of thick brush. After devouring perhaps eight pounds, the cougar loosely heaps leaves and branches over the kill, then retires to a brushy ravine or rocky shelf to rest. Cougars dislike tainted meat, but they keep returning to a kill, sometimes for several days, until it's consumed or becomes too ripe. A fairly fresh cache indicates that a mountain lion is probably nearby.

Until recently, cougars were assumed to be almost entirely nocturnal, and hunters assumed this explained why the big cats are almost never located without dogs. However, a study in Idaho showed the animals to be as active in daylight as at night. Once in a while a hunter or other outdoorsman, upon turning back the way he came, discovers tracks proving that a mountain lion has been trailing him—and in broad daylight. As a rule, the lion is merely inquisitive; attacks are rare. But the trailing may go on for miles because the lion is too cautious to get close and thereby verify that the strange two-legged creature it's following isn't a prey species. Even in cases like this, an attempt to turn the tables and trail the lion without dogs is nearly always useless.

Despite all I've said, there is one way to hunt mountain lions without hounds. The success rate isn't high, but it's an exciting endeavor, and if it gets you no cougar, it may provide some shooting anyway—at a bobcat or coyote. I'm referring to the use of a predator call. Though cougars are much harder to toll in than bobcats, the techniques are the same, and you can apply the tips given in the bobcat section. Just be sure you're in a good cougar area, very well concealed in a spot where you won't be scented, and be absolutely silent except for the calling. Few hunters are aware that it can be done, but cougars have been lured successfully (if not often) with both manual and phonographic calls.

The well-known outdoor writer Byron Dalrymple took part in a successful hunt of this type in Mexico. The callers were the Burnham brothers of Marble Falls, Texas, famous for their calling ability as well as for their design and manufacture of various animal calls. That particular hunt took place at night, when cougars are a bit easier to fool, but expert callers have also managed the trick in the daytime—another proof that cougars are not really nocturnal.

Since mountain lions will happily dine on rabbit when they fail to kill a deer (or when opportunity is hard to resist) the injured-rabbit call can attract them, just as it does the smaller predators. But bear in

Few hunters realize that cougars can be lured with a predator call, either phonographic or manually operated. It's been done in Mexico and more recently in Arizona. This photo shows a lion curiously—or hungrily— approaching an exposed loudspeaker propped in a bush.

Pronghorns

Pronghorns aren't very big or tough—a mature buck generally weighs less than 115 pounds and stands no more than three feet high at the shoulder—yet these animals can be difficult to bring down because they're so fast and wary. One of the finest trophies on record was an Oregon pronghorn buck shot by Eugene C. Starr in 1942 at a distance of 510 yards. That would be too far away for most of us to chance a shot, but the usual range is pretty long, probably between 200 and 400 yards.

You need a bullet with sufficient velocity to provide a relatively flat trajectory, and it should also have weight enough to be somewhat resistant to wind-drift. Out at the target, it should have plenty of retained energy, as well as fast expansion upon penetrating. A muzzle velocity in the neighborhood of 3,000 feet per second is essential, so the minimum cartridge is generally considered to be a .243 or 6mm with a 100-grain pointed soft-point bullet.

A better choice (and I'd bet it's the most popular of all) is the .270 with a 130-grain bullet. This has a muzzle velocity of 3,110 fps, and as far out as 300 yards it retains more than 2,300 fps of that zip. Even at 400 yards, it's still traveling at more than 2,000 fps, and at that distance it delivers over 1,200 foot-pounds of energy. Bert Popowski, a notable authority on pronghorn antelope, has called this caliber "about as perfect for pronghorns and other plains game as any in existence." Which means that if you'd like a rifle for both pronghorns and mule deer, the .270 is a fine choice.

This is not to imply that other calibers won't kill pronghorns cleanly at long range. The .257, .25–06, and the .264 Magnum will all do the job with their 100- to 140-grain bullets. So will a .300 Magnum with a 150-grain bullet.

In any of the calibers mentioned, bolt-action rifles and single-shots probably have an edge over other actions. The first shot is usually what counts in pronghorn hunting, so it's accuracy, not speed of repeat fire, that brings success.

Having stressed the frequency of long-range shots, I must avoid giving the impression that an exceedingly powerful scope is wanted. Pronghorns are high-strung creatures. They don't stand still for very long the way woodchucks do. Although chuck or prarie-dog shooting is excellent practice for a pronghorn hunter, there's seldom a comparable amount of time in which to get a solid rest and a perfect sight picture. Even when browsing or grazing contentedly, pronghorns amble along, like deer but more nervously. There are experienced hunters who take pronghorns with 6X or 8X scopes, but a slightly lower magnification and wider field of view will help the average shooter center the target in the reticle quickly and then hold steadily. I'd say the best choice is either a 4X scope or a variable with settings from 2X or 3X up to 7, 8, or 9. Though you'll probably leave it set at 4X most of the time, a choice of settings may sway you in favor of a variable if you plan to use the same scope-and-rifle combination for other game.

Very few pronghorns are taken with sidearms, but it can be, and has been, done. My advice in this connection is threefold. First, you'd better use the sort of powerful, accurate pistol cartridge that might be chosen for the long-range game-silhouette matches in which a steel-plate target must not only be hit but knocked over at considerable distances. A Thompson/Center Contender single-shot pistol specially chambered for the .30 Herrett cartridge comes to mind. If you prefer a repeater, a good (though expensive) choice would be the Auto Mag pistol chambered for the .357 AMP. And although pronghorns have been killed by hunters using open sights on both of these guns, a 2½X scope should be installed. Second, even with the gun scoped, you'd better become adept at stalking and limit your shots to 100 yards at most. And third, you'd better practice your shooting until you can place your bullets almost as accurately at that range with a handgun as with a rifle. Not many of us ever attain that degree of proficiency.

To find a band of pronghorns with a good buck among them

Les Bowman, a former guide-outfitter and well-known hunting writer, kneels with a fine pronghorn buck that exhibits a wider-than-usual horn spread. Open country is the rule in pronghorn hunting, and most hunters use rifles mounted with 4X scopes or variable models, though a few favor fixed-power scopes with a magnification of 6X or 8X.

usually requires some scouting, and pronghorns have such sharp senses—particularly vision—that when you first spot game, it will probably be at a considerable distance. An important part of your equipment are good binoculars of at least 7X35 specifications. Some hunters prefer 8X35 or 9X35.

If you do your scouting by vehicle, you should also pack along a spotting scope. Antelope trophies are hard to judge, and all the harder without the close look afforded by a powerful spotting scope.

The horns a buck sheds in its first year are puny, but a "long yearling"—approaching its second autumn—may develop 8-inch horns, and in some cases may look like an acceptable specimen, if not a trophy, when viewed at long range. Most does also have horns, but they're usually prongless, sometimes hardly more than bumps and seldom more than a few inches long. The problem, really, is to differentiate between a buck that's almost good enough and one that's quite good.

A hunter wants horns measuring at least 13 inches long and with substantial prongs jutting from them if possible. A horn length of 14

It's difficult to judge a pronghorn trophy, especially at long distance. This is a good buck. The horns are wide and high—as high as the head is long. They're thicker from front to rear than the ears and have sizable prongs.

inches or so is very good, and anything exceeding that is excellent. But because of the lyre-shaped curvature near the tips of antelope horns, length is difficult to estimate. Bear in mind as you examine an animal in the distance that an immature buck's horns don't look as massive or as deeply black as those of a passable trophy. Use your binocular or spotting scope to compare the horn size with parts of the animal's head. On a good buck, the horns are usually thicker from front to rear than the ears, and they should project considerably higher. The prongs should be conspicuous, and the length of an entire horn from base to tip should nearly equal the length of the head. Anything longer than that will be a fine trophy, indeed.

There are five subspecies of pronghorns, distributed from Oregon eastward across the Great Plains and southward into Mexico. More than 90 percent of today's populations are the common "American" pronghorn (*Antilocapra americana americana*). This subspecies and the Oregon pronghorn (*A. a. oregona*) account for most of the finest trophies taken. The rather small range of the Oregon pronghorn is centered in that state's eastern sagebrush regions. If you're hoping for an outstanding trophy, probably the best place to try is there or the plains region, where *A. a. americana* prevails. Wyoming and Montana have the biggest herds, though there's good hunting in about a dozen other Western states.

According to a common misconception, it's futile to hunt pronghorn where there's no sage. In most regions the animals do rely heavily on sage, but only because it's the most plentiful and palatable food left to them by cattlemen and farmers. They can thrive where sage is scarce if they can find the right grasses, forbs, and browse plants. When scouting in arid country, be sure to glass any splashes of vegetation that contrast with the pale desert monochrome, and remember that pronghorns like rabbitbrush, snowberry, snakeweed, saltbush, wheatgrass, cedar, bitterbrush, juniper, and alfalfa. They even like prickly pear, a cactus that often grows where most browse plants are meager or absent.

Pronghorns are exceptionally fleet animals with enormous stamina. They can run at more than 30 miles an hour for perhaps 15 miles without resting, and they can double that speed for a mile or two. This can be a problem because they often spot you while you're trying to spot them. Since there's no hope of overtaking them once they've been spooked, the smart tactic is to count on the fact that they won't run far if not pursued. Try to make a wide circle and come up near them again. This can use up a good part of the hunting day in some instances and isn't guaranteed to work, but you can return to the same area tomorrow and they'll probably still be around.

Most game animals are most easily stalked from above—that is, from elevations higher than where they're standing or moving. They tend to watch for potential danger from below and escape by making their way upward. The reason becomes obvious when you visualize sheep or goats climbing to avoid such predators as wolves. Even deer are likely to move upward, though they can't begin to negotiate the seemingly inaccessible crags where a mountain goat escapes danger. But pronghorns are an exception to the rule. They're accustomed to terrain where any enemy, from coyote to man, can follow and stalk them. In the open plains and semidesert country they inhabit, both predators and prey rely heavily on vision. You may have noticed that coyotes often climb rises to look about for something edible: a rabbit or whatever else might be surprised and caught. Pronghorns look for danger straight out and above even more carefully than they watch any lower terrain.

For this reason it's easiest (though never truly easy) to stalk them from below. In typically open pronghorn country, there's very little cover, but you can work closer to the game by using the concealment of low stream beds, hillocks, gullies, dips, and brush, always staying as low to the ground as possible.

Anyone who has spent much time in pronghorn country has seen the "heliographic" danger signal employed by this unusual species. A pronghorn has a big white rump patch—a bright rosette of long hairs that can be erected by a complex musculature, flaring the patch out several inches in all directions. The result is a white flash, and it's used to communicate alarm, just as a whitetail deer lifts its "flag" when spooked. But from the hunter's standpoint, there are important differences between the pronghorn's rosette and the deer's flag. For one thing, pronghorns sometimes flash their rosettes when merely nervous, before they're really spooked. For another,

This is the kind of shooting that's often demanded in pronghorn country. You want a cartridge with a relatively flat trajectory but with a bullet heavy enough to be somewhat wind-resistant. The bullet should also retain plenty of energy at long range and should expand fast upon pe͠ ͠trating. Probably the most popular choice is the .270 with a 130-grain bullet.

the flash can be seen at great distances on open prairies or desert flats, and when one animal sends the signal, it's repeated instantly by all others within sight. I recall one occasion when I'd glassed a wide expanse of Wyoming grassland and failed to spot a small band of antelope—for their dominant tan color blended with the background—until I noticed several winking white dots near the rim of a far rise. Thus the rosettes can occasionally reveal distant game to an alert hunter.

On other occasions, when the hunter is within range, the flaring white can tell him that he must make his shot right now or forego it. There's no way to be sure whether the animals are erecting their rump patches because they're mildly nervous or because they're jittery enough to run in another instant.

Pronghorns are notoriously alert and almost equally inquisitive. This means their attention can be riveted on one hunter, who serves as a diversionary object, while another hunter works in closer. It doesn't always succeed but is certainly worth a try when a band is feeding or moving in an open area where there seems to be no way to get quite close enough for a shot. Assuming the two partners have been crouching or crawling, one man slowly stands up, moving gently to avoid stampeding the band. He stands there in full view or begins to walk away. While the animals are watching him, the other partner continues to stalk, usually by a circuitous route, since pronghorns have a very wide arc of vision.

A variation on this tactic, useful for a lone hunter, is simply to stand up, walk away, and then circle around to shorten the range.

Still another way to take advantage of a pronghorn's inquisitiveness was taught to early settlers by the Plains Indians, who waved their hands or any attention-getting object in the air to coax the game toward them. Pronghorns are more wary today, having been heavily and efficiently hunted for so long, but the same method sometimes still works. Again, it's worth a try when there's no way to get quite close enough. At this point, you should be hidden by brush, rock, or whatever. You raise your hand into view and wiggle your fingers or flutter a handkerchief. This may elicit any one of three responses. One is a flaring of rosettes and a sudden stampede—a gamble you choose to take and one that makes the hunt all the more exciting. The second possibility is just a mild curiosity on the part of the animals, which seems for the moment to bring about a stalemate. They may look your way, but they don't move. The third possibility is that one or more of the animals will be magnetized by the fluttering object. Often the antelope that approaches is the herd buck, the finest trophy in the band. Slowly, snorting softly, he comes closer while the hunter tries to steady his rifle and his nerves.

But what can be done in the event of the second possibility, the apparent stalemate? The answer is to take another gamble. Rise slowly, in full view. If the animals still don't flee at this point, they can sometimes be approached more closely—not by walking directly toward them but by moving closer on an oblique line, steadily and quietly.

In September (earlier in southerly regions) pronghorn bucks

begin to disperse from their bachelor bands to gather harems. The rut generally lasts well into October. Hunting is apt to be best just before the rut and during its first few weeks. At this time, bucks are in the finest physical condition, bold and active, with their horns fully developed and not about to be shed for quite some time. (Pronghorns are the only horned animals—truly horned, not antlered— that shed their headgear, and actually, they shed only the black outer sheaths, retaining a skeletal core.)

The hunting season varies considerably among states—and also among districts or management zones within some states. But generally, the season coincides with at least part of the breeding season, so you may want to plan a hunt accordingly. The states with the longest seasons are Wyoming, New Mexico, Idaho, and Montana. All four states have hunting during the rut, though New Mexico and Idaho split their seasons. Hunting during the rut doesn't deplete future populations, because any harem master killed is quickly replaced by another. Hunting at this time doesn't make the sport too easy, either, because the mating urge doesn't rob pronghorn bucks of their wariness.

If you do much hunting, sooner or later you're almost certain to top a rise and surprise a band of a dozen or more pronghorns. They'll surprise you, too, of course, but if you aren't flustered, you'll assume a solid sitting or prone position as they run from you. Not only does this give you a steadier shooting platform; it also alarms the animals less than if you remained standing, so they may not move off at top speed. Be ready to shoot, because fleeing pronghorns tend to pause and look back, just as mule deer so often do.

The antelope will race along, single file, with the herd buck at the end, serving as rear guard. This keeps the best trophy closest to you for a shot. Most likely, they'll stop running when they reach the farthest crest, before spilling over it and dropping out of view. The pause ordinarily lasts anywhere from about three seconds to ten. That isn't much time, but you've already settled into shooting position and picked your target, the closest buck, so you have a good chance to get off a careful shot.

If you spot pronghorns without their spotting you, there's a better chance for a successful stalk. All the members of a band may be alert, but one of them—most often an old doe standing on a little rise—is likely to be serving the herd as sentinel. Watch her most

With their rump patches flared in alarm, eight pronghorns streak away. As usual, the herd buck—the trophy—brings up the rear. The animals may be running at 60 miles an hour, but if they aren't severely spooked they'll probably halt atop the next rise, pausing to look back. If the hunter is in position and ready, he may then have a shot at a stationary target.

closely. If you can stalk without revealing yourself to her, you may well get close enough to a buck. Stay low, take your time, and make a circling stalk to take advantage of any rise or screening vegetation. If you can get within 200 to 250 yards, it's time to assume a steady shooting position.

When pronghorns move from one area to another—to a water hole, for example, or to relatively low, protected places at the onset of bad fall weather—they often travel along passes, draws, or sheltered valleys. These are good places to scout, or to wait in ambush if you've seen antelope there before. Note the wind direction and scout the lee sides of hills. Antelopes will often move, feed, and rest on a lee side.

Generally speaking, the best places to take a stand and try to ambush pronghorns if you've tired of scouting is the vicinity of a frequently used water hole, pasture, or salt lick. But you don't want your stand at a high point unless it offers concealment. Just as dips and draws mark a good stalking route, they also mark good ambush places, since pronghorns tend to look out toward the skyline— expecting to see danger far off. Their sight and hearing are their keenest senses and best defenses. All the same, it's wise to wait where there's no strong breeze to carry your scent to the game.

Mountain Goats

More often than not, a hunter on a big-game trip would enjoy collecting a good goat trophy but does not consider the mountain goat his most important priority. He may be seeking a sheep trophy, an elk, a bear, and in some regions he may want a moose or caribou. He chooses his equipment accordingly. A goat can be killed cleanly with a 120-grain expanding-point .25–06 or even a 100-grain hollow-point .243, but I'd prefer something a bit heftier. If I were hunting the high country exclusively for goat, I'd be happy with the .264 Magnum or .270. Either of those calibers would also do nicely for sheep. So would the 7mm Magnum or one of the .300 Magnums. And either of those last two would serve well for any other big game encountered. I think, however, that I must agree with the late Jack O'Connor and several other renowned authorities who refused to forsake the .30–06 for any of the newer cartridges when the objective was an assortment of medium and big game at assorted, but often fairly long, ranges. There may be no true all-around cartridge, but the '06 probably comes closest.

I'm aware that some of our finest hunters use high-power scopes for mountain game, but I feel that 4X is about the best magnification for most of us—partly because of those mixed possibilities I just referred to, partly because greater magnification is seldom needed for a killing shot when you get into position for a goat or sheep.

I've said elsewhere that I believe in using as much scope power as you can handle properly, and I'm not contradicting that principle here. After all, to quote a favorite truism of my friend Jim Carmichel, "you can't hit what you can't see." But how much can most of us handle properly? When I'm winded, shaky, and tense after an arduous climb in thin mountain air, and I have a slight case of trophy fever, I sometimes experience a momentary panic while I try to put the reticle on the game. The higher the power, the narrower the field of view is and the tougher it is to find that sight picture. Having managed to do so before the game moves (perhaps), it's tough with a high-power scope to conquer the apparent wavering of reticle against image. I'm pretty sure the average hunter will reluctantly admit to the same degree of difficulty I experience. For us, 4X is enough.

The classic way to hunt mountain game is with one of the aforementioned powerful, flat-shooting rifles, and there used to be a lot of printed talk about the challenging shots that had to be made at long range. The talk was valid, but a lot of hunting writers must have been embarrassed when archery enthusiasts began taking goats and sheep with the bow and arrow, thereby proving that such game can be stalked to surprisingly close range by a hunter with sufficient skill, stamina, time, and patience. If a species can be hunted with a bow, obviously it can be stalked close enough for a clean kill with a handgun. And a few hunters have been doing that in recent years.

Alfred J. Goerg, a pioneering handgun hunter who died some years ago in an Alaskan plane crash, once killed a fine billy with a .357 Magnum Colt Python. The range was about 180 yards, and he was using the revolver's standard open sights. To understand the degree of skill needed for such shooting, you should be aware that Al's front sight would have covered about 20 inches at 135 yards. I certainly don't recommend open-sight handgunning for mountain game, but there's no doubt that a .357 revolver with a 2X scope can be used efficiently on goats or sheep by an adept marksman. At least equally efficient would be a single-shot pistol such as the Thompson /Center Contender or the Merrill Sportsman in the same caliber or perhaps in a special chambering such as the .30 Herrett. It, too, should have a 2X scope for mountain game. The Merrill, by the way, is available with a wrist-rest attachment that may help steady you for long shots.

It's traditional to recommend a 7X35 binocular for hunting mountain game. This power and size gives you sufficient magnification and sharp optics without reducing the field of view too much. However, such improvements have been made in optical design and construction in recent years that I would now prefer an 8X35, or even perhaps 9X35, for hunting goats and sheep. The field of view is wide enough, and the extra bit of magnification can be a great help in glassing distant slopes or crags. A crucial facet of this hunting is to climb to a good vantage point, thoroughly scan the wide vista of terrain that might hold game, and then—when animals are spotted through the binocular—use a spotting scope to get a closer look at what might or might not be a worthy trophy.

Incidentally, some novice mountain hunters, having read about this scanning and spotting tactic, jump to the conclusion that when trophy quality is thus confirmed, the time has come to shoot. This may be why they're tempted to buy very high-power varmint-style telescopic sights for their rifles. But what most often happens is that a good trophy is spotted at a distance far too great for shooting. The guide and hunter then plan a careful stalk that will (if all goes well) put them within realistic range without spooking the desired animal or spooking others that will, in turn, alert that one.

A good binocular is essential in mountain hunting, because careful glassing is necessary to locate goats, sheep, and other game.

If you don't own a spotting scope, make sure your guide does—or buy one. It's among the most important items of equipment for hunting mountain game. Judging headgear, especially on mountain goats, can be almost impossible without a high-quality optical aid. However, there's such a thing as having too much power in a spotting scope, as well as in your rifle scope. For one thing, you must have an extremely steady position—or a tripod or other rest—to find the game and see it clearly when the image is enormously magnified. For another, the image will suffer a comparably magnified degree of interference from rain, snow, haze, or mirage. And finally, I want my spotting scope to be relatively light and compact. Some hunters use 30X spotting scopes or zoom models. I feel that 20X is about best.

Among all American game, goats are the hardest to judge in terms of trophy quality. This is one of many reasons why an experienced guide is essential. And of course it's one reason why fine optical equipment is also essential. Having provided yourself with those two aids, you need one other: a knowledge of what to look for.

Both males and females have curved, black, stiletto-pointed horns. Because sex identification is sometimes almost impossible at long range, nannies are usually legal game. However, kids remain with their mothers for a full year. No sportsman would shoot a nanny that's accompanied by a kid, thereby dooming the young, but this is not to say that only a billy is an acceptable trophy. For many years, the top score in the Boone & Crockett record book was held by a Canadian nanny with horns over a foot long. Eventually she was displaced by trophies with horns slightly shorter but heavier, more symmetrical, and wider at their maximum spread as well as between the tips (where there's a slight inward curl).

Obviously, then, your spotting-scope evaluation of a distant animal is not to make absolutely certain it's a billy, but to ascertain with a reasonable degree of assurance whether the horns are poor, mediocre, good, or excellent. Anything more than 8 inches long is quite acceptable. More than 9 is excellent, and horns over 10 inches long may qualify for a record book. As a rule, a 9-inch horn is as long as the distance from the animal's eye to the tip of its nose. Visually matching those lengths at a great distance can be difficult, even with a good spotting scope. A combination of other factors should also be

The distance from a goat's eye to the tip of its nose is usually about nine inches. If the horns look at least as long as that eye-to-nose distance—as they do on this goat—the trophy is probably a very good one. Yet a hunter might have to pass up this shot because the animal could easily topple off the precipice and smash the horns or land where it couldn't be retrieved.

considered. The horns should have a fairly uniform backward curve and should look rather thick near the base. Sometimes a comparison can be made if other animals are in view. A female's horns generally rise fairly (though not quite) straight for about two-thirds of their length and then curve back rather acutely. As a rule, a mature male's horns not only curve more evenly from base to tip but are slightly thicker at the base.

If there's any doubt at all about whether a distant goat is worth stalking, the rule is to abide by your guide's decision. After all, he's a better judge than you are, and you're paying for his experience in these matters.

In Alaska, the season on goats opens in August and lasts through December. In the Northwest Territories it's from mid-July through mid-November, in the Yukon from August through October, in British Columbia from August through late November, and in Alberta from late September into early October. Colorado has a separate season for archery (late August through late September) and for firearms (mid-September through early October). Idaho and Montana open the season from early September to late November, Washington from about early September through October, Wyoming from September through mid-November, and South Dakota during most of October.

Knowing the dates of game seasons can help you plan when and where to hunt. This is especially important in this kind of hunting, which requires a great deal of planning and preparation far in advance. Wherever I feel it's important, I'm providing data on seasons, but a book can list only approximate season durations because the dates in some locales change from year to year. On the basis of these approximations, you may cross some locales off your list if the season there is too short, or if you know you can't get away from business at the appropriate time. But that leaves a lot of other states as well as Canadian provinces and territories. You won't want to write to them all for specific dates (nor do you want to pay to apply for a permit in every one of them).

Anyone who undertakes hunting trips should join the National Rifle Association and subscribe to *The American Hunter*, one of the NRA's monthly publications. There are a great many benefits, but the one I'm thinking of here is that each year, one issue of the magazine (usually August) includes a directory of guides and outfitters and an up-to-date, state-by-state listing of hunting regulations, probable opening and closing dates of all the seasons, license and tag fees, etc. The addresses of game departments are also listed. Thus, from one source you can obtain all the current information needed to begin planning a hunt. For information about membership and subscriptions, write to the National Rifle Association, 1600 Rhode Island Avenue, N.W., Washington, D.C. 20036.

The goat seasons open early, partly because some of the best goat habitat becomes inaccessible in November or December. Another reason may be that in most regions, the rut is at its height from mid-November to mid-December. Knowing this can help you decide whether to try for a goat when you're not quite sure of your evaluation as you peer through a spotting scope. Before the rut, it's unusual to find a mature billy mixing closely with the bands of nannies. A trophy male is apt to be foraging or resting alone. A big, dry female may also be alone, having temporarily wandered away from her band, but in either case, a solitary goat is worth very careful examination.

The time you pick for your hunt may depend on a number of factors. In most regions, part or all of the sheep season coincides with the goat season. You'll probably want to check that, as well as the open season for other species. Within that framework, of course, your timing may depend on when your chosen guide-outfitter has openings or prior bookings. You'll have to make an early hunt if the habitat in a given region is inaccessible during the latter part of the season. You may also want an early hunt because the big billies— the best trophies—will be foraging and resting alone. On the other hand, there are regions where the goats are still shedding in early August, and regions where their winter coats are still very short in September. The pelts are prime and most beautiful in the last part of the season, so you may prefer that time if the other factors I mentioned don't interfere.

Alaska is one of the best goat-hunting locales, but only certain parts of the state hold a good population. The species ranges chiefly through the coastal mountains from the southern Panhandle north and northwest to the Talkeetna region above Anchorage, then south into the Kenai Peninsula. There's also a good (transplanted) population on Kodiak Island. Among the lower states, Washington has the highest population and annual harvest—the highest success ratio for hunters. Other very good bets are Idaho and Montana. The number of nonresident permits offered by these states fluctuates from year to year. It's always a good idea to apply as far in advance as the game department allows, and begin planning then by locating and making arrangements with a qualified guide, gathering the necessary gear, practicing your marksmanship, and conditioning yourself physically.

Although goats don't climb or leap as spectacularly—that is, as acrobatically—as sheep, they prefer even steeper slopes and more precarious crags and pinnacles, narrow benches, and razorbacks. They do sometimes come down to timberline, but they like their habitat high and remote. It has often been said that the hardest part of a goat hunt is climbing to where the goats are. As a rule, the hunt begins on horseback. You and the guide ride out from camp on a long, early scouting trip, and when the horses can't get up to a desired vantage point, you dismount and climb. Perhaps after doing this a few times, or doing it for days on end, you see a trophy worth stalking. The meat of a young goat is fair but no real delicacy, so you might as well try for the most impressive billy you can locate.

Having found one you want, you begin the stalk, and that means climbing. You may be successful on the first try, but you may very well not, and that try can consume a couple of hours or the better part of a day. For these reasons, it's essential to condition yourself during the summer before the hunt. You should go into training, as an athlete does, and you should consult your doctor regarding this regime—and in fact, regarding whether there's anything about the state of your health (a heart condition, for instance) that might determine the way your guide conducts your hunt or might even preclude this kind of hunting for you.

A few old billies grow to such prodigious size that, contrary to the normal rule, their sex can be distinguished with a fair degree of certainty. Why these few goats attain abnormal size is uncertain, but they're apt to be loners. Though goats are usually quite fat in autumn, they're not as big as their shaggy coats make them appear. A mature nanny is likely to weigh 125 to 150 pounds, a mature billy

200 to 225. The female will stand about three feet high at the shoulder, the male about half a foot higher. The exceptional males are even taller and heavier. If the distinctive bisonlike hump over the shoulders is very pronounced, you and your guide have all the more reason for thinking you've found a big old thick-horned male.

There are times when tracks and sign can help you locate a worthwhile goat. Tufts of hair clinging to the ground or brush generally indicate a likely goat mountain. The scat, which looks much like that of sheep or deer, may reveal where goats have been feeding. Compacted pellets mean the goats have been browsing on dry, brushy foods, perhaps just inside the timberline. Massed droppings mean they've been feeding on succulent grasses and the like in the high meadows. The squarish tracks are hard to tell from a sheep's, but the lobes tend to spread more than a bighorn's, and the separation widens at a point nearer the rear end. The print is more square and blunt. A mature nanny's print generally measures about 2½ inches across or from front to rear. A large billy's will measure 3 inches or a bit more.

Although the normal procedure is to spot goats from a distance, a few of the big, elderly billies sometimes remain in a small, secluded area until the rut, and they may be well hidden. Once in a while, such a favored area is below timberline on a very rough, timbered slope that provides shade, feed, and spring water. Here an old billy will dig beds in the shale and dirt at the base of a favorite cliff, and before summer is over, he will have beat well-defined trails to nearby springs and feeding areas. If the timber is too dense for glassing and your guide decides the slope is worth a close investigation, trust him. Go in from above, carefully and quietly, moving into the wind if possible. When you do find a billy on such a slope and can get a shot at him, he nearly always turns out to be a good trophy.

Goats are neither as stupid nor as nearsighted as some hunters have concluded. They have excellent long-range vision and are wary of those predators that present danger. A goat on a pinnacle or high bench can see for miles around, but feels safe enough to ignore a man moving in the distance. If the hunting pressure in the area has been light, the animal may also ignore human beings seen somewhat closer—but then again, it may not. The animal's hearing is excellent, too, but a goat is so accustomed to the sounds of rolling stones and debris on the talus slopes that it pays scant attention to such noises. On the other hand, a hunter who snaps a dead limb at the timberline may send his quarry out of sight in an instant. The animal's sense of smell is also keen. Sometimes it doesn't seem so because the air currents are erratic in the mountains and a shifting thermal can swerve scent away before it reaches the goat. All the same, a goat hunter must stalk as cautiously as if he were hunting deer because—despite stories to the contrary—his quarry may be frightened off by a wrong sound, sight, or odor.

Thermals are so tricky and unpredictable among steep cliffs that it's sometimes impossible to stalk into the breeze. Usually, however, you can make a long, circuitous climb, keeping your scent and the sight of you from the game until you're above your target. The final segment of the stalk should be from above whenever possible because goats instinctively know that predators such as wolves, coyotes, cougars, and wolverines will approach from the surrounding low country and can be avoided by climbing where enemies can't follow. The myth that many kids are killed by eagles is just that—a myth. Both bald and golden eagles have been known to catch a very young kid that momentarily wandered away from its fiercely protective mother, but these occurrences are rare. Predation of goats is very light. Their greatest killers are rockslides, snowslides, and occasional missteps while negotiating very high, narrow points. Goats may be our most surefooted animals, but in their habitat some accidents are inevitable. Since the only predators that goats worry about come from below, the hunter's rule is to approach from above. The game's instinct to climb out of danger is so strong that once in a while, when a hunter spooks a goat from above, the animal runs toward rather than away from him.

Sometimes there's no way to get above a goat on its own slope or cliff or canyon wall. And if you do, the topography may block your target below. Look about carefully and see if there isn't a neighboring slope, cliff, or wall that can be climbed so that you can shoot across the chasm or valley at the animal.

There are times when a true sportsman either foregoes a shot entirely or waits in the hope that the goat will move. It's senseless to shoot one standing right on the brink of a cliff where, if he falls, the trophy will be smashed or impossible to retrieve.

Having dwelt on the need to climb, I should mention one unusual exception to this rule. Along parts of the Alaskan and British Columbian coasts, some of the herds forage on cliffs and steep slopes within sight of the ocean. There are guides who specialize in scouting by boat, cruising the coastline with their clients. Now and then, goats have been shot right from the beach. More often, however, the summits are glassed from the slowly moving boat, and when a good trophy is sighted, the guide and hunter go ashore to climb for a shot, as in normal inland hunting. This can be rigorous, but the chance of success is very high.

Salt licks are great attractions to most game, and goats love them. Such licks generally contain minerals besides salt (and sometimes no salt at all). Since there aren't a great many licks in goat habitat, when the animals locate one it becomes a periodic magnet to them. Your guide may know of such a lick, or one may be found during the course of a hunt. An abundance of tracks, droppings, hair, and rooting will make it obvious. The area of a heavily used lick is worth hunting thoroughly and revisiting.

In late summer and early fall, the nannies, yearlings, and kids like to feed and bed on open south-facing slopes. But the old billies seek the coolness of shaded northern sides. The rough north slopes are the places to hunt and glass most carefully during the early part of the season, before the rut causes the sexes to mingle. High, breezy benches and peaks are also worth glassing, and so are unmelted snow or ice patches in shaded gullies.

A goat or a flock of goats will begin feeding early, and by about eleven o'clock, almost every goat will be bedded down to chew its cud and rest. It may rise and move just a little now and then but will stay more or less in the same spot if not invariably in the same bed until midafternoon, when it begins feeding again. This gives the hunter two big advantages. First, if he spots a trophy at any time

Where goats have been foraging or licking salt, goat hair often clings to conifer trees and bushes.

from the middle of the morning until noon or a little later, he can depend on it to stay there until midafternoon, which may give him time to complete a stalk even if the climbing is so tough that rest periods are needed. Second, if it does turn out to be impossible to reach a good shooting position within decent range before the animal leaves to feed, the hunter can return the next day—this time beginning his climb early enough to be at the right spot at the right time. Goats don't like to wander much. Except when traveling to a salt lick or searching for nannies during the rut, a billy seldom moves more than a few miles from his favorite bedding area and nearby feeding areas. And he invariably returns. His bedding area is his home, and that's where you'll most likely find him.

I've said that goat meat is only fair, and that's true, but it isn't bad, either, unless it's that of a very old billy. The flesh of an old one is usually quite tough. Some people worry that it will smell bad, because domestic goats have a rather strong aroma. In the first place, the meat of domestic goats really isn't bad at all when well cooked. In the second place, a mountain goat is not a goat but a type of antelope

The late Jack Keller, an accomplished Northwestern sportsman, rests after reaching the spot where his trophy Canadian billy fell. The climbing is often regarded as the hardest part of goat hunting.

and it has very little odor. Its meat is tasty when pot roasted or simmered long and gently in a stew. Either way, a dose of meat tenderizer is recommended. Whether or not you have a yen to taste mountain goat, I'm of the opinion that it's not sporting to kill a goat for the trophy alone and let the meat go uneaten. Chances are, your guide-outfitter will cooperate in helping to pack it out. In some states he (and you) will have no choice because the law requires that it be packed out.

Sheep

As with goats, a rifle in the 6.5mm class or thereabouts will do for sheep if you're hunting nothing else on the same trip. My own choice, however, would be a .264 or .270, preferably the latter. Jack O'Connor, who was one of our most famous sheep hunters, began with a 7x57mm Mauser but later relied mostly on a .270. This was despite his well-known fondness for the .30–06 in big-game country. His two favorite .270 sheep rifles were bolt-actions, of course, Model 70 Winchesters each weighing exactly eight pounds with 4X scopes installed. With all the riding, scouting, and climbing involved in a sheep hunt, what's wanted is a reasonably light, short rifle. O'Connor liked a 22-inch barrel on his.

Unlike goats, sheep are often the sole object of a hunt or at least claim top priority. Such a rifle is perfect for them. Furthermore, with 150-grain bullets, a .270 will perform very well on elk and even moose. If you'd feel more comfortable with something heavier for moose, bear, or other big game that may be encountered, you can use a 7mm Magnum, .300 Magnum, or .30–06—the same sort of thing I recommended for a mixture of game in the section on goats. But keep in mind that sheep aren't as tough as goats, and contrary to popular belief, they're usually shot at somewhat shorter range.

Jack O'Connor's advice about scopes was also valuable. He conceded that some good sheep hunters favor variable models, the idea being that a variable can be carried at the 4X or 5X setting but turned to higher power for a long shot. And he conceded that he himself had taken a number of good rams while using a 2½X scope. But he called the 4X ideal.

More sheep than goats are taken by archers, and they're also easier with a handgun. ("Easy," of course, is a relative term.) A .357

Magnum with a 2X scope would be an excellent choice. Additional choices are the same ones I suggested for goats.

Although sheep are awe-inspiring mountaineers and inclined to make more spectacular leaps and bounds than goats, they prefer somewhat gentler slopes. Their acrobatic style of climbing or fleeing is simply a result of their hoof structure, which differs from that of goats. Their preferred type of slope doesn't mean they can be stalked more easily or in less time, but it does mean that a long, arduous stalk can eventually put you closer to them. Even though sheep tend to be more wary than goats, most trophy rams are felled at distances of less than 200 yards.

Taxonomically speaking, there are only two species of North American wild sheep. The Rocky Mountain bighorn and the desert bighorn are really a single species, *Ovis canadensis*. More surprisingly, the white Dall sheep and the nearly black Stone sheep also comprise a single species, *O. dalli*. However, because the four varieties differ in horn formation, general appearance, and range, they're separately categorized in the Boone and Crockett record book and, for practical purposes, are regarded as distinct types by hunters, game departments, and guide-outfitters. Within these four types there are numerous, more or less localized races exhibiting more subtle differences. When a sheep hunter speaks of achieving a Grand Slam, he's referring to an unusual accomplishment—the taking of a trophy representing each of the four.

To a certain extent, habits and habitat differ, just as range and appearance do. For example, the desert bighorn has adapted to very arid habitat, and its way of life is quite unlike that of the Rocky Mountain bighorn. Before embarking on a long, costly trip in quest of a trophy ram, a hunter should read all he can about the particular variety he seeks. An excellent book for this purpose is Jack O'Connor's *Sheep and Sheep Hunting* (Winchester Press, 1974).

Bighorn sheep range from the Rockies in British Columbia down into Mexico and east into the Dakotas, west into Washington, Oregon, and California. Those inhabiting British Columbia, Alberta, Montana, Idaho, Wyoming, and Colorado are Rocky

Although desert bighorns and Rocky Mountain bighorns are scientifically classified as a single species, they differ significantly in appearance. The desert sheep are smaller, leaner, and have less massive horns. Shown here is an excellent desert ram with a curl that would be worth taking even if the animal were a mountain ram.

Mountain bighorns. The bands of sheep found in the arid regions of Arizona, Nevada, Utah, lower California, New Mexico, Texas, and Mexico are desert bighorns. (Texas has only a token population and no open season). The species varies from rich, dark brown in the upper mountains to pale buff—almost the color of sand—in the deserts. The tail is darker but has a whitish edging that extends partly down the rear surface of the hind legs. On the darker, northern strains of bighorn sheep, a pale or whitish rump patch is sufficiently conspicuous so that it sometimes enables a hunter or guide to spot game on a distant slope, but the patch is a faint lightening of the coat on the pale southern sheep. North or South, the muzzle and the belly are whitish, and a pale ring usually circles the eye.

The Rocky Mountain variety is America's largest sheep. A mature ram may weigh 300 pounds and may stand more than 40 inches high at the shoulder. The horns are dark, and they curl back, down, forward, and up in a C-shape. On this type of sheep the curl of the horns is tighter than that of the other strains, yet the horns themselves are more massive.

In the arid, sparsely vegetated sheep habitat of the Southwest, a ram cannot attain the size of its Rocky Mountain counterpart. A desert bighorn seldom weighs more than about 180 pounds or stands more than 3 feet high at the shoulder. (Mature ewes of all American varieties are about a fourth smaller than rams and—like immature males—have slender horns that are too short to form more than a half-curl.) In another tip, I'll explain how to judge whether a curl is of legal size or better. Here, for the purpose of comparing the two types of bighorn, let me just stipulate that a Rocky Mountain bighorn with a curl of about 40 inches is a sporting trophy, while a desert bighorn with an outside curl of about 33 inches is a good one.

This bachelor band of mountain bighorns hasn't yet been dispersed by the rut, but the rams have begun their descent to elevations frequented by females and young and they've begun to associate with ewes. One female can be seen in this group. This is a typical band in which rams gather with other rams of the same approximate age and size. If they were seen at a distance, trophy judgment might be very difficult. In such cases, the rule is to abide by your guide's advice.

These are Alaskan Dall rams. Note that their horns are thinner and more flaring than those of the darker varieties of sheep.

Dall sheep are principally an Alaskan tribe, but they also range into northern British Columbia, the Yukon, and the Mackenzie Mountains of the Northwest Territories. In the southeastern part of this range, the white Dalls intergrade with the dark Stone sheep, and color varies from almost white to gray. The pure Stones are dark gray, gray-brown, blackish-brown, or almost blue-black. They range from the central part of the Yukon eastward to the Mackenzie District and southward to the Stikine River in British Columbia. Stones have the same whitish areas as bighorns on the muzzle, belly, and rump. Dark as they are, they're a bit easier to spot at a distance than bighorns. The pale color of the underparts extends farther up onto the brisket and, more important, the whitish rump contrasts sharply with the dark body color, providing a white flicker against the background of a mountain slope.

Mature Dall rams are slightly larger than desert bighorns but seldom weigh more than 200 pounds. The yellowish horns have a graceful outward flare, often with a spread of more than 2 feet. The horns are slimmer than those of bighorns but, because of the flare, the outside measurement of the curl is apt to be a bit longer. Stone sheep tend to grow heavier than Dalls but seldom weigh more than about 225 pounds. Their horns are darker, heavier, closer to the face, and sometimes slightly longer with a tight conformation— midway between the Dall shape and the bighorn shape.

The late Jack O'Connor poses with a fine Stone ram he took in 1971. He used one of his favorite sheep rifles, a .270 Model 70 Winchester.

Where flocks of Dalls and Stones intergrade, there's a color phase of the Dall known as the Fannin sheep, or saddleback. It's darker than other Dalls, sometimes quite gray, and is darkest across the back. This "saddleback" marking is sometimes almost black. Both the body and the horns are apt to be a trifle heavier than those of the white sheep.

Every sheep hunter dreams of taking a full-curl trophy but realizes that he may have to be satisfied with anything better than a three-quarter curl—the legal minimum. Among Dall rams, some of the annual horn growth goes into the outward flare rather than a tight forward and upward curve, so full-curl Dalls are harder to find than full-curl specimens of the other varieties. All the same, it's illegal to take an animal with less than a three-quarter curl.

The hunter or guide must wait for an unobstructed profile view of a ram's head in order to judge the curl with sufficient accuracy.

The base of the horn just about covers the top of the animal's head, from in front of the eye rearward to the front of the ear. The initial growth is upward, but quickly sweeps back, down, and around so that, if the horn were to grow long enough, it would form a full circle when seen in profile. In judging a potential trophy, you're simply estimating quarter-segments of this circle.

If the tip of the horn barely extends back past the ear, as on a very young specimen, it's a quarter curl; if the tip curves down as low as the base, it has formed a half-circle—that is, a half curl; if the tip comes down and forward so that it passes the ear again and is almost under the eye, it's a three-quarter curl.

That legal minimum is hard to estimate at a distance unless you know the knack, which is to visualize a straight diagonal line, pointing down and back from the front of the horn base through the eye. If a continuation of that line would touch the horn tip or any portion of the horn behind the tip, you have at least a three-quarter curl. On a full-curl trophy seen from the side, the tip comes up past the eye to the horn base, completing the imaginary circle.

Usually a hunter wants a set of horns as perfect as he can find. But someone who has already taken such trophies may prefer one or both horns "broomed," for the brooming is one mark of a mountain

METHOD OF ESTIMATING SHEEP'S CURL

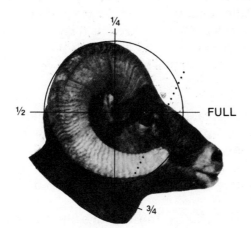

Superimposed on a photo of a bighorn ram, this circular diagram shows how to evaluate a sheep seen in profile. You can see that if the horn grew long enough it would form a complete circle. To judge a potential trophy, you estimate quarter-segments of the circle. If the horn tip extends forward past the ear, it's a three-quarter curl, the legal minimum. If an imaginary line (the dotted line) can pass from the horn base through the eye and then through the tip or any portion of the horn, it's at least a three-quarter curl A full curl comes up past the eye, just about to the horn base.

patriarch. The term refers to horns that have been broken off near the tips. It sometimes happens by accident or during one of the awesome battering fights that take place during the rut, but usually an old ram breaks or files the tips off deliberately when his horns, having reached full or nearly full curl, come up past his eyes and begin to block his peripheral vision. Brooming is more common— and more pronounced when it occurs—among bighorns than among Dalls and Stones, for the flaring horns of the latter varieties are less likely to block their vision.

A hunter who has managed to view a ram from only one side can tell if the animal is legal. However, if he wants anything better than the legal minimum—and whether he prefers the trophy broomed or unbroomed—he'll have to exercise sufficient patience, or stalking skill, or both, to get a look at the ram's far side.

Sometimes the horns can form almost a full curl without truly impressive massiveness or a large diameter across the circle. In judging a distant head, it helps to observe not only how close the horns come to making a full circle but how big that circle is. If the curl is sufficient and the sweep of horn from top to bottom equals almost a third of the animal's height, you're probably looking at a fine trophy.

Many of the greatest trophy rams are quite old—13 or 14 years—but sheep usually attain excellent curls by the age of 7 or 8, sometimes sooner. When you've taken a sheep, you'll probably be curious as to its age. This can be calculated by simply counting the winter growth rings of the horns, which form dark, narrow bands.

Among desert bighorns, most of the finest trophies have come from Arizona, Baja California, and Sonora, Mexico. A majority of the really impressive Rocky Mountain bighorns are taken out of Alberta, British Columbia, and Montana. A great many of the

Larry Koller and a guide measure the basal girth of the horns on a Rocky Mountain bighorn taken in Montana. Trophy measurements include greatest spread, tip-to-tip spread, length of each horn (measured on the outer curve), and circumferences at base, first quarter, second quarter, and third quarter.

record-book Dalls are shot in the Yukon and in Alaska's Chugach and Wrangell mountains. And all of the top Stone trophies have been collected in British Columbia; the area of the Muskwa and Prophet rivers, which is in the northern part of the province, is especially good.

In the Northwest Territories, the season on Dall sheep stretches from mid-July to mid-November. In the Yukon, Dalls or Stones can be hunted from August through October. Alberta has a bighorn season from about the third week of August through November. In British Columbia, the season runs from August to mid-October and includes Dalls and Stones as well as bighorns. Alaska has Dalls only, and the season runs from early August through October. Washington has a bighorn season for conventional firearms during the last couple of weeks in September and for muzzleloaders during the first couple of weeks in October. Arizona has a split season for desert bighorns—from about October 9 to October 25 and about December 4 to December 19. Montana's Rocky Mountain bighorn season lasts from early September until late November. New Mexico opens a season on Rocky Mountain bighorns during a couple of weeks in September and a separate season on desert bighorns during a couple of weeks the following month.

Seven other states—Colorado, Idaho, Nevada, North Dakota, Oregon, Utah, and Wyoming—have mountain or desert bighorn seasons of varying lengths.

The early seasons in the Far North take into account the inaccessibility of some sheep habitat from mid-fall through winter. In other locales, the duration and timing of seasons are based chiefly on the sheep population and the peak rutting time in a given latitude. Regardless of locale, you should begin planning—inquiring about a permit application, locating a guide-outfitter, etc.—as long in advance as possible. In many cases, the season overlaps the season for other species such as goats, moose, or elk, and in a few cases, a single big-game permit covers them all.

In one of my tips on hunting rockchucks, I noted the tendency of most hunters to hold too high when making a long shot at a steep uphill or downhill angle. When the target is a marmot, the resultant miss is no calamity, but shooting high can also cause you to lose a once-in-a-lifetime sheep or goat trophy. Suppose, for the sake of illustration, that your game is standing 250 yards away from you at an uphill or downhill angle of 45 degrees. Now draw an imaginary horizontal line from your muzzle to the point where the game would be standing if the ground were level. That distance, you'll find, is considerably shorter than 250 yards. To be precise, it's only 200 yards. If this is hard to visualize, study the diagram. It has two straight lines stretching out from the muzzle—one along a 45-degree angle to a downhill target and the other on a horizontal plane to a point directly above the target. You'll notice that the second line is substantially shorter. That short horizontal line is the "gravity distance"—the distance along which gravity acts on the bullet. In the example just cited, only enough holdover is needed for a 200-yard shot rather than a 250-yard shot (and with a sheep rifle that will probably mean no holdover at all). This underscores the importance of practicing shots at such angles to find out how to hold in a given situation. A great way to practice is, of course, on rockchucks. If you can't do that, find a slope where the topography forms a natural backstop and practice on paper targets.

A good northern sheep mountain usually has a subtle look that a guide or experienced hunter can recognize. Though sheep and goats sometimes share the same general habitat, sheep prefer more open slopes, somewhat less steep and rough. Look for high, relatively gentle slopes and wide basins close to more rugged or precipitous terrain. The grazing meadows on these slopes will usually command a wide view, and the bedding spots will usually be slightly higher than the meadows. Sheep rarely remain for long where there's no upward escape route or where they don't have a wide view in at least two directions.

Desert bighorns suffer an almost eternal scarcity of forage, shade, and escape routes. This means they may be attracted to almost any canyon, hilly area, rocky bluff, or patch of mountains. However, they prefer their habitat to be as remote and inaccessible as possible, a fact the hunter bears in mind as he scouts. Sheep—especially northern sheep—wander much more than goats, often roaming new slopes from day to day. But since good foraging slopes are

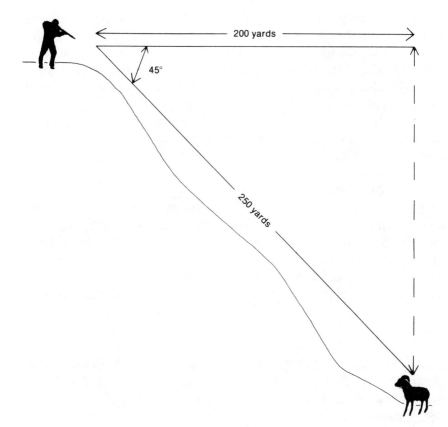

200 yards

45°

250 yards

In the chapter on chucks, a diagram illustrates the physical principle underlying the tendency to hold too high when aiming steeply uphill or downhill. A resultant miss can be shrugged off if the target is a rockchuck—but not if it's a once-in-a-lifetime ram. Here, a correlative diagram shows the principle in operation as a hunter fires at a sheep standing below him on a steep slope. If the sheep is 250 yards away and the angle is 45°, the bullet's drop (from gravitational pull) is the same as if the sheep were on level ground at a range of only 200 yards.

scanty in the desert, the bighorns there may frequent one likely spot for longer periods or return to it more often.

Sheep are primarily grazers. They feed in the open and rest during the day at whatever bedding spots they find. The beds are usually shaded in hot weather but exposed on cool days, when the animals enjoy sunning. Nighttime beds are quite different, for sheep use the same ones again and again, sometimes for years. A well-used sheep bed is a depression about 4 feet wide, and it may be worn down to a depth of about 1 foot. It's usually ringed with droppings and smells of urine. When you discover a heavily and recently used bed, you've found an excellent hunting place.

At first light, sheep begin moving and feeding. They lie down to ruminate and rest by about 9 or 10 o'clock, rise to graze briefly in the early afternoon, then rest again, and feed actively once more from late afternoon until dark. If you spot a band of rams while they're grazing in the morning, the best tactic is to wait them out. Watch where they go and plan a stalk while they're bedded. The brief midday or early-afternoon feeding takes place near the bedding spots, so if you know where they've bedded in the morning, you can count on them to remain there for five hours or more.

Don't be fooled by the fact that sheep prefer to forage on fairly gentle inclines. They can move with astonishing speed and agility. A mature ram can leap about 17 feet on fairly level ground, about 8 feet when ascending, and an easy 30 when jumping downward. When spooked, they can make headlong runs at better than 35 miles an hour. And at times they seem to enjoy negotiating chimney formations or narrow openings between cliffs by caroming from wall to wall. I know that rams have been shot cleanly while running or leaping, but as a rule such shots are chancy at best.

Except for the pronghorn, no American game animal has vision as keen as the sheep's. It's true that a hunter who remains stationary may escape the notice of a ram at fairly short range, but that ram can probably discern a man moving in the open at a distance of 5 miles. The same general stalking techniques apply to sheep and goats, but sheep are warier. Like goats, they're accustomed to the sound of rolling or falling rocks, but the unfamiliar sound of a human voice or the scrape of metal can spook them. A wrong sight or sound at a great distance may only alert rather than alarm them, but the utmost care must be taken as the stalk progresses. Scent is also very important. Unfortunately, sudden wind shifts and thermal drafts are common in the northern mountains. There may be no way to avoid a betrayal of the breeze, but you should remain constantly aware of its direction and strength, trying to avoid letting the game wind you.

Occasionally, the hot, arid habitat of desert bighorns turns the wind into a hunter's friend. You may be able to find a regularly used water hole or mineral lick with a nearby place of concealment at a higher elevation where rising thermals keep your scent from dropping down to the animals. Then the hunt becomes a waiting game, as when you wait on stand for deer.

Another peculiar aspect of desert hunting is that the bighorns there are more inquisitive than other sheep. Perhaps in their open surroundings, where predation is light, strange sounds become an attraction rather than a warning. Sometimes, if a hunter has an obstructed view and can get no closer, he can coax a ram out from behind the obstruction by tossing pebbles. (True, the noise of pebbles falling won't usually spook mountain sheep, but neither will it bring them investigating.) This doesn't mean that desert bighorns are less skittish than other sheep. Cover may be scant, and once a hunter is detected, he may have an exceedingly difficult time maneuvering into range. A band of desert bighorns can keep fading back like a maddening mirage.

Desert bighorns have a longer breeding season than that of any other medium or big game in North America. The rut generally begins in late July and lasts until September or October. The more northerly sheep begin rutting in October. Their breeding activity peaks in November or early December and ends soon after that. The hunting season in most locales extends into the time of the rut, but that's the toughest time to collect a trophy.

Mature rams stay away from the ewes until ready to mate, and then the males are bunched with the females. Although the rams become less wary while preoccupied by the sexual drive, the ewes remain very alert. And if you are successful in staying downwind, keeping out of sight, and making no alarming noise before you can get a shot, you'll find it difficult to pick out and get an unobstructed view of a good ram. To make matters worse, if you're hunting in the North, a late-season trip can be ended by a sudden snowstorm. Such storms can be quite dangerous, and of course they can reduce visibility until hunting is useless.

If you do hunt during the rut, you may occasionally (though not often) locate your quarry by sound. Rutting rams challenge rivals by emitting a deep, rasping blat, and when a couple of heavy rams charge each other head on, the battering of their horns reverberates through the mountains.

A deep blatting sound isn't always a good omen. If you hear it while stalking close, proceed with the greatest care, as the animals may

These Wyoming bighorns were photographed during the rut. Late-season sheep hunting is difficult because the good rams are in close association with ewes and young. It can also be dangerous in the event of a sudden storm.

already be aware of your presence. The challenging call and the alarm call of sheep are quite similar.

As with goats, the object of a stalk is to get above the game. Climb to a point overlooking a grazing meadow or a grazing and bedding basin, and wait for the animals to bed down if they're moving too much or if a closer approach is chancy. If they get nervous, they'll climb, and it's obviously desirable to have them climb toward you rather than away from you.

Before the rut, a few of the old rams wander by themselves, but most of the males travel in bachelor bands. Sometimes as many as a couple of hundred Dalls or Stones dot a single northern sheep mountain, but they're really a loose aggregation of smaller groups. Among bighorns, especially, a band is likely to number from half a dozen to a dozen, and sometimes only three or four. The greater the number, the greater chance there is that one of them will take alarm. Assuming that the trophy heads in two bands look equal from where you're glassing, and both bands present the same degree of stalking difficulty, your chances are probably better with the band that's smaller in number.

Another problem with large bands of sheep is that rams associate with others of the same approximate age. Their horns may be so similar that it's very difficult to judge the best trophy in a big group. Once you've chosen, the others in the group may block your shot.

Prior to the rut, if you spot bands of ewes and juveniles, you can make an educated guess that the rams are somewhere higher. In summer and early fall, the males keep to higher, rougher terrain than the females and young. And even if the rut is imminent, the trophy rams are probably making a very leisurely descent.

When you see a band of rams, try your best to get a view of every animal, not only for trophy-judging purposes but because one may have moved a little way off from the others to serve as a sentinel. If there is one on guard, he may return to grazing with the others after a while, or he may keep watch until the band is ready to bed down. Sometimes—but by no means always—one sentinel will replace another. Since a ram keeping watch is the one most likely to sense danger, you must pay particular attention to him as you make your stalking climb.

If you're detected at long range, you don't always have to give up the stalk. Sometimes the sheep will ignore you. Sometimes they'll retreat at an unconcerned walk or a mildly concerned trot, meaning that they're only nervous and not yet spooked. You can continue a circuitous stalk, but now you'd better be all the more cautious. Remember, the sheep feel secure because they stay close to rugged cliffs or slopes.

Tracks can mark a good grazing and bedding slope, or may lead to the destination of a wandering band. A sheep leaves a narrow trail of prints that can be confused with a goat's or mule deer's. However, a sheep's hoof lobes are not as splayed as a goat's, so the track isn't as blunt or square. Each lobe forms a slightly more definite crescent and tapers to a slightly more pointed front. In soft ground—especially if the ram is headed downhill—the dewclaws may leave twin depressions behind the main track. These will be larger but more closely spaced than those of deer. The prints of the hooves themselves are not as crescented or pointed as those of deer, and they are likely to be slightly larger. In soft ground, a mature ram usually leaves a print 3 to 3½ inches in length.

Locale also helps to identify tracks. Sheep prefer higher country than deer during most of the hunting season, and they avoid the really rugged, highest goat terrain except when pushed there by intrusion.

Another kind of sign is hair—tufts clinging to rocks or vegetation. A Dall's white hair looks pretty much like a goat's, but the terrain plus the combination of other sign may help to identify it. Bighorn sheep have longer, darker hair than deer and shed more of it.

Sheep like to visit mineral licks a couple of times a week. After doing so, Dall and Stone sheep often leave droppings as round as marbles, whereas bighorns then leave elongated droppings. The licking of the mineral-containing earth gives the scat a claylike consistency.

At other times, the pellets are usually bell-shaped, though desert vegetation produces less uniform droppings, and succulent grasses in the northern meadows can produce massed scat.

Desert bighorns leave still another kind of sign where water is scarce. They can survive for long periods without water, but they rely heavily on water holes and, when necessary, obtain liquid from saguaro or barrel cactus by gnawing the plant open or butting them over. They also eat cactus when they can't find enough grasses and forbs, so it pays to notice whether cactus has been disturbed. Like javelinas, sheep may chew up prickly pear, but it's easy to tell a sheep's track from the smaller, more rounded peccary track.

In the North, an important element in glassing is the knack of spotting movement or the flicker of a pale rump or belly patch against a darker background. Sometimes the glint of a horn can also be discerned. In early fall, bighorns occasionally wander down into timber, and it's most important then to watch for partially concealed animals and small movements. As Dalls tend to stay well above the timberline, their white coats are easy to see at a distance, except when the animals are on snow. They wander less than bighorns. If you spot a far-off band, you can feel relatively confident that they'll still be around when you reach the slope. Stones are intermediate in their behavior between Dalls and bighorns, and they're fairly easy to spot because of their contrasting dark and light hues.

Dalls—and, to a lesser extent, Stones—sometimes seem to rely on the leadership of one elderly member of the band. That one probably has at least as good a curl as any of his comrades. Therefore, if you can't be sure which head to try for, your guide may advise you to pick the lead ram. I'm careful in selecting a guide-outfitter for any medium- or big-game hunt, and my rule is to follow his advice in all such matters.

UPLAND BIRDS

Chukar Partridges

Shooting an occasional chukar on a preserve can be interesting sport, but it's not like hunting redlegs in the wild, rough Western terrain where these partridges have established themselves as naturalized Americans. Preserve real estate tends to be more or less horizontal. Furthermore, preserve birds tend to hold rather tightly for a pointer (or even a flushing dog) by comparison with chukars that are born free. For preserve shooting, I like a 20-gauge gun with field loads of No. 7½'s, especially if I'm going to be using the same gun and shells for bobwhite quail. If I'll be shooting pheasants along with the chukars, I prefer No. 6's but will make do with 7½'s.

For chukars in the wild, I stay with the 20-gauge because I prefer a light gun for this kind of hunting, which involves a good deal of walking and climbing. But I can understand why some gunners favor a 12-gauge. My 20 is chambered for 3-inch shells, and I've been happy to use the long Magnums where the cover happened to be very open, the flushes were wild, and most of the shots were long.

However, chukars are neither very tough nor very big. They average about 13 to 15 inches in length, ¾-pound to a pound or so in weight. In other words, they're slightly smaller than ruffed grouse. Therefore, many gunners use field loads both on and off preserves; but for most of my nonpreserve hunting I've been more comfortable with high-velocity loads, and on occasion I've been thankful to have 2¾-inch Magnums on hand, or even the aforementioned 3-inchers. I favor 7½'s because I need all the pellets I can get in my pattern, yet there have been times when I carried 7½'s in one pocket and 6's in another, in case I found the birds insistent about getting up far away. The long shots call for a moderately tight choke, and the bore constriction keeps enough 6's in the pattern.

The logic that applies to loads also applies to choke. Improved cylinder is fine for preserves, but modified is better for birds in the wild. Many devoted chukar hunters like a double, bored improved and modified, with two triggers or a selective trigger for handling both close and long shots. I have a Western friend who uses a European gun with a less common choke combination—improved and full—that can be very useful in chukar hunting. (For that matter, it's also useful for Midwestern pheasant hunting and some kinds of waterfowling.)

When chukars flush, they tend to fly downhill. Theoretically, knowing this should reduce the number of misses. It doesn't. Sometimes they flush well out—or below—you, sometimes so close they almost seem to have sprung from under your feet, and sometimes instead of flying straight downhill, they level off over a hollow or canyon. Most other upland birds are rising when the shot is made, so a gunner who shoots too fast or shoots by conditioned reflex, as if taking a bird on the rise, is liable to miss a lot of partridges. Chukars are as fast as bobwhites, and a change of course at more than 35 miles an hour makes for an elusive target. Obviously, experience alleviates the problem somewhat. If chukar hunting is new to you, try forcing yourself to wait each bird out. Swing with it, of course, but with the expectation that it may well change course as you pull the trigger if you fire too soon. Shoot a bit slowly and you'll probably take your limit more often. By the way, this is one more reason why a modified choke is better than improved cylinder for shooting in natural habitat, and why you may want to use fairly hefty loads.

Shoulder slings on shotguns are popular in Europe and Asia, unpopular in America. Their lack of acceptance in this country has more to do with appearance than with any functional considerations, and quite a few Americans have taken to installing slings on their waterfowling guns, just as they do on shotguns used for deer. In duck or goose hunting, a sling is a great convenience when you have to carry a lot of gear. In deer hunting, it's valuable when you have to walk a long distance, and it can be essential when you have to get into a tree stand. I'm surprised that more hunters don't use slings for Western chukar hunting. A carrying sling is really appreciated where it's necessary to climb steep bluffs, canyons, outcroppings, and the like.

Chukars—also known as red-legged partridges, redlegs, rock partridges, Indian hill partridges, or gray partridges—are native to southern Europe and much of Asia. During a span of almost half a century, most of our states and half a dozen Canadian provinces introduced chukars, usually to supplement American game species that were dwindling as their habitat was altered by farming. Until the mid-1950's, attempts to establish these partridges failed. The releases had been made chiefly in lush flatland farm country, rich with foods for many upland birds though sometimes deficient in nesting, roosting, or escape cover. Chukars can't survive the heavy winter snows that characterize many agricultural areas, and in order to thrive, they don't need lush farmland but semiarid, steep, rocky habitat.

Such terrain is now apt to be good chukar-hunting land. The birds became established when released in canyon country and dry, hilly regions with light snowfall. They can withstand terrible cold but will starve where snow accumulates to a depth of more than a few inches and thus interferes with their feeding. In the semiarid habitat they need, a very dry spring can reduce the chukar population drastically, yet the birds usually recover and they are underharvested in some regions. At this writing, there's a fall or fall-and-winter chukar season in Mexico, British Columbia, and the states of Arizona, California, Hawaii, Idaho, Montana, Nevada, Oregon, Utah, Washington, and Wyoming.

In most years, chukar hunting is best in eastern Washington and Oregon and in western Idaho, near the Snake River. Dates of the open seasons depend on the previous summer's nesting success. Washington's season is likely to be from about mid-September to mid-October, Oregon's from early October through December, Idaho's from mid-September through December.

Male and female chukars have the same coloration: bluish-gray on the upper body, wings, and breast; brownish on the outer tail feathers; whitish on the lower face and throat. The legs, beak, and a narrow ring around each eye are red. Above the beak, a black band extends across the face and eyes, then curves down along the neck and over the upper breast. The belly is buff, and the flanks are a paler buff marked with vertical black and chestnut bars. Many hunters like to know whether a bird is mature and whether it's male or female. A mature chukar has rounded rather than sharp primary feathers. Females have no leg spurs. Only some males have spurs, but if the distance from the tip of the third primary to the wrist joint is more than 5¼ inches, you can assume that you're probably examining a male.

Many references list America's chukars as the subspecies *Alectoris graeca*, a European chukar whose call is a whistle. This is incorrect. Our birds are descendants of Himalayan and Turkish stock of the subspecies *A. chukar*, which does not whistle but clucks and cackles. The name "chukar" is derived from the sound of the most typical call—*chuh! chuh! chuh! chu-kar-a!* This cackling helps maintain contact between members of a covey, and thus keeps the covey together. Occasionally, you may also hear a clucking feeding call—*took, tu-tu-tu-tu*. Listen for these sounds as you hunt. They may lead you to a covey, or indicate a good place to cast your dog, or help you locate scattered singles after you put up a covey.

A reasonably good imitation of a chukar's voice will usually stimulate the birds to reply. In chukar country, you can buy chukar calls at sporting-goods stores. Many hunters learn to call well by using only their own vocal chords, without a mechanical aid.

In semiarid habitat, water is crucial to the survival of birds. Brushy creek bottoms often mark a good chukar area. And most coveys are found within half a mile or so of water. The average number in a covey is about 20, but groups may vary from just a few to about 40. Water holes attract large congregations. In hot weather, check the vicinity of water at midday. And in any weather, check during late afternoon or before quitting at sundown because the birds habitually go to water before they roost.

Good chukar country has recognizable roosting sites. It will have talus slopes, rocky outcroppings, cliffs, canyons, or bluffs. The birds roost on the talus or other steep, rocky places, sometimes under low trees or shrubs. In cool weather they may roost in a circle, facing out, as quail do. Colder weather or wind often makes them roost in rocky crevices, hollows, or caves. For roosting and escape, some of the bluffs, canyons, or other slopes should be fairly steep and at least a couple of hundred feet high.

Good habitat is also recognizable by its foods and by the vegetation used for escape and nesting cover. Chukars prefer to eat grasses, forbs, and grains. They like brush for nesting and shade. And they like the steep, brushy places for escape cover as well as roosting. If chukars are plentiful, you'll probably see lots of sagebrush and cheatgrass. The area is all the more promising if these plants are mixed with bunchgrass, ricegrass, and bluegrass, and even better if there are also herbs or weedy forbs like Russian thistle, filaree, or fiddleneck. Sage is often dominant, but not crucial if there are other shrubby plants such as rabbitbrush, saltbush, or greasewood.

In many areas, farms provide better hunting than that last description would indicate. Some hunters, having read that chukars get along quite well without cultivated crops, avoid farmland and scout only the roughest uncultivated areas. This is a mistake if there are fields of wheat or alfalfa—good chukar foods—close to canyons or steep, brushy inclines where the birds can find escape and roosting cover.

When hunting in the early morning, try the southern-facing slopes—warm roosting sites.

Feeding activity peaks during midmorning, but on comfortably cool days, the coveys may continue to forage (and move) until late afternoon. During the feeding periods you may flush them out of any grassy place or wherever they can find grain.

On a hot day, if you don't want to take a noon break, you should use the midday period to check water, shady draws, and cool dusting spots. Heavily used dusting sites usually display tracks, feathers, droppings, and hollows scratched in the ground.

In late afternoon, look to the water again, and then to the rocky roosting areas.

Since chukars don't burrow down tightly into the grass when roosting, as bobwhites do, they're sometimes seen from considerable distances when roosting as well as feeding. Some chukar hunters carry binoculars and scan the terrain for the gray forms.

Though chukars like to head downhill when airborne, they usually head uphill when running—and they're terrific ground-runners. They've been clocked scampering up slopes at 17 miles an hour. An experienced hunter therefore likes to come at the birds from above.

A young hunter with strong legs and lungs can often force-flush coveys by running down at them. If the birds continue to run and you can't get close enough to put them up, fire a shot. This usually flushes them. It's also wise to fire a shot when a covey flushes too far out. You won't bring a bird down, of course, but for reasons no one seems to understand, the firing of a shot makes them sit tighter when they land again. The noise seems to take some of the run out of them. After shooting, you have a better chance of catching up to the covey (or scattered singles) and forcing a rise.

Some sportsmen who hunt in the style just described like to work without a dog. Their reasoning is that wild chukars are greater gallopers than pheasants, and the average dog just keeps pushing them ahead without getting them into the air. Such hunters drive along back roads to scout an area, glass the canyon slopes, listen for calling birds, and prowl stream beds in dry weather. But those of us who are a bit short of leg or wind prefer a close-working pointing dog that has been trained to respond well to signals and to circle below birds—thereby pinning them or pushing them back up toward the hunter.

When chukars land after a flight, they generally run uphill, just as they run uphill in preference to flying when an intruder approaches. As a rule, you want to get above an area where you see them land. But don't count on this as an invariably successful approach. It may be that heavily hunted birds learn to reverse their tactics, because in some areas they've been observed running downhill. If you fail to intercept them from above, try circling below.

Some hunters prefer to walk up chukars without a dog, but a pointing dog can be a big help if trained to work close, respond well to signals, and circle below the "redlegs" to halt their runs.

On shooting preserves, hunters often take a mixed bag of chukars and pheasants. Whereas free-roaming chukars tend to run and then flush far out if at all, those on preserves tend to hold rather tightly under the approach of a pointing dog.

Though the author is partial to springers for many kinds of upland hunting, he concedes that flushing dogs can be more hindrance than help for putting up wild chukars within shooting distance. However, a springer can often handle chukars on preserves, where the terrain is flatter and the birds don't flush so far out. And this breed is adept at retrieving fallen birds in brush.

If you arrive where you expect to intercept birds—or where you've heard them or simply think there's an excellent chance they're hiding—try just standing still and silent for about half a minute. As with many upland birds, this tactic is a great help when you're hunting without a dog. It seems to panic hidden birds into flushing.

Even when hunting with a dog, it's often necessary to outrace chukars. They simply won't sit tight for a dog, so when you get a point, the best procedure is to rush in before they have a chance to use their legs.

In country where you can see birds on the ground at considerable distances, you can be sure that they also see you. Try to stalk them. If you see them across an arroyo, for instance, retreat, cross where you won't be seen, and come down at them from a higher point on their own side of the draw—that is, from an unexpected direction.

Chukars can unnerve even a very staunch pointer that isn't accustomed to them. In this instance the dog broke and ran but force-flushed the bird within shooting range.

A band of chukars gleans grain amid stubble. Chukars like steep, rocky, semi-arid habitat, but they often visit agricultural fields, particularly wheat and alfalfa. The shooting can be exciting here, but on such flat, open ground the birds will flush way out.

During a feeding or roosting period, note the elevation on a slope where you find your first covey. You'll probably find others at about the same height, so it makes sense to keep working along just above that elevation.

At the risk of incurring the wrath of the nation's grouse hunters, I declare that the chukar is at least as delicious as the grouse. Try stuffing and roasting it—gently, as you'd treat a young and tender chicken. Baste it liberally and often, for any wild bird is drier than domestic fowl.

Rocky outcroppings like this can be trying for man and dog but are often productive of chukars, especially during the warm part of day.

Doves

I've shot doves with a 12 gauge and a 20. A friend of mine uses a 16, which isn't popular anymore because, with today's ammunition, the advantages of the 12 and 20 overlap, doing away with any need for an in-between bore size. With doves, I can't see that it matters at all whether you use a 12 or a 20, as long as your shells are appropriate. I don't hold with the smaller gauges. They produce too many lost cripples when used by less than experts. Generally speaking, I prefer field loads of 7½'s—or sometimes 8's over a water hole or any place where the birds are coming in close and fast, as they often do at the beginning of the season. I switch to high-velocity loads for pass-shooting, or after the first week or so when the flocks begin to fly high and flare at any hint of activity below. In my 20 gauge, I've even used Magnums carrying 1¼-ounce pellets for that kind of shooting.

It isn't that doves are tough to bring down. On the contrary, they're small and rather fragile. But they're erratic fliers, and when they flare or come in high and wide, you want a little extra insurance that you'll hit them with a couple of pellets.

Most writers hedge slightly with regard to choke by saying that either improved cylinder or modified is best for most of us. Well, yes, but which? The answer is both. Improved cylinder or even a skeet boring is excellent when and where the birds are coming in close, as described above. Otherwise, I think a modified choke will help you limit out sooner. I've heard a lot about close, easy flushes while jump-shooting doves, but my own jump-shooting experience has included more long than short shots, so I'd stay with modified for that kind of hunting. If you're an adept trap shooter or duck gunner, a full choke will probably serve you very well for pass-shooting doves. It doesn't work for me because, quite frankly, I'm not a good enough wingshot, but if you hit fast-flying doves at 40 yards plus, the tightness of a full-choke pattern may enhance your sport at certain times, particularly in the last part of the season.

I have an improved and modified over-under that I like as a dove gun, for no better reason than the fact that I've had fun with it and feel confident using it. Confidence has a lot to do with which gun is "best" for any shooter. But there are also more objective considerations. I've already mentioned several different chokes that might be best in different situations for different gunners. And I can recall an occasion in Virginia and more than one in Kentucky when I would have been happy with something close to a true cylinder bore.

This, I assume, is why I've twice observed a gunner enter a dove field with enough gear to outfit a safari—not just the commonly seen folding stool, ammunition box, and ice-filled cooler for storing sodas and birds, but two guns, as well. And it's why a repeater—either a pump or an auto—with a variable-choke device is probably the most sensible choice for dove shooting.

Aside from the fact that you can buy a pump or auto with an adjustable choke, or have such a device installed, a repeater has one other advantage. This is one of the few kinds of shooting in which you really do sometimes get a chance to make a triple try as birds come over.

In states with a daily bag limit of twelve doves, I've heard gunners jokingly refer to the limit as a "box of shells"—meaning they'd taken a dozen birds with twenty-five shells—and they were boasting, not complaining. I've been told that the nationwide average is two doves downed for every five shots fired. Having admitted that I'm a mediocre wingshot, I want to say that my average on doves is a little better than that, and I think I know why. Doves are slim, streamlined, fast, evasive fliers, but they're not that tough to hit if you don't get too eager.

I've sat at the edge of a feeding field, concealed in the same hedgerow with gunners to the right of me, gunners to the left of me, all better shots than I can ever hope to be, yet I was taking more birds per hour than they were. Because in that kind of doveshooting— sitting lazily while waiting for birds to come in over decoys or a water hole or soybeans or millet or a combination of those attractions or whatever—most gunners tend to become impatient and shoot far too soon.

On occasion, I've stuck a decoy into the ground 25 yards in front of me and vowed to shoot at nothing beyond that. And it's been pure pleasure to listen for the gunfire in a hedgerow on the far side of the field and wait for that useless sky-busting barrage to push the doves across to me, right over me. Maybe I don't fire as many shots as some of the others, and maybe they wonder why I'm holding my fire, but I put doves in my cooler and I get to carry home some leftover shells.

Doves are migratory birds, included among the federally regulated species. Federal guidelines (maximums, really) govern the seasons, shooting hours, and bag limits set by states. More than thirty states, including Hawaii, currently have seasons. In a typical year, about seventy shooting days are open between September and mid-January. Even if you know that doves are legal game in your state, you must check the regulations carefully because some of the state options are complex and can vary from year to year. For example, the federal bag limit in recent years has generally been twelve a day in the East and only ten a day in the West, but shooting hours in the Eastern states generally last only from noon until sunset, whereas in Western states, shooting may begin half an hour before sunrise.

Most states split their seasons, and in some instances it's a triple split. That is, there may be hunting in September, again during the last half of October, and finally for a few weeks ending in mid-January. Some hunters don't seem to realize that the rest periods benefit them as well as the doves. In some regions, the birds become very wary after only a week of heavy hunting pressure, and in most regions they become elusive toward the end of the first month. Moreover, as fall progresses, new flocks of migrants join an area's resident birds and earlier arrivals.

It's not generally known that, although there's a breeding peak in spring and summer, doves reproduce somewhere on the continent in every month, nesting from southern Canada to Mexico and Cuba, and in every continental state except Alaska.

In a good hunting locale, most of the September birds are residents, or "natives." A little later these birds are mixed with flocks of migrants, or "flight birds." During the last part of the season, most of the local doves may be transients or flocks that will winter there and then leave. Because of the rest periods, none of these groups is overharvested, and each can establish itself in a given area.

By the time shooting starts again after a split, the birds have become habituated to good feeding, watering, and roosting places, as well as flight paths between these destinations. In some areas the good shooting sites are famous, but just before any segment of the season opens, it's smart to scout the countryside, watching for shifts or newly established sites.

I think hunters give doves too much credit for intelligence—or for the ability to learn how to avoid danger, at any rate. It's true that the birds seem very naive when a season opens and then quickly become reluctant to pour into previously used fields. But this is only partly a result of learned caution. Early in the season, most of the birds you see are local breeders that have established their flight paths and daily destinations. Later on, a lot of them are newly arrived migrants, still unfamiliar with the local attractions and indecisive about where to feed, dust, water, and roost. Decoys are useful at any time but all the more so now. So is concealment. And so is scouting for the most attractive places.

As the season progresses and the action cools a bit, it's also important to be increasingly alert. Doves may approach from unexpected directions, and all of us have had the embarrassing experience of failing to notice them come from behind us and overhead. At such times the gun is apt to come up just a trifle too late. But sometimes you can hear a soft whistle as mourning doves approach. The sound is produced by the air cutting across their primaries. Now and then this warning whistle has alerted me to a bird that I'd otherwise have missed.

So far, I've been generalizing about mourning doves, our most widespread and populous dove species. The closely related whitewinged dove breeds in Texas, New Mexico, Arizona, lower Nevada, and California. (Whitewings also range farther east, and a few are taken as far from their home breeding grounds as Florida.) Southwestern whitewing hunting is usually excellent early in the season, but most of these birds soon migrate. A little later, there are big whitewing shoots in Mexico, for many of the doves winter in South America.

A whitewing is easily distinguished from a mourning dove. To me, it looks rather like a cross between a mourning dove and the related common pigeon. It's a bit stockier than the mourning dove, and its tail is blunt rather than pointed. A mourning dove's long tail (which sometimes induces hunters to give the bird too little lead, shooting behind it) is narrowly edged with white except on the rearmost part. A whitewing's fan of tail is widely tipped with white at the rear corners. As its name implies, it also has sizable white wing patches—white coverts contrasting sharply with the dark brownish-gray primary and secondary feathers.

The warning whistle I mentioned applies only to mourning doves. Whitewings fly silently. However, you may hear either species call, and sometimes you can encourage them to swing close or try for a landing by calling them. The pigeonlike coo of a mourning dove is appropriately mournful, and most of us are familiar with it. The whitewing has a more abrasive, broken tone that sounds somewhat like a rooster. Commercial dove calls are available, and some hunters learn to coo or cackle without a mechanical call.

Doves don't respond to a call as readily as waterfowl or crows, but calling is still worthwhile. In my experience, it has worked best over a water hole and/or over decoys.

The whitewing doesn't twist, turn, and dip as erratically as the mourning dove, but it flies about as fast and is almost as difficult to hit. Flight speeds of various birds are listed in many references, and I've mentioned some of them myself. These speeds are necessarily approximations and can be misleading. A dove usually skitters along at 35 or 40 miles an hour. That's fast enough, certainly, yet a dove isn't really hard to hit at that speed if it's crossing close to you or coming overhead. On the other hand, a strong tail wind can enable a dove to accelerate abruptly to a speed nearer 60 miles an hour. I know of only two ways to counter this problem. The first is to be observant of the wind and the way the birds seem to be flying and—if you find yourself shooting behind your targets—pull ahead a little faster and farther. The second is to handle doves pretty much like skeet targets, swinging with them quickly and giving them plenty of follow-through. Of course, in pass-shooting you may be handling them more like trap targets than skeet targets. But either way, leave your gun down until you're ready to shoot, and then get on your target fast.

Perhaps you've heard or read that doves, like pigeons, carry some dangerous diseases. Occasionally they do, and so do a number of other birds. These diseases include psittacosis and a form of meningitis. But don't worry. The cooked meat is perfectly safe to eat.

In connection with the flesh of doves—which is superlative table fare—several other details demand attention. Some hunters dress their doves in the field. This promotes cooling of the meat, which might be important on a very hot day if you don't store your birds in a cooler or if you have to transport them a long way. With a severely gut-shot bird, it also prevents edible meat from being soured by digestive juices.

But if you do clean your birds on the spot, remember that no farmer (or fellow hunter) wants the field littered with putrifying entrails. Carry a plastic bag for the innards. Don't, however, make the common error of stowing whole birds or edible portions in a plastic bag or any airtight bag. Lay them in the shade or put them in a container that will keep them cool and allow air to circulate. The best container of all is an ice-filled cooler. The faster a bird cools, the better it keeps. Ice water is no good, but a layer of ice chunks or cubes is ideal.

Many hunters save only the breast of a dove (or any similarly small bird) because there isn't much else that can be picked off the bones. I don't usually do this, I suppose because I was raised during the Great Depression, and the rule never to waste a fraction of an ounce of meat was drummed into me. However, if you just "shuck out" the breast, there's no need to clean your bird, or to pluck or skin it. You don't even need a knife if you shuck the old-fashioned way. Just hold the dove in both hands with its breast up. Place your thumbs along the keel—the center of the breast—and press them down and apart. The skin will separate and you can just pry the breast out. A few feathers may adhere to the meat, but they're easily picked off. Before pulling the breast out, some hunters cut off the wings and head. This takes only a moment and does make for a cleaner job.

If you want the whole bird rather than the breast alone, begin by removing the head, feet, and outer parts of the wings—which have almost no meat at all and come off easily at the first joint. Then skin or pluck the bird. Skinning is obviously faster and easier. (Sometimes, in fact, it's hard to pluck a small bird without inadvertently pulling some skin off.) But the skin is tasty and helps keep the meat juicy, so plucking has its advantages. The sooner you do it after killing the bird, the more easily you can pull out the feathers. When I decide to pluck mine, I do it immediately after arriving home. The larger feathers are picked off and the small ones can be rubbed off. When I clean larger species, I work from below the breast and rib cage, the way a store-bought chicken is cleaned. But with anything as small as a dove, I just hold the bird breast down and use a pocket knife to split the back open from neck to tail. Unlike most hunters, I save the giblets—heart, liver, and cleaned gizzard—as they're delicious in a gravy, sauce, or soup.

Disregard the advice found in some cookbooks to the effect that one whole dove or a couple of breasts will make a normal serving per person. Even a big domestic pigeon makes no more than one serving for anyone with a hearty appetite. Mel Marshall, in his excellent book *Cooking over Coals* (Winchester Press, 1971), figures on three doves per person. Assuming the doves are served with plenty of vegetables, biscuits, or bread, etc., I agree.

As Marshall also notes, recipes and cooking processes for doves and pigeons are interchangeable. He includes several excellent ones, including the time-honored Southern style of deep-frying doves in peanut oil. My own favorite is a recipe I developed for woodcock—a braised dish with mild onions, mushrooms, and crumbled chestnuts—and I'll give details in the woodcock section.

Another book is worthy of mention here. It's *The Dove Shooter's Handbook*, by Dan M. Russell (Winchester Press, 1974). Russell provides far more information on all aspects of the dove's life history, management, and hunting than I can squeeze into this single chapter of a book covering many species. And he's an authoritative writer, with long experience both as a dove shooter and wildlife biologist.

Male and female doves look pretty much alike, but if a bird has a definite iridescent sheen on the neck, it's a male. Doves are delicate and short-lived. Whether or not they're hunted, few live more than a year, so most of those you shoot are juveniles, or at least birds of the year. If you're curious, examine the primary coverts—the small feathers partially covering the flight feathers. The younger the dove, the more of these will have white tips. They aren't molted all at once, of course, and the white marks only those feathers that haven't yet molted. If all have been replaced by dark feathers, you can usually tell a bird of the year by the three outermost primaries. If they're new—not faded, frayed, or blunted—the bird is probably a young one.

Doves are primarily seed eaters. Where grain crops are scant or absent, they thrive on doveweed, bristlegrass, ragweed, pokeweed, pigweed, crabgrass, and other weeds and seeds. Baiting is illegal, but if you don't take grain from one place to another and then dump or scatter it on a field to attract the birds, you aren't violating the regulations. In other words, you can "plant a dove field"—as many farmers do, for lease to hunters as well as for their own use—and you can even manipulate the crop more for attracting wildlife than for harvesting the grain. You can cut it, rake it, or leave much of it scattered after machine-picking.

Some landowners plant sunflower patches for doves but, more often than not, when a farmer says he's planted a dove field, he's talking about browntop millet—a favorite of mourning doves. Soybeans have become an extremely popular cash crop, planted for their own sake, and they also draw doves (as well as quail and other wildlife). Newly planted barley and wheatfields attract doves, too, and so do machine-picked cornfields. Other good dove crops include sorghum, rye, buckwheat, peanuts, peas, and cane.

Whitewings like the same cultivated foods as mourning doves, but a lot of otherwise good whitewing habitat is brushy, uncultivated land. There they rely on such wild plants as doveweed.

Waterholes on farmland are among the best places to shoot doves. The water is all the more attractive if it's muddy and if it's adjacent to one of the crops listed in the text. And shots can be made at reasonable range if there's an irrigation ditch, hedgerow, or other natural blind.

Not only do many farmers plant dove fields, but some state conservation agencies maintain such fields as a game-management tool. Supervised public shoots are sometimes held on these state fields. However, regulations and the interpretation of regulations may vary from year to year, so you should check with your game department before the season with regard to legal public and private fields. And, of course, you must ask permission of the landowner before shooting on any private land.

Doves feed actively during the morning (when it's illegal to shoot in many states), then rest and often dust around noontime, return to the fields to feed again between about two and four o'clock, and after that go to water and finally to roost. They actually seem to prefer dirty-looking water. A water hole—whether it's a cattle tank, a pond, a stream, an irrigation ditch, a slough, or no more than a muddy little depression in a field—may be good throughout the shooting day, especially if it's adjacent to feed and to dry dusting spots. So shoot over or near feed during the foraging periods and work the water holes and roosting areas late in the day.

I have a cool, lightweight set of camouflage clothing—hat, shirt, and pants—that I find very helpful when I want to shoot from a spot where there's no concealment. Doves see color and are quick to notice movement or unnatural shapes. However, I've done very well without camouflage in most situations, and many veteran dove shooters never bother with it. It isn't necessary if you station yourself against a tree, bush, hedgerow, or anything else high enough to break your outline or partly conceal you. A ditch may also offer sufficient concealment.

Whether you're sitting at a feeding field or watering spot, decoys help greatly. As with calls, they don't bring birds pitching in the way decoys bring the ducks, but they definitely subvert the caution of incoming flocks, pairs, and singles.

Since the decoys work even if they're impressionistic rather than realistic copies, some hunters make their own out of anything from wood to cardboard. If they're gray and they roughly approximate the shape of a dove, they'll do. However, durable commercial decoys aren't very expensive. Usually I prop a few in trees or on a fence, but more should be stick-ups in a field or near the edge of water. You can have a few of them quite close to your place of concealment.

Before landing, doves often reconnoiter from nearby trees, powerlines, or other high perches. In Virginia, George Reiger taught me a decoy trick that takes advantage of this habit. George doesn't enjoy scrambling around in trees. Like many of the cleverest hunters, he prefers mental to physical exertion. So he has attached a long cord to one decoy and tied a small weight to the end of the cord. He tosses the weight over a tree branch adjacent to a favorite dove field. The weight falls to the ground with the cord attached, and George then pulls on the cord, raising the decoy on the other end up to the tree branch. The decoy doesn't perch on the branch as a dove would, but dangles just under it. From a distance—a bird's-eye view—it looks like it's perched on the branch, and that's what matters.

The decoy is easily retrieved by tossing the weight back over the branch. For all I know, this may be an old Virginia dove-hunting ploy. It was new to me.

Shooting over a Kentucky soybean field one day, I found that I had even more than the usual difficulty finding my downed birds in the standing crop out to my front and in the tangled brush behind me. Watching my fellow shooters, I became convinced that some of them were failing to find as many as half the birds they killed. I asked a game biologist if he had the same impression. He did. It seems to me that in some kinds of cover, a retrieving dog is essential. I would go so far as to support a regulation prohibiting dove hunting without a dog in some areas. (Admittedly, this would be a tricky law to write and enforce, and would have to take into account the use of one dog by several hunters.)

Just as a few dogs dislike retrieving woodcock, a few dislike fetching doves—probably because the feathers come out very easily. A dog may occasionally get a mouthful of feathers and have trouble spitting them out. But even a dog that won't actually pick up a dove will usually locate a downed bird for you—that is, if the dog has a passable nose. And most retrieving dogs will carry doves quite happily, although some have a mild disdain for everything but the game they've been trained on. Labradors seem to be good at retrieving doves (and all game birds, for that matter), but I can't say that any particular breed is best. You can use any dog that's been taught to fetch game for you.

Far too many dove hunters ignore the need for a good retriever. Birds felled in brush or standing crops can be so hard to find that some shooters seem to waste as many as they kill. Few birds are lost when a hunter has a well-trained dog like this Lab.

One caution is needed with regard to the use of a retriever. Dove shooting often takes place on hot days. Your dog should be kept cool and rested, preferably in the shade, and must have water. This is no big problem. You'll probably want to have water on hand for yourself, anyway.

In late afternoon, doves begin to gather in roosting trees like this one, and they can often be flushed from nearby ground cover. However, you should make it a rule not to shoot right at a roost and not to shoot very near one when the light begins to dim. If cut off from their accustomed roosts, some birds spend the night on the ground or in lower vegetation, where they're vulnerable to predation.

Dogs are fine only at retrieving doves, not at pointing or flushing them. These birds simply won't hold for a dog. So if you want to jump-shoot doves or walk them up, you'd better keep the dog at heel. You can often walk them up in a field with a standing crop or, late in the day, in brushy places near the wooded roosts. Where the ground

Camouflage clothing is often a help, but at the beginning of the season when doves haven't yet become wary, a limit can be taken by shooters fully exposed in a crop field.

cover is high, the birds are less inclined to flush prematurely and can therefore be hunted like other upland birds. You will, however, get some wild flushes. And some of those that flush within range will skim along close to the ground until they're far out. Don't expect many of the shots to be easy or short.

I've spoken of shooting near roosting trees and late in the day. There's nothing wrong with that, in my opinion, but I concur with many other hunters who won't shoot right at a roost—or right up until legal quitting time on a darkly overcast day. The doves need their roosts. When cut off from an expected roost site, some of them spend most of the night grounded (where they're vulnerable to predators) or in lower, less desirable roosts. Moreover, when the light gets very dim, shooting results in too many lost cripples. For the sake of good management, sportsmanship, and a clear conscience, I can forego roost shooting or a parting shot in the dark.

Ruffed Grouse

Grouse hunters often speak of snap-shooting—meaning that a ruffed grouse may flush so fast, so unexpectedly, that there's no time for the kind of gun-swing that's effective in most kinds of wingshooting. Instead, you snap the gun up and fire instantly, instinctively, as the muzzle passes the target. For this, you need a light, fast-handling shotgun that fits you well and doesn't tend to get caught in brush or branches as you bring it up. A 12-gauge is fine if you don't mind a few extra ounces of weight, but you don't need that big a bore because very few shots are long, and a grouse is easily killed if you get the pattern on the bird. Nor do you need a lot of repeat firepower, as you'll seldom get a chance for more than a couple of shots.

I'll admit that twice in my hunting life I've missed an opportunity for a coveted double when two birds got up—because I missed with the first shot, brought one bird down with a second, and had nothing left for the other bird. But really, such opportunities are rare. Most of the grouse you see will be singles. Personally, I like a light, short, double-barreled gun—either a side-by-side or over-under—which is also nice in the woodcock alders. I generally use No. 8 field loads. I don't need any more power than they provide, and I do need the wide, dense, uniform patterns obtained with small pellets. When using a double-barreled gun, however, I sometimes load the first barrel with the No. 8 and, for longer, follow-up shots after my frequent misses, I put a high-velocity load of 7½'s in the second barrel. This is a fairly common practice in the grouse woods.

A friend of mine has a 20-gauge over-under grouse and woodcock gun, custom-bored with a true cylinder for the first barrel and skeet choke for the second. He wants as wide a pattern as he can get with the first shot and just a trifle tighter pattern with the second. This works well for him, and it would probably work well for any very fast snap-shooter. Since my reflexes aren't that quick, I prefer the more conventional improved-cylinder and modified combination. A grouse is likely to be on the verge of disappearing in timber or brush by the time I get my gun up, so I want slightly tighter patterns for the longer range at which I bag most of my birds. I believe most shooters will do well with my chosen combination, even if they're a little younger and quicker than I am. Those who use repeaters are probably best served by the improved-cylinder boring.

The "ruff" is the most widespread of nonmigratory American game birds. It's familiar to hunters all the way from central Alaska eastward across the lower portions of the Canadian territories, in every province to the Atlantic, and throughout the upper United States. In the Rockies and near the seaboards it ranges farther south. On the West Coast it ranges into northern California, and near the East Coast into northern Georgia and Tennessee. Along the Rocky Mountain chain, it's found as far south as Utah. The distribution of this species roughly approximates that of aspens, a crucial food source. The best hunting is to be had in New England's woods and farmland, down through the Appalachians, in the woods of the Lake states, in the middle and upper stretches of the Rockies, and in the forested mountains along the Pacific Coast.

In the mountains of the British Columbian coast, where the ruffed grouse is sometimes called the willow grouse, I've walked right up to one that was dusting itself on a logging road, and I've seen a hunter flush one from a low tree limb by tossing pebbles at it. In regions like that, where grouse have never been heavily hunted, the ruffed species has another interesting name, for it's often called "fool hen"—a description reserved elsewhere for the blue grouse and spruce grouse.

Yet this same species is the most elusive game bird in some regions. My previous tip listed the best hunting regions, but "best" can be narrowed down slightly if it's interpreted to mean not only a relative abundance of birds but also challenging birds. In that case, "best" means the Eastern and Midwestern sectors that have been settled and farmed for the longest period. Centuries of wingshooting in those regions seem to have influenced or accelerated the process of natural selection. Only the shy, quick-to-flush birds have survived

The author examines a young ruffed grouse he flushed in a stand of aspens—
the most important food source for grouse in most regions.

there and perpetuated their genes. I've felt a warm satisfaction—pride, in fact—after bagging grouse in New England, central New York, West Virginia, and Michigan. But along British Columbia's Inside Passage, I shoot a ruffed grouse only if I want camp meat.

When a gunner goes hunting in a state far from his home, he's sometimes startled to discover ruffed grouse that look rather different from those he's known in the past. He can tell they're the same species, but he may wonder if he's shot a mutation or a bird that has somehow been altered by pollution or the changing environment. In all probability, he's merely shot a race of ruff that's new to him. There are at least eleven subspecies. In the Eastern and Midwestern regions where grouse hunting is a traditional sport, the prevailing race is the so-called Eastern ruffed grouse (*Bonasa umbellus umbellus*), a predominantly brownish bird, but the most widely distributed is the gray ruffed grouse (*B.u. umbelloides*), a paler variety ranging across Canada and through the Rockies. To bewilder hunters further, a reddish phase of the gray subspecies is most common

This grouse was photographed on a log in New York woods that provided plenty of roosts in the hemlocks. Standing trees are essential, but ruffed grouse are also attracted to stumps and drumming logs like this one.

in dry habitat, at low elevations, and along the southerly fringes of the range. The grays in the North, sometimes called "silvertails," tend to be a trifle larger than the red phase, yet both colors are sometimes represented in a single brood.

An experienced hunter usually examines the tail of each ruffed grouse he bags in order to identify its sex and perhaps its age. (In years when the hunting is good, I invariably seem to take more females than males, and perhaps this is one sign of a healthily reproducing population.) If the tail can be fanned out 180 degrees without opening gaps between the feathers, the bird is probably a male, but the tail's coloration is a more reliable indicator. Its basic color varies from brown or red-brown to gray, with six to eleven dark, pale-edged cross-bars followed by a much broader dark or black subterminal bar and gray tipping. On a male, this subterminal bar is rather uniform. On a female, it's almost always broken at the center by the brown or gray background color because the two central feathers lack the last dark bar.

In this respect, both male and female birds of the year resemble adult hens, but they have a narrower subterminal bar, mottled primaries, pointed (unworn) tips on the two outermost primaries, and a whitish chin patch.

It has been said that grouse are where you find them—an allusion to the fact that they like a fairly wide variety of foods and many different (or different-looking) kinds of roosting and escape cover. Yet these birds have definite general, regional, and seasonal preferences. Thus, experienced hunters note that grouse can be flushed from some coverts year after year, except during their cyclic population declines. And some hunters also have a knack for recognizing new coverts that are likely to hold grouse.

Let's begin with the general preferences these birds exhibit. Mature forests usually have poor hunting, because grouse need openings, edges, and second growth—young trees and brush. Good hunting areas display a mixture of brush, shrubs, and young "pioneer" trees—such as aspen, alder, and birch—that are heralding a new plant succession. Such vegetation provides food. They also need taller hardwoods or conifers for escape and roosting purposes. An area that has been subjected to a controlled burn is

The tail fan at top is a female's. It isn't quite as full as the male's, pictured below it, and the sharp black subterminal band becomes vague—almost absent—on the female's central feathers.

promising because the clearing action of fire encourages new growth. Areas subjected to timbering operations are also promising because logging provides roads (where grouse love to dust and sun themselves), slashings, and clear-cuts. And areas with small patchwork farms or abandoned farms are good because they provide brushy edges, fields, and orchards.

In any grouse region, aspen buds are the most important of all foods, but there are times when the birds will be concentrating on other edibles. And in any region, grouse love fruits and berries. They also love the fall crop of seeds from those fruits and berries. During the hunting season, a deserted, overgrown orchard is always a good bet, particularly if other foods and roosting trees are nearby.

As to seasonal preferences (bearing in mind that grouse can be somewhat unpredictable), the birds tend to forage and roost on high ground—the true uplands—during the early part of the hunting season. As the weather gets cold, they tend to concentrate in the lowlands. Also bear in mind that during the fall certain foods are particularly tasty to grouse or particularly plentiful; this is when they're attracted to beechnuts, acorns, dogwood, serviceberry, bunchberry, wild grapes, willow, maple, hop hornbeam, mountain laurel, thornapple, and apple trees (as well as other fruit trees). Aspen remains important then and throughout the winter. Late in the season, such winter foods as hawthorn, greenbrier, and wintergreen also gain importance.

Then there are the regional preferences, which are really just a matter of the most readily available types of food and cover. Where certain kinds of vegetation are concentrated, the birds may also be concentrated. In the East, tangles of wild grapes, sumac, rhododendron thickets, and blueberry and cranberry patches are sometimes more productive for the hunter than aspens. In the Midwest, the same foods may draw ruffed grouse, and clover patches also seem to be excellent hunting sites during the early part of the season.

Even if you fail to move grouse in the coverts where you usually find them, you can often discover for yourself what plants are attracting and holding them. Just keep hunting the likeliest areas until you finally kill a bird. Then open its crop and see what it's been eating. Of course there's no guarantee that the other local grouse have been feeding on the same things during the same period, but the likelihood is strong.

Grouse are flushed from alder swales somewhat less often than woodcock, but grouse and woodcock are very often hunted together and found together in the same habitat. Both species, for example, like brushy pastures and young runs of poplar or birches.

Since mountain laurel was among the fall grouse foods I listed, I must now debunk the old myth that laurel toxifies grouse meat. Neither laurel nor any other poisonous plant affects the wholesomeness of upland-bird meat. It's perfectly safe to eat even if the birds have been feeding exclusively on laurel.

It is true that the taste of some game meats is affected by the diet of the animals. I've eaten mule-deer roast that had been flavored by sage while the animal was alive. I've eaten fishy-tasting ducks and I've eaten brant—a normally delicious bird—that had been spoiled by a heavy ingestion of unappetizing algae. It's also true that man-made persistent poisons in certain pesticides and fungicides are transferred through the food chain—from plant to fish, bird, or mammal, and thence to man—which is part of the reason why the use of a number of pesticides and fungicides has been restricted or prohibited. But naturally poisonous plants are an entirely different matter. Many game species eat foods that are toxic to humans, but the toxins don't enter the bloodstream and tissues of these creatures, so their meat is harmless to man. A fallacious myth is a poor reason to pass up anything as delicious as grouse.

Many species of wildlife are subject to population cycles, but the ups and downs are most pronounced among snowshoe hares and ruffed grouse. These population cycles are probably caused by a combination of climatic cycles, plant succession, and progressive crowding as the birds in a given locale become more abundant during periods marked by favorable conditions.

At one time, many hunters (and some game biologists) believed that the abundance of grouse in a given season could be predicted very accurately on the basis of the cycles. This isn't quite true. In some regions, a complete cycle spans no more than 7 years, as a rule, while in others the cycle may span 11 years. The average is 10.

A very generalized prediction is possible, however. In most regions, the second or third year of each decade is a good grouse-hunting year—perhaps the best of the decade—but hunting becomes poor by the seventh. I hunted in the state of New York from 1968 through the early '70's. In the coverts I most often visited, birds were scarce from '68 to '71. They were a bit more plentiful in '72, and hunting was fairly good in '73, though not spectacular. In '73 I also had very good hunting in New Jersey and Michigan (though I've been told that the Midwestern and Eastern cycles are usually not

This Michigan grouse stands out clearly in a close-up photo but you'll rarely get close to grouse on the ground, and they're well camouflaged. The flush often comes as a startling surprise. Even when you're hunting with a good grouse dog, you must be alert—ready to mount your gun instantly in response to the sight or sound of a bird flushing from the ground or trees.

quite synchronized). In '77 I didn't hunt in any of those three states, but a friend hunted my familiar New York coverts and reported that birds were again scarce.

It's probably safe to predict a general rise in the grouse population from now until 1982 or '83, then a dip and another rise to a peak 10 years later. But knowing that the cycle may differ considerably in your locale, it's wise to follow the practice of many hunters by keeping a log of when, where, and how many birds you move (not just those you bag, though you'll probably want to note that, too). There's enjoyment in leafing through such a log on winter evenings, seeing once again the sudden flush of a bird or a particularly good performance by your dog (or yourself), and a log covering several years will help you to make an educated guess about grouse abundance in coming seasons. A population decline continues for two or three years, followed by a gradual upswing for at least three or four years, and then the peak years follow.

These are grouse tracks on snow. In winter you can occasionally track a grouse to where it has taken refuge under vegetation or by burrowing right into the snow. But even under those conditions, a flush can be sudden and forceful enough to fluster a gunner.

You've probably heard, read, or seen examples of the "crazy flights" that grouse occasionally make during the so-called Mad Moon of early autumn. Birds have been known to collide with trees and telephone poles and to crash right through windows. Among various theories to explain this abberational behavior, one of the most persistent—and hardest to squelch—is that the grouse are getting high on fermenting berries. There have been authenticated instances of bears and other animals becoming inebriated that way, and I can't prove it never happened to a grouse. The fact is, however, that the birds making the disoriented flights are young ones, sober but inexperienced, confused, sometimes panicked as they disperse from the area where they were born. The dispersal occurs under strong and sudden pressure, for the adult birds in the territory evict the young ones. If they didn't, the habitat would very quickly become overcrowded, and the population cycles would be even more pronounced.

I have a theory of my own as to why the hunting is so much easier early in the season than later on. It isn't that the coverts are "shot out." If that were possible, the following spring's reproduction stock would be depleted, and the cycles would be drastically affected. It's just that during the early part of the season, dispersal is still in progress, and the coverts are relatively full of inexperienced birds of the year that are far less wary than their elders.

Last year a hunter told me about flushing "coveys" of grouse. When I told him that grouse aren't covey birds, that they normally prefer solitude, he was sure I didn't know what I was talking about. Throughout the summer, a hen grouse leads and protects her brood. One September day, a hen dragged one wing and hobbled about as I approached her on a dirt road. She was feigning injury to draw me away from her nearby chicks, just as she would lure any predator away. The grouse family remains together until early fall. And the hunter had seen such families—"coveys," as he called them— because the season had opened in his locale (in Ontario) before dispersal had begun. There are regions where you may move groups of birds during the first days of the season, but don't expect such bonanzas to continue.

Though ruffed grouse can utter a variety of calls, vocalization is chiefly used for courtship in the spring and for communication between a hen and her brood. Nevertheless, there are a couple of sounds any experienced grouse hunter listens for. An important one is the startling whirr of a bird rising. Sometimes a flush really sounds thunderous—and the noise may be the first indication you have that a bird is anywhere near you. Be alert for it, but don't rely on it as a timely and dependable signal to mount your gun. A grouse surprised on the ground usually makes a great deal of wing noise as it explodes into the air. But when a grouse sees you from an overhead perch in a tree, it often leaves as silently as an owl. Grouse like to perch in

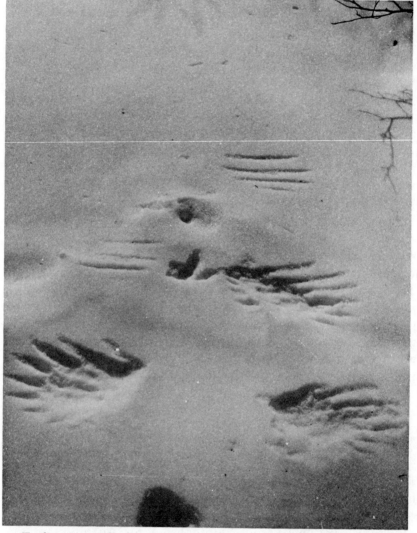

Trailing a grouse is always interesting but it certainly doesn't always pay off. More often than not, the trail ends with wingprints like these, where the bird took off.

hemlocks and other conifers, and when I move through such woods, I look up quite often, remembering missed opportunities when grouse flew over and dodged behind screening timber before I could raise my gun.

The other sound to listen for is drumming. Drumming is heard a great deal more in the spring than in the fall, as it's the male's method of proclaiming his territory—warning other males away and attracting females. But mature male grouse occasionally drum again in the fall, probably to prod birds of the year into dispersing from their territory. The grouse stands on a log or hummock, with his neck ruff erected outward and his tail fanned while he beats the air with his wings. The wing feathers aren't striking anything. The drumroll sound is produced by an implosion of air filling a vacuum he creates with each powerful stroke of the wings. In the woods, sounds of this sort are sometimes ventriloquial, so it isn't always easy to pinpoint their source. But when you hear a drummer, it makes sense to proceed in the direction of the sound, prepared to shoot if a surprised grouse thunders up.

Because grouse won't hold for a close point the way woodcock often do, a good many hunters prefer to work without a dog. Where grouse have been heavily hunted for many years, they tend to flush so wildly that a flushing dog may be useless (though a springer, Lab, or other flushing dog that submits to tight control can be excellent on grouse). And some hunters are convinced that no pointing dog will consistently catch scent and freeze soon enough to hold a grouse for the gun. While I certainly don't agree that an able pointer can't be trained as a really good grouse dog—I've hunted over a few marvelous grouse dogs—I do admit that an experienced dogless hunter can bag his share of birds when and where they're reasonably abundant. To some extent, he counts on luck, but for the most part, he relies on practiced reflexes, a knowledge of the foods and roosting sites I've listed, and a record or memory of coverts that have previously produced well.

A valuable tactic for a dogless hunter is to stop walking frequently and just stand still for a minute, ready to shoot. This tends to panic a hidden bird that has frozen, hoping to escape notice while the intruder moves through its domain. Whether the bird is on the ground or perched overhead, it may then flush. The same tactic works on a number of other upland birds, including woodcock and pheasants. It also works on occasion when you're shooting over a dog. After all, no dog is likely to find every bird. Sometimes a pointer will pass one or will be working one patch of cover while a bird hides off in another direction within range.

I once wrote that "the chief attribute of a good grouse dog is a nose so sharp that the animal freezes into a staunch point at a mere whiff of grouse before getting close enough to flush the bird." I have no reason to retract that, but I ought to add something.

The next most important attribute is the habit of working close to the gun, combined with a willingness and learned ability to obey commands. Although some hunters feel that a fast-moving pointer pins birds more effectively than a slow one, you don't want a wide-ranging quail dog for grouse because that kind of pointer will merely bump birds out of range or beyond screening foliage where you won't even see them dodge away.

The third most important attribute is visible "birdiness." Some dogs give little or no sign that game is near until almost ready to point. Others become excited enough to alert you in advance, and this is a big help with grouse.

Various pointing breeds seem to rise and fall in popularity, or fashionability, over the years. Currently, the Brittany is very popular as a grouse or grouse-and-woodcock dog, and I feel this breed deserves its eminence.

Since a grouse dog must work close to the gun, grouse hunters are inclined to take special care in training their dogs. It isn't that they use any unique training methods but that they use the conventional ones more thoroughly. Any young dog that works too independently of the gun (or an older one in need of refresher lessons) may be slowed down by attaching a heavy chain or even a sash weight to his collar. This can be an especially needed corrective with a dog to be used for grouse hunting.

I also feel that patience is very important in polishing a grouse dog. It's unfair to expect perfect performance from an inexperienced pointer. The dog is likely to become much better after several years of hunting.

A good grouse dog is one like this English setter—a dog that doesn't range too far from the gun, that warns the hunter of impending action by displaying excited "birdiness," and that freezes in midstride at the first whiff of grouse. Currently, the Brit is extremely popular for grouse and woodcock. Though the breed deserves its eminence, well-trained setters as well as German shorthairs can also excel.

Chains and check cords are intended only for training—at least in theory—but a 50-foot check cord can be very helpful if a fully trained dog seems to be acquiring the habit of working too far out. Personally, I prefer to keep a check cord sequestered in my jacket and take it out only when the dog and I are hunting alone or when, for unknown reasons, the dog suddenly becomes abnormally obstinate. My hunting friends are inclined to pass merciless remarks about dogs that have a lifelong need of the leash.

But I suspect that these same friends keep 50-foot check cords conveniently hidden for use in case their own dogs get out of hand.

I like to wear a whistle on a neck lanyard and I make it a rule to bell an upland dog. My dogs and I have always been adept at losing track of one another for brief periods. The bell tells me where the dog is, and my whistle tells him where I am and what I want, in case he's interested.

I think the bell is particularly important when hunting grouse and/or woodcock, because the cover is often so thick that visual contact is intermittent. If the dog works closely enough, I should be able to hear the bell at all times—and when it stops tinkling, I take it for granted that the dog is on point, and I'd better get there fast.

I believe grouse are harder to hit than any other upland bird. This is partly because they so often flush in thick cover where it would be difficult to swing a gun and get on any bird, partly because they often flush so suddenly, and partly because they twist and dodge and seem to know that safety lies in veering behind screening trees or brush— putting cover between themselves and any intruder.

Contrary to some published opinions, however, they're not our fastest upland birds. If you feel an urge to settle any disputes over flight speeds, you can tell your friends that grouse have been clocked, and the timed record speed was 51 miles an hour. When crossing an opening, a grouse may occasionally exceed 40 miles an hour, but in thick cover, it will rarely exceed a mere 25 miles an hour. It isn't speed that makes this target so difficult but the dodging and the cover itself. This is another reason why snap-shooting works well with grouse.

When all these factors (and certainly not any lack of shooting expertise) make you miss a grouse, or when your reflexes aren't fast enough for you even to get off a shot, try your best to watch the bird and mark the area where it comes down. Now is when a pointer may be most valuable in furnishing you with shots. For grouse, unlike woodcock, will hold tighter for a second point. A grouse that flushes wildly the first time may wait for you to come close for another try.

In winter, grouse often burrow completely under the snow, or sometimes they burrow partway down in a sheltered spot beneath a low umbrella of vegetation such as rhododendron. The legs of these birds are feathered almost to the toes, and at this time of year, the toes themselves are fringed with rods of cuticle called penctinations, which provide support on snow and are shed in the spring. Grouse can walk quite well on snow, and they'd rather walk than fly.

When hunting on a snow, you may occasionally see a little oblong crater where a grouse has landed. From there, try to follow its wide (2¼-) or 2½-inch-long, three-pronged tracks. Each left or right print is placed rather precisely in front of the previous one. The bird may have taken off again, leaving only wing prints in the snow at the trail's end, or the trail may give out in tangles of brush or clear ground beneath overhangs. But once in a while, you may follow to where a grouse has dug in. If there's considerable snow on the ground, try to mark down any bird you move as precisely as you can. Working on snow, your dog might otherwise have trouble locating it for a second flush. Or perhaps you're hunting without a dog. Either way, following the tracks can be worthwhile.

Blue Grouse
and
Spruce Grouse

Back in the chapter on small game, I included both gray and fox squirrels in a single section, and I included both rabbits and hares—cottontails, snowshoes, and jacks—in another single section. Why, then, it's logical to ask, have I covered ruffed grouse in a section of its own and relegated the closely related blue grouse and spruce grouse to another section? One reason is that if I grouped the two "fool hens" with the noble ruffed grouse, a number of hunters might refuse to buy this book. I can't afford to take that chance.

A more objective reason is that blue grouse and spruce grouse are quite often shot under very different circumstances and with a rifle or handgun, whereas the ruffed grouse is normally regarded as the proper game for a truly adept shotgunner. To a disciple of the ruffed grouse, carrying a rifled arm into the coverts or killing a bird on the ground or in a tree is a desecration. And to many, the only grouse worthy of the gun is the ruffed grouse.

This is not to say that the blue and the spruce never provide sporting targets on the wing. They certainly do. In fact, some hunters betake themselves and their shotguns to the woods specifically to flush one variety or the other. And many more pack shotguns along on big-game trips so they can enjoy a change-of-pace hunt for blue or spruce grouse.

As with ruffed grouse, a light, short, fast-swinging 20-gauge gun would be my choice. These two species are neither as fast nor as artful in the air as the ruffed grouse, but once in a while the cover is fairly thick, and I don't like to carry a heavy gun in the woods or mountains—or pack any more weight and size than necessary on a big-game trip.

The spruce grouse is usually about 15 to 17 inches long—slightly smaller than a typical ruffed grouse—so I wouldn't fault a hunter for using No. 8 shot. However, I'd choose 7½. For one thing, an occasional flush may be far out when birds are encountered in a clearing or high-country pasture or when they have to be forced into the air by fast footwork. For another, 7½ is a better all-around size for whatever small game you might encounter.

The blue grouse is the largest of the three species. A male is often more than 22 inches long and may weigh close to 1½ pounds. And fairly long shots are more frequent with this bird than with the spruce grouse. In blue-grouse country, I prefer No. 7½ pellets in loadings of no less than 1⅛ ounces (which means I load my 20-gauge with 2¾-inch Magnums). If there's a good chance of a mixed bag— snowshoe hares along with the grouse—I prefer 6's to 7½'s.

With regard to choke as well as gauge, blue and spruce grouse are pretty much like ruffed grouse. You should do nicely with improved cylinder or modified (or these borings in combination if your gun is a double). Incidentally, shotgunners often prefer No. 6 loads in a gun with the tighter boring but like 7½'s in an improved cylinder.

On a big-game hunt, many sportsmen pick the sort of utility sidearm known as a kit gun—a compact, light, but sturdy and accurate rimfire, usually a revolver. Both spruce grouse and blue grouse are commonly seen perched in trees or foraging, dusting, or watering on the ground. And they often remain still enough for a hand-gunner to make a head shot. The kit gun of my choice would be a compact .22 revolver with adjustable open sights. I'd load it with Long Rifle cartridges firing solid bullets at standard velocity, the same ammunition I'd use for hares, in the hope of a mixed bag.
Of course, some hunters pack no kit gun but do wear a centerfire handgun either as a primary arm or back-up gun for whatever big game they're hunting. A centerfire sidearm can also be used on timber grouse, but then head shots become all the more important because a big, powerful bullet can literally disintegrate a partridge, leaving lots of feathers but no meat for dinner.

Quite a few hunters who go into the wooded mountains expressly for these birds prefer a rimfire rifle rather than a shotgun. Instead of trying for flying targets, they hunt for stationary birds both in the

This hunter carries two guns for blue grouse in the Rockies—a shotgun for those that fly, a revolver for those that won't budge from trees. Blues are often hard to flush from overhead perches.

trees and on the ground. For this kind of shooting, you can use open sights, a peep sight, or a low-power scope, depending on what lets you shoot most comfortably. You'll rarely, if ever, need a scope's magnification, but the crosshairs and the clarity of the sight picture may be a considerable help, especially where timber dims the light. Again, I'd use the same ammunition as for hares, and I'd restrict myself to head shots.

A scoped .22 rifle is appropriate for blue grouse if the hunter shoots only at stationary birds.

Wilderness grouse can also be taken by the big-game hunter who packs nothing but his powerful centerfire rifle. In this case, of course, it's absolutely essential to make only head shots. This can be difficult enough to be sporting, indeed. Such a rifle is apt to carry a scope, sighted in at relatively long range. You must learn the amount of hold-under needed—that is, how low to aim so that you can make a head shot when a grouse is perhaps 50 or 60 feet from you. As

Charley Waterman has expressed it, "If you hold too low, your bird disappears in a cloud of feathers." If you're going to use a scoped big-game rifle on grouse, the only practical way to learn where to hold at short range is to practice beforehand on paper targets.

Some big-game hunters handload mild charges for grouse, hares, or other camp-meat targets. If you do this, bear in mind that with such ammunition in your rifle or handgun, the point of impact will be quite different from the point of impact with your big-game loads. You'll still have to do some preparatory paper-target work in order to know where the bullets will strike at short range.

Apart from softer recoil, mild centerfire loads have another advantage—less noise than that of big-game loads. Some hunters

Although both blue grouse and spruce grouse are often taken with rifles and with the sort of utility sidearms commonly known as kit guns, they can provide good shotgunning sport, too, and should not be regarded as mere sources of camp meat. For both of these wilderness grouse, the author favors the same kind of light, short shotgun as for ruffed grouse because a long, heavy gun is a tiring burden in the mountains. A 20 gauge is a good choice, but with shot one size larger than for ruffed grouse.

and guide-outfitters wince at the very thought of shooting "unimportant" game such as grouse in any area where the noise of gunfire might well spook a trophy elk or deer. You just have to exercise your common sense. If everyone in the party has taken his big game, why not have a go at grouse? In that case, obviously, it doesn't matter whether the loads are noisy. If, for one reason or another, you're staying around camp for the day while the others are far off seeking big game, you might as well do some shooting, but then the mild loads are really advisable because your companions (and their quarry) may not be quite as far off as you think. Finally, there are times during many a big-game hunt when no big game seems to be anywhere in the region—or when you're on the way to where you think it is, but you still have a considerable distance to go. At such times, too, I see no reason not to take pot shots but, again, I'd play it safe by using the quietest possible loads.

Some of the foregoing shooting advice is purely my own. Some isn't. I'd have forgotten several valuable details if I hadn't refreshed my mountain-hunting memory by re-reading Charley Waterman's *Hunting Upland Birds* (Winchester Press, 1972). Since that book is devoted entirely to the hunting of winged upland game, it contains more material than I can include here about a number of species. It will be helpful to you no matter what upland birds you hunt, but in my opinion its value is unique with regard to wilderness grouse. A library could easily be filled with published works on the ruffed grouse, but few writers have considered the other species to be worth their attention. I know of no other book that provides such thorough first-hand information.

If, like many hunters, you take as much interest in the natural history of your game as in the hunting methods, then you should know about another book—Paul A. Johnsgard's *Grouse and Quails of North America* (University of Nebraska Press, 1973). A scholarly work but written in terms a layman can understand, it contains intriguing facts about game management and the importance of hunting, as well as biology and animal behavior.

Grouse are often called partridges, and the two species now under discussion are sometimes called timber partridges, timber grouse, wilderness partridges, wilderness grouse, mountain partridges, or mountain grouse. Without question, they do thrive best in timbered, mountainous wilderness.

There are eight subspecies of blue grouse, ranging from the West Coast (as far north as lower Alaska, as far south as upper California) eastward into the Rockies (as far north as Alberta, as far south as Arizona and New Mexico). The populations in the southernmost Rockies are relatively sparse and scattered, but sufficiently plentiful so that both Arizona and New Mexico have open seasons in the early fall. The dusky grouse of the Rockies, the sooty grouse of the Pacific mountains, and the Richardson grouse of the far Northwest and the upper Rockies are all subspecies of blue grouse.

Four subspecies of spruce grouse occur in the same regions as the blue and also eastward across Canada and down into the northernmost parts of the Lake states and New England. The Franklin grouse of the Northeast and the Rockies is a subspecies of spruce grouse, though it has a narrow, grayish or whitish terminal band on its tail instead of the broad orange-brown band characteristic of other spruce-grouse races.

There must be a great many experienced hunters who have never seen timber grouse, so I'd better describe them. The blue grouse has a long, squared tail, black or blackish-gray, occasionally marbled, with a light gray terminal bar. (On the Richardson subspecies of the northern Rockies, the tail is entirely dark.) The male's body is gray, blue-gray, or slaty, darkly mottled and marked with wavy blue-gray lines. His throat and shoulders are streaked or mottled with white. Above his eye is a yellow or yellow-orange comb. On the sides of his neck are featherless air sacs, but the hunter may not see these until he has a bird in hand. Sometimes the sacs are hardly noticeable when relaxed (though they're very conspicuous when a courting male inflates them). Sac color varies with subspecies; some races have wrinkled yellow sacs, while others have smooth purple sacs. A hen has neither sacs nor comb. She's brownish, darkly mottled and barred, and her breast is marked with bars of yellowish-brown.

The little spruce grouse is also brownish, but the male is very dark—often almost black or blackish-gray, with wavy black markings on his upper parts. He has a narrow scarlet comb about the eye,

Where spruce grouse seldom encounter man, they sometimes merit the
name "fool hen," yet they can offer sporty wingshooting. Here, a hunter
using a light over-under returns to camp with Alaskan spruce grouse.

a black throat edged with white, and a black breast patch with a broken white border. His blackish belly is checkered with white or a tawny color. In spring when he's courting or in fall when he's proclaiming his territory, he puffs his neck feathers almost as far out as a ruffed grouse. Both males and females of most subspecies have a black or very dark brown squared tail with a rusty terminal band, but the Franklin subspecies of the Cascades and Rockies lacks the band and has white spots at the base of the tail. Regardless of race, both sexes have little tufts of chin feathers. The hen is brownish, with light and dark flecks and bars, and her underparts are whitish with brown crossbars. When seen on the wing in dim light, she's very hard to tell from a small ruffed grouse. You needn't worry about this. In a state or province where two or more species are common, they can be legally taken during the same season.

Though blue grouse deserve the name fool hen in some regions, spruce grouse are generally more foolish. They often perch in the open and flush only with great reluctance (making them even better targets than blue grouse for rifled arms). This is especially true in the Far North, and Charley Waterman believes it may be due to the fact that the species seldom encounters man in that region. I think he's right, for two reasons. First, even ruffed grouse behave foolishly in remote wilderness areas, while in settled locales they're famous for evasive tactics. Second, in parts of the upper Midwest where hunters are as common as birds, I've seen spruce grouse that were positively skittish.

In the Yukon and the Northwest Territories, the season on grouse (and ptarmigan) opens at the beginning of September, after the seasons on some big-game species have been open for quite some time. In most of the states and provinces where timber grouse are shot, the season opens either before the big-game seasons or shortly afterward. Whereas most animals in these regions drift down to lower elevations as the season progresses, the grouse climb higher when the weather begins to cool. Therefore, if you're going to take your shotgun and go out just for timber grouse, the hunting will be good (and probably a bit easier) early in the season. You may take your limit in the foothills. If not, at least you won't have to climb to the high ridges.

Once the big-game seasons are well underway, timber grouse are primarily birds of the high mountains. They're often found near timberline. Often, too, they're found in the same areas with ptarmigan. They feed heavily on conifer leaves—particularly the needles of Douglas fir and the true firs, but others as well—and they also eat the berries, buds, and broad leaves that attract ruffed grouse. You may find them around blueberries or aspens, or in high, brushy pastures, though most often they'll be in or near evergreen timber.

Normally, neither species takes off as fast as a ruffed grouse (or flies as fast) but they can be just about as speedy when diving downhill off a tree limb or a bluff. And where they have the opportunity, they like to do just that—pretty much the way chukars do. In the timber, most flights are short, but downhill flights can also be very long.

If a timber grouse passes you going downhill, it can be as tough a target as a ruffed grouse in brush, but snap-shooting is seldom efficacious. Swing fast, keep swinging, and make sure to give it plenty of follow-through.

As I've said, these birds flush reluctantly; but when they do flush, they often rise with an even more thunderous wing clatter than that of ruffed grouse surprised on the ground. An unexpected flush can startle a hunter so thoroughly that he never gets off a shot. There are only two things to do about this, at least in my experience. The first is merely to know about it so you can be mentally prepared. The second is merely to experience it a few times. I've never really become accustomed to it, so maybe this isn't much of a tip. But I've found that I get less flustered as I get more annoyed with myself and more determined not to miss an easy shot the next time.

Some shotgun hunters use dogs. A timber grouse holds no tighter than a ruffed grouse under a point, but it doesn't behave in quite the same way. Sometimes it just walks or runs off. (As with pheasants, this can have a depressing effect on staunchness unless your dog is very well trained.) Sometimes it flushes far out, like a ruffed grouse, but it's less likely to make a substantial flight. In fact, it may just fly up into a tree. If you can see it up there, this isn't so bad because you can flush it from a perch. In any event, a pointer can be very helpful if it's a tightly controlled, close-working dog. And a controlled, close-working flushing dog can be just as helpful, forcing the birds into the air as you come within range, your gun ready. What you don't want is a dog that ranges out and continually drives the birds ahead, sometimes clear off the slope you're working and almost always out of range.

To flush a timber grouse out of a tree, you need only toss a stone or stick at it. If this sounds too easy, try tossing a stick or pebble and then mounting your shotgun quickly and smoothly. The first couple of times you flush a blue or spruce grouse that way, you'll be over-confident, and you'll probably miss or fail to shoot in time. The third or fourth time, however, you'll have a good chance of connecting.

What I've just described is the easy part. The hard part is finding the bird in the tree. Sure, it's common to see a timber grouse perched out in the open, visible from a distance as you walk along. But when you scare one into a tree, it's even more common for the bird to light on one of the larger (but fairly high) limbs, close to the trunk. That's where to look. If you fail to find it quickly, I think it's a waste of time to go on searching. There are almost surely more birds in the immediate vicinity.

I've tried flushing them from the ground in the same way—by throwing something at them. Maybe I don't have a good enough throwing arm, but it doesn't seem to work well. I've been told they can be put into the air by firing a shot. This is true of some other birds, but I don't like to scattergun a grouse that isn't flying, and I don't like to waste a shell. The best way I've found is to do my impression of Teddy Roosevelt on San Juan Hill. I charge them, and sometimes they fly pretty well. Sometimes, too, this only trees them, in which case I aim a stick or stone at a perch. And sometimes if the ground is too steep for me to run fast, they simply fade back into more ground cover, in which case I take a few deep breaths and charge again.

These birds are no more covey creatures than the ruffed grouse, but they are quite often found in loose foraging groups, and early in the season—before dispersal—you may find family groups, as with ruffed grouse. At any rate, where you put one up, you'll probably find more.

Sometimes, while hunting with a rifle or pistol, you spot birds on fairly open ground, but not quite close enough for a shot. In this case you don't want to charge in. Just slowly crowd them. These birds are poor hiders. They retreat into bushy cover but often stop where you can see them clearly.

As in most kinds of hunting, you should explore slowly if you think there are birds in the area. Move slowly enough to avoid spooking unseen grouse into a run or into premature flight, and they'll often show little concern at your approach. This tactic works whether you're using a smoothbore or a rifled arm.

In late fall, explore the high ridges. By then, timber grouse tend to concentrate on the upper slopes, so the hunting there in cold weather can be excellent.

With or without a dog, a light snow is perfect for hunting either blue or spruce grouse. Follow their meandering, three-pronged tracks (much like those of a ruffed grouse) from bushes to trees to bushes, and so on. Be persistent. Sooner or later you'll probably flush one or more.

And if you don't flush any but find that the tracks end with a take-off, search the nearest trees. Under these conditions, they seldom go far, and they seem to spend quite a lot of time perching. On snow, a determined and observant hunter can usually find game either under the trees or in them.

Pinnated Grouse

The pinnated grouse, or prairie chicken, is a relatively large bird and not very fast on the take-off—but capable of traveling 40 miles an hour after getting well into the air. It isn't easy to bring a big grouse down when a long shot has to be made. My choice of gun would be either a 12 gauge or a 20 chambered for 3-inch Magnum shells.

Early in the season, before hunting pressure has turned the birds "hawky," No. 7½ shot will do in high-velocity loads or—if you're walking them up or using a dog—even in field loads. But later in the season or when you're pass-shooting, you'll want 6's in high-velocity loads or perhaps Magnums, depending on how the birds are flying where you hunt.

The same kind of advice pertains to choke. When 7½'s are appropriate, so is a modified boring. When 6's are appropriate, so is a full choke. However, I must add that many Midwestern gunners, accustomed to long shots in open fields, use full-choke guns at all times and for everything from prairie grouse to pheasants. A waterfowl gun is often used for these "chickens" as well as for the other two prairie grouse—the sharptail and the sage grouse. In double-barreled guns, modified and full borings are ideal.

There are three subspecies of pinnated grouse. A rather small variety known as Attwater's prairie chicken is found only on the Texas coast; it's endangered and fully protected. The lesser prairie chicken (*Tympanuchus cupido pallidicinctus*) is principally a bird of the short-grass prairies in the lower Plains states. The greater prairie chicken (*T. c. pinnatus*) is most common in the taller grass of the upper Plains states. These pinnated grouse need extensive grasslands for nesting and foraging. Their habits and habitat are much like those of the sharptail grouse, but prairie chickens are less adaptable to environmental change. Their range and numbers were drastically reduced by the plowing and pasturing of the grasslands.

At this writing, only five states have open seasons (though several others are in the process of reestablishing the prairie chicken). The best hunting is probably in Kansas. For a number of years, a season

A hunter and his dog congratulate each other over a brace of pinnated grouse—prairie chickens. The gun is a 20 gauge, choked modified and full. Some hunters load 7½'s in the more open barrel, 6's in the tighter ones.

was opened only in the eastern part of the state, where the greater prairie chicken resides; the lesser, occupying southwestern Kansas, was too scarce to be hunted. Now, however, both varieties are in good supply, and there's a season on both. It lasts about a month, spanning part of November and part of December.

The hunting is also excellent in lower South Dakota, where the greater prairie chicken is the resident subspecies. The season there generally runs from about mid-September through part or all of November, and applies to sharptails as well as the chickens. Nebraska, too, has a concurrent season for its greater prairie chickens and sharptails, from about mid-September through part or all of October. The Sandhills region in the north-central part of the state is usually best for prairie chickens. Texas has a very brief season on lesser prairie chickens—a mere token. The birds there will probably increase in future years. Oklahoma opens a short, separate season for each of the two prairie-chicken subspecies in November, plus a number of archery days in November and December.

Field identification is easy, even for someone who has never hunted prairie chickens before. On the sides of the neck are long, stiff, dark quills called *pinnae*—hence the name pinnated grouse. These pinnae are much more pronounced on the male than the female. Hornlike, they lift above a rooster's head when he inflates the air sac on his neck during the spring courtship and mating rituals on the booming grounds. (Also called *leks*, the booming grounds are flat, open spaces, famous for the fighting, strutting, and dancing of the males and for the loud booming sounds produced when a displaying rooster jerks his head and forcefully expels air from the neck sacs.) When lowered, the pinnae cover the deflated sacs—a bare orange patch on each side of the neck. In addition to the sacs and pinnae, a rooster has an orange comb over each eye. The sacs and comb are brighter on the lesser subspecies than on the greater, and the lesser has lighter barring on its back feathers but more barring on the underparts.

Aside from those differences, the coloration of the two races is about the same. They're yellowish- or buff-brown birds with deep brown and black barring on the body and scapulars. The underparts are pale but darkly barred. The wings and blunt tail are brown. Usually, the tail has very narrow white tipping and there are white spots on the outer wing feathers. The legs are yellow and thinly stockinged with pale feathers. In length, both subspecies are comparable to a ruffed grouse; the lesser is 15 or 16 inches long, the greater two or three inches longer. But they're shorter-tailed and heavier-bodied than the ruffed grouse. A rooster of the greater subspecies may weigh two pounds or so.

If someone asked you to name a 2-pound bird that sometimes flies over pass-shooters at 40 miles an hour, you'd probably think first of a duck. The frequent use of waterfowling guns, therefore, is not at all inappropriate. Yet these same birds are taken on the wing with bow and arrow, a sport whose popularity is evidenced by the Oklahoma archery season. Of course, it would be a rare archer who could kill a pinnated grouse by pass-shooting. Ordinarily, an archer who brings down a prairie chicken relies on the fact that the bird is relatively slow and ponderous when on the rise.

Another flight characteristic can help the scattergunner. The prairie chicken tends to beat the air with its cupped wings in a series of hard, fast strokes, followed by a long glide. In pass-shooting, the target is easiest during that glide.

Bear in mind, however, that even during the glide one of these big, blocky, squaretailed birds may be faster than it looks. As with duck shooting, a common mistake is failure to lead the target far enough and give the gun-swing plenty of follow-through.

Before summer is over, the broods of chicks have scattered and joined foraging flocks of older birds or sometimes formed new flocks. (This is true of sharptails and sage grouse, as well.) By the time hunting season opens, these concentrations of birds, known as "packs" in some locales, are large enough to provide excellent shooting when they're flushed in feeding areas or waylaid en route to such areas. Among their preferred wild foods are knotweed, wild rose, bristlegrass, blackberry, buttonweed, ragweed, clover, oak, bluestem, goldenrod, and flowering spurge.

Among cultivated crops, their favorite food is sorghum, followed by corn, wheat, and oats. Although the plowing of vast tracts has reduced their numbers by robbing them of nesting and escape cover, the crops themselves are magnets for prairie chickens—rich food resources replacing some of their natural forage.

Frosts usually bring flocks to the grainfields. In Kansas, the hunting in and around agricultural fields is apt to be excellent when the season opens because frost has arrived by November. In South Dakota or Nebraska, where hunting generally begins in September, farmland shooting is apt to improve later in the season.

Prairie grouse of all three types feed actively in the early morning, then rest and sometimes go to water during the warmth of the day, then feed again in late afternoon. With the pinnated species, I think the best early-morning method is pass-shooting at a grainfield that has been attracting large numbers of birds. Prairie chickens develop habitual flight paths—somewhat like the flyways used by crows—to their favorite feeding spots. Hunters stationed at strategic points therefore enjoy pass-shooting that's a good deal like duck hunting. In South Dakota, I've heard this classic method called a "stand-shoot"—in reference to the stands taken by the hunters, who crouch low along fencerows, in shocks and clumps of vegetation, and in ditches.

At first light, the birds begin to come in. They're apt to be flying low, yet some shots may be long—first because quite a few may pass far to one side of you, and then because some of them may look so slow that you underlead them and have to make followup shots.

Once the majority of birds have arrived in the feeding fields, there's usually a lull in stand-shooting. Then, before going much further afield, you might walk some up amid sorghum or other crops. After that, walk them up in uncultivated grasslands and brushy prairies and draws where their natural foods grow.

In very open prairie country, pinnated grouse often seem to congregate around thickets or clumps of vegetation on rises or little knobs. Perhaps some of their choice foods grow there, or perhaps a slight elevation gives them a better view of any approaching predators. Whatever the reason, these spots merit investigation.

Few wingshooters pay much attention to tracks, but bird tracks, droppings, and feathers sometimes tell you where prairie chickens or other upland species have been congregating. This photo provides an extra tip, as it's an identification portrait of the big, wide-toed, pheasantlike footprints of a prairie chicken.

Where prairie chickens have the advantage of the good visibility just described, they often flush far out. (For that matter, wild flushes are common even in bottomland cover.) In making your approach, it helps to know that the birds try to rise into the wind.

It also helps to know that they seem to hold better in tall grass than in bushes.

You can walk up prairie chickens without the aid of a dog, but I prefer to use a pointer. For pass-shooting in the agricultural fields, a dog is valuable for retrieving. And when walking the fields and prairies, a dog can often pin some birds that would otherwise get up too soon. It's true, as I wrote in an earlier book, that "the big late-fall flocks will not always wait out a point." I'm glad I had the sense—

Sharptail Grouse

Even if sharptail grouse weren't sometimes hunted together with prairie chickens or sage grouse, the guns for them would be the same. (Incidentally, sharptails are called prairie chickens in some areas.) These are large, open-country birds that are best handled with a 12-gauge gun or with a 20 chambered for 3-inch shells. I like high-brass loads of 7½'s or 6's as a rule, but where flushes tend to be wild, some shooters use shot as large as 4's in Magnum loads.

As with prairie chickens, a modified choke may be the best boring for most areas and situations—that is, the best compromise. But you'll often want a full choke. Either a variable-choke device or a double gun, bored modified and full, can be a great help.

At present, there's a fall season on sharptails in Colorado, Idaho, Michigan, Minnesota, Montana, Nebraska, North and South Dakota, Washington, Wisconsin, Wyoming, Alberta, British Columbia, Manitoba, Ontario, Quebec, Saskatchewan, and the Yukon. In Nebraska and South Dakota, it coincides with the season on prairie chickens. In Colorado, Idaho, Montana, North Dakota, and Washington, it usually overlaps or coincides with the season on sage grouse, but in Wyoming—where sage grouse are traditionally hunted before summer is quite over—the sage grouse come first and the sharptails are hunted in November and early December. Elsewhere, sharptail hunting begins in September or October.

The length of the season and the bag limit depend on censuses of the bird populations. The hunting is excellent in the Prairie Provinces, where the season lasts into or through November. It's also very good in North Dakota and Minnesota, which have comparably long seasons, and in the other upper prairie states, although their seasons aren't quite as long.

This male sharptail grouse, photographed in an Ontario grainfield, vividly exhibits the species' characteristic white wing spots and the feathering that gives the bird its common name. This rooster's deflated neck sacs are barely visible but the conspicuous combs over his eyes proclaim his sex.

The sharptail is about the same size as the greater prairie chicken. A bird of average length measures between 16½ and 18½ inches long, and a big one may weigh two pounds. It's a brown bird but paler than the prairie chicken, with a tan or yellowish-buff body flecked by darker brown and black. The brown wings have conspicuous white spotting. The breast is pale and marked with lateral rows of dark V's. The legs are feathered. In flight, it's fairly easy to tell a sharptail from other prairie grouse. For one thing, it's smaller than the sage grouse. For another, the prairie chicken has a square tail, while the sharptail has a tapered white tail with two dark, long, spiky central feathers. And its body is spotted and flecked rather than barred. The rooster has a yellow or orange comb, and it also has an air sac on each side of the neck. These sacs vary in color from orange or pink to pale violet. As on the prairie chicken, they can be inflated conspicuously. During hunting season, however, the sacs are usually deflated and hardly noticeable.

There are more than half a dozen subspecies. Some of the Northern populations are paler than the others and also more migratory. With the coming of hard frost, all three types of prairie grouse make short migrations to areas of easy foraging that offer some protection from the elements. Brushy coulees and bottomlands then become likely holding areas.

The sharptail's manner of flight resembles the prairie chicken's—slow on the take-off but fairly speedy when the bird is well into the air, and it is also characterized by fast wing strokes interspersed with glides.

Sharptails are similar to prairie chickens in their habits and needs, though much more adaptable to alterations in food and cover. Grainfields offer fine shooting. In a corn- or wheatfield or in wild vegetation that's high enough to make the birds wait out an approach instead of flushing wildly, you can walk them up without a dog. (Of course, such cover also lets a pointer work all the better since the birds are more inclined to hold.) In standing corn or other crops or over a big stubble field, dogless hunters can also work the birds toward one another—or drive them as pheasants can be driven toward standers at one end.

If you spot a large flock of sharptails in a stubble field and you have several companions, try spreading out, surrounding the birds more or less, then moving toward them. They'll probably flush out of range but are likely to scatter in all directions. This means that some will almost surely fly over the shooters. They won't be the easiest targets, but they'll offer some exciting pass-shooting.

When you conduct a pheasant-type drive for sharptails in the fields, both the drivers and the standers should get quite a bit of shooting. For some reason—maybe just lack of experience or intelligence—sharptail grouse seem reluctant to escape by gaining plenty of altitude and then crossing over a long line of hunters. Instead, they're inclined to scatter somewhat aimlessly or fly right along the row of guns.

Sharptails and sage grouse have dancing grounds, comparable to the drumming grounds of prairie chickens, where they perform their spring mating rituals. These spots are flat, open, and some-

The text mentions the usefulness of pointing dogs for hunting sharptails in corn or other high cover where the birds hold relatively well. This picture, showing a Labrador retriever ready to start work, reminds the author to add another tip—that flushing dogs can also push the birds up out of tall cover within gunshot. And like most upland birds, they seem to hold longer and flush closer to the gun once they're scattered.

times beaten almost bare of vegetation. And of course they're marked by tracks, feathers, and droppings. If you find such a spot (or witness the dancing in spring), it may be worth another visit if the hunting season opens in early fall. Both sharptail and pinnated roosters revisit these spots then to assert territorial rights. I've heard that the same places remain productive later on, but I haven't found it to be so. After all, the birds wander or migrate slightly with the coming of cold weather.

Sharptails are attracted to the same crops and other foods that draw prairie chickens, but they also rely heavily on tree buds of certain kinds. This means they can often be flushed out of birch, mountain ash, alder, willow, and chokecherry.

When the birds aren't in the cultivated fields (as they often are in early morning and late afternoon), they're most likely in or near tall vegetation that provides cover as well as food. In addition to the aforementioned trees, rosebush thickets often hold them. So do poplar groves and other clumps of trees and brush, particularly around prairie creeks or potholes. They roost, water, and feed there, and the height of the vegetation disposes them to hold well for a dog—or for the approach of a dogless hunter.

The sharptail is less of a ground-hugger than the prairie chicken. It often roosts high. If you keep your eyes only on the ground and your dog, you may swing too late on sharptails that go out overhead. As in hunting ruffed grouse and timber grouse, it pays to look up frequently into the trees and be prepared for a flush from any height or direction.

Listen as well as look. Prairie grouse cackle when they flush. The sound of the sharptailed variety is a clucking—*"cuk, cuk, cuk."* And the wings make noise on the take-off, too. As in hunting pheasants or ruffed grouse, noise is sometimes the first warning that the gun had better come up.

And, as in deer hunting, it pays to watch the middle distances. Where the prairie cover is fairly open, you can sometimes see birds roosting or feeding. Of course, they can see you, too. This is the kind

A Lab shows off his prowess at retrieving sharptails. These birds are fairly big but their mottled coloration blends right in with the ground cover, so a fetch dog is a valuable help in bringing fallen sharptails to hand.

of situation in which it's particularly rewarding to have a pointer that will circle widely (but under your tight control) and pin the birds while you move in.

Late in the season, when birds seek shelter from strong, cold winds, the overgrown shelterbelts, or windbreaks, or abandoned farmlands often hold sharptails, as do any natural windbreaks on land never cultivated. In open prairie country, by the way, these spots often hold Hungarian partridges together with the sharptails.

Don't forget to poke around abandoned farm buildings or machinery. These, too, provide weather shelters, and the weeds and brush around them provide food—not only for sharptails but for a number of upland game species.

Prairie grouse, like all gallinaceous birds, need to pick grit and like to dust themselves. Sometimes you'll see them doing so along the edges of back roads. Unused railroad rights-of-way—with their dusty, gritty road beds flanked by brush—provide the same advantages plus plenty of adjacent food and roosting cover. A stroll along such a strip often furnishes good shooting and a mixed bag that may include rabbits and two or three species of upland birds. Powerline rights-of-way are also good.

Sage Grouse

With regard to guns, the same general observations apply to sage grouse as to sharptails and pinnated grouse. However, gun and load selection may be influenced by two seemingly contradictory characteristics of the sage grouse. The first is that these big, powerful birds are either physiologically fragile or more susceptible to shock than many species and are rather easily brought down, even when hit by no more than the fringe of a pattern from a field load. The second is that they're the continent's largest grouse—much larger than the related species—and since they tend to become wild flushers late in the season, you may have to reach out for them with a hefty load.

I'd use a 12- or 20-gauge gun, the latter chambered for 3-inch shells. As I've mentioned, there are times when No. 7½ shot is big enough for prairie chickens or sharptails, and in some regions you can hunt one or the other species along with sage grouse. However, 7½'s just aren't big enough for sage grouse. If these "prairie bombers" are on the agenda, No. 6 is definitely the size to use.

Some very authoritative writers recommend field loads, at least in a 12 gauge. That's fine early in the season or wherever you find you can get reasonably close before the birds flush—especially if you shoot fairly fast, before a sage grouse can get up full steam. The rise is slow and labored, but subsequent flight speed is a very different matter—which brings us back to the need for reaching out with something fairly powerful. I prefer high-brass loads. I like 1¼-ounce charges of 6's, and if I'm using a 20 gauge, this means I want 3-inch Magnums.

In a double-barreled gun, a good choke combination is modified and full. In a repeater, modified is definitely best for almost any wingshooter (except perhaps toward the end of the season). Full choke is the only boring used by some Western gunners, self-trained since childhood to bring down birds at what most of us would consider very long range. Unquestionably, a tight bore has an advantage when most of the birds are flushing way out in open country, and if you're using a full choke, you can wait out an occasional close-riser, letting the bird gain some yardage before firing. But modified is better in most places for most gunners on most days. Best, of course, is an adjustable-choke device so you can switch in accordance with conditions.

In most years, 11 states and 1 Canadian province open a fall season on sage grouse. The season lengths and the harvests vary regionally from very impressive to vestigial, depending on the grouse populations. Thus, I'd travel to Alberta for sharptails but not for sage grouse. Nor would I make a long trip to hunt sage grouse in the Dakotas, Colorado, Washington, Oregon, or California. As a rule, the hunting for this species is somewhat better in Utah and Nevada, and considerably better in Idaho. The Idaho season (on sharptails as well as sage grouse) generally runs for a couple of weeks in September and a couple more in October.

Best of all are Wyoming and Montana, whose combined annual kill generally accounts for more than half of the continental sage-grouse harvest. (The continental total averages about 250,000 birds.) Where the habitat is suitable, those two states sometimes have an incredible abundance of grouse. Traditionally, sage grouse provide the year's first upland shooting. In Montana they're hunted concurrently with sharptails, usually from early or mid-September through a week or two of November. In Wyoming they're generally hunted during all of September—a couple of months before the sharptail season opens.

Some hunters prefer the last part of the season, others prefer the first week or two. If you're working with a dog, the cooling weather puts less rigorous demands on the animal (and on you). Moreover, the grouse gather in larger and larger flocks—sometimes hundreds of birds in a very small area. On the other hand, large flocks (at any time of the season) tend to run before a dog or flush far out; the larger the flocks become, the more wary the birds seem to become. And this tendency is intensified by extended hunting pressure.

If you can handle far-out flushes and long shots, you'll find the sport most exciting late in the season. Otherwise, you may favor the opening weeks when you can bag more birds with fewer shells.

Like prairie chickens and sharptails, sage grouse gather on dancing grounds to perform courtship rituals. In this photo of a South Dakota dancing ground, the roosters are inflating their air sacs, strutting, squawking, and jumping for a passive audience of hens. Unlike the other prairie grouse, sage grouse don't return to their dancing grounds in early fall, but they're likely to be plentiful in the same general vicinity where they mated in the spring.

Among this continent's gallinaceous birds, only the turkey outweighs the sage grouse. A mature sage hen is likely to weigh three or four pounds, a rooster five or six—and occasionally well over seven. A hen may be almost two feet long, and a rooster may be longer by half a foot. Both sexes have mottled grayish-brown upper parts, a pale breast and flanks, black bellies, and palely feathered legs. The rooster has a black chin and upper neck with a white V across the throat. His breast is white, whereas the hen's neck and breast are pale but barred with brown. Under the rooster's white breast feathers are two big, frontally positioned air sacs that vary from yellow to olive or reddish-brown. During the springtimè courting rituals, his entire breast and neck are puffed up so enormously that his head may be entirely hidden. At the same time, the hugely inflated sacs are bared. In the fall, the deflated sacs are hidden but the male can be distinguished by his large size, his neck and breast coloration, and a yellow comb over each eye. Both sexes have long, pointed, tails marbled with brown that fan out in flight, but the male's is longer. When strutting in the spring, he spreads the tail feathers into a sunburst shape. These feathers are pointed—like enormous spikes—and one of the bird's colorful nicknames is spiny-tailed pheasant.

Other regional names include sage chicken, sage turkey (a reference to size), and sage buzzard (a reference to the bird's supposedly tough, strong-tasting meat). This species feeds so heavily on sage that the flesh may acquire a strong—in fact, slightly bitter—flavor of sage oil. But you can draw the bitterness out by marinating a bird before cooking it.

I've read many recipes for marinades. They vary in details and proportions, but almost all include the essential ingredients: a minced clove of garlic, a chopped onion, salt, pepper, and wine. I don't agree with most cooking writers that the wine must be white, but it should be dry, preferably a white or rosé. Most recipes ignore one ingredient—a very generous splash of lemon or orange juice—which is another agent that helps draw out any sage or other strong flavor while somehow releasing or intensifying the savoriness of the meat itself. (If you don't use the juice, use a little vinegar; I use both.) I have an unproven theory that citrus juice also slightly tenderizes meat of almost any kind. Other acceptable but optional ingredients include celery seed and cloves. Most of the marinade recipes call for salad oil, which I regard as superfluous at best.

Soak the bird for at least four hours, turning it at least twice. The breast is dark and very big, yet you can cook this grouse by any method appropriate for other large upland birds or for ordinary chicken. However, if it's a big old rooster, you'll probably be well advised to use one of the simmering methods just to make sure it's tender. The result will be delicious.

The size, shape, weight, and consequently laborious lift-off of this species can result in an amusing complexity of shotgunning errors. First, perhaps, a grouse flushes ponderously and not very far out, and the gunner gives it too long a lead, missing an easy shot because the hunter is accustomed to the swifter-rising sharptail or pinnated grouse. The next one flushes unseen and is well on its way before he

Bill Browning, a well-known wildlife photographer and artist, collects a big sage rooster. These grouse are America's largest, but some wingshooters have trouble hitting them because they fly high and fast (after a lumbering take-off) and their size makes range deceptive.

gets his gun up. Now, having realized his first error, he overcompensates and shoots behind it. At the next opportunity, he checks his swing and demolishes a slow riser, but after that, he may fall into the bad habit of stopping his swing. A rising sage grouse sometimes provides an easy target unless it's way out. Yet for the sake of meat as well as sport, the wise shooting policy is to wait a bit, swing smoothly and deliberately, and give it plenty of follow-through, leading it pretty much as you'd lead other prairie grouse. Like the others, this one flies with a series of powerful wing strokes followed by a glide. And like the others, this one can move along at 40 miles an hour. But the glide is shorter than that of the sharptail or prairie chicken, and sometimes the speed is actually greater. Because of its size, the bird just doesn't look like it's moving that fast.

Several writers have stated that sage grouse can achieve 70-mile-an-hour spurts. I can't vouch for this and don't know if they've been clocked at such great speed, but I suppose they could manage it with the aid of a heavy tail wind. Gusty wind is common on open prairies, and you should be conscious of it while hunting.

Range and altitude can also be deceptive because sage grouse are so large. They tend to fly higher than the other grouse, yet sometimes one will accelerate without first rising high; it may, in fact, skim the sage at full speed when the gunner has the impression it's still at its low climbing speed.

One other disconcerting flight characteristic merits your attention. Though the roosters tend to fly relatively straight, the hens twist and gyrate. Don't try to move your gun with these twists or you'll probably miss. The erratic movements aren't great enough to take the bird outside the edge of a good pattern, so just swing and shoot as if a twisting hen were flying as straight as a rooster.

The name *sage grouse* is the most apt of all the descriptive names applied to this species. Sage buds, young leaves, and shoots usually account for at least 75 percent of a mature bird's diet, so when you want to find sage grouse, the first thing to look for is usually sage.

That last tip doesn't imply that sage grouse will invariably be found feeding on sage. Important supplementary foods include grasses and other soft plants—especially dandelions and clover. If you're hunting uncultivated land, and the birds aren't in the sage, watch for these plants and explore any grassy expanses.

The cultivated food most favored by sage grouse is alfalfa. When hunting on a farm or ranch, check the edges of any alfalfa field.

Also check water holes, whether you're hunting on cultivated or uncultivated land. Hunt near irrigation ditches, stock tanks, ponds, creeks, and muddy seeps. Sage grouse will fly a considerable distance to reach water, but they prefer to feed and rest nearby. Most often they're within walking distance of it and seldom more than about half a mile away.

Paradoxically, sage grouse dislike thick cover when it becomes wet. At such times, look for them in more open, drier places. Otherwise, they like to feed and rest where the sage thickens and they can stay down out of the wind. Try the coulees and any wide basins cut by gullies.

From late morning until early afternoon, sage grouse stop feeding and go to rest—as other upland birds do. Gullies and draws are the most common resting places.

Birds there may hold tighter than when feeding—hoping that if they stay still and hidden, any intruder will pass by without detecting them. Sometimes you can panic them into flushing by pausing every few steps, just as you do when walking up other upland birds.

Early morning and just before dusk are the best times to hunt near water. Those are the times when sage grouse come to drink. At other times, hunt the good feeding and resting places, preferably fairly near to water.

Also search for big white blotches on the ground amid or around sagebrush. These mark the surface run-off of saline concentrations known as alkali seeps. Grouse like to feed at or near the seeps. On cold, sunny days, they often rest and bask on the seeps, too, because the white reflects the sun and warms them.

Tracks and droppings are worth watching for, too, especially around muddy water holes. The tracks are like those of other grouse but larger. The ordinary pale droppings don't indicate that birds have visited a spot very recently. These droppings weather so slowly that it's hard to tell how old they are. You may find great accumulations where grouse roosted long ago. But if you find darker, solidified pools (called cecal droppings because they're produced by the cecal ducts at the juncture of the small and large intestines), you can assume the place has been recently used, for this type weathers away fast. Of course, obviously fresh droppings of either kind indicate that birds probably remain in the immediate area.

And you can look for the birds themselves—or parts of birds—in trails and openings amid sagebrush. Even when most birds in a flock are feeding or resting in concealment, in thick brush, one member or perhaps two will often move about in the open. It's possible that a bird moving in the open is performing sentinel duty for the flock, watching for approaching predators. Whether or not this is the explanation, it pays to scan the terrain for exposed birds.

This kind of scouting is reminiscent of pronghorn hunting, and it often takes place in the same habitat. Many sage-grouse hunters, with or without dogs, use binoculars to scan the surrounding area. A 7X35 binocular will serve well enough, but some hunters prefer a slightly high power or a zoom model that can go from 7X to 15X. The lower power facilitates a visual sweep of the panorama, while the high power permits close investigation of likely cover patches. For me, at least, it's a bit harder to spot a grouse's head or protruding beak or pointed tail in a brushy opening than to glass for big game. The use of the zoom feature is roughly comparable to the use of a spotting scope in big-game hunting—providing a close look after a preliminary view with lower magnification.

Quite often, a flock of sage grouse can be stalked almost like pronghorns. If they see movement or hear the scratch of brush plants, they may run or fly, but they're not quite as alert as other prairie grouse.

They usually rise into the wind and then swing around with it.

Some hunters like to approach crosswind when possible, so that the birds won't stretch the range while rising and leveling.

As with other grouse, you must use your eyes as well as your ears because you may hear a flush before you see it. Listen for a clattering of wings and a loud, chickenlike, clucking cackle.

If you're almost within shooting distance of a flock, try dashing in. The birds may defeat you with a ground-run, of course, but the flock may flush, and such a take-off is usually ragged—a few birds rising at a time. When that happens, rush for the late-flushing birds, and you may well get shots at a couple.

On the sage flats, a hunting party can form a line of drivers and a line of standers. The drivers simply move through the brush, taking shots at any birds that get up within range, while the standers fire at the birds that flush far ahead of the drivers.

On a windy day, no more than two hunters are needed to stage such a drive on a smaller scale. One of them works a flat or field by walking into the wind while the other waits at the far edge.

In another variation, one man circles through a thick sage patch, moving in tightening rings, while a companion waits at the downwind edge of the patch for flushed birds to swing toward him.

If you're hunting alone, you'll probably do best by working around waterholes in the early morning, then zigzagging through the thickest sage patches, pausing frequently, next working the lowland resting places if you don't break for lunch, and again zigzagging through thick sage in mid-afternoon.

From several of the preceding tips, you will have inferred that you can take about as many grouse without a dog as with one. Many hunters prefer to work without a dog, since these birds are disposed to flush wildly or make long runs through sage or grass. Dogless hunters enjoy debunking the myth that sage grouse are slow ground travelers, seldom able to slip away from a dog for long, and the equally fallacious myth that when flushed, they don't fly far and can be marked down easily so the dog can work them again. On the contrary, sage grouse often draw man and dog on for frustrating and futile periods, and they may fly several hundred yards. So the dog-less hunters have some logic on their side.

But there's another side. Very often in open country, several hundred yards isn't too far to mark birds down, and scattered singles that have been flushed usually hold at least a little better than the big, nervous flocks first encountered. Besides—or maybe more important—it's more fun to hunt with a dog. And those who use one enjoy debunking a myth of the dogless: that dogs don't work well in sage. The hell they don't. They can sniff out a sage grouse just about as well as they can sniff out any other prairie bird. The decision about a dog depends on how you like to hunt.

I must add, however, that a dog isn't essential for retrieving cripples. (I hate to admit that, because in the case of most upland game as well as waterfowl, I feel that dogs save enormous numbers of game that would otherwise be wasted.) When your shot brings a sage grouse down but fails to kill it, the bird will, of course, try to escape. It can walk pretty fast—I almost said "run." But for reasons I don't understand, evolution hasn't taught these birds to hide well when injured. As a rule (not a hard and fast rule, but a rule, nevertheless) a grounded sage grouse can be seen and overtaken without the aid of a dog. So if you don't have a dog, go ahead and hunt.

If you do use a dog, the animal must be controllable and tightly controlled. Otherwise, when a flock flushes with a few birds going up at a time, the dog will just bump or push away those remaining on the ground. Staunchness and obedience are essential.

I once wrote that "flushing dogs seem to have no special advantage at putting sage grouse up within gunshot, but a pointer accustomed to working pheasants or Hungarian partridge may circle and pin them until the hunter arrives. Even without any circling . . . a few birds will probably hold just long enough." Since then, I've seen a Lab and a springer work well enough to force a retraction out of me. Worse yet, another outdoor writer has stated—with justification—that pointers sometimes have trouble pinning down running grouse. I'm especially embarrassed because I own a springer (or he owns me), and I love the breed.

So, publicly owning up to prior ignorance, I'll revamp my opinion as follows: Either a pointer or flusher can work these birds if the dog has gained some bird sense and can be properly controlled. Either type of dog will be most successful early in the season, before the birds have gathered into huge, nervous flocks and before they've learned escape tactics. Late in the season, a pointer may really have more trouble than a flusher but can be used effectively after a flock is scattered because singles and pairs sit more tightly.

Hungarian
Partridges

If you think of Hungarian partridges as oversized bobwhites that prefer open fields and flush about twice as far ahead of you as quail would, you have a fairly accurate picture of Hun hunting. Because so many shots are long, some wingshooters are partial to No. 6 loads in 12-gauge guns. That combination will serve you well enough if you're better at swinging deliberately on the farthest-out birds in a covey rise than at picking your targets very quickly so you can shoot fast as the birds get up.

But it's a combination that's not for me—nor for most of the shooters I know. Typically, these birds rise 15 to 25 yards in front of the gun. Assuming that your reflexes are no better than mine, you should still be able to get off a first shot at a bird 25 to 35 yards away and a second at 40 or 50 yards. Until a partridge is well away from you, No. 6 is a bit large. I much prefer high-velocity loads of 7½'s. There's nothing wrong with using a 12-gauge gun, but I once had the experience of walking 18 miles of wheat-stubble fields and timothy hay carrying a gun that grew heavier with each step. Ever since then, I've preferred a light 20 gauge chambered for 3-inch shells. As a shotgun grows heavier toward the end of a long day's hunting, I find myself getting it to my shoulder ever more slowly, so my preference isn't based on a mere dislike of toting an extra eight ounces or so.

If you carry a 12 gauge, ordinary high-brass loads will give you 1¼ ounces of shot, and that's plenty. In a 20 gauge, 2¾-inch Magnums will give you 1⅛ ounces. I suppose that's enough. However, my 20 is chambered for 3-inch Magnums, so I can use 1¼-ounce loads—thus equaling high-brass 12-gauge loads—and I like the little edge that gives me. I don't think I've ever put so much shot into a Hungarian partridge that it was spoiled for the table. The opposite is more often true: I need the generous shot charges to get *enough* into a fast-flying bird at 40 yards or more.

Those who use No. 6's, particularly in 12 gauge, are inclined to favor a full choke because they're concentrating on the long shots. In a tight barrel, the 6's will retain a dense enough pattern at 40 yards or more. Since I prefer 7½'s and I try to make my first shot quickly, I favor a modified boring and I feel that modified is the best bet for the majority of shooters.

Someone must be asking at this point why it's so important to hurry the first shot on a covey rise. Well, I don't mean you must truly rush it; this isn't snap-shooting at ruffed grouse. But it is important to mount your gun fast, picking your first target before the stock comes to your shoulder if you expect to bring down occasional doubles or make up for a first miss. Otherwise, you'll really have to rush the second shot. I once hunted with an Ontario guide named John Ouderkirk who could consistently hit partridges at 50 yards, but I doubt that many wingshooters are that good.

Like chukars, Huns are also known as gray partridges, and like chukars, they're naturalized Americans. Eight subspecies are native to Europe and Asia. Ours are called Hungarian partridges because most of our early importations came from the plains of Hungary. The first birds were released in California and Washington shortly before 1900. At first they failed to establish themselves, yet subsequent efforts during the next few decades were spectacularly successful in the same areas and elsewhere.

Field trials for bird dogs in Canada and the United States were in large measure responsible. From the turn of the century until the First World War, field-trialers imported considerable numbers of partridges. Naturally, some escaped the pointers and the guns, and those birds began to breed in their new habitat, producing "accidental wild populations." Hungarian partridges furnished a marvelous test for the pointing breeds. These birds don't hold for a close approach the way quail do. To effectively work them for the gun, dogs must have keen enough noses to scent them at a fair distance, and must freeze into a staunch point the instant they catch that scent, or the birds will flush too far ahead of the gun.

Even on an open meadow or cut-over field, Hungarian partridges are sometimes hard to see on the ground, but they can see you and your dog at a
considerable distance. A good Hun dog like this setter hunts wide enough to
cover a lot of ground but accepts strict control and knows how to come
around on the far side of a covey, holding the birds under a point while the
hunter approaches for the flush.

While the field-trialers were experimenting, Huns also attracted
the interest of game departments that were eager to replace upland
game depleted by forest-clearing and the tilling of former grasslands. These partridges had adapted to Europe's tilled plains. Unlike
some of our native species, they could flourish on open flatlands and
gently rolling prairies where small-grain crops were replacing gigantic expanses of wild vegetation. Though Huns can also thrive in sage
and bunchgrass near streams in the dry lands of the Great Basin,
they usually move or spread their populations to the nearest wheat
and hay.

Today, Washington opens the Hun season from about mid-September to mid-October, North Dakota has a slightly shorter season in late November and early December, and a more substantial fall season is offered in a dozen other states plus eight Canadian provinces: Idaho, Illinois, Indiana, Iowa, Minnesota, Montana, Nevada, Oregon, South Dakota, Utah, Wisconsin, Wyoming, Alberta, British Columbia, Manitoba, Nova Scotia, Ontario, Prince Edward Island, Quebec, and Saskatchewan.

That list of states and provinces represents three major areas of partridge distribution. The westernmost extends from the Pacific Coast eastward to Idaho and Utah. Then there's a central area—the largest—which sprawls across the Great Plains from the Prairie Provinces down through Montana, upper Wyoming, the Dakotas, and adjacent parts of Minnesota and Iowa. The third significant range covers the Great Lakes region.

For a long time, Oregon and Idaho had the largest annual harvest. Then, in the early 1970's, Washington and Montana recorded the biggest harvests. Montana remains one of the best Hun states, if not the single best. The hunting is also excellent in Wisconsin and Ontario, as well as in the Prairie Provinces, and is getting better and better to the east.

Despite the continuing enlargement of the Hun's range, a great many American hunters have never seen this bird. When a Hungarian, or gray, partridge whirrs up before your gun, it doesn't look particularly gray. Your strongest impression is of a wide rusty tail and rounded, blurred, rusty-brown wings. It's a plump bird, shaped like a considerably overgrown bobwhite. It's about 12 or 13 inches long, and you can figure its weight at an ounce per inch. A bird on the wing is most often seen from the rear. If you get a crossing shot, the body looks pastel brown, with some gray on the breast and flanks.

The gray becomes much more conspicuous when a bird is in hand. The crown is buff, the forehead and cheeks cinnamon, the back grayish-brown, the wings and tail barred and vermiculated with rust-brown and gray. An examination of the brown wings shows that the scapulars have bright white shafts. The neck, breast, and flanks are gray. However, the flanks are marked with vertical chestnut barring, and a dark chestnut horseshoe marks the lower part of the Hun's breast.

You can roughly age a Hun. If the bird is a young one, hatched no longer ago than the previous spring, its outer primaries will be pointed. If it's younger than that, the legs may be yellow, but this age indicator often fades to the adult blue-gray color before the wing molt is completed.

Before you can distinguish sex, you'll have to shoot a few birds and practice making comparisons. On a hen, the horseshoe marking is smaller and less distinct than on a cock, and once in a while it's entirely absent or whitish rather than chestnut. To confirm the sex, you have to inspect the scapular feathers closely. A cock's are yellowish-brown with thin, wavy black lines, turning chestnut near the outer edges; a hen's are blackish at the base, with light yellow crossbarring but no chestnut and with the wavy lines only on the outer portions. Most females also have two to four buff crossbars on the scapulars and middle wing coverts, plus a buff stripe along the shafts of these feathers.

Huns don't burst from cover as explosively as bobwhites or fly quite as fast, but there is a similarity in the take-off and flight. As I indicated in my discussion of guns and loads, a single or a covey is likely to be 30 yards out before your gun is up and swinging. At that point, the birds are often no more than 10 or 15 feet high; they don't try for much altitude. Sometimes, however, they do fly fairly far. They may head for another field several hundred yards off. In open stubble, you can usually mark them down. But unlike most upland birds, they'll probably flush farther from you (or farther from your dog) with each successive approach, so close teamwork between hunter and dog is essential. Their average flight speed is about 30 miles an hour. However, they're capable of abrupt spurts and equally abrupt switches of direction—two more reasons why I like to get off a fast first shot.

Flushed grays try to stay together, seldom scattering as haphazardly as other covey birds. But scattered singles and pairs will hold much better for a dog than coveys will, and I learned an interesting trick from John Ouderkirk to force a scattering. What you do (if the opportunity presents itself and you're a good enough wingshooter) is try to bag the two birds that are in the lead. These coveys are family groups, evidently led by the mates whose young are the followers. If you can spot the leaders and bring them down, the others, not yet accustomed to moving independently, will scatter in confusion, fly only a short distance, and then wait out your approach, probably in the hope of hearing the reedy gathering call of the parents.

This is the kind of close Hungarian rise a gunner hopes for but seldom sees. The bird at far right has been hit and is falling. This covey was flushed beside a farm road, where the birds were picking grit in convenient proximity to roosting and feeding areas.

Early in the season, most coveys number from half a dozen to a dozen birds. Where hunting is permitted well into December or January, you may put up coveys of 20 birds. When flushed they'll usually split into two groups that can be marked down and hunted separately. Such coveys consist of two families. This is because the period of courting displays and subsequent mating is approaching. The birds seem to avoid mating with siblings or parents. Therefore, two distinct families often join forces for a short time, until pairing disrupts the enlarged group.

Huns like to roost and rest in grass, hayfields, or brushy edges, and they take shelter from wind around buildings, in draws or hollows, and on lee hillsides. They pick grit on bare spots and on trails and back roads, but I find it very hard to walk up close when they're in these more open places. The roosting, resting, and feeding areas are best. There will be some water near any productive area, but I don't bother looking for it because Huns are less dependent than most birds on frequent watering.

In wild terrain, these birds can live quite well on forb and weed seeds, but small cultivated grains are their favorite foods. Biologists have found that wheat, oats, and barley make up about 70 percent of their fall and winter diet on the Canadian plains—and probably throughout much of their American range. However, food preferences differ slightly from one region to another in accordance with what's most abundant and easily available. In Michigan, for example, corn rather than wheat attracts the most partridges. Using the foods I've listed as guidelines, you can easily discover where—and on what—the birds are feeding in your hunting area.

If you fail to flush coveys out of the small-grain stubble, they're probably roosting in hay or gritting along the dusty edges. Alfalfa is their favorite type of roosting hay.

Too many hunters, though they take great pains to mark down missed birds or those at which they haven't shot, are careless about marking fallen birds. With or without a dog, it's extremely important to mark the fall of a killed or injured Hun. Otherwise, it will often be much harder to find than a fallen bobwhite because, as a rule, it will have been hit and brought down much farther out. Stubble-field terrain may be so bare that you think you can spot anything on the ground at 50 yards or more. Yet these birds can seem to vanish into the very earth if you don't see just where they've landed.

In this scene, both shooters are swinging their guns almost horizontally—
which is common in hunting Hungarian partridges. These birds rise somewhat like bobwhite quail (though not as explosively) and they don't rise high.
The problem is that they flush much farther out than bobwhites. Note the
distance from the gunners to the dog, which has just broken point—and the
dog had pointed the birds from a considerable distance.

A good gray-partridge dog has to display somewhat contradictory
qualities. Huns are typically birds of the flat, wide-open spaces
(mostly open farmland), and an effective dog is one that hunts wide
just in order to cover enough ground. It's true you'll sometimes spot
coveys on low knolls or in stubble fields or low grass, but most of the
time you have to depend on the dog to locate birds. On days when
scenting conditions are favorable, let him move out.

Yet that same dog must accept tight control before you get too
close to the birds, not only because they'll flush far in front of him
but also because they're runners, as Charley Waterman phrases it,
"in a class with chukars and pheasants." Once in a while you may
have the pleasure of seeing a dog that has learned to head off a
running covey. For the most part, you'll have to count on the dog's
obeying signals, circling wide to pin a covey between himself and
you, and slamming into a point at the first hint of scent.

In high weeds or brushy cover, a flushing dog can put up grays close enough, but in most situations, I'd like a wide-ranging pointing dog that's very conscious of his human. My bid would go to a well-trained English setter or English pointer.

Now I'll add a further contradiction. There are times when you'll want to hunt with your dog very close, almost at heel. In wet weather, coveys like to keep relatively dry on minor elevations such as well-drained knolls. From knolls with low cover such as cut-over timothy, they can see you coming for quite a distance. If the weather is not only wet but windy, the birds tend to get "hawky"—even more nervous than usual—and scenting conditions are poor. Now a wide-ranging dog is of little avail because too many coveys will explode into flight before the dog is sure of them. You're better off holding the dog in to help with the few coveys you spot or luck into.

Trust your dog when he acts "birdy" and give him the benefit of the doubt, even if you suspect he's sniffing ground-runners that have left for other fields. Sometimes you'll discover that the birds have come back or settled down and will now hold much tighter.

The habit of return is a Hun characteristic that can be turned to your advantage in other ways. After you've put a covey up several times and finally lost track of it, hunt on for a while and then revisit the area where you first moved the birds. Once they're no longer being disturbed, coveys usually circle back to a favored feeding or roosting area.

An extension of this tactic can help you bag grays from year to year. Like bobwhite quail, they establish small, favorite haunts that are used season after season. When you find productive spots, remember or jot down their locations. The descendants of each family group you find will continue to covey there in succeeding generations.

Learning such covey locations and hunting them diligently is the best way a dogless hunter can bag Huns. Concentrate on weedy edges of stubblefields, draws, low and brushy spots, brush or weeds around buildings, and roosting hay—the places where high cover will help to hold the birds for you.

Pheasants

I used to shoot pheasants with 3-inch Magnum loads of 7½'s—that's right, 7½'s—in my 20-gauge gun. In those years I did most of my ringneck hunting in a part of Warren County, New Jersey, that was characterized by small, brushy fields and weedy meadows interspersed with woods, brambles, and brush thickets. I invariably hunted with a friend and his springer spaniel, a pheasant-wise dog that could head off and flush the most determined runners. My friend and I were young enough then to keep up with the springer, more or less. Sometimes, while the dog was quartering a patch of brush or tracking one bird, we flushed another one somewhere else. But even then, any bird that cackled into the air was likely to be close, partly because the ground cover was dense and partly because we could work through the thickets toward the edges, ready to shoot when skulking ringnecks reached the openings and jumped into the air. In terms of range and vegetation, it was almost like grouse hunting. Few shots were longer than 30 or 35 yards.

In recent years, most of my hunting has been on Pennsylvania farmland and at one New Jersey preserve that has a mixture of brush and big, open fields. To use 7½'s in these more typical circumstances would be a stupidity as well as a heresy. At 40 yards or farther, you need more size, weight, and punch to bring these birds down cleanly and consistently. The ringnecked pheasant is a tough, hardy species. John Madson, one of our most perceptive outdoor writers (as well as one of the most vivid and literate) has described the pheasant as "shingled with galvanized feathers." Like most hunters, I now use No. 6 shot.

When I carry a 12-gauge gun I use high-brass shells, and if I were hunting in still more open country, I might easily be converted to 2¾-inch Magnums. When I carry a 20-gauge gun, I do use 3-inch Magnums and give thanks that my 20 is chambered for them.

Nationally, 12 is the most popular gauge. Although I'm partial to a light 20, I concede that the 12 has an edge for open-field pheasant shooting. In the big Midwestern fields of corn or small grain, quite a few hunters carry the 12 gauge with a high-brass load of 6's for the first shot and high-brass 5's in the magazine or second barrel for long follow-up shots. It's a good idea. In some regions, there's so little call for 5's that the sporting-goods stores seem to ignore their existence, but for follow-ups, this pellet size is worth finding or handloading.

I own two favorite pheasant guns and a semifavorite. (Doesn't everybody have at least three?) One favorite is a 20-gauge over-under, chambered for 3-inch shells and choked modified and full. The other is a 12-gauge pump with an adjustable choke device, and for the roughly average cover where I now hunt, I always choose modified.

The semi-favorite is the 20-gauge Magnum I used to carry in the tight cover I just described, where 7½ shot was sufficient. It has improved-cylinder and modified borings, a combination that's ideal for much upland game but not tight enough for pheasants except in tangled thickets or marshy spots with high, dense reeds and rushes. In my part of the East, there are numerous pockets of such habitat, but I can't recommend the improved-and-modified combination as a generally efficient pair of borings for ringnecks.

I'd say that modified is best for the typical mixed cover in many parts of the country, but full is needed for hunting many of the wide Midwestern and Western fields where 50-yard shots are taken in stride. A couple of my Midwestern friends use their waterfowling guns to good advantage.

In the fall and winter of 1977–1978, 38 states and six of Canada's provinces had pheasant seasons. (My numbers don't include states where pheasants can be shot only on preserves.) Although ringneck populations have declined sadly in recent years, a great many pheasants continue to thrive in a vast region extending from lower Canada down over the United States to an indistinct line running from Chesapeake Bay or thereabouts in the East to Central California in the West, with southerly dips here and there. Below that line, pheasants don't reproduce well. However, there are a number of states both below the line and above it where pheasants either winter poorly or breed poorly, but where the game departments release great numbers of birds annually to replenish the populations. It's almost certain that the same number of states or more will have seasons in future years, though bag limits and season lengths will fluctuate in accordance with pheasant numbers.

The "American" pheasant has a predominantly Chinese ancestry but is really a mongrel, a unique blending of stocks and subspecies from various parts of Asia. It represents a long, very successful experiment in importing and breeding hardy, fast, self-sufficient, adaptable wildlife, reasonably resistant to disease and predation— birds that combine these admirable traits with equally admirable qualities as game and table fare. Pheasants were hunted in Europe in the 18th century, and American attempts to establish them date from the Colonial era. In this country, truly successful importations and releases began in 1881.

Knowing some of this impressive history, many hunters wonder why Southern game departments have had so little success in establishing wild pheasant populations. In the 1920's, the great naturalist and game manager Aldo Leopold first advanced the theory that calcium requirements are the key to natural range. For successful laying, hen pheasants seem to need more calcium than do birds that evolved on this continent. They reproduce as far south as prehistoric glaciation carried rich lime deposits. Beyond that glacial line, they seem to reproduce only where the earth has some other source of the right type of lime. Leopold's theory is still accepted but in qualified form. Pheasants have additional critical breeding requirements, including a favorable average ground temperature and humidity.

The last nationwide tally of pheasant harvests showed the four top pheasant-hunting states to be Iowa, Pennsylvania, South Dakota, and Illinois—in that order. In recent years, those states have usually been the best or among the best, and in all likelihood, they will continue to be. Other very good states are California, Nebraska, Michigan, Kansas, Washington, and Idaho.

Even in the best pheasant states, the birds have declined. Hunters want to know why, and what—if anything—can be done about it.

Owing to farming methods, especially in the Midwest, pheasants attained their greatest numbers in the 1940's. A decline began soon afterward with the trend toward huge single-crop corporate operations and "clean farming" methods, rather than diversified family farms sprinkled with fencerows, windbreaks, brush-bordered potholes, and other forms of cover. The birds were granted an inadvertent reprieve in the 1950's, when the Soil Bank program removed many acres from cultivation. The fallow lands produced big crops of pheasants and other wildlife, but those lands are now cultivated, and farmers are being pressured to increase production still further.

Clean farming results in very scanty winter cover for wildlife. The severe prairie winters are taking a greater toll of birds than ever before. Clean farming also results in severely reduced springtime nesting cover except in hayfields, and the modern method of haying has worsened an unhappy situation. Pheasants are ground-nesters. Alfalfa hay is their favorite nesting cover. A hen will run or fly from approaching danger at most times of year, but when she's laying or incubating her clutch, she's very reluctant to move, and she becomes progressively more reluctant as hatching time approaches. She simply sits tight, hidden in the alfalfa until a high-speed mowing machine, called a "swather," smashes her and her eggs. About 12-million ringnecks are harvested each year by hunters. About 60-million—including hens, eggs, and young chicks—are lost to the swathers.

All that sportsmen can do to help alleviate the situation is to support their conservation agencies and the environmental organizations committed to providing enlarged wildlife habitat. The real hope lies in redesigning the mowing machines. As this is being written, experiments are being conducted with an ultrasonic sound-emitting attachment that seems to scare hens away from in front of the swathers. Other flushing mechanisms have failed. If the device works and can be produced economically, it will save enormous numbers of birds. The swather will continue to smash many eggs, of course, but a hen pheasant nests again after a clutch is destroyed.

Hunters who have shot only pen-raised, "planted" pheasants on preserves often get the impression that ringnecks are big, lumbering, close-flushing, easy targets. If pheasants really are easy targets, American hunters must be abominable wingshooters, for misses are frequent. Ringnecks living in the wild are much warier birds. They prefer to escape by running, not flying, and when they do flush, they're usually much farther away than those flushed on preserves. Moreover, they fly faster. After all, they've been flying ever since they learned how, and their wings are stronger than the wings of birds living in pens. This is especially true of pheasants in areas that have supported a wild population for many years, because natural selection culls out the slow-witted and slow-winged. The elusive runners and fast fliers are left to perpetuate their genes.

If you've hunted only preserve pheasants and are planning to hunt wild birds, you ought to prepare yourself. When you flush your next few preserve birds, wait them out a bit. Let them put some distance between themselves and the gun before you shoot. You may end up paying for one or two released pheasants that you fail to bring home for dinner, but by so doing you'll be orienting yourself to shooting wild birds.

But a pheasant is big and relatively slow as it rises, so why all those misses? There are several reasons, all of which you can counter. A mature rooster usually weighs 2½ to 3 pounds (or almost three), and when you have a crossing shot, you see a bird 2½ to 3 feet long. But it isn't all target. At least half of that length consists of nothing but long tail plumes. A shooter's natural tendency is to lock his eyes on the center of the visible target as a reference point. That is, he swings ahead of the target's center to obtain his lead. But in the case of a cock pheasant, what looks like the center is just about the rear end of the body, where the long tail feathers begin. Force yourself to disregard most of what you'd normally consider the target, concentrating instead on the head, or at least the forward part of the bird. That's your only reference point. Practice swinging ahead of that and you'll limit out more consistently.

Hens are legal game in many regions, since the regulations are based on whether a percentage of the females can be killed without lowering the population's reproductive potential. Hens have shorter tails, and (in my experience) they're not quite as adept as the cocks when it comes to running rather than flushing. For me, they're somewhat easier targets, and I think I'm typical in this respect. However, if you're not used to shooting them, they may give you a bit of unexpected trouble at first. Don't let yourself forget that a typical hen pheasant weighs a pound less than a mature male. Her total length is only 20 inches or so. She presents a smaller target, so you still have to use her front end as your target reference and swing ahead.

Obviously, on going-away shots—which are very common with pheasants—your reference point is the whole target, the bulk of the bird's body. If the bird is rising, you swing through the target, and fire as you blot it out with the gun; but follow through or you may well shoot under it. An incoming shot works the same way. You swing through and blot it out as you would with a Station 8 skeet target. If the bird is going straight away or dipping slightly, you want to shoot under it; that is, you fire as the bird is about on top of your bead or muzzle, or perhaps with just a little air showing between bird and barrel. Remember that the target must literally fly into the shot pattern.

In my opinion, you shouldn't pay too much attention to advice about how much to lead birds—I mean how much in feet or inches. It depends on the individual shooter's reflexes, speed of swing, eyes, and judgment of distance. The right way is to practice on clay targets and preserve birds until you "groove" into the right lead for you. At that point, you probably won't be conscious of leading the targets. You'll just automatically pull the trigger at the right instant as you swing through.

Shooting too soon is another common reason for misses. Many hunters become overeager to fire as the bird rises, because that's when it's moving relatively slowly, and they can't wait to feel the weight of a cackler in the game pocket. This is a bad tactic, as I'll show with two examples of what typically happens.

In the first, the bird towers to 25 feet or so before it levels and starts away, accelerating. That's most common. Well, the towering is slow compared to subsequent flight speed, but it's often fast enough to outstrip the average hunter's gun-mounting and swing. Just as the hunter has swung through and let go, the bird levels and accelerates. The hunter has shot over it, of course.

In the second example, the bird decides—for reasons known only to itself—not to fool around gaining altitude. The hunter's last two pheasants have towered, and he swings his gun skyward, just as he's done twice. But this one skims away at about the level of a shock of corn. For an instant the hunter loses sight of the target entirely. He checks his swing, brings the muzzle down, and fires, by which time the pheasant is 50 yards away. And now the pheasant abruptly rises, putting several feet of air between its belly and the shot string.

I'll admit the possibility that I'm rationalizing because my reflexes are slowing down. If others will admit the same thing and retard their trigger pull by a temporal hair until the bird has completed its grandstanding tower play, I think they'll limit out more often.

There's another argument against banging away as a pheasant clears the ground cover. Every once in a while, a bird holds tight and flushes quite close to you instead of way out. Put a load of 6's into a bird when it does that, and I won't be offended if you don't invite me to dine on it.

And here's yet another argument for waiting a bird out: If it goes out low, and you're hunting with a dog, and the dog leaps or runs after the pheasant, shooting can endanger the dog.

I nearly forgot to mention one last reason for missing, and it's the reason I most often miss. Once a ringneck has leveled off, it can move along at 35 miles an hour or a bit better. That's fast enough, but not so fast that it's a really difficult target (unless it's way out there). Let's say that I've quickly limited out for two days in a row and I'm feeling pretty self-confident. I've now acquired a mental "set" that instructs me to swing with a 35-mile-an-hour target. My next bird happens to be flushed by another hunter, upwind of me. The pheasant rises into the wind (which is normal) and then wheels and flies with the wind (which is also normal). It's a healthy wind the pheasant is riding, and the bird accelerates to 50 miles an hour. I don't even realize it has gusted to 50. Nonetheless, I can take that bird, regardless of my stupid 35-mile-an-hour mental set, *if* I give it a real golf-swing follow-through. Otherwise, I'll waste a shell.

Normally, in walking up pheasants without a dog it pays to zigzag, but you can move straight ahead when working a narrow strip of cover like this planting because the birds have no room to make side-runs. That's the author at left and he's connected with a rooster that rose as it reached the edge of cover.

A big follow-through won't pull you too far ahead of the slow fliers. Some of the shot string will tag them. And it's needed for the sudden spurters.

Pheasants are primarily seed-eaters. Their favorite seeds, of course, include kernels. The cultivated crops that hold the greatest attraction for them are corn, wheat, oats, barley, and soybeans. Where these are lacking, the birds will seek whatever large or small grains are available. In most parts of the United States, their favorite wild foods are foxtail and ragweed. However, a hunter should be aware of other wild foods, as well. On the brushy northeastern farmlands where I've done much of my hunting, I've often flushed them from grape tangles, sumac clumps, raspberries, and blackberries. They like fruit, and they'll visit old orchards. Quite often, too, they're found in lespedeza or goldenrod.

Whether you hunt with or without a dog, a knowledge of good holding cover is just as important as a knowledge of preferred pheasant foods. Pheasants leave their roosting areas at dawn and—during the early part of the season, before hunting pressure has altered their habits and before the winds have become cold and strong—they often sun themselves for a little while in thinly grassed spots or openings amid brush. Then they feed in grain and stubble fields, high grass, brush, and quite often in thin adjacent woods. Some birds are likely to be out in the fields at almost any time, but they feed most actively in the morning and late afternoon.

With the approach of midday, after hunting the corn or grain fields, I generally take a short lunch break and then work thicker cover where pheasants rest out the warmest part of the day. This is a good time to try brush piles, wild-rose tangles, brambles, woodland edges, brushy hedgerows or shelterbelts, and marshy stands of rushes or cattails. There's nothing wrong with the classic calendar picture of the pheasant flushed from corn, yet I really believe I've shot more of them in cattails and over the fringes of prickly brier patches.

Midday is also a good time to look for birds sunning themselves on slopes (lee slopes if there's any wind) or dusting themselves and picking grit in ditches, dry stream beds, old gravel pits, and the edges of dirt or gravel roads.

In midafternoon or a little later, the birds begin to infiltrate the feeding areas in good numbers again, but at this time of day, they seem to prefer feeding in or near heavier cover than in the morning. It's a good time to hunt the edges of fields, near thickets, brush, or other edge-type cover. And it's a good time to try the marshy areas again. As the season progresses, these same areas may also be the best producers during the morning feeding periods, for the birds soon learn to avoid the hunters moving through open fields, and they're also beginning to seek shelter on cold, rainy, or windy days.

Late in the afternoon, pheasants return to the same kinds of dusting and grit-pecking spots visited at midday, and now they're sometimes present in greater numbers. After that, they seek high, thick ground cover for roosting—for example, tall clover, hay stubble, weeds, and brushy edges.

With the onset of fairly severe weather, pheasants spend much of their time in natural shelters—clumps of willow or Russian olive, windbreaks, weedy ditches, hollows, high brush along the edges of sloughs and marshes, sumac and wild-plum thickets, bulrushes, cattails, and so on.

In winter, large numbers of pheasants gather in small sheltered areas. The flocks thus formed are often segregated by sex. Although hens tend to concentrate in greater numbers than roosters, it's sometimes possible to flush two dozen cocks or more out of a brushy or willow-choked ditch. Where only roosters can be legally shot, this characteristic is a decided help to a hunter. By exploring the spots protected from wind, one can often find a cluster or flock of roosters and bag the limit right there.

On windy days, pheasants seem to hold more tightly than usual. Perhaps they're afraid to move about because they can't hear the approach of predators above the sound of the wind and rustling vegetation. Whatever the reason, a dog can work well by moving into a moderate wind, and he then has a better chance of keeping birds pinned until the hunter comes up. (Too much wind, however, will just interfere with scenting, and the dog is likely to bump some birds while others flush as wildly as ever.)

Wind has a greater advantage for a dogless hunter. Because the birds are reluctant to move about, this is the best of all times to employ the stop-and-go tactic that often works even without wind. As you hunt the hollows, thickets, lee sides of brush, and other wind-shelters I've enumerated, stop every 10 yards or so and wait at least half a minute before proceeding. Any nearby birds have undoubtedly heard or seen you approach. Stopping evidently gives them the impression they've been discovered and are being stalked. Instead of skulking away under cover, they often panic and flush.

Rain has almost the same effect as wind. It can ruin scenting conditions for a dog, but pheasants dislike moving when it's very wet, so the stop-and-go tactic is valuable for a dogless hunter in rain as well as wind. It also works well when a lot of dew clings to the vegetation.

If I'm hunting alone, I often walk against the wind. Like most birds, pheasants prefer to rise into the wind, as this gives them lift and control, but once up, they usually wheel and ride the wind. Thus, I've often had pheasants flush far ahead of me, increasing the distance as they rose but then turning to fly back almost overhead. The cover often influences the direction in which you hunt, so bear in mind that walking crosswind can also give you reasonably close shots—crossing shots.

When hunting with a partner, I like to have one man work a patch of cover by walking with the wind while the other man waits downwind, at the far end of the patch. At first the birds will move along the ground ahead of the walker, but they're likely to flush when they reach the far end (or sooner). If they're close to the walker, he'll get a shot. If they're closer to the stander, he'll get a shot as a bird sails along on the wind. And either man may get a chance at a crossing shot.

Late in the season, after weather and hunting pressure have influenced game behavior, I sometimes pass up all thin cover— even corn stubble. Instead, I concentrate on thick, hilly cover, such as woods or shrubs growing on slopes, especially lee slopes. I work my way from the bottom up, toward ridge tops or any balds. When the ground-runners reach the limit of the concealing cover, they usually clatter into the air.

There are areas in flat prairie country where the tactic just de-scribed can't be applied. In that case, I hunt the marshes and the edges of lakes, ponds, sloughs, and streams. I've worn hip boots to hunt pheasants as well as shore birds and waterfowl. Wet bottom-lands can provide as much protection from the weather and hunters as high woods or brush, so either kind of terrain may hold late-season pheasants.

Where lakes or rivers occur in pheasant habitat, late-season birds may also find shelter and concealment on islands. Try island-hopping with a boat or canoe.

I suppose the most persistent argument among pheasant hunters concerns the best breed of dog for the purpose. The fact is, any pointing or flushing breed will add to your pleasure and help you take birds if the dog happens to be a good one and is properly trained.

Among the very popular pointing breeds are the English setter, English pointer, Brittany spaniel, and German shorthair. If a pointing dog is used primarily to hunt tight-holding birds such as quail, or wild-flushing birds such as grouse, too much time spent in the ringneck fields can lead to bad habits. Pheasants are notorious for skulking and running, and this trait is hardly conducive to staunch quail-pointing or to instant freezing at the first whiff of grouse. But all the same, a good pointing dog can be trained to handle pheasants differently from other birds—and very effectively. The dog shouldn't range too far from you, because any pheasants he points won't await your arrival as quail do. But the dog should quarter fairly wide, and then come around on the far side of any birds to block their runs. When that's done, pheasants will flush close enough more often than not.

Among flushing dogs, springers are my favorites. A talented and well-trained springer can flush pheasants out of cover where their ground-running would frustrate most dogs (and most dog-owning hunters). To do this effectively, a springer has to work in harmony with his master but has to exert hard, fast, persistent pressure on the scampering bird. However, some hunters prefer a slower-going, more tightly controlled dog. A Lab is probably best for those hunters, though a springer can be trained to work pretty much the same way. Both breeds are outstanding pheasant-finders. Both are also adept at locating and bringing to hand downed pheasants, and so are the pointing breeds I've mentioned.

Anyone should be able to increase his success rate by following my earlier tips about where to hunt at various times of day and during various parts of the season, but those tips and several others are especially important for hunting without a dog. For example, open fields—even cornfields—can be fruitless unless you have a dog to force the birds into the air. So a dogless hunter pays particular

Several kinds of dogs perform beautifully on ringnecks, but none is better than the springer at flushing them within gunshot, chasing down cripples, and bringing birds to hand.

attention to islands and strips of dense cover. After sizing up an island or strip, he moves through it in a direction to prod the birds toward a point, an obstacle, a thinning, or a bare opening. Such places are where a bird most often gives up running and flies.

Some hunters dislike using their valued pointing dogs on such notorious ground-runners as pheasants, but the birds can be managed by a well-trained pointer like this one. The rooster in the picture had been trapped into flushing within range when the dog circled to its far side and pointed as the gunners approached.

Small thickets or narrow strips of cover are the most productive ones without a dog, because they provide less room in which pheasants can skulk or run.

When working a relatively wide patch of cover without a dog, it's essential to zigzag or you'll merely pass a great many birds without ever knowing they're present. In a narrow strip such as a fencerow, windbreak, or ditch, this isn't necessary. The birds there can't walk to the side without exposing themselves, so they'll either walk a short way and flush or walk to the strip's end and then flush.

If you find a very birdy-looking thicket, try to get into it quietly.

Then, when you think you're probably close to any hiding birds, plow through. When working toward the end or border of a thicket, apply the same tactic—bull ahead. Feeling cornered and charged, the birds are then likely to flush.

Wide patches are more easily worked with one or more partners. One man can move in, toward the center, and then search outward in widening spirals. He may get shots, but he's acting chiefly as a flushing-type bird dog. His partner or partners can wait on the fringes of the patch for birds to come out.

The Illinois gunner at right has a slightly rising straightaway shot that he should make if he swings through the bird's body. If he misses, his partner will have a crossing shot that will require a longer lead and isn't quite as easy as it looks. When seen in profile, half the target is composed of nothing but long tail feathers. The shooter will want to swing well ahead—not ahead of the target's apparent center, as many hunters do, but ahead of its forward end.

The morning feeding hours are an excellent time for the dogless pheasant drives that are traditional in some parts of the country—especially in big Midwestern farm fields. The size of the field determines the number of drivers and standers that can safely and profitably work together. Up to, say, a dozen men might serve as drivers, walking through the field in a wide line, with at least that many "blockers"—and sometimes up to twice as many—waiting at the far end. The driving line should be somewhat "cupped" so that birds won't walk out to the sides. Pheasants can slip between hunters only 20 yards apart. And even when spaced that closely, the drivers should zigzag or waver slightly, not moving too quickly or directly.

The standers at the far end should remain fairly quiet, because pheasants have excellent hearing and vision.

It's usually best to stage a drive toward hedgerows, fences, corners, brush-rimmed sloughs, or abrupt openings. With pheasants, any of these obstacles seems to dictate flight. Patches of tapering cover can be effectively driven in the same manner. The blockers wait at the small end while the drivers move from thick to thin.

I've said that I generally ignore areas of scanty cover late in the season, since most pheasants are then hiding or taking shelter in dense growth—and moreover, thin cover and a blanket of snow provide the birds with good visibility, thus lengthening the distance of flushes. But there's an exception to the rule. With an inch or so of fresh snow, you can frequently track and flush them. They leave big, thin-toed tracks, often more than three inches long. Those of roosters are bigger than hen tracks. Both single birds and groups tend to move over a field rather directly—for example, marching along between rows of corn stubble—until they reach a slight depression or some other little windbreak. Then they mill about to feed or snuggle down on the ground against the lee side of shocks, stalks, hummocks, or just clods of turned earth. Where the tracks form haphazard mazes, try to move with the wind at your back. Chances are, you'll pass several birds without seeing or flushing them, which is all right if you frequently stop and turn around. Do that and an occasional ringneck will cackle and clatter up out of its hiding place.

Normally, wingshooters feel contempt for anyone who "ground-sluices" a bird. However, there's one time when shooting a bird on the ground is an acceptable action and, in fact, the most sportsmanlike thing you can do. It's when, hunting without a dog, you bring down a bird only to discover that it can still walk or run. A dog can usually catch a crippled pheasant, but a man very often can't, and the only thing to do is shoot the bird again—aiming for the head, if possible, to avoid ruining meat.

If a bird is merely wing-tipped and comes down in thick cover, you may not even be able to find it, much less shoot it on the ground. For this reason, when I'm hunting without a dog, I pass up a lot of tough but possible shots that I'd make if a retriever accompanied me. Why chance marginal shots when you'll lose the birds, even if you do bring them down? Losing such cripples is both cruel and wasteful.

Many years ago, an old woodcock hunter verbally skinned me alive because I neglected to drop my hat where I marked a kill down. We both knew I'd killed the woodcock; he'd seen me hit it. But the dog failed to find it, and so did we. It came down on a mat of dead brown leaves and underbrush where it was as perfectly camouflaged in death as it had been in life. The old woodcock hunter was right, and the same rule applies when you drop a pheasant—or any bird—in dense ground cover. Go straight to where you think it landed and, if you don't immediately see it, drop or prop your cap or a handkerchief there. A safety-orange hunting hat or bright red bandanna is best. Anything else can be lost as quickly as the bird itself.

With the marker in place, search the ground and brush for the bird, working outward in circles. Occasionally, you may have to search the same ground over and over for a while, but you'll probably find your bird. Without the marker, you'll soon lose track of the point where the bird first seemed to have come down, and your chance of finding it is much slimmer.

One more suggestion about moving toward a downed pheasant: Do it directly and quickly. Very often, an injured bird is sufficiently stunned to remain there for a retrieve. If you dawdle, it may recover its mobility and sneak away or burrow into thick ground cover where it will die slowly or provide easy pickings for a predator.

Pigeons

The last two pigeons I killed were brought down with No. 8 field loads in a 20-gauge gun. I wouldn't recommend light charges of 8's as normal pigeon loads, but I mention this instance to illustrate that what's right for pigeon shooting depends on what kind of pigeon shooting is being done. Those two birds came to a waterhole where I was shooting doves. In my part of the country it's quite common to collect a mixed bag of mourning doves and "rock doves," or common pigeons. There are dove-shooting snobs who would almost as soon swing on a mockingbird as a pigeon, but I'm not one of them.

In selecting a gun and ammunition for pigeon shooting, you must consider the fact that the common pigeon is tougher than the dove, and the bandtailed pigeon is tougher than the common pigeon.

Rock doves, rock pigeons, blue rock pigeons, domestic pigeons, feral pigeons, common pigeons—whatever you want to call them—are most often shot in grainfields, barnyards, and the like, sometimes over decoys. This is short-range shooting, for which I like 7½ field loads, and it really makes no appreciable difference whether a 12- or 20-gauge gun is used. In many regions, however, these ubiquitous birds have spread into wilder, mountainous terrain where somewhat longer shots are common. For such shooting I'd switch to high-brass loads of 7½'s or 6's, depending on how long the shots might be.

Bandtailed pigeons are a different matter. (And come to think of it, some Western bandtail shooters are, or pretend to be, as disdainful of rock pigeons as the mourning-dove purists.) A lot of bandtail hunting is pass-shooting. The favorite bore is 12, the favorite ammunition high-brass loads of 6's. I must add, however, that early in the season—particularly at water holes or grainfields—high-brass 7½ loads in a 20 gauge are just as efficient. And I don't mind using a 20 gauge for pass-shooting at bandtails, either, but then I want No. 6 pellets in 3-inch Magnum shells.

Choke, too, depends on the kind of pigeon shooting you have in mind. Improved cylinder is right when you're using 7½'s on common pigeons coming to decoys, grain, or water—or flushed out of barnyards. With either 7½'s or 6's, modified is a better choice for longer shots where the birds are wilder. Modified is also right for bandtails around grain or water, and in some situations, it will suffice for pass-shooting. But for most pass-shooting at bandtails, a full choke is more effective if the gunner has skill enough to utilize a tight pattern. In a double-barreled gun for rock pigeons, I'd prefer improved and modified borings, a common upland choice, while for bandtails I'd favor the modified and full combination found in many a waterfowling gun.

Bandtail pigeons are migratory, though the flocks that breed in the lower part of the range shift only short distances in autumn. The species nests from lower British Columbia down the West Coast to Baja California and eastward into New Mexico and the lower Rockies. The birds winter from Puget Sound down into Mexico, with the largest concentrations usually occurring in California, Arizona, New Mexico, and Mexico. Migration begins very early in September, and occurs in sporadic waves. The birds don't habitually use the same flyways for wave after wave or year after year, as some migratory species do, but a hunter can get very good shooting if he knows their favored feeding, watering, and roosting spots (which I'll enumerate in later tips). Migration dwindles in October, after which only the wintering areas retain high populations of the birds.

The three coastal states plus Arizona, Colorado, New Mexico, and Utah have an open season, generally in part of September and early October. The daily bag limit has usually been eight in the coastal states, five in the inland states. Washington, Oregon, and California annually harvest about 500,000 bandtails. Far fewer are harvested in the inland states, and this probably has less to do with the bird populations than with the facts that bandtail shooting is a popular tradition in the coastal states and that a lot of the shooting there is over cultivated land. Forest shooting is tougher, and a surprising number of Southwestern sportsmen are unfamiliar with bandtails as game birds. The season in that part of the country was closed in the 1940's because of declining pigeon populations. It was re-opened (at first experimentally) in the late 1960's after the birds had again become very plentiful. Since then, studies by game biologists have indicated that hunting is having no adverse effect on the number of pigeons. However, in each of the four inland states you must hunt in designated areas and—to help the game departments census the hunters as well as the pigeons—you must obtain a special free permit. So be sure to check in at a game-department office before shooting bandtails in any of those states.

Common piegons—rock pigeons—aren't migratory. Their range is global, and they're abundant almost everywhere in the United States. Descended from domesticated strains of European and Asian pigeons, they're so plentiful in some cities that they've become a major pest species, defacing buildings, occasionally spreading disease (although the cooked meat is perfectly safe to eat), and enlarging the populations of rats and other vermin by serving as supplementary food for them. In several instances they've actually undermined structures such as bridges and overpasses by roosting and nesting in great numbers on the supports. (Where there are no man-made structures, they roost and nest among cliffs; hence the name rock pigeon or rock dove.) In rural areas where they've proliferated, they can be a major agricultural pest and can also be detrimental to wildlife by competing with doves and many other seed-eating creatures.

Unlike their migratory relatives, they receive no federal regulatory protection. And they certainly need none. Most states have no closed season or bag limit. Almost everywhere, a substantial thinning of these birds would be beneficial both to wildlife and to man.

Those who sneer at the idea of shooting common pigeons generally haven't tried it—or have only shot an occasional one. When a couple of unsuspecting pigeons are jumped from a field or wayside ditch, or when they fly low over you, they're rather easy to bring down. But when they become aware of danger (as they quickly do when actively hunted) they're fast, difficult targets. This species is, after all, used in live-pigeon shoots, which are among the most difficult shotgunning matches. Yet the rock pigeon isn't nearly as hard to hit as the bandtail, which tends to fly high and often moves along at 45 miles an hour or perhaps faster. Byron Dalrymple has aptly described bandtails coming in over trees to reach a salt spring as not just flying but hurtling.

Certainly no American needs to read a description of the all-too-common common pigeon, but many hunters are unfamiliar with the bandtailed pigeon. Though it flies faster, straighter, and more gracefully than the common variety, it's a slightly bigger, plumper, bird, about 13 to 16 inches long, with a wingspan of two feet. The color is predominantly gray or blue-gray. The flight feathers are darker, a gray-brown. The head and underparts have a smoky lilac or plum tone that fades on the lower belly. The tail, wider than a rock pigeon's, is bluish-gray from the rump back to a dark gray-brown or almost black subterminal band and is tipped with a broad, pale gray band. The feet are yellow. The bill is yellow but has a black tip. The bandtail is also known as the white-collared pigeon, an allusion to a narrow white streak that crosses the nape of the neck. Some hunters mistakenly believe that only the male has this collar. Both sexes have it at maturity. The female is slightly duller than the male, but a collarless bandtail is a juvenile.

In Washington, Oregon, and California, bandtails are often shot near orchards and around grainfields. In this respect, traditional West Coast bandtail shooting rather resembles traditional South-eastern mourning-dove shooting. The cultivated grains that bandtails seem to love most are wheat, oats, and barley, but they also have a tremendous appetite for waste corn in stubble fields and for grain sprouts of any type. Among orchard fruits, cherries may be their favorites, but they visit other kinds of orchards eagerly, too. They also come in great numbers to such truck crops as peas.

Hunters of the interior Southwestern states more often hunt bandtails in wild, wooded areas, but where the above-mentioned crops are grown in portions of the states open to bandtail hunting, some shooting also takes place on farmland. (And along the coast, some shooting is done in wild as well as cultivated areas.) Because the favorite wild foods of the bandtailed pigeon are acorns and piñon nuts, shooters frequently look for stands of oak and piñon. In some woods, however, these trees grow in such profusion that they fur-nish no clue to specific locations where the birds will concentrate. It pays to know about additional preferred foods and other attractions. Bandtails love hazels almost as much as acorns and piñon nuts, and they also feed heavily on wild cherries, elderberries, dogwood, wild grapes, blueberries, blackberries, mulberries, and manzanita berries. (But in some areas, unfortunately, wild berries are pretty well gone when the season opens.)

Roosting sites are another obvious attraction. Whereas rock pigeons in wild habitat roost in the cracks and hollows of cliffs, bandtails roost in tall trees. They especially like dead trees, or trees with several leafless limbs, because they don't want profuse foliage blocking their vision. From such trees they can watch for hawks and other winged predators. They use these high snags not only as roosts but as vantage points above feed or water. A foraging spot or water hole with at least one big dead tree nearby is a good bet. The first birds to arrive usually alight on high branches, and soon afterward they swoop to the ground or to lower trees and then to the ground.

Doves and pigeons habitually alight on dead trees. Bandtails are especially attracted to such perches, which provide good visibility in case a raptor approaches low over the trees. These bandtails are in the Sierra Madres.

Water is even more important than a high perch with a wide view. As with doves, muddy water is most attractive. Bandtails will pass by a clear stream in favor of a stagnant-looking slough or a muddy puddle.

The best of all water holes is a salt spring or salt seep, or water close to a salt lick. All pigeons and doves, by the way, are fond of salt. Where there are saline deposits, bandtails spend about as much time picking at salty mud as they spend drinking.

A water hole is worth trying at any time but is best rather early in the morning—often around eight or nine o'clock. Bandtails quit foraging earlier than doves or rock pigeons. They begin the day with a dawn (or barely postdawn) feeding, then seek grit, dust themselves, and go to water, after which most of them perch in trees, remaining more or less inactive until the afternoon cools.

They feed heavily again from around four in the afternoon until dusk draws them back to the roost trees. From midafternoon until the light begins to fade, you should have good shooting wherever the preferred bandtail foods abound.

As soon as migrating bandtails arrive in an area and begin to settle in, finding food and water, they can be walked up at grainfields, waterholes, and thickets of preferred wild foods. When flushed, they don't usually rise in a cloud like rock pigeons and whitewinged doves but go up a few at a time, as mourning doves do. This kind of shooting is best very early in the season, because bandtails soon learn to be wary.

While walking through promising habitat, watch the trees as well as the ground. Bandtails frequently alight and perch noiselessly on tree limbs. If you're not alert, you can pass by without noticing or flushing them.

Pigeons don't hold for dogs, and some retrievers seem to dislike fetching them. All the same, a willing retriever can be a big help in locating downed birds in oak canyons, chaparral, and other kinds of thick brush.

Bandtailed pigeons fly high but follow the contours of the land, so ridges are good for pass-shooting as well as for scanning the country for flocks. This hunter is glassing a valley for birds.

Most bandtail hunting consists of pass-shooting from concealment while migrating birds seek food, water, or rest. Because the birds fly high, the best spots are usually on ridges or hillsides near some of the aforementioned attractions that draw the pigeons down. The passing flocks rise and dip, following the contours of the slopes as they search for low feeding and watering spots with high roost trees nearby. A hunter can stay out of sight against a tree, in brush, or behind a boulder.

As bandtails pass over the treetops and rise to fly upslope, they lose a little speed. If possible, that's the best time to pick a target, swing past it, and fire. Try to shoot before the bird dips again.

Even if you can shoot at the optimum moment, you'd better give a bandtail much more lead than you'd give a rock pigeon. Think of it as a fast-flying duck, and get way ahead as you pull the trigger.

In farm country, rock pigeons can be found and shot in quantity by anyone with enough energy and originality to ask a farmer for permission to kill them on his land. If you're courteous and friendly, and observe sensible safety precautions, he'll probably not only thank you but invite you back to hunt other game.

Rock pigeons usually make morning and afternoon trips to grain-fields, feed lots, grain elevators, seed and feed warehouses, or similar cornucopias of easy pickings. The big farm flocks also roost close to feed—sometimes on rocky bluffs, but more often in barns, sheds, and abandoned buildings, on ledges of buildings in use, on roofs,

Rock pigeons are primarily seed-eaters. They're usually shot over grainfields, barnyards, and the like. Where there are no cultivated crops, they often peck about on the ground for wild seeds and fallen nuts. They move about on open ground and can easily be walked up if they haven't been hunted much. Elsewhere, decoys help.

and under bridges. You can get plenty of shooting by waiting near a feeding and/or roosting site.

I have two friends who live in central New York. One is an engineer. The other is a well-known wood sculptor who owns a farm. The farm-owner is perennially besieged by pigeons, and these two men get all the shooting they can handle by standing in a barn entrance, thumping the wall hard, and shooting at pigeons that dive out of the loft or swoop from under the roof. I understand this is a common practice in many parts of the country. It's harder than you might think. The thumping alarms the birds sufficiently to prod them into much swifter flight than is normally seen by idlers tossing stale bread crumbs and peanuts from town-square benches.

Pigeons coming to a grainfield or water hole sometimes fly almost as fast as those rousted roughly from their roosts. As I indicated earlier, I've shot them when I was hunting primarily for doves. Missing a couple of doves isn't anything to be ashamed of, but missing the doves and then pigeons, too, can be embarrassing. When this happens, I try to make sure of the next pigeon to arrive by taking advantage of an almost invariable flight characteristic. An incoming pigeon swoops or dives close to the ground and then swerves upward, slowing on the rise before landing gently. I miss a lot of overhead birds and divers, but I seldom miss a slow upward swerver.

Hunters are so accustomed to seeing tame city pigeons that it's hard to convince them they must stay out of sight. Pigeons are very quick to learn the meaning of gunfire. In some locales, they commonly roost in towns and make morning and afternoon flights to adjacent farm country. In front of a library in one such town, I watched them peck about under the feet of the human residents—completely tame—but when a truck backfired, they left with astonishing swiftness. At grainfields, hiding is just as essential as with doves. The birds pay little attention to any noise but gunfire. After a few shots, though, they'll flare away if they see gunners in the grain. And all pigeons, by the way, have very keen vision.

Their visual power is, in my opinion, at least matched by their lack of mental power. Or maybe it's just a lack of discrimination. Rock pigeons can be fooled—and strongly attracted—by anything that looks remotely like other pigeons or doves feeding or drinking. Commercial dove decoys bring them in. So do the crudest homemade pigeon decoys—wooden, cardboard, or plastic-foam cutouts. Place the decoys near the edge of a water hole or in a field as you would for doves, and put a few up off the ground—in bushes or trees. If they're homemade, paint them gray. It makes no difference that feral pigeons display wide color variations; gray shapes that roughly approximate their own contours will bring them in.

Byron Dalrymple has written that bandtails are as elegant on the table as on the wing. He's right. Hell, I wouldn't be surprised to discover that Pliny had penned the same kind of praise some time ago. There's a real, if subtle, difference between the taste of bandtail and common pigeon. I think it has to do with all those acorns and piñon nuts that bandtails cram into their crops. But I feel constrained to point out that all the famous European squab recipes were originally concocted in culinary tribute to the ordinary rock dove—the common pigeon. Technically, "squab" on a menu means a very young pigeon, not even fledged. Actually, it means whatever pigeon the chef has bought, shot, or filched, and no matter. A farm-fed common pigeon is a gastronomic delight. Try it gently steamed or in a pie. Try it braised or sauteed. Try it however you please or by whatever "squab" or dove recipe you find. But try it.

Ptarmigan

Ptarmigan are members of the grouse family. They're generally a trifle shorter and stockier than ruffed grouse, and you can kill them cleanly with field loads in a 12-, 16-, or 20-gauge shotgun. As to shot size, 7½ will do, and 6 will do a mite better. My reason for recommending shot one size larger than you might expect for such birds isn't that they're harder to kill than ruffed grouse or one of the other timber grouse; they're not. It's just that they're often encountered on rather open ground, where they may flush far out and usually run before they fly.

In some regions and on some hunting trips, there's another advantage to No. 6 shot. As with blue grouse or timber grouse, you may, in a single outing, have a chance to pot snowshoe hares as well as birds, and a load of 6's is right for hares.

Manitoba, one of the provinces where you can hunt ptarmigan, abides by a two-shell-capacity rule for shotguns. You can, of course, plug a repeater to accommodate only two shells, but I imagine a lot of hunters in Manitoba must favor over-under or side-by-side doubles. In a double-barreled gun, an excellent choke combination is improved cylinder and modified. And it's excellent not only for ptarmigan but for many other kinds of upland game. In a repeater, a modified choke is best.

Occasionally, ptarmigan are shot for camp meat by big-game hunters using rifles or handguns. For advice pertaining to these arms, see the section on blue grouse and spruce grouse, the other birds most often taken in this manner. In general, ptarmigan are regarded as game to be taken on the wing—with a shotgun. However, they're related to the various timber grouse and, in remote habitat where they rarely encounter humans, they can be as stupidly trusting as the northernmost spruce grouse. And even those that are accustomed to human intrusion often present stationary targets for rifled arms because high-country birds are commonly exposed in sparse vegetation or bare ground.

All American ptarmigan are Northern or high-country birds. Seven of Canada's provinces and both of her territories have long seasons on them. Quebec's—from late August through April at this writing—is the longest in Canada. Alaska's is even longer—from the beginning of August through April or early May. In my listings of game regulations, I can find only one other state that has a season right now. It's Colorado, where white-tailed ptarmigan can be shot for about a month, from early September to early October.

Charley Waterman is pictured shooting rock ptarmigan near Fairbanks, Alaska. This kind of hunting is often done in rain or fog, and the photo incorporates an extra tip: Follow Waterman's example and pack rain gear.

There are three American species, the whitetail, the willow ptarmigan, and the rock ptarmigan. The latter two are circumpolar in distribution but don't range as far south as the whitetail. Willow ptarmigan are found from northern Alaska down to central British Columbia, across all of Canada, and on the Arctic islands. Occasionally, they appear as far south as upper Minnesota. Rock ptarmigan occupy the same general regions but aren't found quite as far south, except along the Pacific Coast. Whitetailed ptarmigan range primarily from central Alaska through parts of the Yukon and down through British Columbia. A few of them are seen in Washington, and separate populations are scattered through the Rockies—in Alberta, Montana, Wyoming, Colorado, and New Mexico. In the lower parts of their ranges, all ptarmigan are found only at high elevations. Elsewhere, all three species may be found in overlapping habitat, but willow ptarmigan are chiefly flushed at the lower altitudes, rock ptarmigan somewhat higher, and whitetailed ptarmigan at the highest.

The willow ptarmigan and Scotland's famous red grouse, a most esteemed game bird, are two races of the same species. Where willow ptarmigan (or any ptarmigan) are subjected to a significant amount of hunting, they become shy, quick-flushing game birds just as other grouse do. And all three American ptarmigan species are extremely tasty. To prepare them for the table, follow any grouse recipe you happen to like.

American ptarmigan of all three types turn white in winter and have fully feathered legs. When undergoing their seasonal molt, or after they've acquired winter coloration, they often take hunters by surprise because they can be almost invisible when roosting right out in the open. With patches of snow on the ground, the white or spattered brown and white of their plumage can camouflage them completely until they flush.

Ptarmigan often cackle and beat their wings loudly as they rise. As fragments of a snow patch suddenly burst upward, transformed into birds, the sound can increase the startling effect. This commonly flusters gunners who don't know about it until it happens.

Here's a covey of willow ptarmigan in the process of molting from summer plumage to winter-white. At a distance, the birds look like flecks of snow on the ground.

They don't explode into the air very fast or rise very high. Their alarmed take-off is roughly comparable to that of pigeons. But if a hunter isn't constantly alert, they can be up and away before he mounts his gun. Their flight speed, once up, has been estimated at close to 40 miles an hour.

Like other high-country birds, they often drive downward in flight—down slopes or over ledges. For advice on shotgunning techniques to handle this maneuver, see the section on blue and spruce grouse and the section on chukars.

Among all three ptarmigan species, the cock is slightly larger than the hen. A male willow ptarmigan averages 14 to 17 inches long and weighs about 20 to 24 ounces. A male rock ptarmigan averages 13 to 16 inches long, 15 to 19 ounces. The whitetailed ptarmigan is smallest—12 to 14 inches long and seldom weighing over 12 ounces. With a bird in hand, sexual identification is easy except in the case of the whitetailed ptarmigan.

A male willow ptarmigan has a scarlet comb over the eye. His primary and secondary wing feathers remain white all year. His tail remains dark brown except for white tipping and white central feathers. In winter, however, very long upper tail coverts conceal this dark brown splotch. The spring molt turns him primarily chestnut or rusty brown, with dark barring on the back and sides.

The female is combless. In summer she's heavily barred with ocher and dark brown.

By autumn, both hens and cocks have begun to acquire white feathering, as if flecked with snow, but a cock's back is still barred with brown, whereas a hen is more grayish above, white below.

A male rock ptarmigan also has a scarlet comb, but his summer plumage is browner—less reddish—than the willow ptarmigan's and has fine brownish-black markings instead of true bars.

The female is combless, paler, and more coarsely barred. Both sexes retain blackish tails throughout the year.

In early autumn, a hen is brownish with sprinklings of white, while a cock is predominantly ash-gray. Soon both sexes turn white. The cock now has a black streak from the bill through the eye.

Only among whitetailed ptarmigan do both sexes have a comb over the eye. It's red but much smaller than on other ptarmigan and is often completely hidden by winter plumage. Both sexes also have white tails and wings throughout the year. In summer, a cock is mostly brownish, but with black, buff, and white mottlings, vermiculations, and bars. Just above the tail, his rump turns tawny or pale yellowish-brown, and his underparts are white.

The female is paler—more yellowish and spotty.

In autumn, both sexes turn pale cinnamon on their upper parts, with little spots and fine lines of dark brown or black. Their breast feathers are now speckled white, and by winter both sexes are entirely white—pure snow-white—except for their black bills, eyes, and claws.

Both willow and rock ptarmigan migrate short distances to winter in lower, somewhat more sheltered areas. Whitetailed ptarmigan may sometimes drift down a little, but evidently they're equipped to

This is a rock ptarmigan in winter plumage. A black streak running from the bill through the eye marks the bird as a cock, though his scarlet comb is hidden under feathers. The species retains a blackish tail throughout the year, but its white body can render it almost invisible on snow. On bare ground, exposed vegetation, or rock, however, it can usually be seen before it runs or flies.

winter in high, stormy habitat. They're the ptarmigan that can be hunted in Colorado, where the season is in early fall. In more northerly regions, some game departments set seasons that run right into winter, but even then the whitetails tend to stay in the high, least hospitable parts of the mountains, often inaccessible to hunters. Therefore the willow and rock ptarmigan are more often sought.

In winter, a whitetailed ptarmigan is completely snow-white except for its black bill, eyes, and claws. The small red comb over the eye is hidden by a tuft of winter feathers somewhat resembling a bushy eyebrow.

Regardless of species, ptarmigan gather into loose flocks as fall progresses. In some regions, these groups are sexually segregated, evidently because hens need more sheltered—that is, more forested—winter habitat than cocks. Whether you find one sex or both, wherever you flush a few ptarmigan, you're soon likely to find more. But don't count on finding them there again the next day or the next season. They wander.

Only a few years ago, it was rare to find an American or Canadian ptarmigan hunter accompanied by a dog, though dogs have long been used for the purpose in some other countries. Now there seems to be a trend on this continent toward the use of dogs. Whether a dog has much value in this sport depends on where you're hunting and which species of ptarmigan is prevalent. On the high, open slopes where whitetailed ptarmigan abound, you can usually find the birds you bring down without the help of a retriever. Furthermore, either a pointer or a flushing dog can become virtually unnerved by the sight of birds moving all about in the open. All ptarmigan hold fairly well when found in thick ground cover, but when caught in the open, they'll run before they fly. And whitetails generally flush farther out and fly farther than the others. Even a well-trained pointer will often take to chasing them fruitlessly. Of course, a flushing dog is meant to chase them, but will not very often force them up within gunshot when they're in the open.

Rock ptarmigan are encountered in fair holding cover somewhat more commonly, so a pointer can be of some help with them—but is certainly not a necessity. And bear in mind that even at the middle elevations, mountain hunting is extremely rough on a dog. (It's also rough on any normally pampered shotgun, something worth considering when you decide what gun to carry.)

At the somewhat lower elevations where willow ptarmigan are often found, the cover is brushier and a dog can sometimes be quite helpful, not only for locating and flushing the birds but for finding and retrieving any you bring down.

I've been told that in some parts of Canada springer spaniels and other flushing dogs are gaining popularity for hunting willow ptarmigan because they work well when the birds cluster in such cover as willow runs and birch thickets.

I've indicated that willow ptarmigan are bagged at relatively low elevations, but I don't mean they can be normally taken in the bottomlands. The places to search are moist tundra with fairly tall shrub growth, muskegs and burns, amid streamside willows, along the timberline, and in the tundralike openings that are common in high northern forests. All three species eat a variety of alpine and subalpine plants, but you should be sure to check willow runs because this species relies chiefly on willow buds and twigs.

You may find willow and rock ptarmigan in almost the same habitat. If you've been hunting the kinds of places I've just described but have had little action with willow ptarmigan, try climbing just a bit higher to find rock ptarmigan. They're generally flushed from shorter, sparser vegetation on rocky slopes around timberline or a little above. Watch for dwarf birch, as the birch buds and catkins are preferred foods of the rock ptarmigan. Also watch for any berry bushes, as all ptarmigan like berries.

Still farther above timberline, on steep, rocky slopes and ridges, you're likely to find whitetailed ptarmigan. If you're a sufficiently fanatic shotgunner to enjoy wingshooting on that difficult terrain (and your lungs and legs are in good enough condition) look for alpine willow, heath, and mosses—preferred foods of the whitetailed species.

The higher you go, the tougher the shooting will be, for the winds up there are strong enough to make ptarmigan fly erratically.

If you're hunting when the season has just opened (early September in most regions), you can count on putting up singles and small coveys. In all likelihood, any such covey is composed of a hen and her year's brood. But as fall progresses, the birds flock together in choice, relatively sheltered feeding spots. Late in the season you may flush groups of 20 birds from heath, willow, or tundra shrubs and lichens.

Bobwhite Quail

For bobwhite quail, no gun is better than a light 20 gauge, and no load is better in it than an ounce of No. 8's, an ordinary field load. These suggestions are based partly on the species itself—a small, fragile bird that most often flushes close to the gun—and partly on the mix of open fields, brush, and woods typifying bobwhite habitat in most regions.

In some locales, however, bobwhites are more commonly hunted in very dense tangles of foliage where more pellets and a trifle more power may be needed. Quite a few heavy-cover hunters prefer a light, short 12 gauge with No. 9 field loads or even high brass. A heavy charge (or big bore) also has advantages in bobwhite habitat for the opposite extreme—low, sparse cover where a good many shots are surprisingly long. If atypically long shots prevail, something can be said for switching to $1\frac{1}{4}$ ounces of $7\frac{1}{2}$'s.

In some regions the 16 gauge remains very popular, even though modern 20-gauge ammunition has made it seem superfluous to the majority of shooters. It's still a nice compromise between the 12 and 20 for the varieties of cover just described.

In sufficiently skilled hands, a 28 gauge is adequate (and certainly enjoyable to carry and shoot), but the readily available loads in this bore size are rather light, so it might be advisable to handload if you use a 28 for quail. I don't consider the .410 adequate. Admittedly, it can be used effectively by an expert shooter who takes all his birds at close range, but it requires fast-gun handling as well as inordinate resistance to temptation if longer shots are to be ruled out.

With a 20 gauge and No. 8 loads, improved cylinder is all the choke you want. In any gauge from 12 to 28, a true cylinder or skeet boring is probably better for those who use 9's unless the local cover dictates occasional long shots. Those who use double-barreled guns usually abide by tradition, which calls for the improved-and-modified combination. It's a good choice, and can be made better by using ordinary No. 8 loads in the more open barrel and—for follow-ups or long shots—high brass 7½'s in the tighter barrel.

Well over 30 states have a fall or fall-and-winter season on bobwhites, and in some of the remaining states, you can hunt these birds on preserves. Generally speaking, the hunting is best and the most fun (and easiest on both dogs and hunters) in December in the South, November in the North and Midwest.

At one time, the Southeast was unrivaled as a bobwhite-hunting region. In recent years, however, that section has suffered from diminished habitat caused by land-clearing, reforestation, and the modern "clean-farming" practices that give land a manicured but sterile look. Marvelous bobwhite hunting can still be found in the Carolinas, Georgia, and northern Florida. (And not long ago, I had excellent shooting in Maryland, barely below the Mason-Dixon line.) But Southerners take their quail hunting very seriously, and in much of the South, it's difficult for anyone but a local resident to gain access to the most productive bits of land, where traditional hotspots hold coveys year after year.

Possibly the best bobwhite hunting these days can be had in Oklahoma, Missouri, Iowa, eastern Nebraska, Kansas, and Texas. Some of these states have more to offer nonresidents as well as residents. Other states where the hunting is usually fine include Iowa, Indiana, Delaware, and New Jersey.

At one time or another, most of us who shoot quail have come close to killing a meadowlark by mistake. Something that looks like a bobwhite bursts out of tall grass, and the gun comes up reflexively. On close inspection, the two species look nothing alike, but in the air, the plump brown bodies and the facial markings can be deceptive. The signal that warns you not to fire is a wide white border on each side of the meadowlark's tail.

Whether or not they're hunted, bobwhites have a short lifespan in the wild, and few survive long enough to breed more than once.

Juveniles therefore comprise about 70 to 80 percent of the quail harvested by hunters. If you're curious, a juvenile can be identified by its pointed outer primaries and a lot of buffy tipping on the upper coverts of the first seven primaries.

Telling males from females is easier. A male has a white chin and a white stripe across the forehead and rearward from the bill to the base of the neck. These white facial areas are separated by an irregular dark streak—blackish-brown or black—that runs through or under the eye and down to the neck where it blends into the mottled brown bib of the upper breast. The body and wings are mostly mottled brown, but the lower breast and belly are pale or

Separated from his covey, this male bobwhite quail is calling to his comrades—a typical behavior pattern of scattered singles as they regroup. He's in a fringe of Missouri woods bordering low brush and farmland.

white and marked with brown and black specks and scallops. There's much less contrast in a hen's coloring. Her face and chin are yellowish or buff instead of white, and the stripe separating the upper and lower portions is brownish. Her belly, too, shows less contrast; her underparts are specked somewhat like the male's, but the background color is pale buff.

There are more than 20 subspecies within the bobwhite's primary range—the eastern half of the United States and southward into Central America. Some are paler, some darker, but most varieties are much alike, and the description I've just given will suffice for all but the rare and protected masked bobwhite of the Sonoran region. An average bobwhite weighs just six or seven ounces, is 8 to 11 inches long, and has rounded wings with a span of 14 or 15 inches.

These are very plump little birds, and when they explode from cover just in front of the gun, their shapes look to me like winged popcorn—or bumblebees somehow spurted from a hidden catapult. A shape like that shouldn't be able to whiz about at 30 miles an hour or occasionally fling itself out of brush at 50. But it does. This brings me to the most common causes for missing bobwhites; and I'll speak from experience, having missed them for each reason I'll enumerate.

A novice gets flustered at first, even if he's pretty good on other targets, because a bobwhite covey actually seems to explode into the air. Until he gets over being flustered, he may sometimes fail to get the gun up and fire it before the birds disappear into screening cover. The cure for this is simply to put up a few coveys, while also gaining self-confidence and attaining a calm reaction by concentrating on scattered singles.

Having quelled the quail palpitations, a shooter must then concentrate on timing. He's still likely to get his gun up too slowly and then try to shoot too fast. This is the opposite of what should be done—which is to mount the gun fast and then shoot with just a little deliberation. Many experienced hunters like to carry the gun at high port when walking in over a point. (I know one very impressive gunner who carries it that way most of the time, but my arms can't take the strain.) At any rate, the idea is to get the gun up fast so that you can take a little more time getting on a bird and shooting. To me, shooting bobwhite quail seems very much like shooting skeet, and skeet is therefore an excellent kind of practice.

I agree with Charley Waterman, who says that the average covey rise is only about five yards away, and many gunners try to get off a couple of shots before the birds have doubled that distance. When such a shot does connect, it may leave nothing worth eating. If the birds rise at five yards, there's plenty of time to get off a couple of shots by the time they're 20 yards away, and that, as Charley points out, is about the ideal range for bringing these birds down with an open-bored gun. In the fields or low brush (though not in heavy cover), you'll be able to hit them at 30 yards or even a trifle more.

Because bobwhites covey so tightly, and because the need to fire seems urgent, flock-shooting is all too common among those hunters more accustomed to other kinds of game. I don't really think that shooting into departing flocks produces many lost cripples. From what I've seen, I think it produces mostly clean misses. The flock-shooter unconsciously compromises between two or more flying targets as he points his gun, and he ends up shooting the air between them. Often you can pick two targets, one for a first shot and one for a second, but the really important rule is to pick a specific target for that first shot—and don't change your mind at the crucial instant. Practice picking your target as you raise the gun, not afterward, and you'll bag more birds.

Bobwhites seem to go up all at once, in a chaotic burst, but of course they're spaced out on the ground, and they can't synchronize their take-off. Some are closer than others, some flush faster than others. In picking a target, there's a temptation to take one of the nearest or latest-flushing birds. Resist it. Pick one farther out—it will probably be just far enough when you fire—and then you'll have time to swing on one that got up closer or later.

In addition to picking your target and not overhurrying your shot, there's another reason to wait out a covey rise by just a trifle. As bobwhites hurtle from the ground, they often seem to spray in every direction. But when they're hardly higher than your head (and sometimes not that high), all of them usually fly more or less in one direction—toward the nearest high, concealing cover. Thus, you'll know pretty well in advance where you'll be pointing your gun. You'll be set for it, and that's a big advantage. Another is that once the birds are headed in that direction, you'll have mostly straight-away shots or shots at slight angles, which are easier than crossing targets.

Bobwhites don't require quite the kind of snap-shots you often make at ruffed grouse in thick cover, but neither do they give you time for the kind of sustained lead that's common in pass-shooting. For crossing birds, you're better off just pulling the trigger as you swing through the target and follow through. On straight-aways or very slight angles, try just blotting the bird out with your muzzle.

Like many upland birds, bobwhites need small amounts of water frequently. They can make use of copious dew if there isn't much water in a given area, but in arid country, they're invariably bagged along river valleys, near creeks or other natural water sources, or on irrigated lands.

Although bobwhites eat insects, seeds comprise over 90 percent of their autumn diet, so there's little point in hunting where seeds are lacking. The most important food plants are weedy herbs and legumes. Ragweed and lespedeza will always attract and hold coveys. Other preferred wild foods include partridgepeas (very common in Southern uplands), trailing wild beans, smartweed, and beggarweed. Among cultivated plants, the favorites are soybeans, sorghum, corn, cowpeas, wheat, and sunflowers.

Unfortunately, food alone won't keep bobwhites flourishing. The birds need a mixture of food and water, resting and dusting spots, and roosting and escape cover. Patchwork farms (almost a thing of the past) and overgrown farmland edges are excellent for quail. Promising bobwhite habitat is characterized by cover and foods that are used all year. Grasses are needed for nesting cover and, to some degree, for spring and summer feeding and roosting. Although wild foods alone once supported bobwhites, the birds now rely heavily in many areas on croplands for summer and fall feeding. Fields also attract them for midday dusting and resting. But nearby, patches of brush or woods are needed throughout the year for feeding, roosting, and escape cover. In traditional bobwhite country, find these features, and you should find birds.

In a few locales, bobwhites make very short seasonal migrations— just minor habitat shifts. In the Smokies, for instance, they move down from "grass balds" to the lowlands for fall and winter, and in northwestern Oklahoma, they move as far as 10 miles from summer uplands abounding in grass and sage to the dunes and canyons. Regions like these have special attractions for bobwhites. Excellent examples of fall holding spots, besides those just cited, are Oklahoma's plum-thicket bottoms, Florida's palmetto scrub, Georgia's piney edges, and the scrub-oak hills found in New Jersey and several other states. New Jersey's Pine Barrens are also quail-rich. In most regions, too, there are "edge" plants that offer the birds extra foraging sites—multiflora hedges and honeysuckle, for example.

Where bobwhites made short seasonal shifts to cool-weather habitat, as just described, they tend to return to the same patches autumn after autumn after autumn. Where there's no need for them to move, they stay in the same little home territories for generation after generation, except during a spring breeding dispersal. The usual home range for a typical covey of 10 to 15 birds is only a couple of dozen acres—and within that little tract, the covey will have favorite feeding and roosting spots. I knew a Southern gentleman who successfully hunted the same little brush patch—between a small farm and a cemetery—for more than 40 years straight. Traditional covey locations of this sort are common in many areas. Some of them may be well known where you hunt, or you may learn about them from local residents or discover them by exploring the types of land I've described.

When you find a covey location, you can return to it several times in a season, but you and your friends should take care not to shoot all the quail you flush there. Leave at least half a dozen birds for "seed stock," and you'll find a renewed covey in the same place the following year, unless the habitat has been ruined or the reproductive cycle has been devastated by flood or drought.

An English setter remains staunch as his boss closes in to kick out a single. Bobwhites lie very tightly under a point, and all the more so after a covey is flushed and scattered.

Within the bobwhite havens described, you can learn to recognize even more specific locations where a flush is likely. Quail don't like to move farther than they have to. In dry weather, they stray from roosting cover just far enough to feed well. In wet weather, they don't like to move out at all, and you may find more of them in the roosting places than in the fields. A roosting zone is apt to be in brush, tangled grass, or a woodland edge, often on a sunny, well-drained south-facing slope where the ground remains warm in late afternoon. Roosting cover doesn't have to be high; wheat stubble is sometimes used, and so are patches of weedy herbs.

Like most sportsmen, I feel that a good pointing dog is an essential ingredient of truly fine quail hunting. Bobwhites act as if they were invented for pointing dogs, and a large portion of the hunter's enjoyment lies in seeing how well a dog locates and handles them, or how nicely one dog honors another's point. Yet there have been times when I had to hunt quail without a dog or not at all, and any hunting is better than no hunting. Without a dog, knowing the likely spots for a covey rise is all the more important. The higher or thicker the cover, the tighter the birds will hold for a dogless hunter, so the roosting areas are best for an unaccompanied stroll.

Ordinarily, bobwhites move into the feeding fields early in the morning, but on rainy, cold, or windy days, they often delay until late morning. At midday, if the weather's hot, try cool-looking roosting and dusting spots. In cool weather, look for birds taking the midday sun on lee slopes or in thin brush. Late in the day, try the brush and grasses again, and try any thickets adjacent to fields.

"Spoor" is not a hunting aid exclusive to big game. There's a common kind of bobwhite sign that indicates an area where the birds like to roost or loaf. It's an accumulation of bird droppings, forming a circle. Quail commonly roost in a disk formation (often called a "roosting ring" or "pie"), especially when the weather begins to cool. The birds settle in a circle, facing out, bodies touching, in order to retain body heat and watch for predators. Where you find the droppings left by such a ring, birds are probably in the immediate vicinity or at the nearest feeding area.

Because bobwhites hold tightly under a dog's point, quail hunting permits the use of wide-ranging dogs that cover a great amount of ground. Where much of the cover consists of low brush and grasses, mixed with rather open feeding areas and small patches of woods, following the dogs can be tiring exercise. In some parts of the South, hunters still honor the tradition of following on horseback or by horse- or mule-drawn wagon. There and in parts of the lower Midwest, four-wheel-drive vehicles are used, as well.

Bobwhites do occasionally run before they flush if they're close to heavy cover, but this is most likely when they're approached by a dogless hunter or by an ineptly working dog. Bobwhites hold better than most upland birds for a pointer, and the more they're hunted, the tighter they hold. A well-bred, well-trained quail dog quarters the fields thoroughly but without wasting time, combs all the edges, checks all the corners, and explores all the brush patches. Such a dog generally keeps his head up, relying more on airborne scent than on ground scent. You'll get the best performance from the

A setter fetches a bobwhite. These birds can be walked up without a dog, but good pointing adds immeasurably to the enjoyment of quail hunting. A dogless hunter will get fewer shots and have trouble finding downed birds.

animal on chilly, sunny days—not so dry that scenting is difficult nor so wet that birds keep to their roosts. You want the quail active, so that they throw off lingering scent.

As to what breed of pointing dog is best, I'm neutral. English pointers, English setters, Brits, German shorthairs—they can all be outstanding. So can Weimaraners where a very wide-ranging stylist isn't needed. In my opinion, the choice should depend in part on what breed you happen to like, and in part on the section of the country where you do most of your hunting. I'm aware that setters and Brits can excel even in the heat and hair-snagging foliage of Southern palmetto, and that English pointers and German shorthairs can seem impervious to Northern weather, but a breed's physical characteristics still determine whether it's the most suitable dog for a given combination of climate and cover.

When possible, move through a promising area so that your dog or dogs can work into the wind. A dog, like any animal with a predatory instinct, prefers to work that way in order to catch scent, and this lessens the likelihood that a dog will "bump" a covey or a single—that is, overrun the game and flush it prematurely

And when possible, it's also wise to cast the dogs in a general direction that lets them work gradually toward woods, brush, or other obvious cover. You then have an idea of the direction most birds will take after a covey rise, and they'll be all the more inclined to take that direction if they find themselves between a dog and a thicket.

Among inexperienced quail hunters (and pheasant hunters, come to think of it) a common mistake is to move in over the dog too slowly, too cautiously, as if afraid of being surprised and off-balance at the flush. Moving in that way sometimes scares birds into flushing before the gun is close enough, and it sometimes encourages them to run or skulk away on the ground. Move in past the dog quickly, decisively, from a direction that keeps the game's perception of approaching danger concentrated at a single point—the opposite direction from escape cover. This, too, will influence them to fly fairly straight away once they've gone up. They seem to freeze momentarily when approached decisively, and then, when the gun is close, up they go *en masse*.

This tactic of encouraging the birds to fly in one general direction not only gives you more straight-away shots within good range but also herds the quail toward one small landing area. The covey will scatter somewhat, but will alight within a sufficiently limited radius so the dog can easily find singles.

Having noted where some or most of the escaped singles have pitched in, wait a while before hunting them. After alighting, they lie very still for a while, instinctively knowing that movement releases scent. If undisturbed, they'll begin to whistle to one another within less than half an hour, for the danger seems to be gone, and they want to gather into a covey again. Give them a little more time to do so, and your dog will give you another covey rise.

That last bit of advice is by no means a strict rule. If you've marked down a single or two quite precisely, a good idea is to put your

Coveys seem to explode into the air, but they seldom rise much higher than the highest quail in this photo, and most of them will head in one general direction—toward the nearest tall cover.

dog—and yourself—there immediately. Since the bird won't move off through the grass for a while, you know exactly where to find and flush it.

I've never hunted with anyone who used a hawk call, but I've heard about it. The idea is that the shrill scream of a hawk makes bobwhites lie still in their ground cover—reluctant to walk or fly, for fear of being seen by the raptor. Perhaps this helps on big open fields where bobwhites might otherwise flush far ahead or retreat on the ground, but in typical habitat, I can't see that it's necessary.

There are also commercial whistles that imitate the bobwhite's musical voice. And if you whistle well and clearly, you can mimic bobwhites without any mechanical aid. I haven't found that whistling draws any scattered birds, but sometimes it evokes an answer from one or two of them, and you can then move toward the sound. The covey-gathering call of scattered birds is rather like the double-

Each of these Florida hunters has an almost straight-away shot as a bobwhite makes for the pines. This is the easiest shot in quail hunting, and it can be had frequently if a hunter notes the direction of escape cover as he approaches a single or a covey.

or triple-noted courtship whistle for which the bobwhite is named, but mellower and not so piercing. The closest I can come to describing it is *ho-hee, ho-ho-hee*. Each note is higher than the last, and the calls are usually repeated with increasing volume. I've hunted over quail dogs that didn't have to be ordered toward the sound because they recognized and closed in on it eagerly.

Scaled Quail
& Mearns Quail

This book has much to say about the handling of chukars and other species that prefer to run before they fly. I can state from experience that none of them surpasses the sprinting ability of the scaled quail—also known as blue quail, scaly, cottontop, Mexican quail, and (most aptly) blue racer.

Concerning upland game, I find myself in agreement with almost everything Charley Waterman has ever written, and he's done more hunting of desert birds—including scalies—than I have. But in this instance I take exception to his preference for a 20-gauge gun and his willingness to use 1⅛ ounces of No. 8 shot as an alternative to 7½. Our differences probably stem from two facts.

The first is that he's a better wingshooter than I am. He's good enough to center a 20-gauge short-Magnum pattern on a bird that's galloped almost out of range before flying. For me (and most others, I think) 1½ ounces is a wiser choice, and that means going to 12-gauge high-brass loads or 20-gauge 3-inch Magnums. And with the extra bit of shot in those loads to keep the pattern dense, I'd rather use 7½'s than 8's.

The second reason for Charley's willingness to go light is that he's thinking—rightly—of a mixed bag. Scaled quail can be hunted in some areas where Gambel's quail or Mearns quail can also be found. Though my scaly loads are fine for the Gambel's, they're heavy for Mearns quail. Field loads of 8's are sufficient for that species, which is very much like the bobwhite. But you can always carry light loads in one pocket and switch when necessary because (as you'll see) you'll generally know by the kind of habitat when Mearns quail are the game.

As to choke, Charley carries a double, bored improved cylinder and full, for all the desert birds. That's a hard choke combination to find, and the open barrel—though excellent for other desert species—strikes me as being a hair *too* open for the blues. I prefer a modified choke in a repeater, modified and full in a double.

In Texas some years ago, I combined an outing for blue quail with a rabbit hunt. I intended to pot a cottontail or two, but a jackrabbit popped from behind a clump of Spanish bayonet as I was heading toward a covey of scalies. The rabbit's action stampeded the birds through thorn bushes and over bare ground, galloping like roadrunners. I shot the jack, and the noise sent a few of the birds into the air, and I managed to kill one. An odd double—one jack rabbit, one blue quail. And that's another kind of mixed bag that influences my choice of gun and load.

Given the opportunity, I'd much rather collect the blue quail than jacks (or even cottontails), so I'd base my selection primarily on the birds and leave my loads of 6's at home. But the prospect of rabbits would be one more reason to use hefty loads of 7½'s—high-brass shells in 12 gauge, or 3-inch Magnums in 20. The 7½'s aren't ideal for rabbits or hares, but in these loads and with a modified choke, they'll do the job at close or medium range.

Scaled (or blue) quail are probably a bit more adaptable than most Southwestern birds. They thrive in semiarid areas and also in some deserts so dry and seemingly barren that other desert quail, such as the Gambel's, are scarce or absent.

Their native range extends from eastern Colorado and southwestern Kansas down through the Oklahoma Panhandle, the western half of Texas, almost all of New Mexico, lower Arizona, and southward into a large portion of Mexico. In addition, they've been introduced into Washington and eastern Nevada. Overgrazing by livestock has stripped away nesting and escape cover in some areas, but in recent years, the game departments have improved arid-country game management with brush shelters and watering devices, and thanks to these measures the quail have extended their range somewhat.

I can find no up-to-date statistics on the heaviest concentrations, but blue-quail hunting has always been excellent in Texas and New Mexico. I favor western Texas, not on any objective grounds, but because I've had such wonderful sport there. The quail season usually runs from the beginning of November through part of February, and I can tell you the birds are plentiful.

The scaled quail is a trifle larger than the bobwhite—10 to 12 inches long—but it's also a trifle leaner, so the weight is about the same, 6 or 7 ounces. The bird's head is pale grayish-brown with a bushy crest (the cottontop that gives the species one of its nicknames). On a male, this crest is whitish; on a female, it's buff and less pronounced. A male's cheeks and throat are pearly, a female's streaked with brown shafts. Regardless of sex, the upper parts are gray or brownish gray, with narrow white streaks on the wings, and there's a pronounced bluish tone on the upper back, neck, and upper breast. The feathers on the pale underparts, breast, and neck are edged with black, and it's this black bordering that gives the species a scaled appearance. On two of the three geographic races, the lower breast and belly are pale or whitish, contrasting very sharply with the black scallops. Males of the third subspecies, found in lower Texas and Mexico, have light chestnut bellies.

Juvenile scalies have scant crests, barring on the central tail feathers, and buff-tipped upper primary coverts.

In my last hunting book, I ignored the existence of Mearns quail because of their extremely limited distribution. Subsequently, my knuckles were figuratively rapped by Southwestern correspondents who reminded me that these birds are sometimes found in the same general vicinity as scaled and Gambel's quail and can be legally hunted in two states. I can't say I'm enormously impressed, but I suppose the Mearns deserves incidental inclusion here. Its small range is centered in Mexico, and it isn't abundant by comparison with other species, but it's shot in small numbers in southwestern New Mexico—where it's taken along with other quail—and it's harvested in much larger numbers in southeastern Arizona. The high Mearns population in Arizona is attested by the daily bag limit of 15 (but don't expect to take your limit unless you're an exceptional gunner) and a long season, generally running from about the beginning of September through half of Februry. The Arizona season on scaled and Gambel's quail generally runs from about the beginning of October through half of February, so you can see the opportunities for a combination hunt. As a matter of fact,

The text stresses that scaled quail are usually seen on the ground. This picture is not a contradiction but a reminder that the birds also occasionally perch on blowdowns, low fences, bushes, and the like. Even on such perches, they're hard to force-flush; they're less likely to fly than to hop down and run.

the combination can be enlarged still further because both mourning doves and deer can be taken during part of the quail season.

The Mearns is also known as the Montezuma quail, though scientifically, it's only one of three Montezuma subspecies, the remaining two being more southerly. It's also called the Massena quail, black quail, crazy quail, painted quail, and harlequin quail. Slightly smaller than a scaly, it's about the size of a Southern bobwhite, and the hen looks very much like a bobwhite hen. The names just listed describe the cock, which has a very handsome black or blue-black and white facial pattern, including a bright white collar or bib. Numerous round white spots mark his sides, flanks, and belly.

My remarks about combination hunts were not meant to imply that the several quails and other upland game can all be bagged during a short morning stroll through a single little pocket of food-rich habitat. The Mearns has rather specialized requirements, which partly explain its limited distribution. It lives in lovely terrain—terrain that some hunters prefer to that of the scaly: on oak- and pine-strewn grasslands at elevations from about 3,500 feet to a bit over 9,000. Where agriculture has occupied adjacent lands, it will eat corn and other field crops. It has a fondness for sunflowers, but its basic feeding habits are quite unlike those of other quail species. It subsists chiefly by scratching and digging for tubers and bulbs, and it also feeds heavily on mast. A favorite food—and one a hunter should learn to recognize—is the tuber of the chufa, also known descriptively as nutgrass, nutrush, ground almond, sweet-rush, and flatsedge. This quail also has a liking for woodsorrel bulbs.

For years, it was believed that the scarcity of harlequin quail on overgrazed livestock range was caused by the removal of needed foods. To the contrary, the grazing animals dislike some of the favored quail plants (a couple of which are toxic to cattle). On overgrazed tracts, the grasses are removed, and the harlequin foods multiply. But the birds themselves can't multiply because their nesting, roosting, and escape cover is gone. In Mearns country, grass is the only such cover. Coveys of these quail are often flushed from bare ground, but a combination of grass and favorite foods will reveal the most promising hunting spots in the highland strongholds of the Mearns.

Where sharp rocks, hot sand, thorns, and other ground hazards can hurt a dog's feet, some hunters equip their dogs with protective boots, available from dog-specialty suppliers. The grassy highlands of the Mearns quail are not, however, as hard on a dog as the desert realm of scalies, and any pointing dog that works well on bobwhites will serve admirably for harlequins. I suppose a flushing dog would also be fine, but such tight-lying coveys are ideal for a pointer.

The instinctive escape mechanism of the harlequin is to freeze where it sits, flying only at the last possible instant when it realizes it hasn't escaped detection. It therefore holds for a point even more tightly than the bobwhite. But this doesn't make it easy game, for it has two characteristics in its favor.

First, its feathering is such perfect camouflage that you can almost step on a Mearns without seeing it, even on bare ground, and in grass, it's invisible until it takes off. Sometimes a hunter searches the ground until he's certain his dog is only pointing scent left by birds that have departed. On occasion, the hunter may even flail the grass with a flushing whip and put up nothing. Then, when he's given up and is certainly not prepared to handle a covey rise, the birds explode from cover.

The flush itself is the other characteristic that favors the birds. They catapult into the air even more explosively than bobwhites and then fly equally fast. The gun-handling techniques recommended for bobwhites are right for harlequins, but be prepared to have these feathered jesters make a fool of you.

Blue quail are seed-eaters. Like other quails, they have a taste for cultivated grains and seeds. They particularly like sorghum, and they'll also glean wheat, oats, and sunflower seeds, but throughout much of their range, wild foods are more readily available, and thus are more important. Blues like snakeweed, tansymustard, mesquite, wild privet, catclaw, deervetch, lupine, and an assortment of weedy forbs. In combination with such foods, they like thorny ground cover. They move through thickets of spiny plants with perfect ease, and perhaps this cover facilitates an escape from such enemies as

The author holds a brace of scaled quail he gleaned from a covey by sneaking close—using a low rise for concealment—and then charging at the birds to make them take wing.

coyotes as well as raptors. Excellent hunting spots are canyon mouths, river valleys, and weedy washes where the preferred foods commonly grow, and where you'll often have to navigate around clumps of cactus, yucca, Spanish bayonet, and the like. Blues also feed, pick grit, and rest under juniper and mesquite.

Though scalies can do without water for long periods, waterholes naturally attract them. Be sure to look for them at desert seeps, springs, creeks, and cattle tanks. They also need grit and dusting places, but the sandy desert surrounds them, and I've never found them gathering at any special dusting and gritting places. Often they just dust and peck about on the nearest open ground. You can see them from a considerable distance on the open desert flats. In some of the relatively more lush, semiarid regions, I suppose they come to back roads and bare ditches for grit and dust. Where I've hunted them, they don't have to.

Some hunters use dogs. During the hunting season, the danger of snakes is usually minor, but a dog will get scratched up, tired, and thirsty in the desert. A short-haired breed is probably best because of the warm climate. Be sure to have water on hand for the dog as well as for yourself. A dog's feet are more likely to become sore in a desert environment than elsewhere. As previously mentioned, some hunters buy dog boots. I recall that years ago, tender pads were sometimes soothed with an application of fuller's earth, but lanolin and various commercial salves are probably the most practical and effective stuff for softening and soothing dry, cracked pads.

Somewhere handy—in your car, for instance—you should have a first-aid kit with the usual contents for yourself and some for your dog. A weak boric-acid solution or ophthalmic ointment should be included in case your dog injures an eye. Antiseptic dusting powder is the best thing for minor scratches on his body or legs. Before applying it, any puncture or bigger laceration should be cleaned, and hydrogen peroxide is excellent for the purpose. You should also have a small pair of pliers, a strong, clamp-type tweezers or forceps, or a hemostat for removing thorns and such. (Actually, it's wise to have these first-aid items on hand, regardless of where you hunt, but it's especially important in a harsh desert environment.) Serious injuries are unlikely, but if you think there's the slightest danger of a wound becoming infected, a visit to the veterinarian is in order. He may administer or prescribe antibiotics or sulfa drugs.

Among the first-aid items of importance for your own safety is a snakebite kit. I know I said snakes are only a minor danger during hunting season, but warm weather can delay or interrupt their hibernation. One hot December day in lower Texas, a rattler emerged from a rocky crevice almost under my feet. Fortunately, the snake was more careless than I was on that occasion, and I collected its rattles as a souvenir. A snakebite kit is a comforting thing to have in a hunting vehicle, especially in the warm South and Southwest. Snakeproof boots are also a good idea in areas known to have a high population of rattlers—or copperheads or cottonmouths. Though cottonmouths are fundamentally aquatic, they're included here because they often come onto land to seek rodents and birds.

The author snipped this set of rattles from a snake killed during a blue-quail hunt in December, when rattlers in most parts of the country are hibernating. It's a reminder that caution and a snakebite kit are assets for an upland hunter in the warm habitat of scalies, Mearns quail, Gambel's quail, and several other kinds of game.

Those who use dogs to hunt blue quail generally prefer close-working pointers. The first flush is almost certainly going to be way ahead, but quite often you can then mark the birds down—after which you and the dog may be able to pin them for a reasonably close flush by executing a pincer movement. You want a dog that acts very "birdy" when he gets a whiff of game. These quail just don't hold, and from what I've seen, I think the dog's chief use, before a shot is made, is simply to alert you by letting you know he's making game. He may be of more use after the shot, assuming you've connected. If a bird falls in a thorny, tangled thicket, the dog can be a big help in finding and retrieving it.

A hunting friend wants me to qualify that last tip with another, and he's probably right. There are regions where the tall grass of the highlands borders semiarid flats or desert. In these edge grasses or the brushy foothills, you may occasionally find harlequins lower than their accustomed elevations, and you'll often find Gambel's quail and blues. Gambel's quail are runners, too, by the way, but in tall grass, even the blues sometimes hold fairly still for an approach. In this special kind of habitat, a pointing dog will perform on scalies much better than I've indicated. So will a bobwhite gun.

Blue-quail coveys tend to be big. It isn't unusual to see well over two-dozen birds pecking about. When flushed, they stay together more closely than some other covey birds, but a few may come down sooner than the rest of the group or may simply become separated. Mark down any isolated singles. They won't hold really well, but they're worth following up because they'll be less decisive than the main group about picking an escape direction and running.

Personally, I'd rather hunt without a dog when the game is scaled quail. In the open country where I've hunted blues, a dog isn't needed to find them, and it would be a very unusual dog that could help maneuver or hold them for a close flush. If there are coveys in the vicinity, you can find them merely by walking and watching. They move about in the open.

The problem is how to get near enough after you see them. If you merely walk toward them, they merely walk away. Where the ground cover is fairly thick, however, you can sometimes sneak almost within range and then rush them. If you're a fast enough runner, this usually puts a few in the air, and your first shot will put more in the air.

Many Southwesterners consider it perfectly sporting to shoot a first scaly on the ground after rushing a covey. This isn't "ground-sluicing" as the term of contempt is normally interpreted. The "blue racers" can cover ground almost as fast as rabbits, so there's nothing disgraceful about hitting one on the run. Besides, that's often the only way to force-flush the rest of them. Try hitting a first bird as it skitters through desert brush and a second on the rise, and you won't scoff at anyone who uses that method.

Perhaps you just can't run fast enough to force a close flush. The birds finally rise, but at 60 yards and going 30 or 35 miles an hour as they clear the brush. Thus they're out of range before you can get off a shot. They may plop right down again after a low flight of 20 yards, but they may also fly much higher than other quail species. I've seen them 50 yards in the air. And they may disappear beyond the next rise before landing. If they come down after a very short flight, you can simply try again. If they go over the rise, they'll probably be farther away than you think, because they'll come down walking. You can shrug and go looking for another covey, or you can make a wide circle, trying to come at the same covey again from the far side. Sometimes this gets you close enough for a final dash that spurs scalies into the air within gunshot.

In Texas I met a 260-pound ex-Marine who hunted blues by scouting the flats from his four-wheel-drive vehicle. He drove along slowly until he sighted a covey. (Like many game birds, scalies haven't learned that vehicles carry enemies, so you can often get close.) When he spotted a near enough flock, he jumped out and loaded his gun as he ran at the birds. I was astonished at how fast and often that ox-built man could run. Since then, I've learned that many hunters use his method. It works, but it requires plenty of speed, agility, stamina, and a love of shooting blues that surpasses weariness, heaving lungs, a parched mouth, and aching, cactus-scratched legs.

Which reminds me to remind you that Southwesterners who wear thin jeans instead of reinforced brush pants either have weak heads, a taste for pain, or legs composed entirely of callouses.

There's another vehicular hunting method that's much more to my liking. What my friends and I do when we see a covey of blues is to drive around the nearest rise and employ a sneak play. We stop the car and walk back. Quite often, by staying out of sight, we can get close enough to force-flush the quail effectively, surprising them into flying instead of running.

Gambel's Quail

The preceding section included a few tips that pertained to Gambel's as well as scaled quail, but I feel that Gambel's quail merit a brief section of their own. My reasons, however, don't include a choice of gun and load exclusively for the Gambel's. The best choice is the same as for the scaly—a 12 gauge with high-brass loads or a 20 gauge chambered for 3-inch shells. In either gauge, the best pellet size is 7½.

My choke preference, too, is the same as for scalies—modified in a repeater, modified and full in a double-barreled gun. All of the plumed quails (Gambel's quail, valley quail, and mountain quail) would rather run than fly, and they can skitter over the ground at better than 15 miles an hour, so a lot of the shots are long when they finally take wing.

However, their sprinting is not on a par with that of scaled quail, and when they're found in relatively thick cover, or if you hunt early in the season before they've become very leery of hunters, you'll get some fairly close flushes. I must therefore amend my advice to take the early part of the season into account. At that time, an improved-cylinder choke may be adequate. This is another of the many birds for which I like an adjustable choke device on a repeater. Early in the season I would also feel confident using a typical improved-and-modified upland double.

Although several species are sometimes described as desert quail, that designation is the most commonly used alternative name for Gambel's quail. They're found in arid and semiarid country, and in very hilly deserts as well as on the flats. With regard to food (which I'll cover in more detail a bit later) they're very adaptable, but they're surprisingly dependent on water and are usually found near it, and they must have dense thickets for roosting. In desert country, these two requirements obviously help a hunter to focus his attention on the most likely bird-holding zones.

Gambel's quail are found in lower California, Nevada, Arizona, New Mexico, western Texas, and Mexico, plus isolated areas in Idaho, Utah, and Colorado. In addition, Hawaii has introduced the species on the island of Lanai (but has had greater success in establishing valley quail). In all the desert-quail states, the season is generally open in late fall or from later fall into winter, and in some it coincides with the season on one or more of the other quails. Gambel's-quail hunting used to be superb, and it's still very good in the Southwest, but it has diminished somewhat as a result of stock grazing and other land use plus a series of droughts that reduced nesting success.

A typical Gambel's quail is hard to tell from a valley quail. It weighs perhaps six ounces and is 10 or 11 inches long. A jaunty, black, forward-curling plume rises from its head, and it has a gray or grayish-brown back, tail, wings, and upper breast. The sides are chestnut with narrow white streaks, and the underparts are buff. A white stripe over the cock's eye separates his chestnut crown from a black forehead. His throat is also black, set off by a white border that reaches up to the eye, and his belly has a black patch with a pale, irregular border. The hen has a smaller head-plume, a sooty crown, a pale face, and a buff belly streaked with brown.

Juveniles have short plumes, pointed outer primaries, and buff-tipped primary coverts. (The same features mark the juveniles of all three varieties of plumed quail.)

All the quails are covey birds. A covey of Gambel's quail may be composed of a dozen birds or a great many more because family groups sometimes band together. If you come upon a single or a pair, you can be pretty certain that lots more are in the immediate vicinity. Coveys composed of several family groups may number as many as 50 birds.

The favorite foods of all the plumed species are deervetch and filaree. In areas where Gambel's quail are common, you should put

These birds are Gambel's quail, photographed in Texas. A cock is in the foreground, a hen to the rear. In the arid and semiarid domains of this species, look for coveys near water, dense roosting thickets, and the food plants listed in the text.

up birds where these plants are found in combination with dense roosting thickets. Additional attractions for the desert quail are bur clover, lupine, mimosa, various other legumes, and grass and weed seeds. Beans, too, are preferred foods; mesquite beans are the favorites, but catclaw and paloverde also draw these quail. In some regions, so do the seeds of ocotillo, desert hackberry, and prickly pear. Such preferences probably depend on what's most abundant near roosting cover and water. Where farms are in operation, Gambel's quail will raid hay fields for alfalfa seeds and leaves.

The most active feeding periods are in the morning and late afternoon, while midday is devoted chiefly to resting, dusting, picking up grit for the gizzard, and going to any nearby water. These activity periods hold true for all the plumed species but tend to be a bit more precise for Gambel's quail than for the others. In late fall, the desert may remain so hot that the birds feed heavily only before about 9:30 in the morning and after 3:30 in the afternoon. Of course, those are the most pleasant times for a desert hunter as well as for his quarry.

If the noon heat isn't oppressive, there's an advantage to hunting when the quail are bedded. While resting at midday, desert quail are inclined to hold tight and then fly—rather than running as they do when they're caught moving about to feed.

Later in the afternoon, you can often waylay Gambel's quail, waiting on stand for them as if you were hunting deer instead of birds. These quail establish habitual runs from favorite midday resting areas to foraging areas, and their tracks are easy to find in the desert. Look for a profusion of wide, triple-pronged footprints, perhaps two inches long. (The tracks closely resemble those of scaled quail, and where you find one species, you may find the other.) You can just wait there quietly, and you may welcome a bit of loafing after the exertion of desert walking. If the ground cover is sparse, as it so often is on arid land, there's a good chance you'll see a covey coming toward you. When they get close, rush them. They may run, but this often makes them flush.

In contrast to scaled quail, Gambel's quail aren't confirmed ground roosters. They like thickets, not only for overhead concealment, but because they prefer to roost off the ground in the evening if trees or tall shrubs are near their afternoon feeding areas. They mark a roosting site with droppings and feathers, and the adjacent land is apt to show plenty of tracks. The vicinity of a roost offers good hunting in the late afternoon. You can comb it with or without a dog, or you can await the coveys that come strolling or flying in, using the same technique described in the last tip to rush birds off the ground.

Coveys of desert quail can sometimes be located by their sounds. When feeding, they softly cluck and make a noise like growling. When resting, they frequently chatter. And when scattered, the singles emit a crowing sound—"ka-kaa-ka-ka"—a rallying call that helps the covey to regather.

Many Southwestern hunters dispense with the services of a dog, but a well-trained pointer can perform rather well on desert quail. The author's friend Charley Waterman is shown here with Kelly, a Brit that helped Waterman bag Gambel's quail and just about every other American upland game bird.

I haven't made a confirming survey, but I doubt that the majority of desert-quail hunters use dogs. Yet it seems to me that pointing dogs perform fairly well on these birds—better, at any rate, than on scaled quail. When a dog first points a covey, the birds almost invariably run and flush too far out, but Gambel's quail hold a bit tighter after being moved once or twice. The dog will therefore do better on subsequent rises, as well as on any scattered singles.

Coveys may be almost anywhere in a well-populated locale, but a good pointer, even one with little desert experience, will instinctively head for choice holding spots such as mesquite clumps and other thickets, brushy washes and ravines, and runs of willows and such along watercourses. Move in quickly, and be ready to shoot if your dog seems to be making game.

Valley Quail &
Mountain Quail

Valley quail are very closely related and similar to Gambel's quail. Mountain quail, the other plumed species, are larger and often fly higher, but a gun and load that will take one variety of plumed quail will take them all. For a mixed bag, my vote would go to a 12 gauge with high-brass loads of 7½'s, or a 20 gauge chambered for 3-inch shells and paired with Magnum loads of 7½'s.

However, if valley quail are your sole quarry and you're hunting them in brushy lowlands—river bottoms and such—you'll have to make your shots quickly, at fairly short range, and you don't need that much punch. All you want then is about an ounce of 7½'s, an ordinary field load. The gun for such hunting should be light and short—the kind of fast-handling gun you'd pick for bobwhite quail.

By the same token, if you're hunting the valleys for valley quail, you want an open boring for fast, close shots. Skeet or improved cylinder is all the choke you need. But if you're hunting mountain quail in the same area, you'll probably find them higher and on more open slopes where a tighter bore is needed. Some mountain-quail hunters use a full choke. Modified is more to my liking, and it's certainly an excellent compromise for locales that hold both species. Of course, if you have an adjustable choke device at the muzzle, you can match it to whatever cover you're hunting.

Valley quail are equally well known as California quail. Originally, they ranged from lower Oregon down through western Nevada and California to the end of the long Baja peninsula. They've been successfully introduced in the upper part of Oregon, Washington, lower British Columbia, Idaho, Utah, and Hawaii. British Columbia now has a quail season in October and November. California's quail season generally lasts from September or October through part or all

Here you see male (left) and female valley quail, also known as California quail. Though very closely related to the Gambel's quail, this species is found in less arid habitat.

of January. The other states usually open the season from some time in October through part of December or January. Despite habitat reduction, quail hunting remains very good in Washington, Oregon, and California. In recent years, it has been excellent along the Columbia and Snake rivers in Washington, and on the tributaries of those rivers.

The range of the mountain quail is more limited—from Washington, Oregon, and southwestern Idaho down through California into the northern part of the Baja peninsula. The species has been introduced in Colorado, but I believe its status there remains uncertain; probably the species hasn't had time to become well established. It has also been introduced in British Columbia—and with some success. I have no current state-by-state harvest figures for comparison, but mountain-quail hunting is usually best in California. Throughout the range, the seasons on mountain and valley quail run concurrently—which is fortunate as well as sensible, because both species are frequently found in the same locale and, when birds are in the air, a hunter can easily mistake one variety for the other.

An average valley quail is just a trifle heavier than an average Gambel's quail. The male valley quail, unlike the Gambel's, has pale speckling on the back of his neck, but this isn't very noticeable until you get a close view. The only striking difference in the appearance of the two species is that the valley quail's lower breast and belly are pale buff with dark scallops that impart a scaled effect like the scaled quail's. The male's belly is more reddish than the female's, and his plume is black, whereas her smaller plume is brownish. Like the Gambel's hen, she has a drab face and throat without the male's black and white pattern.

The mountain quail is distinctly larger—the largest of our quail species. A typical specimen weighs over half a pound and is about 10 to 12 inches long. It has a unique head plume, composed of two straight, narrow black feathers that stand straight up when a bird is on the ground or perched, but sweep rearward in flight. Male and female are almost exactly alike. The throat is dark chestnut, bordered at the rear with a white streak that reaches up to the eye; there's also a tiny white patch at the top front, between eye and bill. The head and breast are gray or blue-gray, blending into brown or olive-gray on the back, wings, and tail. The belly and flanks are chestnut with wide white, black-edged bars running up the sides. Sexual identification is sometimes dubious, but as a rule, the brown of a hen's back reaches to the top of her head or almost to the top, whereas the male's nape is gray down to the back.

Coveys of mountain quail are usually small—often about five birds, seldom more than 10 or 12. Valley quail are much more gregarious. Most of their groups number from a couple of dozen to about five dozen. I've never seen a bigger covey, but I'm told that it isn't unusual to find hundreds of valley quail in a loose gathering. The word "covey" isn't normally associated with such huge flocks of birds, and I've heard hunters speak instead of bands or droves. These flocks, a joining of many family groups, begin to disperse in late winter, but the congregations are apt to remain intact throughout the hunting season.

A big group naturally spreads out. Sometimes you'll see a loose covey of birds scuttling about with their plumes bobbing as they move through low brush and across bare spots. Sometimes, too, you can see the smaller coveys of mountain quail foraging on the ground, because their primary habitat is more open than that of the valley birds. Both species are sometimes found in chukar habitat. They have the same tendency to run rather than fly, and often they can be hunted and force-flushed in pretty much the same manner as chukars.

When flushed, valley quail sometimes fly very low, even flitting right through sparse brush instead of rising over it. (Gambel's quail, their nearest relatives, play this evasive trick just as often.) At first you may have to overcome an inclination to shoot too high when you're presented with these skimming targets. And if you're hunting with a dog, you'd better be sure of the animal's location before you shoot at a low bird.

Mountain quail rise high and don't seem to fly quite as fast, but either species can fly at 30 miles an hour or so, and both are difficult targets. Sometimes, after climbing high into the air and leveling off, mountain quail dip, and again, you may find yourself shooting over your targets.

A problem with valley quail is that a bird sometimes flushes from the ground only to end its flight on a nearby tree branch before you get off a shot. Your natural reaction is to go after it and flush it again, but this time it may fly an even shorter distance to another tree.

Unfortunately, the only solution I know is to be ready for a fast shot while the bird is in the air.

Another problem is that valley quail are disposed to do the unexpected. Plumed quail are wild flushers most of the time, especially before a covey is scattered. As with all covey birds, the scattered singles hold tighter, but most of them are still quick to flush. Yet a

Although mountain quail spend most of the year on higher, more open terrain than valley quail, the mountain birds drift to lower elevations in the fall. Either or both species might be flushed on a slope like this.

valley quail that finds itself isolated sometimes freezes in place, as still as a woodcock, so you have to be alert for an occasional surprise flush almost underfoot where you weren't aware of a bird's presence.

Mountain quail make short seasonal migrations, drifting down to lower ground in late summer or early fall and sometimes traveling more than 20 miles from the highlands where they nested. By October, a hunter can find them at elevations of 5,000 feet or less, and he may begin to flush them in the same habitat where valley quail are hunted. Either species, for instance, might take off from a canyon rim, particularly if the slope is near grainfields.

The kinds of habitat favored most strongly by valley quail are: brushy stretches along streams, foothills, and valleys quilted with oak thickets, high sage, or other brush; the tangled cover of riverbottom land; high grasses; and weedy thickets. These birds don't roost on the ground if they can help it. They perch in thickets of low trees or tall shrubs. Paradoxically, they feed on rather open ground, not in chaparral or dense woods. And they prefer to feed near water. So it's mixed habitat you want to search. Pay attention to edges and openings in thick cover.

Mountain quail rest and roost beneath shrub oaks and other hardwoods as well as in brush. Like chukars, and sometimes quite near them, these quail are also found foraging on rocky slopes. Although many shots will be over open ground, thick canyon cover strongly attracts them in autumn. As you hunt the mountainsides, it pays to inspect patches of bunchgrass and clumps of rosebushes. Also look amid the oaks, in brushy draws, and along the willows that line many creeks. Mountain quail have the habit of running uphill, as chukars do, before flushing. (Valley quail may employ the same escape tactic, but not to the same degree; in thick, tall bottomland cover, they're more likely to get airborne in an effort to flee.)

If the weather has been dry, you're likely to find valley quail assembled at waterholes and springs at almost any time of day.

Normally—that is, when the fall weather hasn't been too dry—both valley and mountain quail feed most heavily in morning and late afternoon. From late morning through the midday hours, they rest, dust, pick grit, and take on water. But valley quail also seek grit before the morning feeding. At that time and at midday, and once again near dusk, back roads are good places to prospect for them.

This cock is a mountain quail, the largest of our quail species. When the bird is on the ground, its head plume stands erect, as in this photo. The plume sweeps back when in flight. This species flies higher than valley quail but sometimes dips, and either species can fool a hunter into shooting too high.

I've mentioned elsewhere that all three of the plumed-quail species are fond of deervetch and filaree. Other plants with seeds that particularly attract valley quail are mullein, clover, lupine, sage, and wild oats. A large assortment of weedy grasses will draw them, and if there are farmlands nearby, they're also attracted strongly to barley, wheat, alfalfa, and oats.

Mountain quail generally feed a little higher in the same locales. In the overlapping zone between the primary habitats of the two species, both types of quail may be found eating pretty much the same foods. However, the foods that especially attract mountain-quail coveys are sumac, grape, serviceberry, snowberry, hackberry, gooseberry, mullein, manzanita, elder, sage, mountain rye, timothy, acorns, clover, wild oats, timothy grass, bromegrass, and the seeds of locusts and coniferous trees. Among cultivated crops, wheat and barley probably have the greatest importance.

Both mountain and valley quail can be walked up without a dog, or surprised into the air while dusting and gritting along roads or on other bare spots—if you get close without attracting their notice. Your chances are probably best when they're loafing in the roosting areas or when they're feeding in dense cover. I've heard that some hunters have success by driving back roads in a vehicle, then jumping out and loading on the run as they force-flush any coveys they find. It's a technique I've mentioned in connection with scaled quail. I've never hunted mountain or valley quail that way myself, but I see no reason why it shouldn't work well if that's your style.

Personally, I'd much rather work with a dog. I like a pointer for this sort of hunting. A pointer that has learned to handle ground-runners such as pheasants or chukars can often pin mountain or valley quail for a close flush on brushy flats or head them off as they scamper up a slope. The dog can be controlled and maneuvered as for chukars.

I must add, however, that in thick lowland cover where valley quail are often found, and even in higher mountain-quail habitat such as brushy draws, flushing dogs may have an edge over pointers. The flushing breeds have become increasingly popular for hunting the westernmost varieties of plumed quail in recent years.

As with desert quail, the calls of mountain and valley quail can help you locate birds if you recognize their distinctive voices. During hunting season, mountain quail sometimes emit the same loud, fairly shrill whistles that signal their springtime courtship rituals, but the most frequent call is a lower whistle. I once described the sound as *"whew . . . whew."* However, I'm not an accomplished bird impressionist, and the *Audubon Society Field Guide to North American Birds* describes it as "a single, haunting, low owllike, slightly ascending whistled: *woook?*" Well, you'll hear it for yourself now and then where you find coveys of mountain quail, and you will soon learn to recognize it.

Also listen for a series of soft whistles—the conversational notes of feeding mountain quail. And if you scatter a covey, listen for the rallying calls of the singles, which sound more or less like *cow-cow*.

When valley quail are feeding, they cluck softly instead of whistling, and you'll soon begin to recognize this sound, too, if you hunt them often. Their chatter is much like that of desert quail. When scattered, their rallying call has a crowing quality. A Western hunter of my acquaintance says it sounds like *"chi-ca-go."* His hearing or his imagination is sharper than mine, but I guess that's close enough. A few hunters mimic the birds, but it certainly isn't necessary. Just use the sounds as directional signals for yourself and your dog.

Woodcock

Woodcock spend the winter in the Deep South, below the latitudes where ruffed grouse are found, and the Western and Far Northern grouse woods are devoid of woodcock at any time of year. But the two species can be found together over a wide range in pretty much the same habitat, and in those regions, the seasons on them overlap. A hunter who goes out for woodcock may bring home grouse, and vice versa. It would be unfortunate, indeed, if grouse and woodcock were so dissimilar in terms of shooting requirements that a different gun and load had to be used for each. But in my part of the country (and in many other parts) you seldom hear a hunter speak of his woodcock gun or his grouse gun. The term is "grouse and woodcock gun."

For bagging woodcock, no combination is better than a light, short 20-gauge gun with No. 8 field loads. Some upland hunters prefer No. 9 pellets, but most of us consider 8's ideal, and they're certainly a better choice if the local coverts hold grouse. Many of those who use double guns in the grouse woods load the second barrel with 7½'s in high-brass loads. For hunting woodcock at the same time, I'd compromise slightly—using field loads of 7½'s or 8's in the second barrel. You don't really need anything heavier than 8's in a 20 gauge for either species.

A few hunters still favor the 28 gauge, and they most often use 7½'s. If I were hunting in the South—that is, strictly for woodcock—I might switch to that bore size. Frankly, I'm not a good enough wingshooter to have confidence in anything smaller than a 20 where grouse are present, but there are hunters who consistently bag both species with a 28.

I've killed woodcock with a skeet gun, and also with an old upland repeater that had a true cylinder boring. Either of those borings will do nicely, but improved cylinder is best for the vast majority of shots.

In a double, the classic improved and modified choke combination would be my choice. Again, the same gun (a 20-gauge improved-cylinder repeater or a 20-gauge improved and modified double) would be excellent for grouse—and for quail and several other kinds of upland game.

It has been brought to my attention that many hunters in certain parts of the nation have never seen a woodcock, much less bagged one. The best advice I can give them is to move, or if business prevents so obvious a remedy, at least undertake a woodcock-hunting trip. The principal breeding range of these noble yet comic upland birds reaches across eastern Minnesota, Ontario, Wisconsin, Michigan, New Brunswick, Nova Scotia, and Maine. Sizable, but smaller, breeding populations spend the summer in Ohio and to the east, from parts of New England down to West Virginia. Few of the birds breed in latitudes below that, but most of them winter in the Southeast—as far south as central Florida and across the Gulf Coast into eastern Texas. The most enormous wintering concentrations are found in Louisiana.

The birds migrate along three main flyways—one down the Atlantic Seaboard, one west of the Appalachians, and one through the Mississippi Valley. The wide middle corridor is used by the largest numbers of woodcock, but there's woodcock hunting (and usually good hunting) in nearly 40 states and also in Ontario, Quebec, New Brunswick, Nova Scotia, and Prince Edward Island. New Brunswick rivals Louisiana as a famous haven for woodcock and woodcock hunters. The yearly woodcock, or "timberdoodle," harvests are also impressive in Wisconsin, Michigan, New York, and New Jersey.

Migration is accomplished principally by a long chain of short flights, but here and there along the way, open water or a lack of good habitat necessitates flights requiring great stamina. The birds tend to gather in "staging areas" and rest before undertaking these nonstop flights. Thus, large numbers of woodcock gather in well-known locations, resting, feeding heavily to build strength, and perhaps awaiting good flying weather. Probably the most famous of these spots is Cape May, New Jersey, where great swarms of woodcock rest during the hunting season before making the long crossing over Delaware Bay. To anyone familiar with typical woodcock coverts, the bushy barrens behind the Cape May·beaches look like mediocre habitat at best, but the hunting there can be marvelous.

Woodcock are protected by the federal regulations governing the hunting of migratory birds. The open seasons are therefore set within federal guidelines, and these seasons are timed to coincide with the presence of "flight birds" (those en route from breeding grounds farther north) as well as "natives" (those that have summered locally and will soon depart southward). Thus, New Brunswick's season usually begins in mid-September. The season opens a couple of weeks later in the Lake States and New England. In New Jersey it usually opens in mid- or late October. A bit farther south, it opens in November. Louisiana usually opens the season in early December, when the greatest concentrations of birds begin to arrive, and the hunting there ends in early February, when some of the birds begin to migrate northward again.

Usually (though certainly not invariably) woodcock flush close. They're not very fast fliers, and if you hit one with only a couple of pellets, it will fall. Why, then, do we all miss woodcock so often? For one thing, the target is small—hardly bigger than an average man's fist. For another, it will most often rise steeply and erratically, veering from side to side, sometimes spiraling like a corkscrew before leveling and flicking away.

And finally, there's the difficulty inherent in one very common type of woodcock habitat. I don't find the species hard to hit when my dog or I put one up on a pasture, even though it's likely to flush a bit farther out than a bird in thicker cover. But I very often find it hard to hit when I'm in high brush, a dense alder run, or some other thicket of shrubs and saplings. I've bulled my way into dense thickets where I knew there were birds, then backed out in hopeless defeat when I found I didn't have room to swing my gun. Many woodcock are taken in cover not quite that dense, but dense enough to present a gun-swinging problem. One solution is to hunt only the edges of thick cover (and the surrounding area, of course). Another is to have someone go in, preferably with a dog, and try to bounce birds out for one or more waiting companions. Either way, it helps to have a light, short-barreled gun. Sometimes it's necessary to spot-shoot or snap-shoot.

In more open cover, I prefer to wait for the bird to finish towering before I shoot. It won't usually rise much above the alder tops and sometimes not that high. Shooting sooner can result in a rather even ratio between misses and mangled birds without much meat left for the table. But whether or not you hold your fire for a split second, it pays to practice getting your gun up and on the bird fast.

The brown and black mottling of a woodcock's plumage is almost invisible when a bird is on the ground, whether it's in brushy vegetation or sitting right in the open on a brown forest mat of leaves and twigs. When I walk in over a dog's point, I mentally draw a line from the animal's nose to give myself a clearer notion of where the bird will rise. Even so, I'm often a little surprised when a woodcock goes up closer than I expect—or occasionally farther away or off to one side. Flushes can be still more surprising when you're without a dog. Sometimes you hear a bird before you see it. The air passing through and around the three narrow outer primaries of each wing makes a light, twittering whistle (a sound some hunters mistakenly believe to be a vocally produced call). With or without a dog, I use my ears as well as my eyes to hunt.

I also do a lot of ground-watching because, even in fairly thick cover, it's often possible to see a woodcock whirring upward but still very close to the ground, considerably before it's had time to finish towering. Those you're slow to see are the ones most often missed.

The woodcock's long, slim bill is the most reliable way to tell a male from a female, whether you're truly interested or just want to impress a hunting companion. A male's bill is rarely longer than 2½ inches; a female's almost always exceeds 2¾ inches. A male usually has a smaller body, too. In early October, a typical male weighs just a trifle more than 5½ ounces, while a typical female weighs 7 ounces or a little more.

That peculiar bill—whose flexible upper mandible hinges open and shut about midway out from the head—is used to drill into the ground for earthworms. Very sensitive nerve endings in the bill enable the bird to feel for its hidden prey, and perhaps to sense it in some other way akin to taste or smell. Another reason for a woodcock hunter to be a ground-watcher is that a sprinkling of little round "borings" or "drill holes" in a small area indicates a promising covert where birds have been feeding heavily.

The woodcock at right is probably a male, the one at left a female. The male is slightly smaller and has a shorter bill. Hunters often put up pairs of woodcock, but these couples aren't mates, and they may be of the same sex. They're togther only because the same things attract them—worm-rich earth in or near good hiding cover.

Another kind of sign, much more easily and often spotted, is woodcock "chalk"—white spatters of liquid droppings about an inch across, quite conspicuous on the ground, on dry leaves, or on still-green undergrowth.

In parts of New England and below the Great Lakes, and probably in some other regions as well, many hunters are firmly if fallaciously convinced that Canadian woodcock are bigger than those nesting locally. This belief usually gains adherents where most of the native woodcock have departed before the arrival of the transients that summered farther north. Woodcock feed voraciously in the fall, gaining weight to be used as an energy reserve. Some of this is burned away during migration, for the Northern birds travel up to 1,500 miles, and more is used if sudden hard frosts interfere with drilling for worms as the birds rest and feed along the way, or if times are equally lean on the wintering grounds. Woodcock that haven't yet migrated far haven't burned much weight, and if mild weather has permitted them to linger in the North, they've had extra time to fatten up. A little later, flight birds and natives mingle in most areas, and no one can tell them apart. Those bred in the United States are just as big as the Canadians.

Another "mystery" that puzzles some hunters is why they never see any migratory flights. The birds make their way southward slowly, and they fly low, yet they appear in a given locale without being seen arriving, and they disappear a little later without being seen departing. The reason is simply that they do almost all their traveling after dusk. (Some people, having seen woodcock rise nearly 300 feet to circle a meadow or field in the spring, assume they fly high when migrating, too, but only the males rise to impressive altitudes, and they do so only during their courtship flights.) Occasionally a hunter thinks he sees flight birds—migrants—settle into a field at dusk, and he's disappointed if he fails to find them the next morning. What he really saw was a group of woodcock coming to a good feeding field from nearby resting and hiding coverts. If they're gone in the morning, they may have migrated during the night, or they may have gone to rest nearby, safely hidden in brushy edges or woods after a dawn feeding.

Many hunters who have seen the birds flying at dusk believe that woodcock are strictly nocturnal feeders, flushed during daylight only from the resting, watering, and hiding places. The birds do feed at night, but they also feed very actively at dawn, noon, and dusk. Early morning, midday, and late afternoon are good times to hunt the food-rich spots, and at other times the brush and woods are promising. However, the best habitat usually has a close mixture of feeding and resting grounds—which are often one and the same. In productive habitat, therefore, I've never found that the time of day mattered a great deal.

Good habitat has a birdy look about it. Bear in mind that the birds must have water and worms. Also bear in mind that worms don't comprise their entire diet, except perhaps for short periods or in unusually worm-rich earth. They also eat insects and a few seeds and berries (among which, sedge seeds and blackberries are their favorites). Look for seeps, springs, brooks, and marshy bottomlands. Look for dark, soft earth with shrubs, young trees, and openings as well as thickets. Alders and young birches are well known for woodcock flushes because they grow in the right kind of soil and are the right size. The best stands of trees are only 10 to 20 feet high, growing close and rather tangled for concealment purposes, but with open or light ground cover so that the birds can drill for worms. In New Brunswick, most woodcock are flushed from alders, gray birches, and evergreens. A study in Maine showed nearly half of all flushes to be in alder runs. A Pennsylvania study indicated that when the birds weren't in the alder bottoms, they were mostly on slopes with lots of crab apple or hawthorne. In Louisiana, the woodcock are mostly moved from among pines or alluvial bottomlands.

Where the types of coverts just described are lacking, or if they fail to produce flushes, other bird-attracting spots can be sought. The woodcock is closely related to the snipe and belongs to an order of shorebirds, but evolution has adapted it to a more or less upland life and a dependence on earthworms. Life in the uplands governs some of its behavior patterns. For example, on hot fall days, woodcock seek the humid coolness of deeply shaded resting places, and they're often flushed from beneath evergreens. In cool weather, they're often up on sun-warmed slopes, especially slopes that have concealing stands of birch or aspen. Bogs are a common type of shorebird habitat, and boggy fields often have worm-rich earth, so woodcock frequent such fields if escape cover is nearby. Sometimes they're also found on cropland—for instance, cornfields adjacent to alders or similar cover. In old orchards, the fallen apples enrich the soil; I don't know if the richness is what attracts worms, but usually they can be found there in abundance. Old orchards are good places to check for woodcock in the fall and dig for bait in the spring. So are overgrown pastures, where cows, rather than apple trees, drop an enrichment upon the soil.

The author shuffles through the ground cover, trusting the setter's point and expecting to flush an extremely tight-sitting woodcock that he can't see. The bird was there, a little farther ahead and to one side than the point seemed to indicate, and a moment later it corkscrewed into the air.

I much prefer to hunt woodcock with a dog, but I've often had to go it alone. If there are only a few birds in the vicinity, this can be a lot of work for a very small return, but if the birds are plentiful—natives or flight birds or both—it can be worthwhile. Without a dog, you'll pass a great many more birds than you'll ever see because they'll just sit there, quite safely invisible. However, quite a few will flush. A woodcock usually lies tight at a dog's approach and point, evidently relying on camouflage to escape detection by anything it takes to be an ordinary four-legged predator. When a man approaches, woodcock usually fly—perhaps because the size of the man makes him seem dangerously close. Some flushes will be quite far out, but many will be close enough.

At one time I believed that the way to hunt without a dog was merely to move slowly through the coverts, ready to shoot. I had, after all, put up quite a few that way. But there's a better way, and shamefaced honesty compels me to admit I learned it from a friend who had never hunted woodcock before. We were walking through

A female woodcock (or "woodhen," if you prefer) lies amid ferns and dry leaves at the base of this birch, but you'll have to look closely to find her. Relying on her camouflage, she sat motionless while the author photographed her. This is why dogless hunters pass many birds without flushing them or knowing of their presence.

normally productive coverts without seeing anything to shoot at, and he reasoned that occasional halts would panic a woodcock into flying, just as the stop-and-go technique pushes up pheasants and some other upland birds. He tried it and almost immediately put up a pair. He shot one, and I brought down the other. After that we hunted slowly, on a zigzag course, pausing often, and we had much better success.

The mention of that pair reminds me that it's very common to flush doubles. They're not mated birds, as many hunters suppose. Woodcock aren't monogamous, nor are they mating during hunting season. They migrate in loose groups, many of which are composed entirely of males or females. When a hunter puts up a pair, he has to be a fast and accurate wingshooter in order to collect both birds; most often, he kills one or none, and that's why few hunters find out that such pairs, at least as often as not, are birds of the same sex.

Among dogless hunters, a common mistake is to struggle through the thickest patches of alders and the like in the expectation—or hope—that at least a shot or two can be had where the woodcock are supposedly concentrated. Birds may be there, of course. They may

In the North, the fringes of alder runs and young birches are the best-known resting places of woodcock, but this Louisiana pine thicket is an equally typical covert. Additional types of concealment cover and feeding areas are described in the text.

be anywhere around. But there are four reasons not to bull through a jungle. First, it will whip and scratch your face, knock off your hat or glasses, tear your clothes, and generally make you more miserable than hunting is supposed to. Second, if birds do go up, you won't necessarily see them in all that screening vegetation. Third, if you do see them, you may not be able to swing your gun without catching it or yourself in the tangles. And fourth, many more woodcock are flushed at or near the edges of such coverts than in the dense parts. They're attracted and held by the combination of fairly open feeding ground and concealing brush.

My personal feeling about dogless woodcock hunting is that I can't do it without feeling a bit guilty. I hate to lose a downed bird—kill a creature, in other words, without bringing it home to eat. To do so, it seems to me, is not only wasteful but callous. And a fallen woodcock can be extremely hard to find unless it lands on open ground. I've shot some I never found and then gone home wishing I'd missed. It's true that some dogs seem to dislike carrying a woodcock, but even those dogs will locate a fallen bird for the hunter.

It's possible to hunt woodcock with flushing dogs. Labs are occasionally used, and at one time springers were among the most popular of breeds for the purpose. A woodcock will usually sit tight until the dog is quite close and then fly, well within gunshot. (But don't let anyone tell you that woodcock never escape by running on the ground; sometimes they most certainly do.)

Having paid my respects to the flushers, I must put aside my bias as a springer owner and fancier long enough to admit that close-lying birds like the woodcock are ideal game for a good pointing dog. I don't think it matters whether you prefer an English setter, English pointer, German shorthair, or Brittany spaniel. Any good pointer can do the job. The best dog, of course, is one that has the right qualities for hunting grouse. Such an animal will help you take both species.

For hunting most upland game, the first part of the season is very productive. I don't find this to hold true for woodcock in some of the best regions. Early in the season the weather may be too warm for comfort or for good dog work. What's more, so many leaves may still be on the trees that it's hard to see a woodcock rise and harder to hit it. I'll take the crispy cool days toward the end of the season when the trees have lost enough leaves that I can see what I'm missing.

I've seen and tried numerous woodcock recipes, but none (in my opinion and that of friends) is better than an unusual concoction I developed from several old methods of preparation. To make this you need a small, mild, coarsely diced onion, plus about half a cup of fresh diced mushrooms and an equal amount of diced chestnuts for every three woodcock. (Some people use only the breasts; I use the whole birds, split in half.) After slitting the hulls of whole, raw chestnuts, I boil them, but only because peeling roasted chestnuts is too messy and too much bother. I then dice the chestnuts, the mushrooms, and the onion. I sauté these ingredients together in browned butter in a moderately deep saucepan or Dutch oven. While they're browning, I braise the woodcock in a fairly shallow pan, using a small amount of bacon or lard—no more than is needed to grease the pan—and adding a generous splash of dry red wine before covering it. I add the braised birds, liquid and all, to the sauté, which I then simmer over a low flame, with the pan covered, for another 10 minutes or so. This sort of dish should be seasoned to individual taste. Personally, I prefer a gentle seasoning—salt, pepper, and a generous pinch of thyme—because I'd hate to overwhelm the delicate flavor of the birds and the chestnuts.

Turkeys
The Big-Game Birds

What constitutes a proper turkey gun depends chiefly on the prevalent type of habitat and style of hunting in a given region. In some states it also depends on what's legal, either statewide or within certain game-management zones or special-regulations areas. Assuming that both rifles and shotguns are legal in a given state, it's valid to generalize that turkeys in the most typical Eastern habitat are more often seen at shotgun range than far off, and they're usually running or flying before the gun can be brought to the shoulder. In many Western areas, it's common to see the birds at distances more appropriate for rifles than for smoothbores.

The wariness of turkeys, especially the males, is legendary, yet there are woods where you're going to shoot them at close range or not at all. The first time I saw a bowhunter scatter a flock and then try to call them back in the Pennsylvania woods, I thought he was about as absurd as Don Quixote tilting at windmills. But after I'd been in those woods for a while, I realized that a good archer (if he was also a good hunter) had almost as strong a chance of connecting as anyone else, because a bird would have to be just about within range to be seen.

While browsing through the regulations of various states, I noticed that several now have special archery seasons on turkeys in the fall, or fall and spring, or split between fall and winter. This goes to show that the range can be short in fall or winter, though turkeys don't respond to calling as eagerly then as during the spring mating frenzy.

On the other hand, I was invited on a one-day turkey hunt in Texas one autumn, and I swear I saw at least four dozen turkeys that day but was unable to take one because I was carrying a shotgun. Only toms (or bearded hens) were legal. Although one flock of hens and juveniles came within 60 yards of me, the only legal birds I saw were well over 80 yards away. With a rifle, one gobbler would have presented an easy head shot. But with my shotgun, I decided I'd be a fool and not much of a sportsman to bother firing. I felt foolish anyway, because either kind of firearm was legal, and I could have walked back to our pick-up for a rifle if only I'd put one in the truck's gun rack when we set out.

Let's discuss shotguns first, since they're most often used. A full-choked 12-gauge gun is a good choice, and generally it ought to be used in conjunction with No. 4's or 5's. The 4's are probably best for body shots, which comprise the majority of turkey kills. Generally those who favor smaller shot (and some of them use pellets even smaller than 5's—that is 6's, or in a few cases 7½'s) make it their rule to aim for the head. Turkeys are the "big game" among upland birds, and the use of a shotgun is considered sporting when they're on the ground or in trees so—depending on local habitat—head shots aren't necessarily beyond the ability of the average hunter.

Since turkeys are such big, heavily feathered birds, I believe in using heavy charges. I don't think 3-inch Magnums are essential in 12 gauge, but I'd use short Magnums, or at least high-brass loads. The 16 gauge, which is still quite popular in parts of the South, is fine with the maximum 2¾-inch loads, and so is the 20 with 3-inch Magnums.

Hunters who scout the hills or take stands overlooking fairly open valleys can, and often do, use rifles. A .22 rimfire Magnum will serve nicely in some parts of the country, but a lot of turkey hunters prefer centerfires for the sake of relatively flat trajectory at occasionally long range. The old .22 Hornet is excellent, but these days I'm sure more hunters use .222's.

Some old turkey hands use open-sighted or peep-sighted rifles. I prefer a scope. I've heard of hunters using high-power scopes, but I don't see the point in that when 2½X gives you all the magnification you need plus good clarity, a wide field of view, and ease in finding the sight picture quickly.

Quite a few hunters use combination arms that provide at least one smoothbore barrel plus a rifle barrel. The least expensive and most readily available are the over-unders sometimes called "turkey guns," with one barrel of each persuasion. There are also three-barreled guns, known as drillings, which are made abroad. Most of these provide side-by-side shotgun barrels over a rifle. Naturally, such arms are a bit heavier than conventional rifles or shotguns, but in most turkey-hunting situations, you don't need a very fast-swinging gun.

Some of the European drillings are made with rather fancy graduated leaf sights. It's true that a low open sight facilitates the use of the smoothbore barrels—and some of these sights automatically fold down flat, completely out of the way, when the barrel selector is positioned for shotgun use. That's very nice, but for turkey hunting, I agree with the many hunters who prefer to mount a scope on a drilling. Some of them use "see-through" mounts so they can peer under the scope when firing one of the smoothbore barrels, and some just practice with the scoped gun until they can use the smoothbores effectively despite the tube riding atop the rib.

If you don't think you can hit the bird's head when using a rifle, there are three aiming areas that should give you a clean kill. When you have a profile view, you can aim right at the base of the wing. A turkey won't always come directly toward you in response to calling—in fact, the approach is more likely to be oblique or crossing—but when you do have a facing shot, your target is high on the breast. And when you see a turkey from the rear, the place to aim is roughly the center of its back.

A good-sized male turkey is perhaps 40 inches long from back to tail and has a wingspread of more than four feet. Despite its size, it's not an easy target. A gobbler on the ground can run at a speed of at least 20 miles an hour, disappearing into brush before you have much time to shoot. He can lift off as fast as a grouse and fly 40 miles an hour.

There are half a dozen races of wild turkey. The native range of the Eastern subspecies extends from lower New England into the South and Midwest; that of the Florida subspecies from the Deep South far enough northward for interbreeding with the Eastern strain; that of the Rio Grande turkey from the Southwest down into Mexico (and, through transplanting, in states as far off as the Dakotas and California); that of the Merriam turkey from the Southwest into the lower Rockies (and, again through transplanting, in a number of Western states); that of the Gould's turkey from Mexico into small portions of the Southwest; and that of the Mexican turkey far below the border.

Generally speaking, geographic differences in size and coloration are minor. However, the Eastern and Merriam varieties are the largest. An adult gobbler, or tom—that is, a male—of either strain weighs about 15 to 20 pounds, a hen 9 to 12. The Florida turkey is dark and comparatively small, whereas the Rio Grande subspecies pale and long-legged.

As a rule, only gobblers—males—are legal game during the spring turkey season, and many states also stipulate gobblers only when a fall season is opened. The most reliable sexual mark is the "beard" hanging or jutting from the breast of a mature male. The Texas turkey shown here is of the Rio Grande subspecies. He's probably young, as his beard is only a few inches long. A few hens grow beards, and those that do are legal because they're so hard to tell from males.

Domestic strains, bred for size, are principally descended from ancient Mexican stock, domesticated by Indians long before Europeans arrived on this continent. By the 1920's, wild turkeys had become rare or extinct in many regions of historic abundance, and calamity nearly resulted when domestic birds and hybrids were released to replenish the populations. Game biologists have since learned that "wildness"—a combination of survival traits—can be genetically lost, and interbreeding with domestic birds can undermine a wild population.

The wild birds had been devastated by timber cutting, forest fires, farming, and market shooting. New techniques of habitat management and bird transplantation brought about a reversal of the decline at least as dramatic as the salvation of whitetail deer earlier in this century. Birds were captured with drop-nets and rocket-nets in baited clearings, then sown like seed in new or depopulated areas. They need relatively mature, open forest. Such woods, once obliterated for settlement, were reappearing in many areas and have been maintained at the proper stage of development. In most geographic regions, forests of that kind offer the best turkey hunting.

In 1974, I wrote that turkeys could be hunted in 35 states. Their dramatic revival has continued. They're found today in parts of the country where they never before occurred. In 1978, 38 states had a spring turkey season and almost 30 had a fall season. Some of these states have large commercial preserves where proper habitat is maintained and good hunting can be had for a fee. In addition, all of them have public and private lands that support huntable populations of turkeys.

The spring season in Southeastern states is open in March and/or April; in most other states, the months are April and May. In several Western states, the fall season opens in mid- or late September. In most other regions, turkeys can be hunted some time in October and/or November—in time to try for a Thanksgiving turkey—and in a few, the season lasts into the winter. The preserve seasons generally stay open longer than the regular seasons. Arizona, Arkansas, Florida, and Missouri are the states with special archery seasons in fall and/or winter, and Arkansas allows either firearms or bows and arrows during an April hunt.

Many states require the purchase of a special turkey permit in addition to the regular gun- or bow-hunting license. The proceeds are used for game and habitat management. Some states allow turkey hunting only during part of the day—usually morning—and a few open the season to residents only. Bag limits also vary. In some states, you can take only gobblers (or bearded hens unavoidably mistaken for males). In others you can take either sex, at least during the fall hunt. In some states with high turkey populations in proportion to the available habitat, you can take more than one per season, while in other states, the limit is one a year. As you can see, it's essential to check any state's regulations for a number of details in addition to the open season.

In a number of states—such as Idaho, Washington, and Oregon—there's an open season and fair hunting, but nothing much by comparison with the really good turkey states. Almost certainly, the hunting will gradually improve there. A few years ago I wouldn't have traveled a hundred miles to try for a turkey in New York or Vermont, but now those states are quite good. Also quite good and steadily improving are Arkansas, Missouri, and Oklahoma. Even better are Arizona, Colorado, Nebraska, New Mexico, Pennsylvania, South Dakota, and Wyoming. Just about all of the Southeast is excellent, but the best states in that section are Alabama, the Carolinas, Florida, Louisiana, and Mississippi.

Texas is generally considered the best turkey state in the Union. The states that reported the highest harvests of birds in 1977 were Pennsylvania, Alabama, and Texas.

But of course, such statistics are hard to interpret because you must take into account the estimated population of birds in a state, the number of hunters who spend any significant amount of time trying to bag them, and the amount of accessible hunting land. For example, Pennsylvania has a population of about 100,000 turkeys in the best years, but they're spread out over more than 15,000 square miles of habitat, and the density of birds in the most productive woods seldom exceeds 10 turkeys per square mile. Turkey hunting isn't usually easy, nor is it necessarily easiest in the states with the most birds. The reported hunter-success ratio in 1977 was highest in Colorado, Wyoming, Florida, North Dakota, Oklahoma, South Dakota, Kansas, and California.

The federal government and state game departments deserve much of the credit for the turkey revival, but so do the 30,000 or so members of a private non-profit conservation group, the National Wild Turkey Federation. This organization of sportsmen has been doing for turkeys what Ducks Unlimited does for waterfowl and shorebirds, and what the Izaak Walton League and Trout Unlimited do for fish. In addition to working for beneficial regulations and promoting and contributing to conservation efforts, the Federation keeps its members informed of trends, events, supplies, and services connected with turkey hunting. If you don't already belong to this organization and you're seriously interested in the species (which would have been our national bird if anyone had listened to Ben Franklin or to us younger voters), you might mail an inquiry to the National Wild Turkey Federation, P.O. Box 467, Edgefield, S.C. 29824.

In the shade beneath a forest canopy, the iridescent washes of bronze, copper, purple, and green on a turkey's feathers may be entirely lost, so that all you see is a big black-looking bird (or sometimes a silver-gray ghost if the turkey is retreating). Sexual identification can be difficult, yet it's crucial if the state restricts hunting to gobblers.

During the spring rut, behavior sometimes helps establish sex because a tom that approaches in answer to a call may strut and display in response to what he takes to be a hen's invitation. He may stretch his head forward as he looks about, and he'll jerk it forward while uttering a long, loud gobble. Intermittently, he'll peck and scratch at the ground as if completely unconcerned with females, but when he struts, he'll tuck his head almost against his back, puff out his body feathers, spread and drag his wings on the ground, and cock his tail up and spread it in a magnificently wide fan. Any time you see this, you can be sure of the bird's sex. Get set for a shot.

Whether or not a tom struts, there are physical characteristics to identify him. Most important is the beard hanging from a male's breast. Composed of peculiarly modified feathers, it looks like a narrow, stiff, miniature black horsetail, usually about eight or nine inches long and occasionally longer. A bird of the year has a beard no more than a few inches long. (Though it grows throughout a male's life, it doesn't indicate age reliably because the "hair" tips break or wear away.) A few females also sprout beards. Such hens are usually counted as legal "gobblers" because they're so hard to tell from males at a distance and in forest light. Most hunters save every turkey beard as a trophy, and some mount them on wall plaques or in display cases.

Here you see a gobbler strutting, dragging his wings, and fanning his tail before a receptive hen. When you see a turkey "displaying" like this, you know it's a gobbler, even if you can't see his beard or his pink head and neck.

Males also have leg spurs, typically an inch long at maturity and so hard and sharp that Indians sometimes used them for arrowheads. However, you must have astonishing vision if you can notice the spurs at shooting distance through twigs, brush, or forest litter. Moreover, a bearded hen may have spurs.

A female's head and neck are different from a male's. She usually has some fleshy neck folds and protuberances, but they're negligible by comparison with a male's. And her head has a shadowy, bluish-gray cast, produced by fine, whiskery little feathers. An adult male has a naked head with wattles hanging from chin and throat, and with fatty lumps called caruncles adorning the throat and neck. He also has a fleshy lobe, called a frontal caruncle, leader, or snood, right above his bill and often hanging down over it. His crown is quite pale. The rest of his head and neck are pinkish, with a pale blue facial tinge. During the spring rut, his feathers brighten and his wattles redden and swell. When he struts, these wattles may flush quite red. The head and neck color and growths may furnish reliable sexual identification in good light, but the beard is usually regarded as the confirming feature, and in many states a beardless bird is illegal, even if it proves to be a male.

In states where there's an early fall season, good turkey-hunting land has grasses and brush to support insect life, for at this time of year, both the adults and the juveniles may still be eating quantities of insects. In the spring, too, good habitat usually has some brush or swampy places. And regardless of season, there must be ponds, creeks, seeps, or swamps to provide water. Whether a hunt is in fall, winter, or spring, most of the best spots have stands of hardwoods that supply mast—acorns, beechnuts, or hazelnuts. Where these favorite foods are lacking, however, conifer seeds are heavily utilized. But bear in mind that at some times of year or in some regions, mast may be scarce or absent, and very different foods will attract turkeys: chufa grass, sumac, wild grapes, dogwood, ragweed, and all sorts of berries. Though wary, the birds will also come to farmlands for corn, sorghum, or oats.

Specific foods and feeding periods are most important during a fall hunt, when sexual attraction won't keep the gobblers moving about or draw them as eagerly to a call that sounds like a hen's yelp. Although turkeys feed intermittently throughout the day, and you might find them in the woods at any time, they forage most intensively for a couple of hours after dawn and before dusk, and those are the best hunting times.

A productive area must have appropriate roosts as well as foods. Turkeys prefer to spend the night in tall trees, usually more than 60 feet high and situated on a ridge or at the edge of a clearing so that no obstructions will interfere with emergency flight. In most regions they like oaks, cottonwoods, pines, spruces, and firs. In parts of the South they roost in cypresses over water (a natural moat to impede the approach of any predators). Sometimes they use the same trees for several successive nights. Sometimes—why, I don't know, unless it's just a matter of instinctive caution—they switch every night. But even when they switch, roosting sign is worth looking for because these birds usually stay within a fairly small area throughout the year.

Roosting sign is composed of molted feathers and quantities of droppings. I wonder if many hunters realize that droppings reveal the dropper's sex. A hen's scat is looped, spiraled, or bulbous; a tom's is longer and straighter, with a knobby twist at one end.

Near roosts and in foraging areas, you may also find the big triple-toed tracks, sometimes more than six inches long. If a footprint is more than 4½ inches long, it was probably made by a mature gobbler, and if the stride is over 11½ inches long, it was almost certainly made by a mature gobbler. Also watch for scratchings and diggings in mast where the birds have been foraging.

Another worthwhile kind of sign consists of dusting spots. These are shallow ovals, not easy to spot but sometimes marked by feathers, droppings, or tracks. Favored places for dusting are under sumacs or small trees and beside logs or burned brush. In scouting for such sign—or for the birds themselves—pay attention to old roadsides and trails, which the birds sometimes use not only for dusting and gritting but for easy traveling between foraging areas.

In the Pennsylvania woods near my hunting camp, and probably in most regions, a primary hunting method in the fall is to locate and scatter a flock (which is apt to be composed of hens and juveniles) and then call. The birds are listening for one another as they regroup, and calling will often lure one into view of your hiding spot. To locate a flock, hunters generally scout for scratchings and the other kinds of sign I described in mast high up on slopes, atop ridges, and on high flats.

There are more methods than you ordinarily see described in magazine articles—which tend to emphasize the drama of calling. For example, as you scout for a flock in woods known to hold turkeys, it pays to stop occasionally, hide, and call, even if you've neither seen nor heard any indication of birds. This is because other hunters may already have scattered a nearby flock, in which case you have a good chance of calling in a bird.

In a few areas, the use of dogs is legal. A turkey is not going to lie to a point, nor will it let a flushing dog get near enough for a flush within gunshot. But a dog can locate and scatter flocks more efficiently than you can, after which both you and the animal must remain still and hidden while you call.

The proper calling sounds to rally scattered turkeys in the fall are clucking, gobbling, and trilling. There are instructional records and tapes, as well as numerous books, to help you learn the right sounds to use both in fall and spring. (I'll have more to say about this later, in connection with spring hunting.)

Another autumn method is to still-hunt, pretty much as you would for deer. In its pure form, this technique isn't very productive. That is, a hunter doesn't often get a shot at a bird spied while he slowly stalks through the woods. But if the still-hunter gets no shot during his stop-and-go progress, he can occasionally hide and call for a while, or he may find sign or even get a glimpse of a distant bird, and he can then wait on stand, either calling or just watching and waiting. Still-hunting is best in bottomlands where there's screening brush, and on brushy slopes. When working the slopes, move to the summits every few hundred yards to scan the opposite hillsides.

Good stands are generally near the edges of fields or clearings, or overlooking small, openly wooded valleys, or near old roads, trails, or burns.

In some regions, turkey hunters refer to stand-hunting as "roost-hunting," or "roosting." I'm not sure whether those terms originally alluded to the fact that the hunter himself roosts in one spot for a while—preferably a fairly high spot with a good view—or to the fact that a particularly good place for a hunter to roost is near a previously discovered turkey roost. It pays to scout a turkey area thoroughly, then go on stand near a roost well before sunrise. The birds may start calling while it's still dark, and they'll probably begin moving at first light. If you don't take a turkey from such a stand in the early morning, you can try again very late in the afternoon—just in case a turkey goes to roost early.

On the basis of scientific evidence, there's some disagreement as to how well turkeys can discern colors. But they can definitely distinguish big patches of unnatural color intensity, and they can spot the slightest movement at long distance. You must be concealed when you go on stand. You'll probably find plenty of natural blinds—logs, boulders, blowdowns, clumps of brush, etc.—but it's not a bad idea to pack along a roll of camouflage netting to improve such blinds. Sometimes, too, you can enhance a natural blind with fallen branches, brush, and twigs.

Camouflage apparel is also a great help. Most hunters wear a camouflage-pattern jacket, pants, and hat. Some wear a camouflage face-net or mask, or blacken their faces and hands with burnt cork, or apply camouflage grease paint, which is available at many archery-equipment outlets and some general sporting-goods stores. A few hunters go further, wearing camouflage gloves and even camouflage-pattern tennis shoes instead of conventional boots.

I'll take ordinary boots, thank you. As I mentioned in relation to quail hunting, in some parts of the country I'd choose snakeproof boots and would pack a snakebite kit just in case I intruded on a rattler. This can be important during the spring season, and there are regions warm enough during the fall season so that rattlers won't be hibernating.

Other recommended gear includes a bird knife with a gutting hook. (In warm weather I prefer to dress a bird as soon as possible.)

Not long ago I saw a rather realistic hen-turkey decoy on sale in a sporting-goods shop in a Southern turkey-hunting area. I can't claim to know from experience how effective such a decoy would be, but it would be worth a try. It certainly can't hurt when you're trying to toll in gobblers during the spring season.

A Pennsylvania turkey hunter brings home Thanksgiving dinner. His camouflage coveralls and hat are an asset both in fall and spring. The most common fall technique is to locate and scatter a flock and then call the birds as they try to regroup.

If you've never attended a turkey-calling contest, you've certainly read about them. I think they've added an extra dimension of fun to the sport and, by helping to popularize it, they've promoted game and habitat management. But they've also helped to establish a mystique of calling that may need deflating. I've heard experts who sounded more like a hen turkey then a hen turkey could ever hope to, and I'm sure such virtuosos bring home more turkeys than the run-of-the-mill hunters. But it's just not true that calling must approach perfection in order to fool an arrogant, sex-hungry gobbler. That notion discourages a lot of hunters from trying a most interesting and rewarding sport. The fact is, even mediocre calling works, and even a tin-eared duffer like me can learn to call tom turkeys.

The best way to learn calling is from an experienced turkey-hunting friend or guide. (And professional guides can be hired in many locales, now that the turkey populations have revived.) There's even a Turkey Hunting and Calling School—or maybe more than one, but this is the only one I know about. It's conducted by Westervelt Lodge, Gulf States Paper Corporation, Tuscaloosa, Alabama 35401. You may want to send an inquiry about costs and reservations, preferably well before the next spring season, which is in the last half of March and much of April in Alabama. My guess is that some of the other commercial preserves also offer instruction.

The next best way to learn calling is from instructional records or tapes, and I suggest that you use these in conjunction with one or more of the books devoted to turkey hunting. Among the good books is *The Education of a Turkey Hunter*, by William Frank Hanenkrat (Winchester Press, 1974). This isn't the usual how-to book; it's a hunting autobiography by a man with a lifelong passion for hunting turkeys—but it includes all the turkey-hunting tricks of the experts, so it's really a complete course in the subject.

In scanning the nationwide hunting regulations, I find that at least one state makes an emphatic point of prohibiting electronic turkey-calling devices in the field. I've been told that many other states also ban records and tapes for turkey hunting. I agree with this regulation; the records and tapes should be used as learning tools. Once you've learned, it's much more satisfying and sporting to bring

These North Carolina turkeys are feeding in a baited field where game biologists have hidden a capture-net. Through capture and transplanting, game departments have built up turkey populations in a great many new or depopulated areas where suitable habitat supports thriving flocks.

turkeys into view with a manually operated call. These great game birds merit the necessary skill and effort—and, as I've said, it isn't as difficult as it's supposed to be. But if you disagree, check your state regulations before taking a phonograph into the turkey woods.

There are old-timers who can yelp like a hen turkey by using nothing but their own vocal chords, or can do so convincingly by blowing through a pipe stem. There are others who get a good sound by scraping a home-whittled cedar peg across a thin, chalked slate or by blowing or sucking a hen turkey's wingbone from which the ends have been cut. For most of us, the commercial calls are better. Anything homemade requires instruction from a practiced hand in making and using it properly. With practice and attention to the manufacturer's instructions, most commercial calls will yelp nicely, and some will gobble.

The basic types of store-bought calls are boxes with hinged handles, boxes with separate strikers, tubes, slates, box or wingbone suction calls, aluminum-groove calls and diaphragm yelpers. Some are more popular (or traditional) than others in various regions. The diaphragm type takes some practice to make it sound right, but it has the advantage of leaving both your hands free, and it can be quite realistic. It's a vibration device, worked between your tongue and the roof of your mouth. My impression is that the most universally common calls are the wooden or slate-and-wooden box calls.

The box calls sound best in dry weather, but they work well enough on humid days, and the birds are most active in drizzly or overcast weather. However, turkeys avoid moving through really wet foliage, so on days like that, a good place to hide and call is near a clearing, trail, or back road where the birds can move toward you without getting their feathers very wet.

A drizzle is fine, but during a hard rain I think I'd find something else to do because turkeys take shelter and hardly move during a downpour.

In the spring hunting season, sexually receptive hens call to any available males by uttering rather plaintive yelps, which sound something like *keowk, keowk*. This is the most basic and frequently effective call—the one you should take greatest pains to learn from a teacher or instructional recording. But it isn't the only sound you need. When flying from a roost, turkeys sometimes yelp more softly, and they often cluck and trill while feeding. An imitation of these calls isn't important (though it might attract a gobbler's attention) but once in a while such sounds may help you locate birds. More important is the gobbling and yodeling of the males—sounds used to warn other males away and respond to calling females. The basic gobbling sound might be described as a high, throaty *gl-obble-obble-obble*, sometimes preceded by or combined with a more yodeling *grrrddle* sound.

Some experienced hunters can tell a big gobbler by its voice. Yearlings have high, hoarse voices, and they aren't very vociferous. Mature birds have deeper voices and they call more.

Calling is usually best when there's little or no breeze. When rustling wind can cover the sound of approaching predators, turkeys remain still and hidden. On calm days they're active, and their gobbling can sometimes be heard at a distance of more than half a mile. It can be very hard to tell how far away a gobbler is, but as a rule the best tactic in response to a gobbler's distant call is to get close fast. Try to get within what you think is a couple of hundred yards, and then sneak into a natural blind and coax him closer.

Answer a gobble with a yelp or two, and then be quiet and wait. You should soon hear another gobble, and it may be best not to reply this time. Use the call sparingly, answering perhaps every third gobble. If the tom doesn't soon come close, some hunters either move on or try to stalk toward another, closer hiding place. I'm of the school that believes in waiting a long time. I think the intermittent conversation with a cautiously approaching but interested tom is worth at least half an hour.

As the bird comes nearer, the silent pauses may lengthen to more than five minutes, or he may become completely silent. Domestic turkeys are the only trusting kind. Besides, a gobbler knows that a hen will come toward him—meet him halfway, so to speak—so he may just stop and scratch about, not even bothering to strut or call when he's near. One hunting tactic in this situation is simply to wait him out. Another is to attempt a closer stalk. Another—and it's a good bet—is to gobble or yodel at him instead of yelping. This sounds like a rival male has moved in on the hen that was yelping, and the urge to chase away the competition may prod him into view.

With variations based on locale and conditions, the basic spring hunting technique is to scout for roosts or roosting areas and then take a stand near one of them well before sunup. The turkeys may have shifted to the other side of the nearest valley, but that's the chance you take. At this time of year the wintering flocks, or droves, have broken up. The yearling toms are mostly foraging in small, quiet groups. Some of the hens are wandering about alone, probably listening for eager toms, but most females are in little cliques of three or four. The mature males have picked out small strutting-and-gobbling territories, and a gobbler will get to his ground early to defend it from rivals, advertise his presence with loud displays, and search about for females.

Crows—Pest Species or Game Birds?

There was a time when I wrote about my fondness for shooting (or shooting at) stationary crows with a .222, but that fondness has waned. Crows are no longer classified as a "pest species" but as migratory birds, subject to federal and state regulations. Some states permit the use of shotguns only. Moreover, my part of the country has become too thickly settled, even where rifle shooting is permitted, for me to feel safe firing a rifle at a crow anywhere but on the ground. A target perched as low as a fence rail has to be passed up.

However, there are still regions, particularly in the West, where a rifle can be used on crows. At modest ranges, a .22 Long Rifle cartridge is accurate enough, though centerfires have always been more popular—not for the sake of power but for accuracy at longer range. It's an exciting challenge to pot crows at typical chuck-shooting distances. Out to about 150 yards, the old .218 Bee or .22 Hornet will do for those who revere tradition. The .220 Swift will stretch that a bit, and the .17 Remington will stretch it a bit more.

At ranges beyond 200 yards, shooting crows with a rifle is much like shooting chucks, and the same rifles are recommended. The .222 is perhaps most widely used.

The right scope depends on your region and your style of hunting. If shots can't be safely taken at much more than accurate rimfire range, a 4X scope is a good choice. Where fairly long shots are frequent, a 6X scope is preferable.

Few people shoot crows with a handgun, but it can be done. Several accurate single-shot pistols are chambered for appropriate cartridges. For example, the Thompson-Center Contender is available with a barrel chambered for the .218 Bee, .221 Remington, .22 Jet, .22 Hornet, .22 K Hornet, or .222; and the Remington XP–100 handles the .221 cartridge. If equipped with a 2½X scope, one of these pistols can knock over crows at reasonable ranges.

Smoothbores, of course, are the usual armament. The most common mistake among crow hunters is the use of shot that's too large. No. 7½ pellets are marginal, and anything bigger is oversized. The most experienced crow hunters generally use 8's or 9's in a 12-gauge gun, and many use a 20 gauge. No. 9 skeet loads are excellent. Crows are surprisingly fragile creatures, and you don't need big pellets to bring them down. What you need is the dense, uniform patterns available with small shot.

Probably the second most common mistake is using guns that are too tightly choked. It's true that many masterful crow gunners use a full choke, but these shooters are skillful enough to center the small full-choke patterns on the birds—and they're able to make killing hits on higher or more distant crows than most of us should try for. Keeping the pattern dense at such long range is the only advantage of the full muzzle constriction. The majority of us will miss or merely wing-tip too many crows if we rely on a full choke to compensate for chancy shots. A modified choke is generally about right.

The previous two tips bring to mind a paradoxical problem in crow hunting. Crows are both larger and smaller than they look. Hunters who haven't had much experience with them tend to underestimate the size of the targets. The continent's most plentiful, most widely distributed, most migratory, and most hunted subspecies is the common crow (Corvus brachyrhynchos). It's also the largest. A typical mature specimen is 18 or 20 inches long with a three-foot wingspread. Most of us are so accustomed to seeing smaller blackbirds that we don't expect anything that big.

Thus, when a crow comes in over the trees, it looks so large that we think it's close, while it's still at long range or coming over high. I think the shooters who find crows tough to kill are often shooting at them too soon—underestimating the distance and therefore taking shots at borderline range. Glance at your decoys now and then. Their size and placement will help you judge the distance of approaching crows.

But I've said that they're smaller than they seem, as well as larger. It's true. Beneath the long feathers, their bodies are smaller than those of pigeons. This is yet another reason to let them come close and use a choke-and-shot combination that will deliver a dense pattern.

A shooter who underestimates the size of a crow and therefore underestimates the range is likely to lead it insufficiently. This can be exasperating because the next bird may come driving in low, and this

Comfortably ensconced in a natural blind close to a flyway, the author's wife uses a plastic crow call designed by the late Bert Popowski. She has a second, higher-pitched call to vary the cries and—on windy days—to carry the sound farther. At right, a stuffed horned owl, ancient and ragged but still lifelike, is being used effectively in conjunction with two plastic crow decoys. This is a common rig in parts of Oklahoma and Texas.

time the shooter is likely to overcorrect himself, giving it too much lead. Crows can be tricky fliers, sometimes wheeling and careening, but they seldom fly faster than 30 miles an hour. If you let them come in and swing the gun smoothly ahead of them, you don't have to lead them by much. Some of us don't consciously lead our birds at all.

Traditionally, the crow has been considered a destructive pest. Where flocks are very abundant, they can inflict tremendous damage on grain crops and occasionally on orchards. They also prey on the eggs and hatchlings of desirable birds, ranging from waterfowl and upland game to songbirds. However, such prey constitutes less than one percent of their diet under normal conditions, and where they aren't too abundant, their crop depredations may be almost counterbalanced by their avid appetite for destructive insects.

They may remain controversial, but legally they're no longer varmints. Several years ago, the United States signed a pact with Mexico that brought the migratory species of Corvidae (jays, crows, and magpies) under the provisions of the Migratory Bird Treaty Act. In its original form, the law prohibited the shooting of crows except where the birds were committing or about to commit some depredation on agricultural crops, ornamental or shade trees, livestock, or wildlife. Sportsmen in some locales seem to be unaware of an option later added to federal guidelines. Each state can either protect crows fully, except in cases of real or threatened depredation, or can treat them as migratory game birds—with a season running up to 120 days, a longer season than for many migratory species. The open days can be consecutive or, because shooting is prohibited during the spring nesting peak, a state can split its season.

Missouri, a good crow-hunting state in winter, runs an unsplit season from about the second week in November straight through about two weeks of March. Mississippi opens the season from early November through February. Some states keep the season open longer by establishing "rest days" when birds may not be shot. In Tennessee you can shoot crows from June through February, but only on Fridays, Saturdays, and Sundays, and in Virginia you can shoot them from August through February, but not on Sundays, Mondays, or Tuesdays.

The split seasons also work very well, providing fine sport during some months when normal game-bird seasons are closed. At least nine states have now adopted this arrangement. Two of them, Pennsylvania and Rhode Island, permit crow hunting only on Fridays, Saturdays, and Sundays.

Pennsylvania and New Jersey, where I do much of my hunting, typify the different ways of conducting a split season. In Pennsylvania, crows may be hunted on weekends, Friday through Sunday, from early January until mid-April and from early June through late August. As in a number of states, no other game can be legally hunted on Sundays, so crows have enlarged the weekend sporting possibilities. In New Jersey, the season runs from the beginning of August through September and from early January through March, and you can hunt on any day except Sunday.

Many states have chosen the other federal option, opening no game season on crows but allowing shooting when depredation is committed or threatened. Some states take the official position that crows within their boundaries are always committing or about to commit depredations. Arizona, Maryland, and West Virginia—to name a few—use this approach in order to protect their crops.

So do the two best crow-hunting states, Oklahoma and Texas. Their stance is not a strategem to mock federal law but a realistic attitude where the wintering grounds of crows include local roosting areas occupied by, literally, millions of the birds. Crows can be shot there in spring and summer, but few are. In winter, when the roosts fill with migrant crows, the motels fill with migrant sportsmen.

Migrating crows funnel into Oklahoma and Texas from breeding grounds that stretch from Alberta to Ontario and from Montana to the Mississippi. All of our states have crows, but in some regions, the birds are less plentiful or make only short migratory flights. In general, the best crow hunting is in winter on the grain-growing farmlands from lower Kansas and Missouri into Arkansas, Oklahoma, and Texas. In some years, it has been estimated that up to 60 percent of the continent's crow population winters in those last two states. The same traditional roost areas attract the birds each year. If severely disturbed, the crows temporarily move from their roosts, but they don't go very far. The peak of the season is from late December to mid-March.

The most famous of all roosting areas is around Fort Cobb Reservoir in Oklahoma. This enormous roost has hosted up to 10 million birds in some seasons. Fort Cobb is north of Lawton, southeast of Oklahoma City, off U.S. Route 62. The motels in the area cater to crow hunters during the winter. The shore of the reservoir—the actual roosting site—is maintained as a refuge. The best shooting is in the sprawling feeding areas and along the flyways that the birds habitually use to reach those areas, roughly from 15 to 50 miles in all directions from the refuge. You'll probably be able to find a guide; if not, local conservation officers can direct you to good locations, and so can the Department of Wildlife Conservation at Oklahoma City. There are fine public hunting areas (state lands) as well as private farms. Here, as well as in the other recommended states, most farmers welcome crow shooters, but if you fail to ask permission first you're trespassing.

In Texas, the heaviest concentrations are in the Panhandle and south of it, from Shamrock (just west of the Oklahoma line) down to the area of Sweetwater and neighboring Colorado City (due west of Abilene). Other parts of the state have big roosts in the rice-growing areas and where good stands of roosting trees mark the coastal prairies. Near Houston, for example, there's excellent shooting around Sealy and southward along the Brazos River. In this state, the best sources of information are the city chambers of commerce. Probably the biggest roost, holding several million birds, is the one near Shamrock, which is situated at the junction of U.S. 83 and Interstate 40.

Missouri formerly vied with Oklahoma and Texas but has lost a lot of prime winter roosts, its bottomland hardwoods, to agriculture. However, it still has a number of roosts that hold thousands of birds apiece. For example, there's one near Puxico in Stoddard County that generally holds about 15,000, and another near Malta Bend in Saline County generally holds about 10,000. The best areas are along the Mississippi and Missouri rivers. For a free annual survey of recommended roosting areas, you can write to the Missouri Department of Conservation, P.O. Box 180, Jefferson City, Mo. 65101.

Federal guidelines permit the use of "electronic" calling devices— that is, phonographs—for hunting crows. However, any state has the prerogative of prohibiting such devices. Check the regulations before you take a phonograph hunting.

Unless you have a friend who's an experienced crow-caller, the best way to learn calling is from instructional phonograph records and tapes—plus a lot of listening to live crows in your area. At first, the cries of these birds may sound monotonously alike, but crows have a big repertoire of communicative sounds. There are gathering calls, feeding calls, fighting calls, warning calls, and distress calls. On a couple of occasions, I've used a battery-operated phonograph, not just for learning purposes but to do the actual calling. Though it works well, I don't think it's quite as effective as using mouth-operated calls once the technique is mastered. The phonograph is loud and very lifelike, but it can't switch sounds instantly to fit a changing situation.

I have a pair of mouth-operated calls, one higher-pitched than the other, and some hunters carry three manual calls to vary the tone. On humid, windy days, the high-pitched call carries farther without losing clarity, while on calm, clear days, the low pitch carries far enough and imitates most crow cries more realistically. There are two other reasons for carrying two calls. First, crows sometimes get wise to the tone of a particular call and stop responding to it. Second, a flock will naturally retreat when the shooting starts but will sometimes return to a come-back call that has a new voice.

Three basic sounds are all you need, and by far the most useful is the loud, wailing distress call, a series of well-spaced *caws*. Use your diaphragm to push air forcefully from your lungs while you use your vocal chords, mouth, and cupped hand to impart resonance and a moaning quality. The late Bert Popowski, a champion at this, described it as saying "oooh, oooh, oooh" through the call, while blowing hard enough to make the reed vibrate fully. This usually brings crows to investigate. If they do so cautiously, you may be able to coax them closer by keeping up the repetition but adding more pounding excitement, or by switching to a mixture of babbling and occasional long notes that often signals the discovery of food, or by interspersing the more strident (but not too high and choppy) fighting and scolding notes.

The second important call is the aforementioned "comeback." Intermittent gunfire won't scare crows off for very long, unless they've seen you or one of them has been stung by a pellet. Even if you've downed a few, the others can sometimes be brought back by a four-note sequence: two fairly short, punchy blasts followed by two slightly longer ones (but not as long as the distress wail). Try to get a commanding sound into this—as if a crow were yelling for comrades to return and share a new discovery. Use it sparingly, with a rest after a couple of quick repetitions. Then switch back to the distress call.

The third important sound is a "mourning" call that crows seem to utter in sympathy when one of their number is crippled and moves about on the ground, dragging a wing. Occasionally it's also heard over a dead bird. It's lower-pitched and more drawn-out than the distress call. Crows will gang in the sky over a grounded cripple. Use this dirge for a short period to bring the crows wheeling, and then switch back to the more urgent distress call to bring them right over.

The notion that feeding crows post sentinels is absurd, since each bird stands guard for itself, but advance scouts do frequently precede a flock in the air, and they can somehow warn the flock away from danger without sounding the usual alarm. One, two, or three birds may come over first, cautiously, before the others are in sight. If they come in close enough for me to be sure of my shots, I bring them down. The others will come searching for them. But if I'm not sure I can kill them, I stay hidden and hold my fire. If missed or shot-stung, they'll turn back and warn the others away.

Crows have excellent vision—in full color—and they're sensitive to movement and reflections. Moreover, if you're skeptical about their vaunted intelligence, try pointing a stick or broom handle up in the air next time crows fly over. If they've been shot at, they'll veer away from anything that looks like a skyward-pointing gun. It's a good rule to stay hidden until the instant you're ready to shoot, and keep your gun down. Very often a blind isn't quite enough concealment. Wear camouflage clothing, or at least clothing that will blend with your hiding spot.

Very often you can find a natural blind in a desirable location, but at some time during the day—most often in the afternoon—you may be cruising the countryside looking and listening for crows, and the choicest spot you find may lack sufficient concealment. For a portable blind, all you need is a roll of camouflaged wire mesh. I like to hunt with three companions and two such blinds. We try to set up the blinds about 100 yards apart in shady tangles along the upwind edge of a flyway. With two men in each blind, each hunter takes birds only on his side.

If one man is a particularly adept crow mimic, he does all the calling for his blind, but there should be at least one caller in each blind. Facing downwind, we know the calling will carry far. Besides, when birds prepare to dip low or land, they most often approach into the prevailing breeze.

In the North, tall conifers surrounded by open spaces often seem to be favorite roosting sites, though hardwoods and mixed stands also hold a great many birds. In the South, clumps of willows are often used, and in some western locales the birds are willing to roost in fairly low shrubs. Almost any grove may be used if water is nearby and food supplies are within flying distance.

Since food is a key to location, you can scout the countryside for grainfields as well as roosts. Crows are more or less omnivorous, but they have strong preferences for certain crops, such as corn and peanuts. Other preferred foods include wheat, sorghum, oats, barley, rice, acorns, cherries, and apples. Fields with substantial quantities of waste grain are always promising. So are the feed lots used to fatten livestock. And in some areas, so are slaughterhouses. Crows use habitual flyways between the roosts and feeding areas, and these flyways offer the best sites for a blind. Never shoot near the roost itself. You ought to stay at least a mile away to prevent the birds from temporarily abandoning the roost. I don't mind shooting closer to a feeding field, because it takes a lot of shooting to dissuade crows from returning to a rich food source.

Flyways are sometimes very sharply defined—with big flocks repeatedly moving along distinct, narrow corridors. I don't shoot from right under one of these flight lanes. Instead I pick a spot well off to one side for my blind and decoys. The fringes of the flights and the pods of stragglers will come over me or can be enticed over, and they offer plenty of fast shooting. On the other hand, the big concentrated flocks in the main corridor often ignore decoys and calls. In part, this is because the birds themselves sometimes make so much noise. And in part, it's probably because a bird hemmed in by many other birds all flying in one direction is reinforced in its purposefulness and is unlikely to change course.

Crows start leaving their roosts about dawn, and the next few hours generally offer the best shooting along the flyways.

After lunch, if you haven't had enough action for the day, the best tactic is to cruise the area, using your ears and binoculars to locate crows in the fields or up in the trees, where they occasionally retire for a rest. Get fairly near these places and start calling. The birds often move from field to field and will fly toward the sound of other crows.

By midafternoon, some of the flocks start grouping with others in "staging areas"—often woodlots adjacent to feeding fields. These aren't roosts, but merely gathering spots where they merge for the flight to the roost. You may get some good shooting near these places—or in the woods themselves—in late afternoon, but crows going to roost don't respond to calls and decoys as well as morning flights.

There are two primary ways to use crow decoys, and from personal experience, I'd say they're about equally effective if used in conjunction with skillful calling. If the calling leaves something to be desired, I favor the use of plenty of big black decoys—stick-ups propped in the ground, plus quite a few up in trees and shrubs or on fence posts where their silhouettes can be seen at great distances. Those on the ground should look like a feeding flock in a stubble field, and they should be out in front of the blind so that approaching flocks will dip toward you into the wind. When you begin to toll the birds in, you can add kills to your stool. Some hunters add every bird downed, but I'm a bit conservative about this. I don't want to be in the open continually, propping birds in lifelike positions, and I have a notion that crows can sometimes tell that a lot of dead birds on the ground are a lot of dead birds on the ground. So I try not to overdo it.

The second basic type of stool is the owl or owl-and-crow rig. Owls and crows are enemies, and when several crows spot an owl, they'll mob it. At one time, mounted owls were commonly used as decoys, but even a moth-eaten old "stuffed" owl is becoming hard to find. Inexpensive lifelike plastic models of horned owls work very well and are available wherever crow decoys are sold. An owl all by itself will attract crows if perched conspicuously, but you have to call attention to it. Start with the distress call, and then mix in some shorter, angrier-sounding blasts—a fighting call. An owl decoy on a pole or in a tree will do, but even better is to enhance the tableau with two or three crow decoys. These are propped in front or more or less on the sides, on branches a little higher than the owl. Now it looks as if the crows are harrassing the owl and calling for reinforcements.

The raven, a scarce and fully protected species, is closely related to the crow. There's seldom any danger of shooting a raven by mistake because most ravens now inhabit wilderness areas. (They're extremely vulnerable to persecution and do not benefit from human activity as crows do.) If you do hunt in an area still inhabited by ravens, you can easily distinguish them from crows. First, ravens are considerably larger and look more hawklike in the air. They flap less and soar more than crows, and when soaring, they hold their wings flat out, whereas a soaring crow angles its wings upward. A raven can also be distinguished by its thicker bill and shaggy throat ruff. At a distance, the bill and throat ruff may not be clearly visible, but the tail will be. A crow's tail is fan-shaped. That of a raven is wedge-shaped, widening and then tapering again.

DEER

Whitetails

Because whitetail deer are hunted in a fairly wide variety of cover, a rifle and load appropriate for one region may not be a wise choice for another. In thick Northern woods, for example, the .30-30 Winchester and .35 Remington cartridges in lever-actions are almost as popular as they are old, and lever-actions chambered for the .32 Winchester Special are still seen frequently. In the relatively open terrain in parts of the West and Midwest, .243 bolt-actions (and other bolt-actions in that general class) are quite popular, especially among hunters who use the same rifle for shooting prairie dogs, chucks, or predators. I'm not saying that .30-30 lever-actions aren't used on Western prairies or that .243 bolt-actions aren't seen in the Northeastern timber; they certainly are. But I'm putting more emphasis here on common sense than common practice.

To keep this tip clear and simple, I'll restrict it to cartridges and discuss action types separately. The famous cartridges I've just mentioned are good enough, but I don't consider any of them best, even when used in the appropriate setting. I've said before that the .308 is probably the best rifle chambering ever employed for whitetail hunting, and nothing has happened to change my mind. I need only add that too heavy a bullet can detract from its efficiency on whitetails. A 180-grain bullet is fine for elk, but it expands too slowly to produce consistently clean kills on game the size of a whitetail. The 150-grain bullet in the .308 is just right. I consider it ideal in brushy or timbered country, and more than good enough in open terrain, even though several other cartridges will equal its performance in Western hunting.

There are, however, a number of other calibers that merit recommendation, and you may have reason to choose one of them on the basis of cover where you hunt or employment on several different kinds of game. The .44 Magnum is excellent at short range—

that is, in brush or timber. Some hunters like the idea of having the same chambering in a handgun and rifle, and this is easily done with the .44 Magnum. (Incidentally, I know of at least one manufacturer that offers a .357 Magnum rifle, and of course that's a marvelous handgun caliber, but I doubt that it will ever gain wide acceptance as a rifle chambering.) Other excellent cartridges are the .270, .280, .284, and .30-06, and these have a couple of big advantages. First, they can be used effectively on a variety of game, from pronghorns to sheep to moose. Second, they'll perform well at short or long range, in woods or on the plains. As with the .308, just be sure to use a bullet weight that's appropriate for whitetails. I'd call 125 grains minimum, 165 maximum, 150 ideal.

Still other cartridges—including some with lighter bullets—are excellent in open terrain where velocity can be a critical factor. In addition to the aforementioned .243 and the 6mm with 100-grain bullets, there are the .25-06 with 120-grain bullets and the .264 with 140-grain bullets. Then there's the too-soon-forgotten 6.5mm Magnum with 120-grain bullets. Just once—some years ago—I used a 6.5mm to kill a Texas whitetail. It performed so well that I was sorry it failed to achieve greater popularity. I could list a few more cartridges, but I think I've named the best of them for whitetails.

Now, what about the type of action? In timbered country, the levers are still favorites, partly because they're light, short-barreled, and quick-handling, and partly because they're handsome and romantically traditional. But they have several serious drawbacks. They restrict your choice of cartridges, some of them present scoping problems, and their factory-installed open sights aren't exactly the best aiming equipment to be had. I'd be content to use a lever-action in timber, but only if it had a scope or peep sight installed.

Pump rifles are all right, too, and they come in a slightly wider variety of chamberings. Autoloaders, which come in a still wider variety, have the advantage of the fastest possible repeat shots, but I wonder if that's as desirable as many hunters suppose. I've seen too many shots rushed with autoloaders, and I've seen volleys fired as if the shooter thought his object was to take a beachhead instead of a deer. Some writers have speculated that the use of autos may increase the number of injured and unrecovered game animals. They may be right, though the fault is the shooter's, not the rifle's. For sporting purposes, I think the real advantage of the autoloading system (and it's certainly a minor one) is convenience and ease of handling rather than speed.

The bolt-action comes in more calibers than the others and, generally speaking, it's the most accurate of the lot. Having taken deer with a scoped bolt-action both in tangled brush and in open country, I'd be pretty hard to convince that it doesn't handle fast and smoothly enough for any kind of cover. As for repeat fire, a skilled rifleman can get off an *aimed* second shot with a bolt rifle almost as quickly as with an auto.

The most popular rifle-scope magnification for deer is 4X. I like that power for long shots in open country. I even like it for some of my woods hunting, but only because it lets me make a careful, last-second appraisal of antlers. While using a 2½X scope, I once passed up a spike buck because I couldn't see his spikes clearly. He was legal, all right, and a few minutes later he became venison for a hunter on a ridge above me. All the same, a 2½X or a variable is best for most woods hunting. There are a few locales where the brush is so thick that you may not want a scope at all, in which case a peep sight is in order.

Among handgunners, the three most popular calibers are .357 Magnum, .41, and .44 Magnum—as well they should be. Personally, I like the .357 because I can take its recoil easily, and I can use light .38 Special loads in it for target practice.

A scope is an unwieldy encumbrance on a handgun, and some hunters just won't use one. They argue that whitetails can be taken by bow-hunters, by shotgunners, and by hunters using "primitive" arms—percussion guns and even flintlocks that usually employ open sights—so a proficient marksman should be able to kill a deer cleanly with an open-sighted handgun at reasonable range, which generally means 75 yards or less. I'm hardly qualified to refute that argument since I've used an open-sighted .357 Magnum revolver in the woods. However, I feel constrained to add that a scope can be a great help (and can stretch the range somewhat) in open terrain. Some shooters favor a 2X scope. I think 1½X is probably sufficient for whitetails, though I've had much longer shots at mule deer, and I can understand why the 2X is gaining adherents.

Many hunters have the impression that handgun hunting for deer is allowed in only a few Western states. On the contrary, it's permissible at present in 28 states, Eastern as well as Western, and a couple more may change their regulations to accommodate handgun hunters. Check with the game department of the state where you plan to hunt. And don't just check whether sidearms can be used at all but *which ones* can be used. Many states have caliber restrictions—quite reasonable restrictions, to assure that adequate cartridges will be used.

Actually, you must check your state regulations carefully no matter what type of arm you want to use. There are special seasons for archery and for hunting with muzzleloaders. There are more than a dozen states where deer hunting with a rifle is prohibited, or hampered by severe restrictions, or permitted only in designated areas. Generally this means you must use a shotgun during the regular season. In some states you can use either buckshot or rifled slugs, while in others you must use slugs. And this sort of thing can get complicated. Virginia permits only slugs in some counties, only buckshot in others. As a rule, all those restrictions aren't as unreasonable as they seem. In very densely populated areas, a rifle bullet travels too far for safe use. Obviously, Virginia considers even rifled slugs to have too great a lethal range for safety in some areas. On the other hand, buckshot is the least efficient of all ammunition for deer under normal circumstances, and is likely to be outlawed where slugs or bullets are considered safe. No doubt this prohibition has reduced the number of wounded and unrecovered deer. For the same reason, there are restrictions in most states on rifle caliber and/or shotgun bore size.

With a shotgun, repeat fire is often crucial, even if the first load connects. Double-barreled guns are fine for small game, but I much prefer the extra shots in a pump or auto for deer. (Several companies also make bolt-action shotguns, and they, too, are good on deer.) Besides, doubles present scope-mounting problems, and not many of them have the right chokes for buckshot or slugs.

Shotguns intended specifically for deer hunting with rifled slugs usually come with rifle-type open sights. These are far better than an ordinary shotgun bead for slug shooting. In fairly open woods where you don't have to rush your shots, you may find that a peep sight serves you better yet. A good many hunters prefer a low-power scope—usually 2X or less. I approve of a scope for anyone who can use one effectively, but for fast shots in thick woods, I myself do just as well with a peep.

In parts of the Southeast where the cover is very heavy, a hunter can spend a great deal of time in the bottomland woods without ever seeing a deer, much less getting a shot at one. This is the region— from Florida's panhandle up through the lower halves of Georgia, Alabama, and Mississippi—where packs of hounds are traditionally (and legally, of course) used to push deer across openings or relatively sparse brush where hunters wait on stand. It's also one region where buckshot is more efficient than slugs, and buckshot is most often used except where the law decrees slugs only. Here, a pattern of pellets is surer than a single projectile because the cover is so thick, the deer are moving, and the range is usually short enough that the pellets don't lose much energy before striking. I'll have more to say about the use of dogs, but first let's finish all the details about guns and ammunition. In most states, guns from 12 to 20 gauge are legal. A 20 will do, but the 12 is obviously best, whether with slugs or pellets. My buckshot choice is the 3-inch Magnum 12, as the shell carries several more pellets than the shorter 12's.

In the South, No. 1 Buck—a medium pellet size—is the favorite, as it puts a few more pellets into the pattern than the larger sizes. But some hunters bank on more energy per pellet on target, so they use No. 0 or even "Double 0," the biggest. Those are the sizes—0 and 00—that are most popular in the North, where thinner cover makes for longer shots. Personally, I prefer No. 1's. "Medium" is a relative term, and No. 1 Buck isn't exactly puny. No. 4 Buck, the smallest, is much bigger and heavier than No. 4 birdshot. Some hunters chamber a load of small buckshot for the first shot and keep loads of bigger shot in the magazine for follow-ups. The theory is that the extra pellets in the small size will provide multiple hits and probably bring a deer down, but they may not kill it; the larger pellets will supply more energy per hit for a longer second shot or coup de grace.

A cylinder boring used to be deemed the only good choice for buckshot, as the slightest choke so drastically deformed the big pellets that they patterned erratically. In today's shells, powdered plastic filler cushions the pellets and reduces deformation so effectively that gunners favor a full choke for delivery of a tight pattern. Though a full choke is usually best, every gun performs differently with various shot sizes and brands of ammunition. I have a gun with an adjustable choke device that patterns best at the modified setting, particularly with the largest buckshot sizes. It's essential to pattern your gun before hunting, not only to check on this, but to check whether it shoots high (or anywhere but point of aim), as many guns do. If you have a variable choke, you can experiment to see which constriction works best with your chosen ammunition. If you can't adjust the choke, you can experiment to see which ammunition works best with your gun.

Hunters frequently argue about the maximum effective range of buckshot. The knowledgeable ones don't like to try for deer at more than 60 yards or so, but you can answer the question for yourself—and more precisely—when you do your patterning. Actually, the maximum effective range is the distance at which you can consistently get more than three pellets into a 20-inch area (the size of a deer's heart and lung zone). If your gun won't do that with your chosen pellet size, try the next smaller size or, if you have a variable choke, try another setting.

Some of today's slug guns are cylinder-bored while others have a slug boring that's close to cylinder. An open boring is best for slug shooting, but a modern rifled slug will not ream out a full choke or harm it in any way. An American-made 12-gauge slug has a diameter of no more than .695-inch, and it will slide right through. Even the German-made Brenneke slugs will do no harm, though the fit may be tighter. The Brennekes have a reputation for accuracy, but they're expensive and not readily available, and the standard American type will do just about as well when fired in the same gun by the same shooter.

I like to sight in a slug gun at 100 yards or nearly that, even though I don't expect (or want) many shots at quite that distance. With slugs, I'm worried about the chance of a clean kill at anything more than about 75 yards. But if the slug hits point of aim at 100, it won't be more than three inches above the line of sight at 50. So if I sight in at 100, I don't have to hold low for short shots. At 100 yards, by the way, a slug group that measures about eight inches across is satisfactory, so this isn't quite like sighting in a rifle. Even at half that distance, a three-inch group is tight enough to satisfy me. To call this accuracy is a semantic stretch, but it's good enough to take deer in appropriate shotgunning cover where the range is short—or where, at least, you should restrict yourself to short shots.

Most slug guns have short barrels, which make them smoothbore carbines, an asset for this kind of brush shooting. And they not only have rifle-type sights but sling swivels. When you're dragging a deer out, you have your hands full, and a sling is a great help. Moreover, I consider it a necessity when I shinny up a tree with a self-climbing tree stand.

About those Southern hunts with hounds. Unlike other forms of deer hunting, they don't require an early start in the morning. The hunters in a camp or club get into the woods around nine in the morning for a run lasting a couple of hours, and then repeat the procedure in the afternoon. A good drive is likely to employ about eight hounds, with a handler-driver to every two dogs. At the end of the tract to be driven, the standers fan out in a rough arc, taking stands at intervals of perhaps 100 yards.

The dogs should have keen noses, but not too much speed or aggression, because the object is to stir the deer up and move them toward the drivers, but never to panic them. The game should be made alert to the intrusion, mildly nervous, but never terrorized. Apart from humane considerations, if a deer is pushed too hard, it will double back, sneak out to one side, or run too fast for anyone to get a shot in the thick cover. No single type of hound is considered best, and mixed breeds predominate. They work noisily to keep the game moving, but slowly to avoid overtaking it.

Generally, the drivers are 200 to 300 yards behind the dogs, and any whitetail is apt to be 300 to 500 yards in front of the pack. Shots have to be made quickly, at briskly moving deer, through any relatively bare spots in the cover. Most such shots are made at considerably less than 50 yards, and the limit should be no more than 75.

There are 17 subspecies of whitetail deer in Canada and the United States, and almost as many more from the Mexican border through Central America. The North American varieties range in size from the tiny, scarce, and protected Key deer of southern Florida—animals weighing an average of about 50 pounds—to the Northern whitetail, the only subspecies that frequently weighs more than 200 pounds (although occasional specimens of several other races attain enormous proportions). The Northern whitetail is found in some of the finest deer-hunting regions—southern Canada, New England, New York, Pennsylvania, Wisconsin, Michigan, and Minnesota. But the biggest whitetails don't always come from those regions or belong to that subspecies. The Dakota whitetail is another big one. So is the Virginia whitetail, which is found throughout the Southeast. So is the Kansas whitetail, which is found in eastern Texas, Oklahoma, Kansas, Nebraska, Iowa, Missouri, Arkansas, and Louisiana. Many of the record antlers, by the way, represent Northern and Kansas whitetails. In recent years, Missouri has been an outstanding producer of big whitetails.

Bear in mind that the ranges overlap, that natural interbreeding occurs and that a great deal of transplanting and restocking was done early in this century when the deer herds in many regions had been severely depleted. Many of today's deer are mixtures of at least two subspecies, and we probably have more whitetails in North America now than at any time since the discovery of the New World. The mature forests that once typified much of the country supported few deer. Whitetails need brush, edge habitat, and young second growth to give them cover and plenty of reachable browse, so they've benefitted from human settlement in many regions.

However, the deer herds have become too big for the carrying capacity of the habitat in numerous locales. This results in winter starvation. High winter kills are one reason why antlerless deer seasons have been found desirable. Malnutrition can also result in stunting but, nationally, the average size remains fairly impressive. A mature whitetail buck is likely to weigh between 135 and 165 pounds, a doe between 125 and 150. (These are live weights, generally about 25 percent more than the field-dressed weights.) And every now and then, someone takes a buck weighing well over 200 pounds. There are a few records of whitetails weighing almost twice that much.

Some of the smaller varieties of whitetails are worth a hard-hunting effort. For example, the Coues, or Arizona, whitetail—sometimes called fantail in reference to the very large tail—is an elusive animal, difficult to hunt in its arid domain. It seldom weighs much over 100 pounds and doesn't have a huge rack, though it's ears are big enough to make it look somewhat like a mule deer. It has adapted to the Sonora Desert and mountains of northern Mexico, Arizona, New Mexico, and southeastern California. Most whitetails are incapable of surviving in such arid country, and they're scarce or absent in much of California, Nevada, Colorado, Arizona, Idaho, and the drier portions of Washington and Oregon (though mule deer and blacktails are abundant in some of those areas). The Arizona whitetail gets much of its water from cactus, but waterholes are always worth scouting or waiting at. I don't have harvest figures, but hunting for the Coues whitetail is fairly good in New Mexico and better in Arizona.

Another small but particularly interesting subspecies is the Carmen Mountains whitetail, whose range is limited to the Carmen range on both sides of the Rio Grande. This means it's found in the Big Bend region of Texas. These deer have such evenly forked antlers that they often look like undersized muleys. They aren't hunted much because most of their habitat falls within the boundaries of Big Bend National Park, where no hunting is allowed. Apparently, no interbreeding occurs with the much larger Texas whitetails. They're separated by a buffer of semidesert where only mule deer occur.

I've mentioned some of the best-known hunting regions and types of deer, but Texas merits a separate comment. Texas has more whitetails than any other state—an estimated 3½ million and an annual harvest averaging over 350,000. There are four subspecies, with overlapping ranges and some interbreeding. The Texas whitetail, found in the western part of the state, is the most numerous and the largest of the southerly races. The antlers are slender but widespread, and a couple of Texas whitetails are among the top heads in the Boone & Crockett record book.

This Tennessee hunter is about to collect a fine whitetail buck. Note that even at close range a buck's rack can be hard to make out if the animal is standing among trees, because the antlers blend with the lacework pattern of branches and twigs.

There's more than one way to tell a whitetail from a mule deer. Antlers are the most easily visible indicator, though not always the most reliable. A whitetail's main beams curve rearward, out, up, and forward if they're beyond the spike stage, and usually hook inward near the tips. The tines grow upward from these beams. A muley's main beams fork and then fork again, each beam forming a pair of Y shapes like the crotches of hardwood trees. Usually, though certainly not always, a muley's antlers are higher than a whitetail's, in proportion to their spread, and the brow tines tend to be smaller, though the total rack may be much larger.

A muley's ears are, of course, larger than a whitetail's, but they aren't always much help in field identification. The tail is a better mark of recognition. That of a whitetail, sometimes more than a foot long, is wide and pennant-shaped. Its rear, or outer surface, is the tannish color of the animal's back, sometimes flecked or streaked with black. The inner surface is bright white. Those inner hairs are longer than the outer ones, so you may see a white border. And when the tail goes up, as it does when the animal is alarmed, you'll see plenty of white tail and whitish inner rump; hence, the name of the species. A muley's tail is much narrower—rope-shaped. At the top it's brownish, but the major portion is white, and it has a black tip about two inches long. Blacktail deer are a subspecies—or rather, two distinct subspecies—of Far Western mule deer. Each of these races has a narrow cylindrical tail, shorter and a bit brushier than that of other mule deer. The skimpily haired underside of the tail is white. The outer surface is black or dark brown, often looking like a vertical black stripe. Neither mule deer nor blacktails raise their tails high to show a conspicuous white flag, as a whitetail does.

A whitetail of either sex can be aged accurately by a couple of laboratory methods involving either tooth sections or eye tissue, and it can be aged roughly by a layman who has learned to judge tooth wear. But the notion that a buck's age can be seen in his antlers is a partial misconception. A "button buck" is usually a deer in his first autumn—born the previous spring. By his second autumn he'll probably be a spike buck with fairly straight antlers three to six inches long, but if the browse in his habitat is ample, nutritious, and mineral-rich, he may be a forkhorn. The forking more often develops during the third summer—that is, on his third set of antlers— yet two-year-olds occasionally have six or eight points. Although it's true that in the majority of cases the antlers are largest, heaviest, and adorned with the greatest number of tines in the fourth or fifth year, it's equally true that after the third year, the number of points indicates nothing but the quality of the habitat. And even in good habitat, an old buck, no longer producing the hormones of his youth, may revert to spikes or fail to sprout any antlers at all.

In most parts of the country, dogs are neither necessary nor legal for driving deer, but there are locales where the traditional drives are so big and noisy as to be reminiscent of the Southern hounding method. I recall one in the Jersey Pine Barrens that involved more than two dozen men. This is a shotguns-only state, with buckshot permitted in 10- or 12-gauge guns, or slugs in any gauge from 10 to 20. Most of the men used buckshot because the cover was very heavy and any shots were going to be fleeting. The area to be driven was a big, dense woodlot bordered by a small field and several narrow dirt roads. Thus the standers were able to station themselves in a very wide U formation along the roads and part of the field at the downwind end of the lot, and any deer driven from the woods would have no choice about where to emerge. They'd have to cross the openings. The drivers also formed themselves into a wide U, with the flankers slightly in advance to reduce the chance that a buck could cut out to the side without being spotted. Then the drivers beat their way through the woods, whooping, kicking at deadfalls, and in a couple of cases even blowing whistles. Before they'd gone halfway through, out came several whitetails, including two nice bucks. They were in high gear, but both were downed.

Such big, noisy drives are generally conducted where the cover is dense and shotguns are used. However, the same beating technique is sometimes adapted to rifles. In this case, safety dictates very wide intervals between standers and also between drivers, and the men must abide by strict rules as to who may shoot, when shots may be made, and in which directions. Generally, this is practical only where the tract to be driven is sizable and the woods are fairly thick. One man should captain the drive and should give a prearranged signal to begin and end it.

The more traditional Northern style is a small, quiet drive. This works best in relatively small patches of cover—less than a square mile—where the woods can be combed thoroughly by the drivers and where the edges have good visibility for the standers. Notches, swamps, brushy valleys or gulleys, and woodlots are good examples.

STANDERS

WIND DIRECTION

WOODLOT

DRIVERS

In this diagram of a typical whitetail drive through a woodlot, the broken arrows show the probable direction of deer movement. The short arrows identify the drivers and show the direction of their movement. Standers wait at the downwind end of the woods, as the hunters want game to scent the drivers but not the standers. The lines of standers and drivers are roughly cupped to outflank deer that emerge at the sides rather than the end of the woods being driven. In reality, of course, the woodlot would be much larger; it's reduced in the diagram to show all elements of the drive.

Usually half a dozen or so men participate, half as drivers and half as standers. If one end of the tract to be driven has high ground—a ridge or slope—the standers can station themselves there. The deer will tend to head upward, and chances are good that the men above won't be scented or seen too soon. If there's no high ground, the standers should be at the downwind edge. The drivers have the wind at their backs. They *want* to be scented in order to push the deer toward the standers. As in the bigger, noisier drives, both the standers and the drivers work in broad, shallow U formations to intercept game moving out to the sides. Again, good organization is necessary, and one man should captain the proceedings. Whereas a big, beating drive works in very thick cover, a small, quiet drive works much better in thinner woods. If there is too much commotion, the deer may slip right back through the line of drivers, or come steaming out at 35 miles an hour. But quiet movement will gently prod the deer along, walking or trotting, so the standers (and occasionally a driver) will have a chance for a well-aimed shot. If proper safety precautions are observed, this type of drive is fine for rifle hunting.

The truth is, you can't really drive deer; that is, you can't herd them, you can't force them to emerge where or when you'd like. All you can do is stir them up and get them moving more or less ahead of you. Often they'll circle back or flank out. But if you proceed as described here, the men in the U formations will get shots. The standers will get more shots than the drivers, so the jobs should be switched on the next drive.

Very small drives are practical where the terrain is right. For example, one driver can walk the bottom of a long ridge, while a second driver, hanging back just a bit, moves along in the same direction about halfway up the slope. Far ahead and fairly high on the slope should be one stander. And one or two more standers should be stationed along the crest. Any whitetail on the slope is likely to move ahead of the drivers and upward—toward the men on the crest or the man part-way up.

A variation of this is a three-man drive along a ridge, with no standers at all. One man moves along the crest of the ridge, while the two flankers keep ahead and a couple of hundred yards down on each side. Any deer bedded or browsing high on the ridge will move

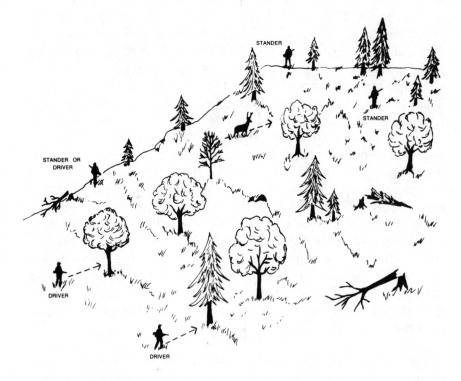

A fairly steep, long ridge is good terrain for a deer drive involving few hunters. One man walks the bottom of the slope. A second driver, hanging back a bit, moves in the same direction on a line about halfway up. A stander stations himself far ahead and high on the ridge to intercept the game being pushed toward him. It helps to have at least one more man up on the crest. Usually he takes a stand but, depending on the terrain and the progress of the drive, he may combine the functions of driver and stander.

When a deer has been spotted and can be tracked, three partners can work effectively. One trails the game directly while the others work ahead and to the sides. A whitetail is likely to become aware that it's being stalked, and usually it will circle around. This will often cause it to cross one of the flankers and present him with a shot.

out ahead of the man at the top and probably veer around to one side or the other, so one of the three hunters should get a shot. I've heard it said that this kind of drive works best if the wind is at your back because a deer will try to circle around to get upwind of the center hunter. In my experience, it's better to move into the wind. That way the deer won't catch scent long before you get close, and most often he'll still move to one side or the other, giving someone a shot.

If a deer has been spotted and can be tracked, a three-man drive of that sort can be staged, regardless of whether the animal is on a ridge. One man trails the deer directly, while his partners work to the sides and a little ahead. Usually, a whitetail will soon become aware that he's being followed and will cut to one side, trying to circle around. This means he'll probably cross one of the flankers.

A simple three-man drive along a ridge requires no standers. One man moves along the crest. The flankers keep slightly ahead of him and a couple of hundred yards down on each side. Deer high on the ridge will move out ahead of the man on the crest and usually cut to one side or the other—across one of the flankers.

Another kind of three-man drive works where deer habitually use an upward-sloping saddle or pass to reach high ground. Two of the men work their way up from the bottom along such a natural funnel, spreading out enough that one of them has a chance for a shot if a deer veers off course. The third man waits above, at the upper end of the funnel.

Three men, or just two, can stage a circle drive. One of them is the stander, and he moves as quietly as possible to a chosen stand—preferably an elevation such as a big boulder, stump, or log pile. A

Where game trails lead from low feeding to high bedding grounds by way of an upward-sloping saddle or pass, a three-man drive can work. Two of the hunters move from the bottom up along the natural funnel, keeping far enough to the sides for a shot if a deer turns off to the left or right. The third man waits at the top. Since game doesn't stay precisely on such deer runs, additional flankers will add to the chance of success.

second man simply moves in a wide circle around him. If there's a third man, he moves in the same direction but even farther out. The width of the circle depends on the cover. In thick stuff, a driver may be no more than 100 yards from the stander. In thin woods, the outer driver may be a quarter of a mile away. The basis of this maneuver is that a deer will try to circle around a driver. If there's only one driver, there's a chance the animal may circle away from the stander and never be seen, but just as often he'll circle in toward the stander. And if there's a third driver, farther out, either he or the stander may get a shot.

Just two men—without any stander—can sometimes drive a deer into position for a shot. The partners start walking together, into the wind. But one hunter soon stops while the other moves ahead. In dense woods, the lead man should be perhaps 60 or 70 yards ahead, in thin timber 150 or more. The lead man moves slowly, stopping now and then, making enough noise to alert but not panic a deer. The rear man follows as silently as possible. A deer will circle around and behind the lead man, trying to get downwind to catch a whiff of what's making the noise. And that will often bring the animal into view of the rear man.

A lone hunter certainly can't drive a whitetail, but if he's quiet and persistent, he can sometimes get a shot by tracking one, particularly on a light, fresh snow. The deer will usually be moving more or less into the wind, so he won't scent the hunter behind him too soon. Don't try to stay right on the deer's tracks. The animal will meander somewhat, following the easiest route or making detours to browse, and if he does become aware of you, he'll either run off—far ahead—or go off to one side. Your best bet is to parallel his trail on one side and then the other, making long, wide S-curves so you cross his trail frequently. If he goes high and into dense thickets, he may be preparing to bed down, and from there on you must move very cautiously, very quietly, hoping to jump him from his bed. If he shows no indication of bedding, sooner or later he'll make a slow browsing detour while you close the distance, and you may have a chance to get a shot.

Still-hunting—simply stalking through the woods quietly—is the most difficult and least productive method, but it does sometimes work, and it can be a great relief for a lone hunter after a couple of hours on stand have turned him numb and bored. I know a man who simply walks through the woods at a brisk walk, quietly but quickly, and no season goes by without his collecting venison. His way wouldn't work for most of us. It works for him because he hunts the same woods every fall, scouts them thoroughly again just before the season opens, knows where and when the deer are likely to be moving or bedded, and can shoot his rifle accurately almost as fast as if it were a shotgun. He literally jump-shoots his whitetails. But for the average sportsman, still-hunting means moving so slowly and pausing so frequently that occasionally it takes half an hour to cover 200 or 300 yards. An experienced still-hunter pauses, watches, and listens more than he walks. And he doesn't walk at a steady pace, because deer have superb hearing as well as a marvelous sense of smell. To a deer, a steady walk means the approach of a human. It's better to take a few steps, pause, take another couple of steps, and so on. This sounds like the uneven, leisurely movement of a browsing animal.

In addition to the sound of walking, some other noises can fool a whitetail instead of giving warning. A few hunters can emit a whistl-

Sometimes a lone hunter can track a deer successfully, particularly on a light, fresh snow. As a rule, it's a mistake to follow the tracks directly or to move noisily or too quickly. The deer will weave, detouring to browse or take the easiest route. Moreover, there's a very good chance that the deer will sooner or later become aware of you and veer off to one side. You'll therefore increase the likelihood of getting a shot if you parallel the trail on one side and then the other, making long, wide S-curves in order to cross the deer's tracks periodically.

ing snort like that of a buck, and if a rutting buck is nearby, the sound may bring him to investigate what sounds like a rival. A few also use calls to imitate a doe's calflike bawl. In my own experience, neither kind of calling has been very effective, but it's a fact that a whitetail is inquisitive enough to investigate almost any sound if it doesn't scare him. I know of hunters who use predator calls—the rabbit-in-distress squealers—to lure whitetails. This sort of thing works best during a rest from still-hunting or at a well-concealed stand, and it may be more effective than most hunters realize. All of us are occasionally guilty of giving up too soon. A deer responds very slowly, very cautiously, like a cat coming to a call. A buck may come within 40 yards but take half an hour to get there.

A better-known calling strategy is the Southwestern technique of "rattling" for bucks. A hunter makes himself comfortable in a good hide and rattles, bumps, and rubs a pair of heavy antlers collected during some previous year, making a sound like rutting bucks fighting each other or "shadow-boxing" a sapling. There's no particular time limit, but rattling works best if you pause every few minutes, resting from your exertions just as bucks do. There are several theories as to why this technique seldom works on Northern whitetails, but no matter; it does work in the Southwest.

Another Southwestern custom is the use of towers, sometimes called "high-sits." Wildlife soon accepts the presence of these elevated stands, which put a hunter up where he won't be seen or scented. It's possible to rattle for bucks from a tower, but rattling is more often done from a natural ground-level blind, and the towers (which originated long ago in Europe and are still used there) are employed chiefly as look-outs and shooting platforms. They command a grand view of game trails and browsing areas.

In other parts of the country, tree stands are used in the same way. Sometimes a hunter who owns wooded land builds a large, comfortable, permanent stand in a tree overlooking deer runs. In most regions, it's illegal to put up permanent stands on public lands or to mar the trees in any way.

This is one reason for the growing popularity of portable, "self-climbing" tree stands. Another obvious reason is that you can easily

A deer stand doesn't have to be up in a tree or in a concealing blowdown if the terrain is such that approaching game won't scent or see the hunter. Here, an Ontario hunter takes aim from a rock outcropping that's sufficiently high and downwind of a game trail.

change locations with such a stand. But this kind of contrivance is by no means flawless. On a typical model, an extension from the platform goes around the tree trunk to grip it. You slip your booted feet into straps on the platform and shinny up. When you get high enough, you shift your weight outward, and the platform stays put until you hug the tree again, shifting the weight inward and thus loosening the contrivance to shinny down. If you're careful, it isn't at all dangerous once you get the hang of it (which you can do in two minutes by experimenting and practicing with the thing just a couple of feet off the ground). All the same, I bought a safety belt as an accessory with my stand.

I also bought an accessory hand-piece that helps me shinny; without that, scrambling up can be difficult for anyone who isn't young and wiry.

A bigger problem with tree stands is that they bite into tree bark. In experimenting with mine, I found that it marred live beeches but did no harm at all to rougher, thicker-barked trees like oaks and maples. Where I do most of my hunting there's no law against these stands, but I'm subject to arrest if I mar a live tree. I therefore use my stand only on dead but solid trees or on live ones with resistant bark.

Portable, "self-climbing" tree stands are excellent whitetail blinds. The better models won't damage trees such as maples and oaks, which have thick, rough bark. The photo shows a hunter in New Jersey—one of the states with a shotguns-only rule. His shotgun has rifle-type sights and a carrying sling, both of which are just about essential for this kind of hunting.

Tree stands are especially popular among archers, because a bow—even a compound bow—has such a short effective range that hiding and camouflage are crucial. Don't let anyone tell you that deer never look up. They look up to nibble twigs, they look up in response to any sound from above, and they occasionally look up when climbing slopes. But a deer isn't likely to catch your scent if you're at least 15 feet off the ground, and the game seldom looks up that high unless you make a noise. In case it does look up, you want to be unnoticeable. Bow hunters and a few others wear camouflage coveralls and hats. Some also wear camouflage head nets or hoods, or daub the exposed parts of their skin with camouflage grease paint or burnt cork.

I'm a burnt-cork man myself. It's cheaper than grease paint, easy to use, and readily available (though the grease paint can be bought at many archery-equipment outlets and some general sporting-goods stores). I even have a pet type of cork—the kind that comes in some sherry bottles and has a plastic or wooden cap at one end. A capped cork is less messy to use. I hold the capped end, char the other end, and then just smear on the charcoal.

Like most mammals, deer are color-blind, so why bother with camouflage? Because a deer is accustomed to seeing the broken, dappled, amorphous shapes characteristic of brush and foliage, and can instantly spot large patches of a single unnatural tone. Many states require hunters to wear a certain expanse—say, 200 square inches—of bright orange, called "safety orange." Most states exempt bow hunters from this requirement, but in heavily hunted areas where the archery season and firearms season on deer overlap or run concurrently, it isn't a bad idea for an archer to wear an orange cap. When he's on stand, his head will be high enough above ground so that the orange won't spook a deer. By the way, you can now buy orange hunting garments printed with darker splotches in a camouflage pattern. The orange stands out like a beacon for other hunters, but all a deer can see is the camouflage dappling.

A 7X35 binocular is another highly recommended piece of equipment. Though it's a common accessory where the vistas are wide and long, it's seldom seen in brush and thick second-growth timber such as the Pennsylvania woods where I often hunt—and I'll admit I've neglected to take mine along on occasion. Yet a binocular can be very helpful even in fairly thick cover. It won't let you see through a screen of shrubs and scrub, of course, but it serves another purpose there. It helps you perceive parts of the deer in the brush and dim little openings amid foliage. I seldom see a whole deer in my woods unless the animal is hightailing away, crashing over or through all obstacles. I have a couple of favorite (that is, productive) stands where I often loaf for hours. Every once in a while as I sit there I scan the surrounding rhododendron jungles and picket-pin thickets of young oaks with my binocular. What the naked eye sees as the base of a sapling the glass may reveal as a deer's leg. What looks like small branches may be antlers.

This obviously effective type of camouflage is popular among bow hunters. Burnt cork can be substituted for the headnet. In many whitetail states you must wear an established amount (perhaps 200 square inches) of blaze-orange for safety during the firearms season, but if you cover the rest of yourself with camouflage, you'll be noticed only by the hunters, not the deer.

With or without a binocular, a crucial aspect of deer hunting—especially in timber and brush—is knowing how to look and what to look for. Next time you're still-hunting through the woods or waiting on stand, note how far you can see. Then shift to a distance half as far. Between that halfway point and the limit is where you'll see most of the deer you get a chance to shoot at. I've had deer appear almost next to me, seemingly out of nowhere, as they approached through thick cover, but the middle distances are generally the most productive. While concentrating on those middle distances, practice picking out individual objects, separating one plant or rock or limb from another, distinguishing between items. And then you'll find you can pick out exposed parts of deer that many hunters—perhaps most—never see at all. Most of the big ones that get away don't escape because of missed shots but because they remain still or sneak past hunters without being seen.

The year before last, my wife missed a chance at a good buck because she moved too soon after a pair of does crossed her path. A buck was following them, and when she moved, he bolted before she could raise her rifle. Quite often during the rutting season a buck will be accompanying or following one or more does. Sometimes he's right behind the object of his desire, sometimes quite a distance in the rear and moving very cautiously if a lot of hunters have been in the woods. When I see a doe during the bucks-only season, I make it a rule to wait as silently as possible for quite a while—sometimes 20 minutes or more. And I don't just watch the trail taken by the doe. Everyone knows that deer establish regular runways between feeding and bedding areas, and it's easy to see heavily used trails. But I've noticed that some of the big bucks stay off those conspicuous trails, traveling parallel to them in a rough way 20 or 30 yards to one side.

Deer have an extraordinary ability to perceive motion, and whitetails seem to be better at it then muleys. I'm willing to bet that an alerted whitetail buck can detect the blink of an eye at 50 yards in good light. But if the deer hasn't already been made nervous by an alien scent or sound, he probably won't toss up his tail and bound away. He's more likely to stand still and gaze at you for a few moments, trying to discern what moved. Your best chance then is to remain stock still until he loses interest—having decided that the movement was only a small animal or fluttering leaf. Then, when he looks away, raise your rifle or shotgun smoothly.

Because deer have such an exquisite sense of smell, many hunters sprinkle their boots and the area around a stand with a few drops of commercial scent, or "deer lure." One popular type is a sexual musk, another smells like frostbitten apples, and a third combines both scents. I've seen bucks lift their snouts and curl their lips, picking up the aroma of receptive does that have recently passed, and then, unerringly, follow the glandular musk trail. I've never seen a buck do that in response to a commercial lure, but I think these scents have definite value. Whether or not they actually attract deer, they do mask human scent. Personally, I favor the apple or combination type, but I can't claim my experience proves one kind or another to be most effective.

Add this tip to the hunting methods described in the text: In flat, open Western terrain, a pick-up truck can be transformed into a safari-type hunting vehicle by mounting an old auto seat on its bed. The hunter pictured is outdoor photographer and writer Pete Czura, chatting with Texas guide Joe Martin. Both Czura and the author spotted good whitetails while cruising with this truck, and subsequently made one-shot kills.

When a whitetail buck is moving, or seen in shadow or through foliage, his rack can be very hard to judge. Most hunters are satisfied with whatever is legal—a doe during an antlerless or "party-permit" season, a three-inch spike if the law allows bucks only. But if you're looking for a good set of antlers, there are guidelines. When a deer is seen from the rear, a rack wider than the body will be excellent. From the side or front, note whether antler height is comparable to the distance from chin to bottom of brisket. A height of antler comparable to tail length is also a good indication. Other favorable signs are thick-looking bases and a sweep that seems large for the size of the head.

The author kneels beside a Texas whitetail he killed with a 120-grain 6.5mm Magnum. Even lighter bullets, such as a 100-grain .243, are adequate in open country like this, though he doesn't recommend them for hunting in timber.

Preseason scouting can be of enormous value, not only in finding heavily used deer runs but also in finding good browsing areas. Whitetails are known to eat more than 600 kinds of vegetation, but unless deep snow has forced them to yard up, they'll be near one or more of their preferred fall and early-winter foods—acorns (especially those of white oak), apples, waste corn or truck crops, maples,

The author's brother spotted this Maine doe in August, foraging in a logged clearing where second growth had sprouted, lush and low. Such areas are always promising, and a summertime hike provides a pleasant means of scouting for them.

hickory, beech, berries, white cedar, hemlock, witch hazel, sumac, aspen, sassafras, wintergreen, dogwood, basswood, and birch. Naturally, preferences depend in part on what's most abundant and closely available, so it pays to do a lot of late-summer and early-fall observing. In the South and parts of the Midwest, for instance, the list of preferred foods also includes grapevines, greenbrier, mountain laurel, rhododendron, sweetbay, honeysuckle—and so on. In the Southwest, live oak, mountain mahogany, buckthorn, buckbrush, and several other plants are very important.

Deer browse intermittently throughout the day, but they feed most actively at night in the lowlands. By first light, many of them are climbing to higher ground, and a few have probably reached the benches, high flats, and ridges where they'll bed down, rest, and chew their cuds. As the air warms, thermals carry scent and sound upward. Early morning is therefore a good time to be on stand fairly high up, overlooking a gap, slope, bench, timber edge, funneling valley, or any other obvious route from feeding to bedding areas. If you've scouted well, you can often position yourself close to a game trail or an intersection of game trails. You should be upwind and far enough away so you won't be easily detected and will have a reasonably clear view.

This doesn't mean you must be up a tree. One of my favorite stands is a big boulder on a wooded Pennsylvania hilltop where I've seen so many deer that I stopped counting long ago. The boulder is easily climbed but puts me high enough to be inconspicuous. A bluff or cliff edge is often good. So is a concealing tree or low tree crotch, a hillside tangle or blowdown—anything that will break up your outline. Complete concealment is not only unnecessary, it is seldom possible.

In cold weather, whitetails are partial to south or lee slopes that offer warmth, sun, and protection from wind. Such a slope is especially promising if it has seeps or springs that maintain and nourish browse plants.

I like to get high on a hill, bluff, or outcropping above a good slope, but I don't go directly to such a stand for fear that I'll drive deer ahead of me and right over the crest. Instead, I start out as early as possible and circle around, coming over the top from the far side.

I usually remain on stand until midmorning (unless cold forces me to move sooner). Then I do a bit of still-hunting until lunchtime. By then, most whitetails are bedded down in thickets or other spots of concealment. When possible, a buck generally beds down facing his backtrail, and this usually means facing downhill. Therefore, I work the high flats and ridges and then still-hunt my way down, slowly and quietly, trying to approach from above.

In late afternoon, I often wait on stand at a lower elevation, waiting for deer to come down toward the feeding areas. That's also a good time to hunt near springs, ponds, or streams, for deer will detour or stop to take on water. However, if the first snows have fallen, they're surrounded by a water source, and I concentrate on areas where tracks show the deer to be concentrating.

Many hunters are convinced that they can tell a buck's prints from an adult doe's. Disillusionment may be painful, but a big doe can

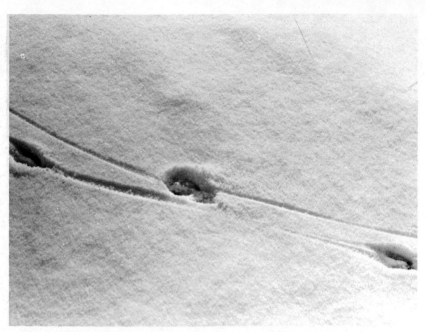

Ordinarily, a whitetail buck's tracks can't be reliably distinguished from a mature doe's—regardless of what you may have read or heard. But on thin snow like this, the tracks do reveal the sex, because only a buck drags his feet for a considerable distance with each step, making long, narrow marks in front of each print, as shown here.

leave 2½-inch tracks that look just like a buck's. They say a big buck's hoof lobes sometimes splay so widely that the front of the print is as wide as the rear or even wider. Well, a heavy doe often has comparably splayed hooves. About the only time you can reliably tell sex by tracks is when a light snow has fallen. In an inch or so of snow, a buck drags his hooves as he lifts them, leaving a long, narrow mark at the front of each print.

Buck rubs are one sure indiction that bucks are in the area. The rubs are long, polished scars, low down on saplings and bushes, where a buck has polished his antlers and, in the process, rubbed the bark away. There's a belief in some regions that the smaller a rubbing sapling is, the bigger the buck that used it. This isn't true. A buck with big antlers prefers a substantial sapling. Rubs mark good hunting areas because a buck will return to a favorite rub.

Unless there's snow on the ground, bedding spots are much harder to spot than rubs—they're just shallow depressions where

Going into the rut, a buck polishes his antlers. Buck rubs, usually seen low on saplings and shrubs, are a sure sign that antlered whitetails are in the vicinity.

the leaves have been pressed down by the animal's body—and deer don't return to the same beds. They do, however, return to the same small bedding area, so if you find a bed, the vicinity is worth hunting.

A deer usually urinates upon rising from a bed. A doe urinates to one side of it, but a buck wets the middle of it. If you find a freshly wetted bed, a buck is probably nearby.

Sometimes a rutting buck makes a wallow. It isn't a big, reeking mess like that of a bull elk, but it can be recognized, for the deer will have scuffled up leaves and earth and will have urinated in the depression.

Salt licks look rather like rootings, as deer actually eat the mineral-impregnated earth.

Deer-browsed vegetation can also be recognized, even when it's so low it could have been browsed by rabbits. Deer have no upper incisors, so they rip bites away raggedly, whereas rabbits snip off leaves, buds, or shoots cleanly.

It's well known that whitetails utilize a small home range and habitually use the same routes between feeding and bedding areas, following terrain contours that provide some cover and easy traveling. This is always worth bearing in mind, but don't put too much stock in it when hunters are thronging the woods during the first couple of days of the season. For one thing, all that disturbance stirs the deer up. For another, all those hunters are lying in ambush along the runs, blocking the deer from their usual haunts. When this happens I give myself three choices. One is to get on the ridges or high flats very early, before the other hunters do, in the hope of waylaying game before the blockade is formed. The second is to hunt lower than usual, most often taking a stand in a bottomland thicket or brushy swamp, because the presence of hunters will turn the deer back into such hideaways. Since all the people walking through the woods will keep the deer moving, there's a good chance a buck will come to me. The third is to avoid such areas altogether and hunt where I won't have so much company. Studies show that most hunters seldom go more than about half a mile from the nearest access road, and a lot of deer take refuge farther in.

On windy days, deer hardly move, and the hunting is tough. But if it's raining, I know one kind of place worth still-hunting, and that's a lowland thicket, such as a hemlock swamp where the wind hardly reaches and the interlaced tree crowns keep the animals from getting quite as drenched as in the open woods.

Unless your shot kills a deer outright or you know for certain that you've missed, the only humane (and productive) course of action is to go to where the animal was and look for a blood trail. Deer don't succumb quickly to shock, and they don't always flinch or jump when hit. Even when struck in a vital organ, a deer often runs more than a hundred yards. If struck elsewhere, the animal can keep going for some time. Find the blood trail and then wait a few minutes. A wounded deer tries to keep moving if pursued. If left alone, the animal will soon lie down, and the longer it lies there, the less able it will be to rise and flee again. This is known as "stiffening up," but what really seems to happen isn't so much stiffening as weakening with the gradual onset of shock. You then have a much better chance of finding your game quickly and being able to approach for a finishing shot if necessary. A short wait is therefore humane as well as efficient.

I once hurt my hand badly when an apparently dead buck tossed his head, swiping at me with his antlers. Approach a downed deer cautiously. Even if the eyes are glazed, I generally touch an eye with a long stick just to be sure, and I'm ready to fire a coup de grace if there's any sign of life.

Some hunters begin field dressing deer or other big game by bleeding it—slashing the jugular vein or severing the carotid arteries at the juncture of neck and chest. This is unnecessary. The bullet (or arrow) has already begun the bleeding process, and sufficient blood will be drained in the process of field dressing.

Many hunters also cut off the knobby, swollen musk glands from the inner surface of the hock joints to avoid tainting the meat. This, too, is unnecessary if you take care not to rub or cut the glands while dressing out the deer. There's nothing wrong with cutting away the glands. My old friend Joe Martin, a retired Texas guide and a great hunter, always does it. But you just don't have to if you're careful. Actually, it's more important to avoid getting hair all over the meat—or to wipe off as much of it as possible. Maybe bacteria cling to the hair, I don't know, but I do know that excessive hair can sour otherwise good venison.

Technically, "field dressing" means the removal of the innards below the diaphragm that separates the heart and lungs from the lower organs, while "hog dressing" means the removal of the heart and lungs as well, and the severing of the windpipe and esophagus as high as possible. Field dressing is a little faster, and it keeps the heart (which makes delicious eating) safe and clean inside the carcass while you drag your deer out. I prefer hog dressing. It takes only a little longer, makes the carcass slightly lighter, and speeds the cooling process, which is important in producing tasty, tender venison.

The author's friend Joe Martin, a very skillful hunter and guide, begins dressing out a whitetail, and his kneeling position demonstrates an extra tip. A deer's hind legs tend to get in the way as you make your initial cuts, but you can easily keep them spread by bracing your own legs against them.

To dress a deer, you need only a small, sharp, single-edged knife. Position the carcass on its back, preferably on a slight incline so that the hindquarters will be a trifle lower than the head. Begin by slitting the skin all the way around the anus. If a local bucks-only law requires the scrotum to be left in place, just make a small detour as you open the body; otherwise, sever the genital root between the bulges of the rump, cut off the genitals and, with a forefinger pressed along the back of the blade to guide it and prevent pricking the intestines, run the knife along with the cutting edge up to slit the belly all the way to the chest. Now free the diaphragm by cutting around the ribs. Reach in as far as possible to cut the windpipe and gullet. After a few finishing cuts to sever the remaining connections, you can roll the organs and viscera right out of the carcass. A good deal of blood will drain out with them.

Like most hunters who enjoy cooking and eating game, I pack along a plastic bag in which to carry a deer's heart and liver. Both are delicious.

If a deer has been gut-shot or you've punctured the viscera during dressing, you may have to wash out the body cavity. Otherwise it's much better not to wet it. Instead, wipe it dry with a clean rag, moss, or leaves. The thin blood glaze that forms not only helps to seal the meat from blowflies but is desirable during the early stage of cooling and aging. Flies and other pests can also be repelled by sprinkling the exposed flesh liberally with black pepper, but if a deer is going to hang in camp for a while before butchering and refrigeration, it can be better protected by a wrapping of muslin.

I carry a hauling rope, which first helps me drag out my deer and then enables me to hang it at camp. Some hunters cut behind the tendons of the hind hocks and push a gambrel stick through so that they can hang a deer head down. I think it cools and drains better head up, and with a buck, the antlers are convenient for tying the hanging rope. I raise the deer as high as possible to foil four-legged thieves, and I prop the body cavity open with sticks in order to promote cooling.

Mule Deer & Blacktails

Hunting books—including this one—commonly speak of "mule deer and blacktail deer" because, from the hunter's viewpoint, they're two closely related but distinct types of game. The two types are actually three types: mule deer plus the Columbian blacktail and the Sitka blacktail. Yet the three are all one species, for the two blacktail races are subspecies of mule deer. Having clarified this sometimes confusing point, I hope I can also clarify the sometimes bewildering advice found in hunting books about the arms used for muleys and blacktails. Both, of course, are Western game, but you'll sometimes find an author discussing long-range shots and typical rifles for Western shooting in one paragraph, then listing rifles suitable for Eastern brush in the next.

This is because most mule deer inhabit open terrain, whereas the blacktails are found in brush, scrub, chaparral, and timber—including dense rain forests. The rifles and cartridges I suggested for whitetails in timber are equally appropriate for blacktails. Those I suggested for Western whitetails in relatively open country are also fine for mule deer, but I must add a couple to this list because a mule-deer rifle is often used for other Western game.

Both the 7mm Magnum and the several .300 Magnums are fine not only for mule deer but for goats, sheep, elk, and moose. (And so are the .270 and .30-06, which I did mention in the section on whitetails.) Since mule deer are bigger than whitetails, some hunters prefer heavier bullets, but 150 grains is really quite enough: I'd reserve 180-grain bullets for elk. In fact, the choice in .270 is between 130 and 150 grains, and many hunters choose the lighter bullets for muleys.

Most mule deer are probably taken at ranges close to 200 yards, at least twice the distance of the average shot at a whitetail. You may therefore want to sight in your rifle at longer range than for whitetails. My scope choice would be a 4X or 2X–7X variable. But for blacktails in brush country I'd be satisfied with a 2½X scope and I'd do my sighting in at 100 yards, just as I would for whitetails.

The same handgun recommendations I made for whitetails apply to mule deer—and this time blacktails are included.

Fortunately, there are no shotguns-only laws in the mule-deer and the blacktail states. Smoothbores are not normally used on muleys, nor should they be; the range is much too long. Sometimes, however, they're used for Columbian blacktails, especially in California's thick scrub. The shotguns and loads I recommended for whitetails are right for these blacktails, too.

The Sitka blacktail ranges from southeastern Alaska into northern British Columbia, and the Columbian blacktail ranges from British Columbia down into California. Together these two subspecies account for about 1½ million of America's eight million or so mule deer. Some biologists recognize nine additional subspecies of mule deer, but various geographical groups are so much alike that many biologists lump them together into fewer races. From the hunter's standpoint, there are just two main types, the Rocky Mountain mule deer and the smaller, paler desert mule deer.

Rocky Mountain mule deer range from the three westernmost Canadian provinces down into the Southwest and from the Pacific states eastward through the Dakotas, Nebraska, western Kansas and Oklahoma, and west-central Texas. Desert mule deer range through the deep Southwest and northern Mexico, including all of Baja California.

Just as the Boone & Crockett record book lists Coues separately from other whitetails because Coues' antlers are smaller, blacktail records are listed separately from mule deer because blacktail racks are smaller. All of the top-record blacktails are from California, Oregon, Washington, and lower British Columbia, representing the Columbian subspecies, which develops more impressive antlers than the Sitka variety. All of the top-record mule deer represent the Rocky Mountain type, though some were taken as far south as New Mexico, where very big, heavy-antlered muleys inhabit the mountains and high plateaus.

In weight as in several other respects, blacktails resemble whitetails. They don't often scale more than 150 pounds (live weight). Columbian blacktails at the lower end of their range tend to be small; those in British Columbia are heavier-bodied, though not as impressively antlered. Sitka blacktails also tend to be small. An average buck mule deer in the Rockies may weigh 200 pounds or so, and much heavier ones are occasionally taken. Though the biggest mule deer are said to be British Columbian, those with record-book racks usually come from the United States. Desert muleys are less impressive both in antler and body size. I shot one in Texas that dressed out to a little more than 170 pounds, which means his live weight was probably about 215 pounds—very large for the desert race. His antlers would have been fantastic for a blacktail but weren't close to a record-book score for mule deer.

Muley bucks often band together in bachelor groups both before and after the rut, and in many regions, you'll see such groups during hunting season. On one occasion I had a choice of five bucks, three of them so much alike that trophy judgment was difficult. A trophy whitetail with typical antler conformation may have up to seven points per side, but a typical mature muley has only five to a side, or if brow tines are lacking, as they often are, he has just four—a double fork on each side.

In judging a mule-deer trophy, a major factor is that exceptional antlers usually have a boxy appearance, the spread being about as great as the height, and the beams are heavy, the tines long. If you get a front view, try to check whether the first fork on each side is out beyond the big ears. A good muley rack also looks at least half as long vertically as the animal's shoulder height.

A whitetail rack with an inside spread of 20 inches is outstanding, but a truly exceptional muley rack has a spread closer to 30—substantially wider than the animal's body. Seen from the rear, a muley's pale rump patch can help you judge. It's about a foot and a half wide on a big buck. If the antlers spread out half again as wide on each side, they must have a spread of about 30 inches. Even if you first see your deer at a great distance, a specimen like that is worth an arduous stalk.

Instead of yarding up like whitetails when heavy snows come, mule deer migrate seasonally, shifting from high summer pastures to

Mule deer, not quite spooked but aware of the photographer, head up a slope in a typical Montana wintering valley. The closest animal has a very good rack. Note how high and wide it is by comparison with the body.

lowlands where snow rarely hampers movement or browsing except for short periods. Desert muleys, having no snow to contend with, remain in one general area throughout the year, and so do the coastal blacktails in those regions where snowfall is negligible. Elsewhere, the extent of travel depends on climate and terrain. Usually it's more of a vertical than horizontal shift. There are at least a couple of herds—two I know about in California—that migrate about a hundred miles, but in most regions, the autumnal descent covers only a few miles. Travel is along passes, saddles, and other natural funnels that are easily traversed and have plenty of grazing and browsing vegetation. Even where the migration is very short, the trails become well marked, and they provide good hunting.

In summer, mule deer on the plateaus graze more than they browse. High-country snowfall therefore governs their migration. When a foot of snow flattens the grasses, they go down to seek the kinds of winter browse familiar to experienced deer hunters: snowberry, bearberry, serviceberry, mountain mahogany, oak, cliff rose, jack pine, cedar, fir, poplar, sage, snowbush, buckthorn, bitterbrush, and juniper.

This fine muley buck was killed by the late Larry Koller, a highly esteemed hunting authority and outdoor writer. The rifle was a .264 Winchester Magnum, a good choice for mule deer (and whitetails and other game, too) in open country. Koller's hip holster holds a .44 Magnum revolver, another good choice.

Although it helps to know the major browse plants that muleys favor, cover is more important than food in locating mule deer in most locales. Food doesn't concentrate them as tightly as it does Eastern whitetails because the kinds of browse I've mentioned are apt to be scattered all about the hills and flats, while cover may occur in more widely separated clumps. For this reason, brushy draws, canyons, and lowland flats are promising, and a hunter should especially seek those with dense concealing vegetation such as oak, cedar, or piñon.

As a general rule, the best bucks stay high at first, lingering behind the other deer, so hunters climb to the plateaus for them during the early part of the season. But in some locales, the migratory parade has been reversed by the advent of four-wheel-drive vehicles and access roads leading up onto the plateaus. A couple of days of heavy hunting pressure will cause many of the big bucks to vacate their favored haunts, and under those conditions, they're among the first deer to migrate.

A Western version of stand-hunting has always struck me as one of the best ways to try for a trophy mule deer. Sometimes called "nesting" or "nest-hunting," the procedure is simply to go on stand—or "perch" for a while—on a promontory overlooking a migration trail. Whether the big bucks hang back at first or join the migratory vanguard to get away from first-week mesa hunters, they're bound to appear along the trails—as are summer-heavy does, an obvious fact but one worth noting in case either sex can be legally taken.

A nest hunter needs a good binocular. But then, in my opinion, so does any deer hunter. My choice would be a 7X35 or 8X35 glass.

Hunters glass high-country trails and bedding areas used by mule deer. Until the snows deepen, muleys prefer grazing to browsing, and plateaus like this offer fine hunting before they migrate to their winter range.

Where early-season hunting pressure isn't too severe, a good general rule is to hunt mule deer high in the mountains and on mesas and cool north slopes during Indian summer weather. As the weather cools, hunt a bit lower. Then, as snow accumulates at the upper elevations, scan the warmer south slopes, and finally the lowland flats, draws, and canyons.

Mule deer have an undeserved reputation for being more naive—more trusting—than whitetails. Where they haven't been hunted much, they do occasionally act foolish, but their reputation for unwariness is based only on the fact that in open country, they sometimes have too little cover to let them skulk and hide as whitetails do. Under such circumstances, they rely on keeping space rather than cover between themselves and anything that alarms them. Like pronghorns (though to a lesser degree), they're accustomed to seeing some of their predators at a distance and checking to make sure the distance is sufficient. Often a spooked mule deer will pause and look back, just like a pronghorn buck, before disappearing over a rim or into a thicket. A hunter who can judge range has a good chance at that moment to collect his deer.

Where cover thickets are sparse and no recent hunting pressure has made the deer nervous, muleys sometimes bed down wherever they happen to be feeding. But even in tall grass or low brush, a deer can blend so well with vegetation as to be almost invisible. Muley hunters, like whitetail hunters, must learn to spot small exposed parts of an animal's body, a bit of leg, a pale rump or chin patch, an antler, the black of the nose or eye.

Desert muleys often bed in any handy shade. I took one on the open slope of a shallow coulee. In mountainous country, bedded deer are harder to find. They often bed high on slopes or shady ridges that give them a good view of anything approaching and where rising thermals carry warning sounds and scents to them. Sometimes, too, they bed just inside forest edges or deep within dense conifer stands.

During the warm midday bedding hours, dark evergreen woods can provide good still-hunting, assuming you can move very quietly.

As with whitetails, sheltering woods are also productive during rain or snow.

In thinner cover, still-hunting is best at daybreak, again before dusk, and in rainy, snowy, or very overcast weather. I haven't found it important to work downhill, as for whitetails, because muleys don't have the same pronounced habit of nocturnal feeding in the lowlands followed by a dawn climb to the summits. But it is just as important to hunt into the wind when possible, and to move slowly, quietly, and with pauses.

The author (right) and guide Biddy Martin roll over a Texas mule deer that was jumped in a shady draw on a hot afternoon. Before dressing the animal, they'll position it so that the head is a little higher than the hindquarters.

Muleys often browse in groups and move in columns. Bucks tend to lag behind the does and fawns when they're ambling along. When browsing or grazing, they usually face in several directions, and they're alert. Whitetail hunters often notice a deer flicking its tail before raising its head in suspicion. I've never seen muleys give this warning or flag their tails when fleeing, but I've noticed that they often lick their noses (an action that sharpens scent reception) and look all about before moving away. Freeze when you see a deer do that, and be ready to raise your rifle and shoot when he looks away.

On wide prairies and desert flats, scouting is often done on horseback or from a vehicle, as for pronghorns. Pretty much the same techniques can be used. Take your time and glass the terrain carefully. More mule deer are overlooked than seen.

Where there are mountains and woods, muleys can be hunted by means of fairly small, quiet drives of the sort often used to hunt Northeastern whitetails. Good sites for such deer drives include cedar or piñon woods cut by ridges or draws, thickets or wooded basins cut by streams, and thick stands of oak, aspen, fir, or lodgepole pine where deer browse and congregate for shelter. If there are no obvious crossings or openings, a hunting party may decide to use no standers. Everyone is then a driver, each man moving the game about for every other hunter.

Another form of driving works well when muleys are browsing and hiding in brushy canyons or draws. One or more drivers can then work through the brush, while at least one hunter on each side of the canyon watches for deer to come up into the open. A variation can be worked without any drivers in the brush. A man walks each rim, tossing stones down into the canyon to prod the deer out. In the case of a small draw, a lone hunter can do this; he may get a shot whether a muley tops out on his side or climbs the opposite slope.

Obviously, many of these techniques can be applied to blacktails, but sometimes blacktails are hunted by the same tactics I described for whitetails, and sometimes they can be taken by still other tactics. In British Columbia, for example, some hunters use calls to mimic a nervously bawling fawn. Columbian blacktail bucks take no more part in rearing or protecting young than bucks of any other race, but curiosity can bring either a buck or doe to investigate.

Blacktails don't make long or well-defined migrations in the manner of other mule deer, but they do tend to move toward lower ground in fall or winter. Like whitetails, they congregate near preferred foods. These differ substantially with region, but some of the most important ones can be listed: oak, bromegrass, fescue, wild oats, filaree, manzanita, buckthorn, berries, ferns, mountain mahogany, acorns, and any other plentiful nuts. Northern blacktails browse on conifers and other evergreens; in the southern part of the range, they're attracted to cactus.

In rugged terrain and in rain forests, blacktails sometimes establish game trails as obvious as those of whitetails.

Among the best places to hunt Columbian blacktails are moderately old burns or clearcuts in thick forest. An opening attracts deer when it has sprouted brush, shrubs, grasses, ferns, and low browse plants, such as trailing blackberry, huckleberry, vine maple, and so on. Such a clearing edged by tall, thick timber is ideal,

On parts of the West Coast where the deer season opens in summer or very early fall, Columbian blacktails like this one may still be in velvet, though the antlers have hardened. The weather may be hot and much of the cover is very thick. A good place for a deer stand is downwind of a clearing—an old cut or burn—where low browse plants blanket the ground.

since it provides the deer with escape and concealment cover as well as rich browse. Pick a stand with a good view downwind of a cut or burn, and use a binocular to scan often, trying to pick out animals or just antlers moving through the slash.

Where it's possible to move very quietly, still-hunting the slopes can be productive. Blacktails often travel along ridge crests. Slopes above streams are especially good.

Columbian mule deer spend much time in thick, tangled stands of red alder, cedar, and similarly dense woods bordering bottomland creeks. Such woods are difficult to hunt. They're too noisy for still-hunting in many cases, and visibility is too limited for stand-hunting in just as many cases. However, the thickets can be driven effectively if standers are positioned along the creeks as well as up on the hillsides above the jungle.

Oregon's season is in October. Washington has a split season that begins in September. California has a split season that begins early in August for riflemen and shotgunners and early in July for bowhunters. The very early blacktail season, actually beginning in summer, means that the deer are not yet rutting when they're hunted. This increases the difficulty of hunting, because the animals aren't preoccupied with breeding—they're less active and more wary than during the rut. Thick foliage and summer heat add to the difficulty. There's nothing much that can be done about any of this, except to dress sensibly and pack a full canteen of water.

Also be sure to pack a compass and map. I consider that essential in any wilderness hunting, but it's worth emphasizing here because a big Pacific forest is the kind of place where getting lost is easier than getting found.

Along the coast of the Alaskan panhandle, Sitka blacktails often come down to the shoreline forest edges and occasionally even venture out onto beaches. Some hunters and guides spot deer or look for deer sign by cruising about the coastal islands or up the rivers from the tidal flats. It's neither legal nor sporting to shoot deer from a boat, but you can scout from one and beach the boat when you find a good spot to hunt.

This Sitka blacktail, taken at Prince William Sound, weighed 186 pounds field-dressed. It's an unusually big buck. Most Sitka blacktails are smaller than other mule deer; their average size is that of a typical whitetail.

Alaska has a five-month season (August through December), a limit of four deer per year per hunter, and a hunter-success ratio of 60 to 70 percent. As a rule, both bucks and does are legal game after mid-September. The antlers of Sitka blacktails are small, often with only one fork on each side, but the meat is tasty, and a hunter can turn an expedition for blacktails into a combination trip for one or more kinds of bigger game because the seasons overlap.

During the early part of the Alaska season—until about mid-September—most of the good-sized bucks are up on the summer range. The best way to find them is to make an overnight trip, camping near timberline so you can get an early start hunting the high, open slopes. On the way up, there's arduous climbing through dense undergrowth, and coming down with a deer isn't any easier. Some hunters butcher their venison on the spot, boning it out to reduce the load.

In early November, Sitka blacktails become concentrated at lower elevations. Visibility has improved by then because deciduous trees and shrubs have dropped their leaves, and as the rut begins, the deer lose some of their wariness. November and December are the months when Alaskan hunters take the greatest number of blacktails.

In November, most of the deer won't yet be near the beaches. They'll be just about at the snowline. But with each succeeding snowfall they drop lower, to where warm temperatures bring rain instead of snow. You can hunt lower and lower as this happens.

Stands of old spruce and hemlock, especially along beaches, are the likeliest places to find Sitka blacktails after snow has blanketed the lowlands. The snow doesn't accumulate as deeply under the sheltering conifers, nor does the temperature dip as low along the coasts, and if there are abundant browse plants—especially blueberry bushes, augmented by forbs—near the spruce or hemlock shelters, the deer are usually plentiful there.

I mentioned the use of deer calls to lure Columbian blacktails in British Columbia. Now let me add that many Alaskans use deer calls to lure Sitka blacktails. Loud blasts will bring deer of both sexes. It may be that curiosity draws them. However, calling works best during the rut, and Don McKnight, a research chief for Alaska's Division of Game, believes that vocalizations may help bucks and receptive does find one another for breeding.

Some hunters produce a bleat by holding a grass blade stretched between their clenched thumbs and blowing across it—an old Indian trick. Some use a rubber band between two notched sticks. Some use commercial predator calls, and some use commercial quail calls, which can be made to utter a high-pitched bleat. Whatever call you choose, pick a stand where you have a wide view and where your scent isn't likely to be carried toward the deer.

Calling works best on calm days; in windy weather, your scent will be blown to the deer while your sound will be drowned out by the various forest noises.

Deer calling requires patience. I've said before, in connection with whitetails, that deer respond slowly and cautiously. Try a series of three long and two short bleats, then wait at least 10 minutes and try a couple more, then wait at least another 10 minutes before moving on. You can still-hunt as you move from one calling stand to another.

Dress for rain when hunting Sitka blacktails. The weather is apt to be more wet than cold. Unfortunately, rubberized parkas and rain pants make for noisy movement, so a lot of Alaskans dress in wool, which retains warmth when wet. I would, however, wear a waterproof hat and waterproof boots.

In the section on whitetails, I told how to dress out a deer. The procedure is the same for blacktails and mule deer, but since mule deer are such impressive trophies, I think this is a good place to add advice about handling any head you may wish to have mounted. If you've practiced on at least a couple of game heads you don't care about and have studied a good book on the subject—for example, Waddy McFall's *Taxidermy Step by Step* (Winchester Press, 1975)—then go ahead and skin your trophy. Otherwise, leave skinning to the taxidermist. Either way, you'll want to cape and sever the head, leaving enough hide for a full shoulder mount.

Use a sharp, fairly short knife. Holding it with the cutting edge up, use the point to slit the skin straight from the top of the withers up the nape of the neck to the center point between the ears. At the lower end of this cut, make another cut completely around the body—down behind the shoulders and across the forelegs at the bottom of the brisket. Then peel the hide forward to the bases of the ears and jaws. By doing this, you save plenty of hide—the cape, as it's called—undamaged and still attached to the head, for a generous mount.

Now, with the carcass on its back, sever the neck right behind the jaws. You don't need an ax or saw, and using one might accidentally damage the hide. Just cut into the axial joint between the skull and spinal column, grasp the head at the antler bases, and twist the head off. Rub plenty of fine salt into the exposed flesh and also into the flesh side of the cape. Then freeze it as soon as possible.

On guided big-game trips, an experienced guide usually handles such chores. And with some kinds of trophy game—sheep, for example—he may completely skin the head and pack it out separately from the horned skull. Let him. Or rather, thank him. He's good at it. You assumed when you contracted with him that he knew his business, and this is part of it. But with deer and some other antlered species, you may be hunting on your own, and you'd better know how to cape a trophy for yourself. The procedure I've outlined applies not only to deer but to other antlered game as well.

WATERFOWL

Geese

I've known hunters who could knock down geese with 20-gauge guns, but even an exceptionally good wingshooter ought to be using a 12 because that's what it takes to kill geese cleanly and consistently. Moreover, the 12 should be chambered for 3-inch shells, as long Magnums are a definite help where pass-shooting is the dominant method—especially in places where long shots are common and the species large.

Until recently, the standard cartridge for geese over decoys was a 12-gauge high-velocity or Magnum No. 4 load. The standard for pass-shooting was a 12-gauge Magnum carrying shot of the same size or, in blinds situated where big, high-flying geese could be expected, No. 2 pellets. The 2's probably saw more use than the 4's.

With the advent of steel shot, the selection has changed. In hard-bottomed fields and marshes, waterfowl pick up and eat spent lead pellets along with their natural grit. Because they retain the pellets in their gizzards, they can succumb to lead poisoning. At the time of this writing, the use of steel shot is mandatory in many areas and, in future seasons, it will be required in still more areas along all four of the federally mapped flyways that blanket the country.

The substitution of steel for lead has been controversial. Objections to it include the fact that it is ballistically inferior and therefore increases the number of birds that are merely wounded rather than killed outright. Among those that escape, many die slowly. However, it's believed that the number of birds killed by lead poisoning exceeds the probable increase in lost cripples that may result from the use of steel. Another objection is that steel loads are more costly, and still another is that they can damage the barrels of some older shotguns. The expense of the ammunition is something we'll just have to accept (while hoping, of course, that manufacturing costs can eventually be lowered). Fortunately, steel shot doesn't significantly shorten the barrel life of currently manufactured American shotguns, or other guns having comparable barrel thickness and hardness.

The rule in selecting steel-shot ammunition is to obtain performance roughly equivalent to that of lead by using pellets one or two sizes larger. A No. 4 steel load comes close to the No. 5 or No. 6 lead-filled cartridges you might once have used for close-in duck shooting. A No. 2 steel-shot load is substituted for No. 4 lead and can therefore be used for pass-shooting ducks and for close-in goose shooting over decoys.

However, for pass-shooting geese you should substitute No. 1 steel loads for No. 2 lead, and many hunters use this larger size in steel even over decoys.

A 30-inch full-choke barrel is the right kind for goose shooting. The full choke gives you a tight, dense enough pattern to bring down birds at a considerable distance, and a long barrel helps you point and swing deliberately as birds come over but often remain quite far out. You want the same kind of barrel you'd use for trap shooting, and for the same reasons.

If jump-shooting were as efficacious with geese as with ducks, there would be plenty of use for more open-bored guns. But jump-shooting is rare. The cover is usually too sparse where geese feed or rest, and the birds (particularly Canadas, but some other species as well once the season's opening salvos have conditioned them) are too alert to let you get within flushing distance.

However, I know some old-timers who use double-barreled guns, choked modified and full, not for jump-shooting but for shooting over decoys. Though something can be said for their choice, I wouldn't think of firing steel shot through one of my fine but middle-aged doubles.

In connection with steel shot, several precautions are in order. The loading of steel shot for safe and efficient performance is tricky. Don't experiment. Don't remove the pellets from a shell and try to use them for concocting handloads. Don't ever fire steel shot at a hard surface, as it will ricochet much more than lead. For patterning, use conventional patterning paper in front of a safe backstop. (I use a high earth mound.) Take care when preparing game for

The most abundant, most widespread, and most hunted geese are Canadas. This one was photographed in Wyoming. The several subspecies that migrate chiefly along the Western flyways aren't quite as big as the Canadas in the East and Midwest, but they're big enough that they usually look closer and slower than they really are. Gunners therefore tend to shoot behind them— the most common kind of miss.

cooking to remove any pellets you find, and take even greater care when eating the game. It's uncomfortable enough to bite down on a lead pellet; a steel pellet between your molars can cause real tooth damage.

At least one brand of ammunition lists another precaution on the box—to wear shooting glasses, especially if you're a left-handed shooter using an autoloader with a right-hand ejection port. This is chiefly to minimize the possibility that residual powder particles might reach your eyes. I happen to be left-handed, and I've used both lead and steel shot in an auto with a conventional right-hand port. I didn't notice any difference at all. I need prescription lenses to see where I'm shooting, so the ammunition manufacturer's warning was unnecessary in my case. I don't think it matters at all whether you're using steel or lead; if you don't ordinarily wear glasses, then it's a good idea to wear shooting glasses regardless of what ammunition you're firing.

Federal regulations require that a gun for waterfowl hunting must hold no more than three shells, including a chambered cartridge. Most repeaters hold more than three, but they're legal if a magazine plug is installed to reduce the capacity while hunting ducks or geese. I think most hunters know this, but I've decided it's worth mentioning for those who are unaware of it and also for the many others who may not know that quite a few states have followed the federal example by limiting shell capacity to three for all kinds of game, not just ducks and geese.

Most waterfowl are bagged at distances between 25 and 50 yards. Though geese are shot at distances close to 50 more often than at 25, it's best to forgo shots at birds over 60 yards away (and 50 is a more sensible limit for a gunner of average ability). Old hands curse at novices who indulge in "skybusting," but the old hands have forgotten that judging altitude is a skill learned by experience. Judging horizontal distance is difficult, too, over fields or water where reference points are lacking. If you find range estimation troublesome, there's a rule of thumb that works for the larger species: A goose whose head is obliterated by your shotgun's front bead is more than 50 yards away. Also try to educate your eye by setting out range markers—a stake driven into the mud or a decoy placed at a known distance from your blind.

The plumage of a bird in the air furnishes another key to yardage. It's possible to identify many kinds of wildfowl by their colors, shapes, and sizes at a substantial distance, but a goose (or duck) is probably no more than 45 or 50 yards away if you can see its plumage pattern in really sharp detail.

During the first segment of a split season in Maryland, I once hunted geese in 70° weather, and I've also hunted them on that same Eastern Shore when the temperature stood at 21°. I usually go prepared for the worst. Wildfowl are active in wet, miserable weather, and they tend to fly low—giving you more shooting—on dark, dreary mornings. Your gear should therefore include a rain parka or similar wet-weather garment and (in most parts of the country) warm clothing. When shooting over fields, I wear insulated, waterproof boots because puddles, sloughs, wet ditches, and bogs are likely to be all about. When shooting over water, I wear chest-high insulated waders. Having a retriever along doesn't do away with the need for waders; you'll want them when you're moving about in the water to set out decoys, and sometimes when you're getting out of or into a boat.

Geese and ducks have astonishingly good vision. They can spot movement, abnormal reflections (such as the glint of sun on your glasses or gun), and unnatural colors. Anything that looks alien can flare them long before they come within range. You'll generally be shooting from a blind but, even so, your clothing and gear should be olive-drab or reed-colored or camouflage-patterned. Some hunters go so far as to paint the barrels of their fowling pieces or wrap them with appropriately colored tape. I've never found this necessary, but I've certainly found it essential to keep my gun and myself down out of sight and still until ready to shoot. I usually wear a billed or broad-brimmed hat to hide my head and keep the sun off my glasses. Generally speaking, if a boat is used, it should be hidden near the blind (some blinds are built to permit the mooring of a boat underneath), or it should at least be covered with something to camouflage it. Waterfowling boats are usually painted an olive or reed color, and many are further disguised by being thatched over with reeds, straw, or the like.

A blind should be camouflaged with vegetation natural to the immediate site. This material often has to be brought there from a slight distance because the ground adjacent to the blind should not be denuded or scarred. Geese (and ducks) have an uncanny ability to spot man-made disturbances.

There are, of course, many different kinds of blinds. Best of all are natural "hides," which may range from rocks to fringes of beach myrtle, willow, rushes, hedgerows, overgrown ditches, corn stalks, clumps of brush, slash piles, or any other natural concealment. But since geese often congregate where cover is scant, constructed blinds are commonly necessary. On land, these include pit blinds and trenches that keep a hunter's head below the level of ground cover until he rises to shoot, as well as above-ground blinds camouflaged to look like hedgerows, clumps of bushes, stands of corn or reeds, etc. Over water, they include—most commonly—raised, thatched, boxlike affairs that often contain a shelf for ammunition and small items of equipment, and/or a bench for the long periods of sitting and waiting that are an inherent ingredient of waterfowling. The regional variations on these blinds seem almost countless.

The positioning of a blind can be extremely important. Good locations are between roosting waters and feeding fields (preferably close to where the birds feed) and on waterways where geese and ducks rest and sometimes feed. Another good location is right in or adjacent to a feeding field if the field is big enough so that shooting won't soon discourage the birds from coming to the area.

But there's more to it than locating a blind where the birds want to go. While there are good pass-shooting sites where birds may move close from all directions, the prevailing wind can be important where birds descend to feed, especially if you're shooting over decoys. Birds use a head wind to help them brake and control their maneuvers, and all waterfowl therefore prefer to fly into the wind when they drop down to land or make a low "inspection" pass (as you hope they will over decoys). With a breeze in your face, geese or ducks aren't disposed to pass close and low in front of you—over your decoy spread, for example. Instead, they'll turn and seek another nearby, attractive place where they can come down into the wind. Or they may approach from your rear, in which case they're often too high as they come over the decoys and are likely to just keep traveling or come down far beyond your rig. Even when fog or an overcast brings them in low, I dislike having many of them come from behind me. I've known long-experienced hunters who could seem to watch all directions at once, but I just get flustered while they get the birds. It's much better to have the prevailing wind coming from behind so that the birds—breasting it as they descend—come mostly from out front.

Very little wind can be just as good as a breeze coming from the rear. A lee shore, for instance, is a fine place for a blind. In a spot like that, any slight wind usually comes from behind—from land to water. Most of the geese or ducks will then come in over the water, toward the decoys and blind. Many will make low passes over the blocks, and some may attempt to splash down. (Once I shot a brant as it hovered, almost still in the air, about to drop among the decoys; a second one landed among the blocks, then leaped up again as I killed the hovering bird—and my partner brought down the second brant as it rose on the wind.)

Books have been devoted to the single subject of decoys. There are so many kinds that they defy description. Among stick-ups, there are full-bodied decoys, "shell" decoys, shadow decoys, and even stuffed birds. Among floating "dekes," there are blocks made of wood, plastic, rubber, and other materials. Both stick-ups and floaters come in models representing resting birds, "sentinel" birds, feeding birds, preening birds, and sleeping birds (with the head tucked rearward over the back or partly under a wing). There are also homemade decoys ranging from beautiful woodcarvings to plastic bleach bottles, rags, mud lumps, and bunched newspapers.

Then there are "confidence" decoys. Usually these represent a different species from the one being hunted, and they're placed near or with the standard decoys—coot blocks used together with duck decoys, for instance—to add realism and give incoming waterfowl a secure feeling that the place below is a safe feeding or resting haven used by their own kind and those that normally associate with them. Some old-timers go to interesting extremes with confidence decoys. Occasionally I still see a stuffed gull propped on the bow of a scull or the corner of a blind. The idea behind this ploy is that a gull would take off if a man were close to it, so the sight of a gull lulls waterfowl into accepting the standard decoys as real.

I'll have more to say about decoys and decoy spreads in the section on ducks, and also in connection with certain species of geese. Right here, however, I want to offer a few general guidelines, since I can't describe all the available kinds of decoys in these pages.

First, there's no need to have decoys in a wide variety of poses. Most of those in your set can be in a standard resting or feeding position. But I'm convinced it does help to have at least a few of them in an alert position and one or two in a sleeping position.

Second, decoys come in more or less standard and also extra-large dimensions. I prefer slightly oversized decoys. Birds in the air can't judge the proper size of birds on the ground. Big decoys either look close or look like rather large birds, so the somewhat exaggerated size doesn't reveal them as false. Their advantage is that they can be seen and their species recognized by flying birds at a great distance.

Third, while there's no need for realistic plumage patterns on the decoys representing certain species, there is a need for realism in the colors of Canada-goose decoys and most kinds of duck decoys. I

In big stubble fields, stick-up decoys are very effective. These Saskatchewan hunters have taken their limit of Canadas over shell-type stick-ups. No blinds are visible because the shooting was done from pit blinds.

don't mean detailed realism, but impressionistic adherence to color patterns.

Many of the plastic commercial decoys feature a molded texturing to simulate the texture of feathers. No one will ever convince me that birds can discern feather texture from the air, but the roughness of the decoy surface is helpful because it's nonreflective. If you make your own blocks, use flat decoy paint, not glossy paint, as shiny decoys can flare birds instead of attracting them.

While shooting from a blind facing a little water hole in the middle of a sprawling Delaware cornfield, I've had Canadas come to a rig of only six goose blocks and a pair of mallard decoys. But if the water hadn't been there, I'd have preferred at least a couple of dozen stick-ups. As a general rule, you can figure that the bigger an expanse of field or water is, the more decoys you need to make a convincing stool. When you're shooting ducks, the dabbling species ("puddle ducks") are apt to take a close look at a small set, whereas most of the diving ducks ignore anything but big rafts of decoys. With geese, I haven't found that the species has as much to do with the requisite number of decoys. *All* geese prefer to feed and rest in big flocks. The more decoys you set out, the more enticing they are, and this is especially important when they're set in big open spaces.

Now I want to quote a cogent paragraph by a very authoritative outdoor writer, Grits Gresham. In *The Complete Wildfowler* (Winchester Press, 1973) Grits wrote this about decoy rigs:

> Pardon my sacrilege, but I think that the intricate pattern sets advocated by some hunters and many writers are more important to them than to the ducks. With rare exceptions, the wild ducks themselves hew to no rule of thumb in positioning themselves on the water. Neither do geese, on land or water.

I heartily agree. This is not to imply that certain simple decoy arrangements don't help in special instances (as I'll explain in a moment), but a lot of old hunters have an unwarranted faith in special "fish-hook" patterns, "teardrop" patterns, etc. If these formations are skillfully set out so that they don't look unnaturally regimented, they work about as well as a somewhat more haphazard scattering.

What's more important is a natural, unregimented appearance combined with good aerial visibility. For this reason, each block should normally be several feet from its neighbors, and the decoys shouldn't all be facing the same way. On water, the current or breeze often turns them all in the same direction, but you can generally correct this by experimenting with the anchor lines. You might, for example, drill new holes or attach new fastenings to a couple of them at the rear instead of the front, and attach the anchor cords there. Another way is to affix two decoys to opposite ends of a slat, facing the blocks in different directions. A single anchor line, attached to the slat, will then suffice for two decoys.

The spread must look inviting as well as natural. That is, there ought to be room for approaching geese or ducks to pitch in. Otherwise they may just give your decoys a cursory look from far off and then move away to other landing sites. Again, this is more important on water than on land. In a field, the birds can almost always find space enough. In a cove, on the other hand, they must spy at least a little elbow room. So when you set out your decoys, leave one or two wide openings in the set.

This brings me to those special instances that call for more careful arrangement. Some of the best water locations are partly sheltered—rimmed—by land, and unless a flight of birds comes directly over, whether by chance or in response to calling, your decoys may be mostly invisible, or not enough may be visible at a distance to be truly inviting. A spit, sandbar, or crescented shore line often hides part of a rig. In that case, line out "stringers" of decoys, at angles from the main part of the stool, in order to draw the attention of flights coming from the sides. Even in fairly exposed locations, I've found that a few separated decoys, somewhat bunched or else strung out from the rest, will draw attention to the main body. Splitting your spread into a couple of ragged groups increases landing space, aerial visibility, and the inviting look.

Wind direction affects decoy placement. The nearest decoys should be about 20 yards from your blind. Most of them should be out in front if the breeze is coming from behind you, though a few should be in any shallow little pockets where waterfowl would be foraging, even when the bulk of the flock is at rest. A crosswind changes the desired set-up. If the prevailing breeze is from the right, most of the decoys should be somewhat to the right of the blind (or to the left if it's blowing from the left). That way, approaching birds will cross right in front of you as they drop low because they'll head upwind to visit the stool.

I like to have a good retriever on hand even when I'm shooting geese over dry land. Once in a while, a goose that's hard-hit will sail a considerable distance instead of just tumbling down. And often a goose that's hit but not killed can run and seek cover after striking the ground. To go after those geese on foot takes much time and effort, and—a more important consideration—such birds aren't always found.

Over water, especially deep water or water with a strong current, the value of a retriever is more obvious. For hunting geese, the most popular breeds are the Labrador, golden, and Chesapeake Bay retrievers. They have the strength and size to manage big, heavy birds, and they also have stamina, strong swimming ability, eagerness, intelligence, and resistance to cold. (The same breeds—and particularly the Lab—are most popular for hunting ducks, but some others, such as the springer spaniel and the water spaniels, can be just about as good.)

If you don't have a dog and you're hunting over a small, calm body of water, you may be able to retrieve your own waterfowl without wading in or using your boat. Some hunters carry a long, strong line with a weight at one end. The line can be swung and flung to snag birds before the current carries them away. Some hunters use an old fishing rod for this purpose, snagging their birds with a fairly heavy casting plug. It doesn't match having a dog, but it does reduce the number of times you must leave the blind.

Boats for waterfowling—Barnegat sneakboxes, Merrymeeting sculls, layout boats, Louisiana pirogues, square-ender john boats, canoes, airboats, etc.—are too numerous to describe here, but two suggestions will help you make a choice if you need a boat. First, read the chapters devoted to boats in two or three books on duck hunting. The authors may not agree with each other, but they'll give you useful information. Second, and probably more important, notice what kind or kinds of boats other hunters favor in the region where you want to hunt. There are major regional differences in design, based on the types of local water, cover, and prevalent waterfowl species. A big seaworthy vessel might be needed to reach open water for some of the diving ducks, and the same kind of boat might be best when you head out to a blind for brant, but you don't need or want one for reaching any other goose blind. If much of your shooting is over water, you might want a small, easily camouflaged craft, but if your hunting site is far from your launching site, you may want a larger boat for toting decoys.

Since geese are harder for me to hit than any other birds (including ducks and grouse), I consider myself a qualified authority on the reasons for misses. I believe that most misses occur when a gunner stops his swing or simply fails to lead his bird sufficiently. Both mistakes stem from the size and manner of flight of geese. They beat their wings more slowly than ducks, but often they're flying at least as fast. Then there's that matter of size, which makes both speed and range deceptive. You can always assume that geese are flying higher and faster than they look. If you've used the techniques I mentioned to judge range and you're still missing, try doubling your lead. Depending on your style of mounting and swinging a gun, you may have to get out in front by one bird length or several. Several is more common. And then, as you fire, you may still be shooting behind the bird if you don't emulate a golfer's exaggerated follow-through.

I've been told that Cree Indian guides are unsurpassed at calling geese with nothing but their own vocal cords and a cupped hand. I haven't had the good fortune of hunting with one of these Canadian guides, but I've hunted on Maryland's Eastern Shore with two aging sportsmen who could vocally mimic Canadas, snow geese, brant, and even ducks. I think the only way to learn this almost-lost art is simply to hunt enough, listening carefully to the birds and to any companions who have mastered the technique. Most of us will do much better with the classic type of goose call, a wooden cylinder enclosing a vibrating reed. Basically, it's a bigger, deeper-toned version of the classic duck call.

There are other types, of course, including one that I find easier to work convincingly. This is a bellows call, a rubber device that you shake or manipulate like a miniature concertina instead of blowing into it.

Probably the best-known goose sound is the double-noted, resonant honking of Canada geese, whose voices will attract some other species as well. But there are many species of geese, and their voices are by no means alike. Some yelp, some bugle, some cackle. Instructional phonograph records are available at sporting-goods stores, but the records I've heard are devoted only to the most hunted species—chiefly the Canada. Although such records are helpful, the best way to acquire skill is to spend plenty of time in a blind, listening to the birds and to other hunters, and spend equal time practicing. Do not, however, practice while you're in a blind with another hunter who is presumably present in the hope of limiting out. Inept calling can cause geese that are pitching in to make a sudden, wide detour. Also do not take a phonograph into a hunting area; electronic calling is just as illegal (and unsporting) as baiting.

Before I give you a few suggestions regarding individual species, one more tip is needed to clarify those suggestions: Don't assume that if I mention a species it will be legal game next season on the flyway where you hunt. You must check the regulations. I hunted Eastern brant one year when they were plentiful, and the bag limit was four a day. There was no open season at all the following year because the brant failed to reproduce in adequate numbers. Long periods of drought on the breeding grounds of some species, or ice on the breeding grounds of others, can deplete the populations. So can habitat reduction along the migration corridors and on the wintering grounds; so can a poor crop of preferred wild foods (such as eelgrass in the case of Eastern brant).

Brant are small geese, hardly bigger than plump mallards, and they're usually shot over decoys along both the Atlantic and Pacific coasts. No. 4 lead shot or, where steel is mandatory, No. 2 steel shot is sufficient.

The American, or common, brant is the Eastern variety, and the black brant is the Western bird. Both species are chiefly marine in their feeding behavior. They don't normally graze on land, as most geese do, but feed on offshore beds of vegetation. Eelgrass is the mainstay of the Eastern birds, but where it isn't abundant enough, they also feed heavily on sea lettuce, widgeongrass, and cordgrass. When you kill your first brant of the day, you may want to examine the down around its vent. If the down shows a green tint, the birds have probably been feeding chiefly on sea lettuce or other algae, which will have a calamitous effect on the normally tasty meat. In that case you may want to hunt other game for a week or so. If the down is white or tan, the meat will be good because eelgrass and the other grasses I mentioned have been the primary foods.

Black brant depend less than the Eastern birds on eelgrass, though they eat it when they find it. They subsist primarily on widgeongrass, surfgrasses, and various other aquatic plants— sometimes, unfortunately, including algae that may have the same effect on their meat as sea lettuce has on Eastern brant.

Brant feed most actively when the tide is at half-flood or half-ebb, and morning tides are usually best because the birds are hungriest then. When resting they tend to be wary, but during feeding periods they seem to be distracted by hunger and will pitch in among decoys fronting an island or seashore blind where their foods grow. Black-and-white decoys that mimic their own appearance are most effective, but they'll also come to scaup or canvasback decoys, and the raft can be made more enticing by putting a few Canada-goose blocks to one side of the smaller decoys.

Brant honk and grunt, and they'll respond to short blasts on a goose call or to the feeding chatter of ducks, reproduced with a duck call. They'll come to decoys without calling, but restrained, intermittent vocalizations add to the attraction. Just avoid making a single ducklike squawk, as that sounds like their own alarm signal.

Like scaup (and pronghorns and caribou), brant are fascinated by fluttering objects. If they trade about near your blind but refuse to come close enough, you can sometimes wave them in by raising a handkerchief or cap just above the blind.

Canada geese of one subspecies or another migrate along all of the continent's major flyways. The number of subspecies is disputed, but at least eleven are widely accepted. They range from the little cackling goose, about the size of a brant, to the giant Canada, which sometimes weighs twenty pounds. An average common, or Atlantic, Canada goose weighs between seven and twelve pounds. Generally speaking, the smaller, darker races are Western, the larger, paler ones Eastern and Midwestern. The ranges of some races overlap, however, and there's considerable interbreeding. In the East, I suspect the size may slowly increase because of hybridization with the giant Canada, originally introduced from the Midwest.

The term "honker" is usually applied to the medium or larger varieties; some of the smaller ones yelp, cluck, and cackle. It's wise to listen to the birds in a given region before trying to call them.

Regardless of subspecies, the Canada goose has a white chin strap, and some hunters make the mistake of using this marking as a range indicator, rising to fire when they can see it sharply. Several years ago at Chestertown, Maryland, four companions and I used a range-finding instrument to test the efficacy of this range indicator. We proved that the chin markings stood out plainly before the geese were within 65 yards of our blinds. A much better indicator is the pale stippling or barring on a Canada's gray-brown breast. When these subtle markings become clearly visible, a goose is definitely within range.

Most geese prefer to graze on land, and the habit is more pronounced in the Canada than in any other species. However, watery feeding sites should not be overlooked, because Canadas eat wild rice, sedges, pondweed, and a large variety of other aquatic and shoreline plants. On dry land they eat assorted wild grasses, seeds and grains, clover, buds, berries, and even the nuts that often attract mallards, black ducks, and wood ducks. But cultivated crops draw them in the greatest numbers. Corn is the most important, probably because it's so abundant and widespread. Depending on what's grown in your hunting region, you may bag just as many Canadas from a blind at the edge of wheat, alfalfa, soybeans, barley, oats, or rice. Fields near roosting waters are always most productive, unless heavy hunting pressure has begun to keep the birds away. In that case, you may do better from a blind in the nearest marshland.

In winter, when stubble fields are covered with snow or picked almost bare, better shooting can usually be had along shorelines where wild vegetation grows close to the water. Wind-protected spots—in the lee of bars, tall grasses, shrubs, trees, banks, or hills—are most promising.

Hunting for Canadas (and other species of waterfowl) is best on cloudy or stormy days and during the week just before and after the new moon. When the moon is full or nearly so, or when there's plenty of starlight, geese do much of their feeding at night. The next day, most of them rest on the water, and few are in the air. When they feed actively during daylight, the greatest numbers begin to get airborne shortly before sunrise, and a hunter will see the most activity during the first hour or so after legal shooting hours begin. If he fails to limit out in the morning, a good time to be back in the blind is from midafternoon until legal shooting hours end.

Canada geese are usually intelligent, alert birds, so decoy spreads must be lifelike. Since grazing geese don't keep their heads down constantly, some of the decoys should have their necks bent while others should have their heads up. It's important to have several near the edges of the spread in an alert, head-up attitude because a few of the birds in a feeding flock of Canadas serve as sentinels. Bagged geese can be added to a stick-up spread, but if they aren't propped in lifelike positions, they'll warn incoming Canadas away.

When hunters talk about snow geese, they usually mean lesser snows, which are far more abundant than the greater snow geese of the Atlantic Coast—more abundant, in fact, than any American geese except the Canadas. Immature snow geese are ash-gray with brownish mottling on their heads and necks. Adult birds of both subspecies are snow-white (though waterborne chemicals and mud often stain their heads and breasts rusty). They have broad black tipping on the wings.

Size and geography are the only means of distinguishing the two varieties in the wild. Greater snow geese are the size of small Canadas—averaging five to 7½ pounds, measuring about 2½ feet long, with a five-foot wingspread. Lesser snows are a trifle smaller,

Most American hunters think of the Gulf States as the shooting grounds for mixed flights of blue geese and snow geese, but during the early part of the wildfowling season, the shooting is excellent to the north, around James Bay and Saginaw Bay. These Ontario hunters have taken their limit of blues and snows.

averaging four to six pounds. Snow geese of one variety or the other nest from northern Alaska to Greenland. The greater snows migrate along the Atlantic Flyway. Many of the lesser snows migrate along the northern Rockies. Some of them fan out westward, to California, while others turn southeastward, flying primarily down the Mississippi Valley and spreading out along the Gulf Coast from Texas to the western tip of Florida's panhandle. Large populations winter in Nevada and Utah and in the Mississippi Valley from lower Illinois southward. The very best hunting can be had in the Gulf Coast rice fields (particularly those of Texas and Louisiana) and in California's grain-growing regions.

For some years, the lesser snow geese have been extending their range northward and eastward. No doubt some of them are interbreeding with greater snows and augmenting the Eastern populations. It's fairly safe to predict that the future will hold new hunting opportunities in areas where snow geese have been protected or haven't been traditional game.

So much has been written about snow-goose shooting on the rice flats that a hunter might wonder if snows can be hunted anywhere but on agricultural fields. It's true that these geese love rice (and corn, soybeans, and other crops), but the shooting can also be excellent in wild marshland. These snow geese, photographed in California, are gathering to feast on cattail roots.

Snow-goose hunters are generally familiar only with the smaller subspecies, which migrates on the inland flyways. They may be surprised to learn about the rather different habits of migrating and wintering snows along the Atlantic. Though snow geese everywhere forage in meadows and grainfields, the greater snows gain more of their sustenance from saltgrass, horsetail, cordgrass, and similar plants growing in a few inches of water, either salt or brackish. They often fly low over coastal blinds. They'll come to white decoys, of course, and they'll also come to rigs of floating or stick-up Canada-goose decoys.

The lesser snows on the Gulf Coast are so fond of rice that the agricultural fields have become famous hunting grounds. (A good many other kinds of waterfowl also visit the rice flats, but not in comparable numbers.) These snow geese also feed in the marshes on cordgrass, panicgrass, and cattail and bulrush roots. Stubble fields are extremely attractive to snow geese, and some of the best hunting places on the Pacific Flyway are the fields of oats and barley. On Utah's Bear River marshes, the hunting is excellent near wheat or bulrushes. Additional wild foods that attract the snows are buffalograss, glasswort, horsetail, saltgrass, and wild barley. Regardless of region, they'll also glean fields of corn, rye, soybeans, or sorghum; in this respect they're like Canadas, and the two species often feed in the same fields.

Snows are frequently shot from blinds intended primarily for Canada geese, but there are strong regional preferences for other methods. In California's San Joaquin Valley, I found that most hunters used pit blinds (which are also very popular for Canadas) in stubble fields, rice flats, and the edges of marshland, and I noted that profile, or shadow, decoys were sometimes used. On the bars, flats, and bogs of the Mississippi delta, a lot of hunters continue to use the traditional mud decoys. These are just mounds adorned with white rags or pieces of paper. Blinds include pits, trenches, or any handy depression or vegetation. For some years, the "Texas method" has been spreading to new regions; I know it has reached Louisiana and Utah, and by now perhaps it's common in California. The standard Texas decoys are rags: old napkins, diapers, shirts, bedsheets, anything white. There's no blind in the usual sense. The hunter himself serves as a giant decoy, either wearing white coveralls or draping himself in a sheet.

In the Gulf Coast rice fields, the most effective snow-goose stool is a very generous scattering of the aforementioned white rags. Each white-camouflaged hunter lies on his back or side while watching for flocks to arrive. He might choose to lie in a depression or next to a slight rise that will conceal part of him, but it isn't necessary. When birds come over, he fires fast. Migrating snow geese often fly very high, and they're speedy, but when eager to come down and pick waste grain, they drop fairly low and decrease their speed. Thus, they often fly only 30 yards or so over the waiting gunners. They're probably going no faster than 40 miles an hour, and many brake their flight and attempt to land. Hungry for rice and easily fooled by the white-rag decoys, they become far less wary than Canadas, and they often ignore obvious signs of danger.

Full-bodied decoys are the most effective stick-ups for geese, but one-dimensional decoys—sometimes called profile, silhouette, or shadow decoys—are less expensive, easier to transport, and effective if placed where they'll be seen by geese coming down to rest or feed. This hunter sets them out near food and water hemmed by steep slopes, a spot where incoming flocks will drop low.

The description I've just given makes snow-goose shooting sound too easy, so I'd better mention a couple of difficulties involved in this white-rag method. You lie on the ground until birds are overhead or at least within range, and then you sit up fast to fire. This business of sitting up fast repeatedly, and firing from that position, is—for me, at least—the greatest difficulty. The strain on leg and back muscles interferes with a smooth swing and follow-through. I've said before that it takes obstinacy and liniment to endure this pleasure except when the geese come in such great numbers that a limit can be quickly bagged; otherwise, lying flat in a rice field can soon make a hunter feel stiff and old. As in most wildfowling, the experience is a combination of the absurd, the miserable, and the delightful.

A second, less serious difficulty is that when snow geese descend on a field, they may be low and relatively slow, but they're more acrobatic than other geese. They can tip, tumble, or twist abruptly as they simultaneously drop and decelerate. You may track an easy target only to have it switch down or sideward as you swing through and pull the trigger. Soon, however, you begin to "read" your birds and take them before they fool you. After that it takes far fewer sit-ups and much less ammunition to bag your limit.

Snow geese have higher, shriller voices than Canadas. After listening to them, you can mimic them by using the same standard mouth call used for Canada geese and controlling the tone and duration of the cries—almost yelping instead of honking. But you can also toll them in with conventional Canada honks. For that matter, I've noticed that they come to rag-strewn feeding fields in assault waves without any vocal inducement, especially for a little while after sunup. If you don't limit out then, try again shortly before sundown, when they head back to water.

The blue goose isn't a distinct species in the accepted sense, but a color phase of the lesser snow goose. In Texas and along the Gulf Coast, the flights are often mixed—white birds accompanied by dark ones. There and elsewhere, blues also travel in flocks of their own. The greatest wintering concentrations occur in Louisiana. They don't migrate as far west as their white relatives but are fairly abundant in some of the states blanketed by the Mississippi Flyway.

A typical blue goose has a white head and upper neck, usually amber-stained, and some white on the rump. The body is mostly gray or grayish-brown, the wings a mixture of grayish-blue and darker gray with some white streaking. There are many color variations because blues interbreed with lesser snow geese. If you shoot a piebald goose in an area frequented by snows and blues, you've bagged a hybrid.

Where a few blue geese mingle with their white relatives, both varieties visit the grain fields, and blues in all regions will come to conventional white rags or three-dimensional white decoys. (They'll also come to brant and Canada-goose decoys.)

However, where blues outnumber snows, or where flocks consist entirely of blues, they're more often shot in marshes than in fields. Many are shot around James Bay during the earliest stages of migration, and soon afterward around Michigan's Saginaw Bay. There they feed heavily on cattail roots, horsetail, and grasses.

Between Saginaw and the Gulf marshes and fields, blue-goose hunting is negligible because these birds make few rest stops.

When they reach the Southern marshes, they're extremely hungry—hence, extremely active. You should get plenty of shooting from a blind in a spot where they can find one or more of their favorite foods: bulrush, cattail, cordgrass, saltgrass, and spikerush. You'll also get excellent shooting on the Mississippi delta's mud flats, where blues feed gluttonously on rice, cutgrass, sorghum, and flags.

On some of the shallow, reed-choked Gulf marshes and bayous, you can reach good shooting sites by using a shallow-draft sneakbox, john boat, pirogue, or the sort of air-propelled boat used in the Everglades. There are also extensive wetlands at Louisiana's famous Vermilion Marshes and elsewhere that are too soggy to be crossed on foot but too shallow for a boat of any kind. Wide-wheeled homemade "marsh buggies" were once common, but now hunters can buy all-terrain (amphibious) vehicles that are nicely suited to navigation on quaking bogs.

The "specklebelly," or whitefronted goose, looks like a blue goose at a distance, but a hunter won't mistake one species for the other

The author (left) and his friend John Falk, a well-known writer and authority on gun dogs, kneel with a day's limit of brant. In many areas, a seaworthy boat is needed to reach the best spots for hunting brant (and sea ducks, as well). The one in the background has plenty of room for hunters, gear, and decoys.

because the specklebelly's neck and head are dark except for a white forehead patch around the bill. The name whitefront alludes to this patch. The name specklebelly alludes to splashes and specklings of dark brown and black against grayish-white on the upper belly or lower breast. Toward the rear, the belly whitens. The body is predominantly grayish-brown with some pale barring, dark gray wings, and a dark gray or brown tail tipped with white. The bill is pinkish—not as red as that of a blue goose or snow goose—with some light blue at the base and a pale orange tone around the nostrils. The bill's black saw-toothed edging, called a "grinning patch," is less pronounced than that of blues and snows.

In autumn, specklebellies migrate along the Pacific and Central Flyways to Washington, Oregon, California, and parts of Mexico, and they also follow the Mississippi Flyway to Texas and Louisiana. Good numbers are seen along the Gulf Coast, but they're more plentiful throughout the West. One of the finest areas for hunting whitefronts is the Big Bend of the Platte River in central Nebraska.

In Nebraska and again when the birds reach the Gulf, many specklebellies are bagged in the marshes, where they feed on such vegetation as panicgrass, sawgrass, and various sedges. But they prefer to graze on drier ground if heavy hunting pressure doesn't deter them, and they love grains, both wild and cultivated. Among their staples are wheat, rice, barley, and wild millet.

In California's Sacramento Valley, whitefronts are often shot over stubble fields where they feed with snows and cacklers (a diminutive Western race of the Canada goose). In Texas, too, they're often shot together with snows over the rice fields, and they'll come to white-rag decoys. They'll also come to decoys representing other kinds of geese, or rigs mixing goose and duck blocks. When mingling with other species at rice and wheat fields, they seem to lose their caution and behave pretty much as snow geese do. But when they're on the marshes, they're more wary than most geese. I think they're at least as cautious as Canadas. Even if your

Stand-up blinds like this one are effective in cornfields. They're camouflaged with cornstalks. A variation is a hedgerow blind camouflaged with shrubs or other bushy vegetation.

marsh blind is fronted by a good spread of decoys, you'll probably have to take most of your specklebellies by pass-shooting.

This North Carolina hunter may be thanking his dog for the day's bag of Canadas. A good retriever and a set of goose blocks are among the essentials for shooting geese over water. The author prefers slightly oversized decoys because they get the attention of birds flying high and wide.

In some regions, whitefronts are better known as "laughing geese." Their rapid, clanging flight notes, rather like hysterical laughter, are hard to mimic. Trying to do so is probably an exercise in futility anyway, because these birds become silent or almost silent as they circle suspiciously, deciding whether to alight. Unless other species are also passing, it's better to remain silent than to chance revealing your human identity by trying the persuasion of a goose-call on specklebellies. Just wait quietly. If nothing alarms them, they'll probably circle lower and lower until they're within range.

Ducks

Waterfowling entails long-range shooting, for the most part, but there are exceptions. More often than not, the various species of diving ducks are bagged at medium to fairly long shotgun range, even when taken over decoys. Among the dabbling ducks (or call them dippers or puddle ducks or surface ducks or pond-and-river species if you prefer), mallards, teal, gadwall, and several other species are often bagged at surprisingly short range—say fifteen to thirty yards. Such close targets aren't always a result of jump-shooting; dabblers sometimes approach very near over decoys.

At the edge of a narrow slough and again on several small ponds, I've seen mallards repeatedly fly between the decoy rig and the blind, thus passing well within twenty yards of me, and I've had many shots at ducks directly above me, no more than a dozen yards over my head as they prepared to pitch in amid the stool of decoys.

You want one kind of gun and load when such close, fast-swinging shooting predominates, and quite another kind for long-range ducking. Normally, my duck gun and my goose gun are one and the same—a 12 gauge, chambered for 3-inch shells, because I need all the help I can get when pass-shooting. For almost all of my shooting over decoys I like the same gun with slightly lighter loads, 2¾-inch high-velocity shells. But when I'm using decoys at one of the puddle-duck blinds I just mentioned, a 20-gauge Magnum is really preferable. Sometimes it's preferable for jump-shooting, as well. During a grouse hunt, I once flushed a wood duck from a creek in such tight cover, at such close range, and so unexpectedly that I was very glad to be carrying a light, fast-swinging 20-gauge upland gun. That sort of experience isn't unusual.

Where lead shot can be used, No. 5's or 6's are about right for close-in decoying or jump-shooting. For most of the shooting over decoys, however, and for pass-shooting, the lead-pellet size is 4.

A hunter in Manitoba picks up a duck he brought down right at the fringe of his decoy spread. Note that he's using only about a dozen blocks, set in water he can easily wade. The dabbling species of ducks can be attracted by small rigs in the shallows.

As I explained in connection with geese, steel shot is now mandatory in a great many areas (and will soon be required in still more areas) in order to prevent the poisoning of waterfowl by spent lead shot swallowed as grit for the gizzard. If you have to use steel shot, the recommendations I just made become invalid. You must then use a 12-gauge gun, substituting No. 4 steel duck loads for the No. 5 or 6 lead-pellet loads, and substituting No. 2 steel shot for the No. 4 lead shot that was formerly standard for pass-shooting and most decoying.

A fuller discussion of steel shot, and some precautions regarding its use, can be found in the section on geese. Also see that section for details regarding clothing and gear, and don't forget that for ducks as well as geese, your gun must hold no more than three shells. Most repeaters require a wooden magazine plug to temporarily reduce their capacity.

Having committed the mild heresy of mentioning an upland gun for duck shooting under certain circumstances, I might as well go on record as believing that a 28-inch barrel with a modified choke is usually best for jump-shooting dabblers or shooting them over decoys in the small-water situations where they come as close as upland birds. In fact, for very close work, a 26-inch improved-cylinder barrel can be advantageous. The 30-inch full-choke barrel that dominates wildfowling literature is for pass-shooting and for decoying where the ducks don't crowd you. Obviously, this long, tight barrel is also necessary where geese and ducks are hunted together.

When steel was first introduced, there was a lot of talk about the supposed need to abstain from shots at ducks more than 35 yards away. Steel was alleged to lose energy and velocity so fast that it would only produce cripples at ranges beyond that. Lately some writers have gone to the opposite extreme, describing steel-shot kills at 60 yards. Perhaps an exceptional wingshooter, using a full-choked gun, can kill a duck at 60 yards with steel shot, but even with lead shot, I think that's too far for most of us to try.

The truth is, a skillful gunner can kill ducks (and I mean consistently retrievable ducks, not cripples that sail off and are lost) at ranges up to perhaps 50 yards with lead shot. For most of us, 40 or 45 yards may be a safer limit. And steel shot kills cleanly at 40 or 45 yards if the pattern is well centered, so the only change that steel should make in the lives of typical duck hunters is to discourage the too-common "skybusting" tendency. I don't like the performance of steel shot as compared with lead, but it can be used very effectively at sensible ranges.

This, once again, brings up the subject of range estimation. If it gives you trouble, you can—to some degree—teach yourself distance judgment by setting out markers and then noting size and details of appearance as birds pass these markers, which can be decoys, driven stakes, fishing bobbers, or perhaps just landmarks or trees at a known distance.

A good rule of thumb is that a duck's plumage pattern is discernible, even on a dark day, by the time it flies within range. Some shooters seem to think this means a duck is within range as soon as it's recognizable. It doesn't mean that at all, as you'll realize if you reflect that a pintail (to cite just one example) is recognizable long before it comes into range, its identity revealed by its raked, pointed wings, quick but deep wingbeats, long neck and tail, the spear of its central tail feathers if it's a drake, its long overall profile, and even its general colors if the day is clear. A duck probably isn't within range unless you can make out the *details* of its color pattern.

Shape, flight characteristics, and color pattern are crucial to identification. You can't shoot a duck until you've made certain it's among the year's legal species on your flyway, and even then you may want to hold your fire. Under the point system of bag limits, taking a given species or taking a hen of a given species may finish your shooting for the day, whereas a drake or another species won't limit you out. You'd better have the current regulations at hand (or memorized) and, if you're not good at field identification, you ought to practice with the aid of a field guide.

Two types of guides are valuable to a duck hunter. One is the relatively thick, weighty, detailed volume of normal book size. I wouldn't bother taking a book like that into a blind with me, but it's an excellent reference that belongs in your home library. Examples of this kind of reference book include *North American Ducks, Geese & Swans*, by Donald S. Heintzelman (Winchester Press, 1978) and my own *Hunter's Field Guide to the Game Birds and Animals of North America* (Knopf, 1974).

The other type is the very compact guide, usually less detailed but easily pocketed and arranged for very fast reference. Among those I can recommend are: the *Top Flight Speed Index to Waterfowl of North America*, by John A. Ruthven and William Zimmerman (Moebius Printing Co., 1968); The *Audubon Society Field Guide to North American Birds*, by John Bull, John Farrand, Jr., M.D.F. Udvardy, and Susan Rayfield (Knopf, 1977); and an excellent little booklet entitled *Ducks at a Distance*, by Bob Hines, published by the U.S. Fish and Wildlife Service. Recently revised and enlarged, *Ducks at a Distance* is available for $1.80 from the U.S. Government Printing Office, Washington, D.C. 20240.

In my discussion of geese I stressed the importance of retrieving dogs, and I named the most popular breeds—the Labrador, golden, and Chesapeake Bay retrievers. The same comments apply to duck hunting, but a few additional breeds deserve mention here. One of the finest, in my estimation, is the springer spaniel. Most American sportsmen think of the springer only in conjunction with upland hunting, chiefly for pheasants. Yet there are water trials for springers, and in England—the breed's home—a springer is expected to be adept at handling assorted game, including ducks.

Two other, far less famous breeds that also merit consideration are the American water spaniel and Irish water spaniel. Both are fine performers. And the fact that the Irish water spaniel looks rather like a chocolate-colored French poodle reminds me that the standard poodle was a favorite duck dog in Germany and France many years ago. Quite a few breeds—poodle, cocker spaniel, Irish setter—were once bred almost exclusively for the field but have been transformed, more or less, into bench-show dogs and nonworking pets. There are some whose field abilities have been show-bred right out of them. However, I had an acquaintance who used a poodle to fetch ducks, and the dog was pretty good. If you have a pup that doesn't happen to be a name-brand retriever but does like the water, you might give him a try, applying the training methods that are used for standard water dogs.

On the central part of the Mississippi Flyway, I once met a grizzled hunter who could make his ordinary, mouth-blown wood-and-reed duck call screech like a banshee. I didn't think it sounded like anything remotely related to a mallard or any other duck, yet that man certainly tolled in mallards, along with occasional gadwalls and other species. I understand from John Madson, an eminent outdoor writer and hunting authority, that this shrieking style is known as a "highball" call and is used to get the attention of high-flying ducks that might otherwise ignore decoys. I'm more accustomed to a lower, gutteral feeding chatter—a few quacks followed by a staccato chuckle—for mallards and several other species. Maybe a piercing wail would be effective in my part of the country, too, when ducks come highballing over. Maybe, and maybe not.

Some species have very different voices, of course, and you have to listen to them for a while before you can mimic them persuasively. But in addition, and for reasons that escape me, a single species will respond well to very different calling styles in different regions. So it pays to listen to other hunters as well as to the ducks.

The best way to learn duck calling is to share a blind repeatedly with a skilled companion. Instructional phonograph records can also help; they're not legal (or sporting) in a blind, but they can be used for home-practice sessions. Plenty of practice is needed, because the tone of a call can be drastically altered merely by the way you cup your hand over the end of the call.

Some hunters have "tin ears" or else an inability to reproduce the tones they hear. I'm one of those unfortunates, so I speak with authority when I say that it's better not to call than to call poorly. Inept vocalizations flare ducks instead of bringing them in. I use a call on desperate occasions when I'm alone or with an equally inept caller and the birds aren't approaching anyway. Sometimes I man-

These are lesser scaup—also known as bluebills or broadbills—photographed on wintering waters in Texas. The size of this raft (and it isn't a particularly large one) indicates why diving ducks require a great many more decoys than the dabbling species. You want to mimic their big feeding and loafing concentrations.

age to lure passing ducks, and I seem to be improving with years of practice. But more often I leave the calling to a companion who's a better wildfowling musician.

A common calling mistake is to overdo it. Your object is to turn the ducks toward your decoys or blind, but the closer they come, the more likely they are to recognize a false note. So, once you've succeeded in turning a passing flight, keep quiet. If the ducks don't keep coming your way, then you can coax them by calling again.

There's an old belief that diving ducks are less suspicious than dabblers, and I think there's a grain of truth in it. However, the exceptions almost outweigh the rule. Among the dabbling species, the gadwall is a trusting creature. Among the divers, scaup are paradoxically wary and inquisitive. Often they inspect a raft of decoys but either swing wide or settle on the far side of the stool. I remember this happening repeatedly one morning on Maryland's Eastern Shore. Finally my companion, a very experienced scaup gunner, coaxed a couple of birds into lifting off the water and flying closer by purring at them. A mellow, catlike purr is a characteristic call of the scaup (or "bluebill" or "broadbill," equally common names for the species). Later, he teased one into making a low pass by gently waving his cap above the blind. A scaup's curiosity makes it vulnerable. All the same, we had few shots that day. Even the supposedly trusting species can be very wary, especially after exposure to early-season gunfire.

With regard to camouflaging yourself, staying low and still until ready to fire, and taking account of the prevailing winds in situating a blind or decoys, the same recommendations I made for goose hunting apply to ducks.

For the sake of success (though not of comfort) a blind supplied by nature is really better than the average man-made structure. Any natural hiding place where ducks pass or congregate abundantly will serve well; it can be driftwood or a rock pile on a shore line, a hedgerow or brush clump, a ditch, high reeds, waterside shrubbery, or just a sand pit. Since nature doesn't always provide complete concealment, I've helped ensure my shooting by carrying along a roll of chicken wire as a portable blind-enhancer. It can be quickly opened and staked in high vegetation, and it can be thatched in advance or on the spot. Some hunters stretch camouflage cloth over the wire or weave reeds into it. A roll of cane or bamboo can be used the same way. I once used a dilapidated bamboo shade taken from an oversized porch window. With the addition of straw, it was fine.

In some of the best hunting spots, nature supplies no concealment at all, and a permanent man-made blind is in order. Since ducks often avoid new or unnatural structures in familiar terrain, it's best to build such a blind before the season opens. In my experience, the most effective blinds have been old ones, repaired and recamouflaged with thatch or brush as needed.

If the shooting is to be over decoys, either a standing blind of this type or a pit blind is often located on a point, island, bar, or cove shoreline adjacent to feeding or resting waters. Ducks like to rest and/or feed in the lee of a shore.

In deciding on a type of blind to be used, you must take into account the prevalent species of ducks, the habitat, and the kinds of blinds that have become locally popular because they've proved efficient. There are many types in addition to pits and thatched or otherwise camouflaged enclosures. Sea ducks are often shot from elevated "reef blinds"—boxed wooden platforms on pilings that permit a boat to be moored underneath, out of sight. Reef blinds look like big elevated huts, and they're certainly conspicuous, yet they don't alarm the ducks. Erected long before the autumn migrations, they're accepted by the birds just as other old structures and topographic features are accepted.

Along the mid-Atlantic coast I've seen sunken "curtain blinds," their tops just above the surface. Though walled with concrete and rimmed with wide, flat wings ("curtains" to help keep waves from spilling in), they have to be pumped out after every high tide. I've also seen low but commodious reed enclosures, staked into a cove to hold a line of shallow-draft duck boats such as Barnegat sneakboxes. A smaller version—a pair of staked aquatic hedgerows that will hide a single boat—is fairly common in many regions. And there are also floating blinds, moored to the bottom and brushed or bushed over to look like islands. Regional differences are worth heeding, as they're based on experience.

For general recommendations about the placement of decoys, see the section on geese. To those recommendations I'll now add a few specifics concerning ducks. I've had mallards and other dabbling ducks (including woodies early in the season, before the simultaneous increase in hunting pressure and wood-duck wariness) swoop down eagerly to less than a dozen decoys set out in a pothole, pond, or other shallow pocket of food-rich water. I'm sure half that number of decoys would have sufficed, although it never hurts to use several dozen where there's room for them. The dippers often feed in small groups, so the sight of just a few lifelike blocks can attract any number of them.

This doesn't generally work with diving ducks, however. They gather in big groups, or rafts, on wider and generally deeper water. I don't think a meager decoy spread arouses their suspicion, but I do think it represents an abnormally small group, settled temporarily on water that isn't choice for feeding or resting. Thus, the diving ducks tend to ignore anything less than a good-sized raft of decoys.

The best procedure is to set out as many as you can afford, or as many as you have the time and means to transport. Use several dozen or more if you can leave them out overnight or set them out before the flights begin to come over at sunup. Many hunters add a few to their collection each year to replace those damaged or lost and to enlarge the spread.

It's usually best not to bunch your decoys too close together, because if each block is surrounded by a few feet of water surface, it's more easily recognizable from the air, and there are landing spaces that look inviting. As with goose decoys, a wide gap or two in the spread also invites birds to pitch in.

However, the dabbling species habitually slip down into little openings on ponds and creeks that look too crowded to hold even one more bird. For these puddle ducks, I've just read about a decoying trick I haven't tried. It's simply to bunch the decoys in a tight group, using just enough anchor cord to reach bottom so that the blocks can't swing around too much and get tangled. The idea is to mimic a behavioral peculiarity of puddle ducks. When they first alight on water, they come down scattered—spread out rather haphazardly—but immediately swim into a temporary cluster while looking about for possible danger. The cluster soon disperses as they feed, cruise about, or just rest. A tight stool of decoys therefore has the natural look of puddlers that have just set down.

The trick is worth trying, and I will, but with a slight modification. I'll use at least a dozen and a half decoys, and although I'll cluster the majority of them, I'll strew some farther from the nucleus, as if the ducks had already checked for danger and begun to fan out. This will look just as natural and should be more inviting since it leaves easy landing spaces and conveys the message that the feeding site has been inspected and found safe. Beyond little experiments like this, I really don't believe in careful decoy arrangements. It's important only to place them naturally, make sure they're highly visible, and set them so that approaching ducks will be close to you when they fly into the wind as they drop down.

A decoy trick that involves no special formation is to mix sets representing a couple of different species that normally associate with each other. This enhances the natural look and conveys a picture of a spot with plenty of food for both species. The two kinds of decoys must, of course, be appropriate to the habitat, and they shouldn't be thoroughly mixed because each variety of duck will tend to stay closer to its own kind than to another species. You might, for example, set canvasback and scaup decoys in a loose double raft, with one species vaguely to the side of the other so that only a few cans and bluebills are actually mingled.

I've also had excellent results when I used goose blocks along with the smaller duck decoys. However, I then segregated the species a little more definitely, floating the goose blocks a short distance from the duck blocks. In a feeding field, geese mingle pretty freely with ducks, and I've often seen Canadas and mallards flocking together in corn stubble. On the water, geese are a trifle more clannish. They associate with ducks but don't quite mingle if there's room to form a separate group.

Since various species of ducks feed together and will come to decoys representing more than one variety, you don't always have to be selective about the kind of blocks you set out. Decoys representing one species will attract another that uses the same kind of habitat. Let's say you've bought or made a dozen or more black-duck decoys. As the hunting season progresses, blacks begin to favor coastal salt marshes, and they're seen in reduced numbers over fresh potholes and creeks. You're hunting late in the season, and your blind is on an inland farm pond that black ducks seldom visit any more. You can set out your decoys there anyway. You needn't acquire new ones, because the same blocks will attract mallards and pintails to a shallow pond.

For me, the most pleasurable duck shooting is over decoys, but pass-shooting can also be exciting, especially for the first hour or so of legal shooting time on a morning after a moonless or stormy night. When there's no night light, ducks don't do much nocturnal feeding, and they're very active early the next morning. If the morning is overcast or rainy, so much the better because the birds will tend to fly low.

Waterfowl, like deer and crows, habitually use the same routes between resting and feeding areas. A little observation will reveal where most of the ducks in a given locality are flying. A flyway between roosting water and a foraging area may be just a few hundred yards long or several miles long. The major portion of a long one is often unproductive because when ducks have to fly a substantial distance, they do so at a proportionately substantial altitude. On a short flyway, you may be able to get good pass-shooting by hiding anywhere. On a long one, your natural or man-made blind should be close to where they rise or descend.

The best pass-shooting I've ever had was near to posted refuge waters where ducks couldn't be hunted. Waterfowl quickly learn that no shooting is ever done on certain waters, so they gather in great numbers at sanctuaries. A blind that's legally located outside the posted zone but fairly near it and also near a feeding area is one where the action is intense.

There are two basic, or most popular, methods of jump-shooting. The more common technique is to stalk to the brink of a creek, river, slough, swamp, pothole, or wooded pond in order to flush ducks from the water. You must be quiet and stay low or the ducks will take to the air before you get within range. "Stalking," in this instance, sometimes means crawling. In the woods, however, I've sometimes just walked to the edge of a creek or pond and put up mallards or wood ducks.

The other basic method is to use a canoe, duck boat, skiff, or even a raft to float-hunt a waterway. The craft should be low above the surface and camouflaged with brush or reeds; otherwise, its approach will spook the birds off the water before you're within gunshot. In effect, such a boat is a mobile blind.

A Labrador retriever threads his way through a decoy spread to fetch a mallard drake. Even on small, shallow waters, good retrievers are usually needed to prevent the loss of crippled birds.

Scientifically, the dabbling ducks are members of the tribe (sub-subfamily) *Anatini*. The North American species are the black duck, gadwall, mallard, pintail, shoveler, all three kinds of teal (bluewinged, cinnamon, greenwinged), and the American widgeon, or baldpate. The wood duck is the sole North American member of the *Cairinini*, the perching tribe, but is usually grouped with the dabblers because of its similar eating habits, habitat, and distribution. The ruddy duck is our lone representative of the *Oxyurinia*, or stiff-tailed tribe. Though capable of impressive dives, it feeds in the shallows—chiefly in fresh marshes but also in brackish and salt

The author's friend Len Wright holds a grouse (right) and a greenwinged teal. The seasons on upland birds and waterfowl overlap in many regions, and dabbling ducks such as teal or woodies may go into an "upland" bag. Unlike most duck hunting, this short-range jump-shooting is best done with an open-bored gun.

water during the hunting season. Behaviorally, it's more like the dabblers than the divers. The ruddy isn't highly regarded, but it often goes into a mixed bag. It's so stupid about avoiding danger that in some regions it's known as the "booby" or the "deaf duck."

The canvasback, redhead, ringnecked duck, and greater and lesser scaup belong to the tribe *Aythyini*—the pochards, or freshwater diving ducks. These scientific classifications are no guide to habitat. The ringneck and lesser scaup are seldom seen on salt water except in the South, but any experienced hunter knows that the can, redhead, and greater scaup are often bagged on brackish or salt water. (For that matter, the black duck prefers salt marshes in winter, though as a dabbler it's supposed to be a pond-and-river species.)

The bufflehead, all species of eider, American and Barrow's goldeneye, harlequin, oldsquaw, and all species of scoter are divers, and most scientific authorities now classify them as belonging to the tribe *Mergini*, the sea ducks, a category that somewhat incongruously includes the mergansers. Here again, scientific references can mislead a layman. The goldeneye, especially the Barrow's goldeneye, is often bagged over fresh lakes and rivers far from the sea.

As I did with geese, I'll offer a few additional tips about major species. In reading them, remember that the inclusion of information about a given species doesn't necessarily mean that it can be hunted in your locale. Bag limits and other restrictions change from year to year, depending on breeding success, harvests, current state of the wintering habitat, and similar factors. In some years, a species may be fully protected along one or more of the nation's major flyways.

In some sections of the country, including mine, both ducks and duck hunters have been pampered ever since the introduction of mechanical corn pickers. The waste kernels and cobs are so copious that mallards, Canada geese, and hunters seem to forget the existence of other waterfowl foods. A cornfield that's hunted day after day can be abandoned by the birds even if it isn't picked clean. (This is one reason why I'm in favor of split seasons or the "rest days" that interrupt but stretch the season in some states.) Other important mallard foods include wild rice, pondweed, smartweed, wild celery, wild millet, bulrush, primrose willow, duckweed, spikerush, culti-

These mallards were surprised near the edge of a little creek. High-banked creeks or those with high streamside vegetation or sharp bends provide good jump-shooting because a hunter can stay hidden while he stalks into range.

vated rice, sorghum, oats, buckwheat, and barley. Obviously, cornfields aren't the only farmlands to try, and if the local farm blinds are all owned or leased by people who need neither your friendship nor your money, you may find better hunting around lakes, sloughs, ponds, and streams. Don't just look for the prairie-type potholes featured on calendars. Mallards love acorns, beechnuts, and hickory nuts. Wooded waters often hold mallards as well as wood ducks.

For as long as any living hunter can remember, the country's finest mallard-shooting area has been around Stuttgart, Arkansas, in the oak flats, flooded rice fields, and reservoirs. You might want to write to the chamber of commerce for advice about arranging a hunt.

Most cornfield shooting of mallards is a matter of pass-shooting or shooting over decoys from a pit or standing blind. Another kind of "cornfielding" is especially productive during winter snow flurries. Near dusk on the day before you plan a hunt, scout the fields to find out where most of the ducks are congregating. Be there at sunup the next morning, clad in white coveralls or draped in a sheet, as if you were waylaying snow geese. Hunker down in a shallow pit, trench, or furrow. Whether or not you use decoys, you should get some early-morning shooting.

Swamps, flooded oak flats, and similar wooded areas are excellent places from which to call dabbling ducks. A site like this provides natural concealment and, to a duck, looks like a perfect place to roost and feed.

Mallards are rather alert, so jump-shooting is best at waters that are wooded or rimmed by fairly high grass, reeds, or brush to conceal your approach. However, I've also done well at streams where high banks or bends covered my stalk.

Not many pintails, or "sprig," are taken by pass-shooting because they tend to fly too high. However, both decoying and jump-shooting work well. In the North, sprig often go into a mixed bag with mallards. Small, wooded waters in farm country are usually good. They don't forage on land as much as mallards because they can't walk as well, but down on the rice fields of Texas and Louisiana, they come swarming in with snow geese.

Pintails aren't very loquacious. They can be mimicked, and I've seen them respond to mallard calling, but I think it's as well to remain silent and let your decoys do the luring.

Decoying is also the best way to attract bluewinged teal. These birds are quick to flare off when a call mimics them ineptly. Silence or an imitation of mallards is a wise choice for anyone who hasn't mastered their soft, chirping calls. Jump-shooting works at the edges of reed-bound waters, but decoying is better. These birds, though spooked by wrong sounds, will make pass after pass over decoys even after a couple have been shot down—or at least they will early in the season.

Cinnamon teal are jumped a bit more easily, but they don't feed or fly in large groups, and they're generally put into a mixed bag by hunters decoying other puddle ducks. In Mexico, however, they're a major attraction for visiting hunters, and the guides know the best places for decoying or pass-shooting.

Greenwinged teal are more widespread. They're hunted on all the major flyways. With other teal, jump-shooting may call for a fairly open bore, but greenwings require a tight choke because they flush at long range. On Maine's famous Merrymeeting Bay, jump-shooters lie low in special sculls to sneak up on the ducks, while on the rice flats of the South and the tule-choked sloughs of California, poling is a common method. Greenwings also decoy readily.

Pass-shooting at wood ducks, mallards, and many other species can be excellent in the early morning or again near legal quitting time if you know the habitual flight paths the birds take between roosting and foraging areas. This Florida gunner is bagging his ducks near swamp water where the birds roost.

Like mallards, black ducks feed both in the water and on land. They like wheat, corn, and other grains, as well as aquatic vegetation and the nuts and berries that attract mallards and woodies. Early in the season, a farm pond with an adjacent stubble field is a fine spot for decoying. I like to put most of the blocks in the water, but I also scatter a few nearby in the field to give the impression that the birds are feasting on grain.

Later in the season, I'd rather hunt blacks on the salt marshes where they spend much time in winter. I set the decoys fairly close to the blind, and I resist the temptation to fire too soon as the birds begin to circle down. Black ducks are very cautious. I try to wait until they're low, but often they'll alight on the far side of the decoy spread, which is why I set the stool close. On occasion, I fail to get a shot before the ducks touch down on the water. In that case, I wait a bit and rise in the blind to flush them. Unlike diving ducks, which generally take off with a run, they tend to leap up. They're fast, but they give you an instant at the top of that leap when there's a good chance of bagging one.

Gadwalls aren't hunted heavily in most regions. They're generally just included in a mixed bag. However, they come eagerly to puddle-duck decoys, and they're vulnerable to jump-shooting because they lack the wariness of most dabbling species.

American widgeon, or baldpates, are also called whistlers (as are goldeneyes). Not many hunters try to mimic the triple whistling note of the widgeon drake—*heew, heew, heew*—which is uttered repeatedly both in flight and on the water. The important thing is to recognize it; and you will, after hearing it a few times. You can identify it when the ducks are still a couple of hundred yards away, and it's a cue for you to crouch low in your blind and stay still until the ducks are within range.

Baldpates are so high-strung that I doubt if many are bagged by jump-shooting. They will, however, come to decoys and can also be taken by pass-shooting. If you're hunting them together with other dabblers, be careful about your calling. Loud, startled quacking resembles their alarm signal.

Woodies, too, can often be located by their voices, though calling them isn't very productive. Their flight call is a mellow hooting, and their feeding chatter consists of squeaking, clucking, and chirping quacks. When in cover they aren't very wary, so you may be able to approach the sounds through the woods and get some jump-shooting. Even if you alert them prematurely you may get a shot, because they sometimes scatter in all directions, and it's likely that one may fly right over you.

There are two better ways to take wood ducks. One is to decoy them along with other puddle ducks early in the season. After a while they begin to avoid decoys and blinds, but then you can use the second method. This requires scouting for a few days to map out their habitual routes between roosts and feeding areas. They often fly to a feeding area at dawn, and by the time shooting is legal, there may be few or none in the air. Since you know where they'll come when dusk approaches, you can pick a good hiding place for some fast jump-shooting just before legal quitting time.

Ringnecks are closely related to scaup (and are better table fare). Like scaup, they can dive deep for succulent vegetation, yet they prefer to feed where feeding is easier and where they can rely on cover rather than wide expanses of water for safety. Good ringneck-hunting spots are wooded ponds, swamps, sloughs, and creeks. They'll come to decoys representing the dabbling species you'd expect to find in such habitat as well as decoys that imitate divers. My first experience with their reaction to decoys so unnerved me that I wrote about their charging at the blocks "as if attacking." Ever since then, I've felt that a modified rather than full choke is best for such ducks on the little brush-lined water holes. The same ponds, by the way, afford good jump-shooting at ringnecks, and I'd use a modified choke for that, too.

Both greater and lesser scaup migrate along all four of the continent's major flyways. Lesser scaup are more abundant on Midwestern lakes and marshes, and they almost monopolize the Mississippi Valley. In the West, the two varieties seem to be about equally abundant. In the East, greater scaup are more plentiful; they're the broadbills, or bluebills, that are commonly taken from boats or blinds on brackish marshes or out on salt water. When a hunter from one region talks to a hunter from another about how or where to hunt scaup, confusion can result because the greater scaup is vir-

Jumped from a pond next to a cornfield, these ducks are mostly pintails and mallards, but widgeon and other species are also present. To stay within the law (especially when bag limits are governed by a point system), you have to know what you're shooting. It pays to practice identification with the aid of a field guide.

tually a maritime bird while migrating or wintering in many regions, and the lesser is primarily a freshwater duck.

Scaup (both kinds) like big waters, but early in the morning and again very late in the day they prefer to feed close to shore. Those are the two times of day when jump-shooting them can be a practical way to try for a limit. At other times, decoying is best. However, rafts of scaup aren't very wary when they're out on big water diving for food. Sometimes a duck boat can approach within range before the birds leave. There's a maddening suspense about this; you keep wondering if you can drift close enough to get a shot or two when they rise.

Lesser scaup tend to be more alert than the greater variety, perhaps because they often have to forage on smaller bodies of water where predation is greater. Yet they decoy about as readily as greater scaup, and both varieties can sometimes be coaxed closer by an imitation of their cat's-purr call. Lesser scaup are quieter than greater scaup, and unless they're startled, they don't croak as the greaters often do. A raucous sound, much like the name "scaup," is a flight call of the greater race. If you make the mistake of using this call as lesser scaup approach, you'll probably flare them.

Buffleheads are also known as "butterballs," but on the West Coast, many hunters deem them inedible when they've been feeding on dead fish during spawning runs. Elsewhere, they're adequate table fare, but no competition for a corn-fed mallard. Their nickname has more to do with shape than taste.

Buffleheads sometimes drop right in among decoys without any preliminary passing or circling. Don't let them alight in the hope of shooting when they rise again. Too often, they dive. Sometimes, too, they leap up again unexpectedly. They can leave the water almost as steeply as dabbling ducks, and they can dive down and then come up flying.

When the name "whistler" is applied to the goldeneye, it doesn't refer to a flight call but to the whistle of wind in the wing feathers. Since goldeneyes utter only occasional quacks and squeaks in flight, hunters listen for the whistle of their wings.

Scaup show little or no interest in goldeneye decoys, but goldeneyes come readily to scaup decoys, so where there's a chance of a mixed bag, you can set out a broadbill rig. Goldeneyes are too wary to be taken often by jump-shooting, yet they pitch right in among decoys placed 30 yards or more from shore.

Wintering flocks of common, or American, goldeneyes are partial to coastal salt ponds, bays, and marshes, but they also frequent lakes and rivers. They feed chiefly on crustaceans, insects, and fish. You have a better chance of bagging them if you understand their peculiar ways of feeding and flying. When traveling, they prefer to follow shorelines, but almost always over the water, a little way from shore. Good blind locations are therefore on points and islands or on the water itself. When feeding, they frequently fly upstream and then

A small, camouflaged duck boat is, in effect, a mobile blind. Its deck can be thatched or strewn with reeds and marsh grasses, the same vegetation that surrounds it.

ride the current down, diving to feed along the way. Oddly, they tend to fly along the windward side of a river or lake, but they prefer to feed on fairly smooth water, and they lift off when they reach white water.

So the best blind location for whistlers is not only out a little from the general shoreline but on the windward side or downstream end of a point or island—not on the lee side, as for most waterfowl—and another good choice is to place it on smooth water close to a rough or windy stretch.

The Barrow's, or Rocky Mountain, goldeneye occurs in two widely separated populations, Eastern and Western. The Western birds are considerably more abundant. Many of them fly down through the Rockies into Colorado while others migrate into central California. They're most plentiful along the Continental Divide. They decoy more easily than the common goldeneyes of the Midwest and Atlantic Seaboard, and on alkaline mountain lakes, where they're attracted by abundant crawfish, they're easily jump-shot.

Oldsquaws, or "grannies," are hunted mostly by New Englanders and often go into a mixed bag with scoters. (Sometimes the two species also go into a mixed stew.) In recent years, Chesapeake gunners have begun to take an interest in both species, and a special sea-duck season in Maryland has considerably lengthened the wildfowling season.

The name oldsquaw, like "granny" and several other nicknames, alludes to the fact that this species is the noisiest of waterfowl. Flight and feeding calls include hoots, yodels, whistles, and honks. After hearing them a few times, you'll recognize their voices, which can alert you to incoming birds. There's no need to master their repertoire of scolding cries, for they decoy eagerly without the persuasion of sound effects.

Both scoters and oldsquaws gullibly approach "poor man's decoys"—gallon plastic bleach bottles painted black. Interestingly, bluebills will also come to such crude decoys if a broad white band is left around the middle of each bottle. Bleach jugs for bluebills can be tolerated on the basis of financial necessity, but handsomely realistic scaup decoys are traditional, and some of us feel a twinge of embarrassment about substituting primitively daubed by-products of the supermarket. The jugs seem more appropriate—and, in fact, are establishing a tradition of their own—for hunting scoters, which are better known in most areas as "sea coots."

A few of the sea ducks seem to contradict the rule that wildfowl are hard to deceive. For stupidity, none of them can beat the scoters, though oldsquaws and common eiders are slow to learn about danger. A good sea-coot rig consists of four strings of, say, 15 black-painted bottles per string. Spaced about a yard apart on each string, the bleach jugs are trailed from a strong anchor line. One string is floated aft of the boat, another out beyond the bow, and the remaining two on the sides, with the farthest bottle only about 30 yards away. You need no camouflage. In fact, you can just sit upright in the boat until ready to shoot, if you stay fairly still. Flying fast, the birds often turn away before crossing the decoy strings, but they're low and within range. And sometimes oldsquaws, eiders, or brant will make a pass at the same decoys.

SHORE &
MARSH BIRDS
Snipe

The common snipe—also called jacksnipe and Wilson's snipe (after the 19th-century ornithologist Alexander Wilson)—is 10 or 11 inches long and weighs less than half a pound. It's roughly the size of the closely related woodcock, but trimmer. Without question, snipe are tougher targets than woodcock. They flush farther out, catapult into the air, and their initial flight is a faster, twisting, zigzag course.

You don't need much in the way of power or pellet size to bring down such small birds. What you need is a light, fast-swinging gun that will throw a sufficiently wide, dense pattern to hit an erratically moving target. To hunters who haven't had much snipe-shooting experience, the small, careening birds look farther away than they really are, an illusion that can lead to "overgunning." A 20- or 28-gauge gun is just right with field loads of No. 9's.

The temptation to use too much gun is usually accompanied by the temptation to use too much choke. The ideal snipe gun is a double with improved and modified borings—the classic grouse and woodcock gun. If you're using a repeater, the requisite compromise is an improved-cylinder choke.

The North American subspecies of snipe has an enormous breeding range—from northern Alaska across most of Canada, and as far south as California and Colorado in the West, Pennsylvania and New Jersey in the East. A few of the birds winter in the middle tier of states, but the majority migrate farther south. They use all the migratory flyways traveled by waterfowl, and they're abundant enough to be hunted in a majority of states. Being migratory birds, they're included in federal hunting regulations. Generally the daily limit is eight, but few shotgunners are good enough to count on filling the limit.

Though snipe sometimes eat worms, they forage in boggier habitat than woodcock, and their mainstays are insects, insect larvae, and freshwater snails, augmented by such vegetation as smartweed, bulrush, panicgrass, sedges, and other marsh plants. Like woodcock, they bore into the ground for much of their sustenance. And although their preferred ground is spongier than typical woodcock habitat, they, too, are spurred southward by autumn frosts. Snipe hunting is best during the first month or two of fall in much of Canada and the upper states, where the season typically runs from early September to early November.. Because the birds migrate a little later along the Pacific Flyway, the season there commonly opens from October through December. Snipe migrate as woodcock do, traveling at night, stopping frequently to rest or feed, and sometimes lingering for weeks in choice habitat. Thus, a good many of them don't arrive in the Deep South until December, and the season there is open in the winter.

A snipe on the wing resembles a woodcock, but with narrower, more pointed wings and an orange-looking tail. The sexes are alike.

Some time ago, I read an article that advised snap-shooting at wild-flushing snipe, as the author considered these acrobatic fliers too difficult for long shots. On the contrary, most old snipe hands wait out their birds, and doing so reduces misses. A snipe usually twists and zigzags for only 10 yards or so, then flies a fairly straight course.

If you wait for a fast-flying bird to straighten out, won't it be beyond range? No—or not often—if you walk the bogs with the wind at your back. Snipe almost invariably leap into the wind and then fly across or into it, usually staying low. If you flush one from the windward side, it will probably fly across or toward you. And if you wait for the twisting to stop, you'll get mostly broadside shots.

Assuming you've failed to mark down a missed bird, hunt elsewhere for a while and then return to where you flushed it. Snipe tend to come back to a resting or foraging site quite soon.

Excellent hunting areas are usually short-grass bogs, swamps, flooded meadows, grass patches in and around marshes, and the shores of streams and lakes. Best of all are meadows almost covered with a thin film of water but with scattered hummocks or brushy tufts that provide cover. During migration, snipe rest and forage not only in freshwater habitat but on brackish and salt marshes.

Walking boggy terrain in warm fall weather can be hard, sweaty work. Dress lightly. Most snipe hunters wear rubber boots. A few (whose feet and legs are evidently impervious to the onslaughts of insects and scratchy plants) wear old tennis shoes.

You can flush snipe within range simply by walking a bog or other likely stretch, and you may have heard or read that a dog is no help. It's true that most snipe will flush before a dog gets close, and it's true that some dogs dislike retrieving snipe. (Some also dislike mouthing a woodcock, sora rail, or dove.) But during the market-shooting era, many snipe hunters used dogs. Scenting conditions are poor over water, yet a dog can help at least a little in locating birds, and once in a while a snipe will hold tightly for a dog. More important is the dog's role in finding snipe that have fallen in tall reeds and the like.

Snipe look much like woodcock but are trickier targets, especially on open flats where they may flush at a considerable distance. Often, however, they soon return to the vicinity where they were flushed and, like the one shown here, may make the mistake of passing close to a hunter.

Coots & Gallinules

"Coot" is one of many regional names for scoters, which are three species of diving ducks. I'm speaking here of a very different bird, the common, or American, coot—also known as marsh hen or mud hen—a species belonging to the family of rails and gallinules. Though it has a ducklike appearance, its toes are not webbed but fringed with spatulate lobes that help in paddling, diving, and walking through reeds and over floating vegetation.

If I were to choose a gun exclusively for coot (a somewhat preposterous "if"), it would be a 12 gauge, and I'd prefer 1¼-ounce loads of 6's or 7½'s. Most hunters take coots either as an incidental bonus during a duck hunt or as a change of pace from duck hunting. The typical duck gun is a 12 gauge, but it isn't usually loaded with 6's or 7½'s. Depending on the locally prevalent ducks and methods of hunting them, the shells might be high-velocity loads of 4's, 5's, or 6's. Where steel shot is required for hunting waterfowl, a hunter is likely to be using the nearest equivalent steel-shot load—No. 4.

A modified choke is probably best—or modified and full in a double-barreled gun. Typical duck guns are full-choked, as they should be for many kinds of duck hunting, and using a full-choked gun for coots is good practice for duck shooting.

The coot is about 13 to 16 inches long, with rounded wings and a heavy bill somewhat like a scoter's and more like that of the gallinules. It's a thick, short, whitish bill with a couple of brownish spots near the front and a brown shield running up the forehead. This frontal shield is believed to be a protection from the sharp, stiff blades of marsh grasses. The sexes are alike; they have black heads and necks, blackish or dark gray bodies, somewhat lighter underparts, a white patch under the stubby tail, a thin white border along the rear edges of the wings, and olive legs. In the air, the legs trail behind the tail and dangle slightly, providing a quick mark of identification for a hunter who has to decide whether he can shoot. This is the only ducklike marsh bird that appears black with a white bill.

Coots are more abundant than any of our true ducks except mallards and pintails. They breed in lower Alaska, Canada, and the Northern states, chiefly from Indiana westward but with some breeding colonies in the East and the South. There's also a resident population in Hawaii. The Northern coots migrate southward to winter chiefly in the Gulf States and along the Pacific Coast. About a million a year are harvested, and many more would be taken if they weren't considered second-rate game by so many hunters. They're plentiful almost everywhere, although about half the annual harvest comes from the Mississippi Flyway. Seasons in most states are long and run more or less concurrently with duck seasons.

The daily bag limit is generally 15 in Alaska and along the Central, Mississippi, and Atlantic Flyways, 25 on the Pacific Flyway. This doesn't indicate that coots are most plentiful on the West Coast, but that gunners in that part of the country haven't learned to appreciate them. The limits are generous because coots are underharvested. Since they compete for space and forage with some ducks, a larger harvest might be desirable.

Coots, like some fish-eating sea ducks, are supposed to make poor table fare. Nonsense! Although they eat a few insects and small shellfish, they subsist during the hunting season almost exclusively on aquatic vegetation and shoreline seeds and grasses. They're so partial to wild rice that in parts of the Midwest they're called rice hens. Coots provide fine eating when skinned and trimmed of fat.

Another basis for low esteem is that coots are trusting (though they don't come to decoys) and are slow to get airborne. Jump-shooting is most common, and different with coots than with ducks. One jump-shooting tactic is to pole a boat through tall rushes and reeds toward open water. If a flock is feeding near the advancing boat, many of the birds can be herded toward the opening, and when they get there, some will take off. They can't leap from the surface like ducks because their feet—only lobed rather than webbed—don't provide enough push. The birds run across the water, their wings flapping as they gain momentum, and they may be more than 40 yards out when they get into the air. Often they're shot when only a foot or two above the water.

Some shooters disparage coots as being slow in the air. Usually, these shooters change their minds if they can be persuaded to waste a few shells on coots, for these birds fly about as fast as pheasants, and a pheasant at 40 yards is certainly a sporting target. They stay low, occasionally surprising a gunner with a burst of wind-driven speed.

Coots forage in flocks, often very large flocks, and they're more often seen on the water or on a shoreline than in the air. Jump-shooting is generally good wherever preferred foods grow: pondweed, bulrush, naiad, widgeongrass, muskgrass, wild celery, or wild rice. When Midwestern Indian rice harvesters come beating through this plume-topped grass in the shallows, they often push out great numbers of coots. Sometimes hunters wait on the open water for the birds to emerge and make their running take-offs.

Although coots nest on fresh water, their migration routes and wintering grounds encompass brackish and salt marshes, bays, and estuaries, as well as fresh marshes, bogs, shallow ponds, creeks, and rivers. Any of these provide excellent shooting.

Many readers may have been puzzled by my statement a few paragraphs back that coots don't come to decoys, for coot blocks are a common sight on some waters. The purpose of these decoys is to attract ducks. Quite often, ducks feed and loaf with coots. The coot blocks are generally used in conjunction with standard duck decoys.

One of the most productive coot-hunting methods is to walk, pole, drift, or scull along a reedy shoreline. A flock is likely to be feeding in the shallows close to shore. As you approach, a few birds at a time will swim out, run across the surface, and take off. Although many hunters walk the muddy banks, I prefer to approach by boat from open water. This pushes birds toward shore, where they lift into the air.

Gallinules are a trifle smaller than their close relatives, the coots, but they're easy targets because they fly slower and even lower. They share the habitat of coots and rails. Most often they are taken incidentally by someone hunting rails, coots, or ducks. The gun, load, and choke recommendations I made for coots can be applied to gallinules.

"Water chicken" and "mud hen" are among the common nick-names for the gallinule. Its body looks like that of a small chicken, but with longer legs and very long toes that enable it to wade the shallows or walk right over lily pads and other aquatic vegetation. There are two species, but one of these, the purple gallinule, is comparatively scarce, has a limited range in this country, and has not been legal game in recent years. It nests from the Southeast and Gulf States to Ecuador and winters from the Gulf States southward. A hunter should be able

Coots flock and feed in the shallows and along shorelines. Jump-shooting gunners sometimes walk the banks or use a boat to push the birds toward shore and force them into the air.

The common gallinule is slightly smaller than the coot and is mostly gray and olive-brown, with a red and yellow bill. It has a white side streak and white wing edges that help to distinguish it from the protected purple gallinule.

to identify it if only to keep from shooting one by mistake. The head, neck, and underparts are a rich purplish-blue. The wings and short tail are dusky, the back is olive or bronze-green, and the large bill is red, with a yellow tip and a pale blue or bluish-white frontal shield running up into the crown. The legs are yellow or yellowish-green.

The common, or American, gallinule is the huntable species. It's almost entirely slate-gray, often nearly black but with an olive-brown wash on the back and a paler area on the belly. A long white streak runs rearward on each side of the body, and the wing edges and primaries also show some white. The frontal shield and bill are bright red, tipped with yellow. The legs are greenish-yellow except for a garterlike red band just below the body. Among gallinules as among coots, the sexes look alike. Juveniles are duller and paler than adults, and have a brownish bill and frontal shield. Avoid shooting juveniles, as it's easy to mistake an immature purple gallinule for a young common gallinule.

The breeding range of the common gallinule extends from upper New England and the Great Lakes to central California and down over most of the United States, the Caribbean, and parts of South America. Birds in the upper part of this range migrate in September and October; some of those nesting farther south migrate in October and November, while others seem to be year-round residents. North America's populations winter chiefly in the lower states. They're especially abundant in Alabama, Mississippi, and Louisiana. Since they travel the same flyways as ducks and geese, they're found in most states during the waterfowl season, and the bag limits are generous.

Gallinules are primarily seed-eaters, and favored plants include duckweed, rice, wild rice, windmillgrass, and knotgrass. Like rails, they tamp vague but visible paths through the dense marsh grasses. They don't gather in flocks, but sometimes as many as a dozen can be found in a small, rich feeding area.

Another trait held in common with rails is a reluctance to flush. You may hear the birds around you in the high marsh vegetation, rustling and grunting, cackling, or clucking. As you approach, they retreat, invisibly. Sometimes you can push them hard enough to make them take off. They swim with their heads bobbing, as coots do, and they run with their bodies stretched forward and wings raised for balance, like barnyard chickens. Occasionally you can pole toward one, herding it to open water or high ground to make it take off.

Rails

There are four huntable species of rail—the sora, Virginia, clapper, and king rail. The smallest is the sora rail, which is comparable to a bobwhite. The Virginia rail is a trifle bigger. The clapper is about the size of a coot or small duck, and the king is a bit bigger, about 15 to 19 inches long with a wingspread of more than two feet. Even though the king rail is twice as large as the sora, a 20- or 28-gauge gun is appropriate for all the rails. They don't fly high or fast.

Field loads are all you need. I'd be satisfied to use No. 8's for all species, but many hunters prefer 7½'s for the two larger rails, and 9's are really best for the little soras, especially in high, dense cover.

I've been reading some of my own writings to refresh my hunting memory, and I find that several years ago I suggested using a cylinder- or skeet-bored gun for all rail shooting. Although I still think a very open boring is right in most instances, I must now qualify that advice. Last September, hunting clappers on a big Virginia salt marsh, I used an over-under, choked improved and modified. On that big, open marsh, the rails didn't always rise close, and those borings helped.

Rails can't be hunted on the Pacific Coast, where they're neither plentiful nor widespread. The federal migratory-bird regulations permit an open season on all the other flyways, but many hunters—especially along the Mississippi and Central flyways—scorn rails as low, slow fliers. The sport is popular and traditional only on the Gulf Coast and along the Atlantic Coast from Connecticut southward. In most of the Northern states, the season lasts from early September to early November. In some Southern states, the season is the same as in the North, but more commonly it runs from early November to early January. Rails are underharvested, 50 bag limits are very generous.

The sora (also called Carolina rail, Carolina crake, and chicken-billed rail) is the most widely distributed of the group. It nests in most parts of Canada and the upper United States, and winters from the lower reaches of the breeding grounds to Peru. Soras usually nest on fresh marshes, but when they're migrating or wintering you can also find them on brackish or occasionally salt marshes.

The species is a plump little wading bird with a short yellow bill that marks it as being primarily a seed-eater. The others have long, slightly downcurved bills for grabbing insects and manipulating shellfish. All the rails are brownish birds with long legs, short rounded wings, and short tails. The sora has a black mask covering the front of its face and throat. The breast and the sides of the head and neck are gray. The belly is crossbarred with black and white. The crown and body are brown, with quaillike black and white mottling on the back and sides. The legs are yellowish-green. The sexes are alike among rails, but juveniles are drabber. If you shoot a sora with a buff breast and no black mask, it's a bird of the year.

The Virginia rail breeds throughout lower Canada and the upper United States, and winters from the Southern part of the country to Guatemala. It resides chiefly in fresh and brackish marshes, but in winter it also visits salt marshes.

It has a darkly crossbarred belly, a darkly streaked brown back, paler, grayish head, and white throat. It's rustier-looking than the sora, with a rich chestnut breast, reddish legs, and a long reddish bill. Juveniles have dark, almost blackish breasts.

Clappers breed primarily from Connecticut to the Carolinas and winter from New Jersey to Florida and along the Gulf Coast. They're the most plentiful rails on the grassy salt marshes of the South. Of all the marsh birds, these are the ones most commonly called marsh hens, and there are locales where you have to call them that if you expect another hunter to know what you're talking about.

A clapper's long, slender bill is grayish-yellow or sometimes dull orange. It's head and body are grayish-brown. Brown and black streaking makes the back look quite dark. The belly and flanks are crossbarred with narrow white and broad dark, irregular bands. The legs are gray-green. Juveniles are considerably darker than adults.

The king rail breeds from Minnesota to Massachusetts and just about all points south. It winters in the Deep Southern states, from the Atlantic west across the Gulf Coast and in regions still farther south. Like the Virginia rail, it sometimes visits salt marshes in fall and winter, and occasionally may be flushed in the same habitat as soras and clappers, but it prefers freshwater marshes, bogs, and ditches.

The king rail, largest of the four huntable rail species, is so reclusive that hunters seldom bag a limit. With its long, reddish bill it looks like an oversized Virginia rail, but the plumage has a less rusty color and the breast is somewhat paler.

The king looks pretty much like an oversized Virginia rail, but not as rusty in color, with a somewhat lighter breast and a face that's sometimes dark. Birds of the year are darker than the adults.

For soras, excellent hunting locales include the Connecticut River near Essex, Connecticut, and along the Patuxent in Maryland. In the marshes near the mouth of the Housatonic in Connecticut, you may put up a few Virginia rails as well as soras. Around Cape May, New Jersey, the marshes are well populated with both soras and clappers. The Virginia salt marshes that I've hunted hold plenty of clappers, and the fresh marshes of that state hold plenty of soras. Among all the clapper marshes, the best are probably those stretching from Beaufort, North Carolina, down to the South Carolina border and from Charleston to Port Royal Sound, South Carolina. The marshes around St. Simon's Sound, Georgia, and St. Augustine and Tampa in Florida also have an abundance of clappers. The clapper and sora are the most abundant and most hunted. I can't imagine setting out exclusively for the reclusive kings or Virginia rails.

Although rails are deep-bodied when seen in profile, the expression "thin as a rail" wasn't inspired by a rail fence but by the appearance of these birds as seen from front or rear. Their bodies are severely compressed laterally—an evolutionary adaptation that helps them weave through dense rushes and reeds. Sometimes they seem to do so invisibly, and I'm sure a hunter passes many more than he ever sees. They're feeble fliers, yet their thin bodies make an occasional straight-away shot a trifle harder than it looks.

There are three more consequential reasons why rail shooting is often harder (and more fun) than the uninitiated suppose. First, a shooter used to upland birds or waterfowl tends to lead the birds and also to shoot high. You can't give these slow fliers any lead, and you'll soon learn that a rail may dip or make just a short flight, descending when you expect it to rise or fly straight. Second, in the cordgrass of the big Virginia and Carolina salt marshes, the birds often flush far out unless the tide is so high that they're "islanded." And third, in the tall, dense wild rice or bulrushes where soras are often hunted, you may get no more than a fleeting glimpse of a flushed bird.

The classic method of hunting is to shoot from a shallow-draft skiff or similar small boat. Usually an experienced hunter or guide, called a pusher, poles the craft through reeds or along reedy banks—swiftly, because a slow approach will cause the birds to retreat under cover rather than fly. The shooter either stands near the bow or uses a high seat near the center thwart. Quite often, the pusher sees a bird flush before the gunner can, and he alerts the gunner with a call such as, "Mark right!" If the boat is still moving, the shot can be tough, so a good pusher is both strong and adept at stopping the skiff.

In many areas, outboards have replaced the traditional poled skiffs. However, it's illegal to shoot from a boat with a running motor, and almost impossible to bring the boat to a quick stop. We used an outboard last year, threading our way through narrow channels during a very high tide, staying close to the bank and nosing the boat into land for a fast shot every time a bird came up out of the stalks.

When ground cover is available, rails will retreat through it instead of flying. This means that rail hunting—especially for clappers and soras—is good only during a couple of days a month, and then only for a few hours when the flood tides are so high that the birds have little ground on which to run. With the expanse of thick cover submerged, rails are often visible before they fly. And even when they're not visible, an approach flushes them because they seem to feel safer flying than swimming away.

It helps to know the kinds of marsh vegetation that attract rails. Soras feed heavily on wild rice, bulrushes, and sedges. Virginia rails seek live prey amid the same or similar plants, but often on more brackish waters. Clappers are very fond of hiding and hunting in cordgrass. King rails sometimes interbreed with clappers where fresh and salt marshes occur together. In such habitat, they, too, hide in cordgrass, and they also hunt shellfish and insects amid the same kinds of freshwater vegetation where soras feed on seeds. Early in the season, an experienced hunter pushing through lush stands of wild rice like those on the Connecticut may look for areas where the husks are darkest, because soras like ripe seeds. Later on, he may look for clearings where the rice grass has been flattened by wind or boats, because the birds are drawn to easy foraging, provided by downed stalks and floating seeds. If you hear an old pusher mention "oats," he means wild rice.

Skiff-pushing, though traditional, isn't the only method. When the tide isn't very high, you can walk up clappers or soras on marsh islands and tidal flats and along tidal creeks.

You can also use a flushing dog, such as a Labrador retriever or springer spaniel. I've released a retriever to work long, narrow islands while I walked or moved along the banks with a boat.

New Jersey hunters, working the salt marshes with a dog, bag a clapper rail. The smaller sora rail nests on freshwater marshes but during hunting season is plentiful in the clapper's brackish or salty habitat.

Sandhill Cranes

Crane hunting usually means high, difficult pass-shooting. Misses are frequent, and I have an unhappy suspicion that unrecovered cripples are more common than they should be. All a crane hunter can do about this is to shoot very carefully, learn to judge range—remembering that lesser sandhill cranes can come over so high they look no bigger than high-flying geese—and exercise considerable self-restraint.

You can hardly be "overgunned" for lesser sandhills. On windy days, a good many cranes will fly over at relatively low altitude—which can mean just within range of a 12-gauge Magnum firing maximum loads of No. 2 shot. Some hunters use 10-gauge Magnums.

A full choke is needed for most of the shooting. In some regions, however, hunters have revived the once-common practice of using stick-up crane decoys. These decoys can occasionally bring birds close enough for the use of a modified choke, so there are a few shooters who carry double-barreled guns, bored modified and full.

Two subspecies of sandhill crane—the greater sandhill and the nonmigratory Florida sandhill—are scarce and protected. A greater sandhill crane can be distinguished from the lesser only by size but, fortunately, neither of the protected varieties occupies the same regions as the lesser sandhill crane. Because of continued habitat destruction, seasons on the lesser subspecies are sometimes curtailed.

The birds nest in Siberia, Alaska, and northwestern Canada, migrate chiefly along the eastern slopes of the Rockies, and then spread out along several flyways to wintering grounds stretching from the Gulf Coast to central California. Federal regulations restrict hunting to states where only lesser sandhills are seen during fall or winter. Alaska currently has a bag limit of two and a season that generally runs through September into early October. The bag limit in recent years has been three in federally designated parts of eight more states—the Dakotas, Montana, Wyoming, Colorado, New Mexico,

Oklahoma, and Texas. The seasons vary, depending on average migratory and arrival dates. In some of the lower regions, hunting begins in late October or early November and continues almost to the end of January. For several years, a free federal permit has been required in addition to a hunting license; its purpose is to enable the government to conduct a harvest census.

In most years, the shooting has been best in eastern New Mexico and western Texas, particularly around the Muleshoe Wildlife Refuge, southeast of Muleshoe, Texas, near the New Mexico border. A hunting acquaintance tells me that the shooting has also been exciting in North Dakota during several past seasons.

Both hunters and official game regulations often refer to lesser sandhills as "little brown cranes"—a confusing name since only birds of the year are predominantly brownish. Both male and female adults have brownish-gray primaries tipped with black, gray underwing feathers, dark gray backs with rusty tipping, and mouse-gray underparts. The gray color pales on the belly, neck, and head, and a bright red unfeathered cap extends from the pointed black bill back over the eye. The brownish juveniles lack the bald red patch. A mature specimen weighs seven or eight pounds, stands more than three feet high, and has a wingspread of at least five feet.

It's easy to distinguish cranes in the air from other big wading birds and waterfowl such as large herons, swans, and geese. First, listen for their loud, low-pitched, fluting flight calls—*k-rrr-oooo, ku-rrroooo*—interspersed with rattling or throaty clacking. Cranes don't respond well to calling, but their own voices announce their approach.

Second, watch for their very long, outstretched necks and long black trailing legs, which distinguish them from waterfowl.

Third, watch for the short tail, coloration, and manner of flight, which differ from those of herons and egrets. Cranes raise their wings high instead of lowering them in deep downstrokes, and the flapping alternates with hawklike glides.

Some hunters shoot only when a crane is gliding, because then the bird is probably going no faster than about 45 miles an hour. With a tailwind or when beating its wings hard, it can attain a 60-mile-an-hour speed. A headwind lowers the speed and improves the shooting—a fact to remember when picking a blind location.

Migrating cranes, or those flying between resting and foraging areas, fly in columns, V formations, and large, shapeless groups—clouds of

The lesser sandhill crane is a large, fast, high-flying bird that poses problems in judging range. The most successful crane hunters generally are experienced pass-shooters who have done a great deal of goose hunting. They favor 10- or 12-gauge guns with maximum loads.

cranes. They begin to drop down when approaching feeding areas. They roost in shallow water but eat less animal matter than most wading birds. They seek bur reeds, grasses, and various kinds of aquatic vegetation, all of which are most attractive if growing near farmlands. During migration and while wintering, they make daily flights to stubble fields to feed heavily on such crops as corn, wheat, sorghum, rice, and other grains. (In far Northern regions, they also rely heavily on heatherberries and unwary lemmings.)

The best crane shooters usually are hunters who have done considerable pass-shooting at geese. They have learned to judge range and speed, and they can lead a bird by a sufficient distance without thinking about it. It's commonly necessary to lead a fast-flying crane by several bird lengths.

BIG GAME

Bears

Most of the bear hunting in America is for the black bear, a smaller animal than the grizzly or the Alaskan brown bear (which is a coastal variety of grizzly). Not only because of the size but also because of habits and habitat, different guns and methods are used to hunt blacks and grizzlies. I'll begin with recommendations about arms for hunting black bears and then offer separate advice about arms for the bigger species.

Black bears sometimes visit my Pennsylvania deer camp—drawn by food odors and looking for garbage. Everyone has heard stories about bears raiding dumps and campsites, occasionally mauling or killing someone. Perhaps because of these incidents, a good many people have a notion that bears wander arrogantly about the woods, unafraid of humans, and may be encountered almost daily where they're abundant. This is unfortunately true in and around parks and other areas where the bears aren't normally hunted and where human ignorance and carelessness have produced a "bear problem." Elsewhere, bears are secretive creatures that are adept at avoiding human contact. In most hunting areas, sightings are much less frequent—least frequent of all when you're actually seeking bears. With the use of hounds or bait, the hunter-success ratio is fairly high. Where neither of those aids is used, the success ratio is so low that most black bears are killed in chance encounters by hunters seeking other game—most often deer.

That fact leads to the obvious conclusion that a black bear can be killed with a deer rifle. Quite true, but not all deer rifles are sensible choices if you're hunting specifically for a bear. For humane reasons as well as your own safety, you want a cartridge with a bullet that will produce a clean, quick kill when put into the chest cavity or through the shoulder. A bear is considerably tougher than a deer, and I have little confidence in a rifle that doesn't deliver at least a couple of thousand foot-pounds of energy at 100 yards. I'd consider the .270 to be a reasonable minimum on a planned bear hunt. Most of the .30-caliber cartridges are fine, and any of the bigger calibers would do nicely, though they're not really needed for the black bear.

Some of the hunters who use hounds—particularly in the thick, swampy Southern forests—prefer a smoothbore. A full-choked 12-gauge shotgun is a logical choice with No. 0 or "Double 0" buckshot. However, I don't like to put extra holes in a hide, not even small holes, if it can be avoided. There are hound hunts in which the gunners wait on stand (as in some other types of hound hunting mentioned in this book) and a shot is made when a bear runs past a stand. This explains the use of a shotgun. However, in most regions where hounds are used, the hunters follow the dogs until the bear is treed or otherwise brought to bay. For this, a shotgun isn't needed. I'd rather use a rifle or a powerful sidearm. A handgun chambered for the .357, .41, or .44 Magnum is excellent.

The choice of proper rifle sights depends on the woods and the hunting method. In very dense timber and with hounds, I'd probably use an open sight. In woods not quite as thick but too brushy for a scope, I'd prefer an aperture sight. In more open cover and without hounds, my choice would be a 2½X scope.

For grizzly hunting, not even a .270 is powerful enough to give me the confidence I want. The .30-06 is a good choice, especially if other big game is to be hunted on the same trip. As the late Warren Page remarked, the old .30-06 remains the best all-round big-game rifle. Other good choices are the several .300 Magnums, .338, .350 Magnum, .358 Norma, and a few even more powerful cartridges, such as the .375 H&H. The heavy Weatherby Magnums are also fine. One other that merits inclusion is the .308 Norma Magnum—though not the *standard* .308, which is fine for black bears but inadequate for grizzlies. The calibers I've listed here are appropriate for brown bears as well as for the smaller inland grizzlies.

I've known guides who carried open-sighted woods rifles, but these were "back-up" guns, to be used only at close range in the event that a client needed fast help in finishing a bear. I've also seen hunting films in which grizzlies were taken at short range as they caught salmon in spawning streams. (And once I missed a chance at a black bear quite close to me on a spawning stream in British Columbia.) These streams sometimes provide opportunities for relatively close shots, especially in late afternoon when grizzlies seem to fish most actively. But an open-sighted rifle is wrong for grizzly hunting, nevertheless.

Like most big-game hunting in the Northwest, the quest for a brown or an inland grizzly often requires much scouting and glassing of open, distant terrain—low brush, balds, tundra, berry-covered slopes and meadows—the kind of habitat where 250-yard shots are as common as those made at 50 yards. A scope is needed. The best magnification is probably 2½X. Some hunters understandably favor a variable-power scope so that they can crank up the magnification when they come to open terrain that's likely to offer only long shots.

This necessity of scouting open terrain for big grizzlies means that a 7X35 or 8X35 binocular is another vital item of equipment. In addition, you or your guide should have a fairly powerful spotting scope. This is all the more important if the hunt will include antlered or horned big game whose trophy status is difficult to judge at long distance.

Now let's examine hunting methods, beginning with the ways of taking black bears. There are 18 subspecies and, even within a single subspecies, not all individuals are black, the name notwithstanding. One rare and protected race, the Kermode bear of west central British Columbia, is creamy white. A subspecies called the glacier bear, or blue bear, is hunted at Yakutat Bay on Alaska's gulf coast; it has a thick, lustrous bluish-gray coat that's sometimes so dark it appears to be silvery black. In the East, most of the bears are black with a tan or grizzled snout and often with a white blaze on the chest. Color variations are more common in the West, where a black bear may be brown, tan, cinnamon, or blond; brown is a common color in Alaska and California.

In a few regions, you may encounter either a black or a grizzly (though black bears go out of their way to avoid grizzlies). If you've filled a grizzly permit, or if grizzlies aren't legal game in such an area, you can't kill one except in self-defense. Since neither color nor size is a sure indication of species, you'd better be able to differentiate by shape. A black bear lacks the grizzly's shoulder hump, and its forehead and snout are rather straight, whereas a grizzly's face is somewhat concave.

Black bears are distributed throughout Alaska, all of Canada except the northernmost portions, most of the wooded regions of the United States, and parts of northern Mexico. However, certain types of forests are much more productive than others. Although black bears are occasionally seen fairly high on mountains—in the upper coniferous zones—they don't stay there for long. The hunting is always much better below an elevation of about 7,000 feet. Good habitat usually has mixed stands of hardwoods and conifers. It must have adequate watering places, as well as dense bedding and hiding thickets interspersed with relatively open spaces where the bears can eat fruits and grasses. The species is omnivorous, but more than three-quarters of its diet is vegetation. In some areas, overpopulous bears damage orchards or lumber so severely that landowners publicize their welcome to sportsmen who hunt bears.

The hunting stories I read as a boy left a strong impression that the Far West was exclusively grizzly domain, while the Eastern timberlands were the real strongholds of the black bear. Actually, the black bear is no longer so populous in the heavily settled parts of the East, and it fares far better in parts of the West. Hunting seasons and, to some extent, methods are governed by the abundance of the species. Not long ago, Pennsylvania (which has usually been a good bear state) temporarily suspended its season because younger bears were being harvested each year. A sow's first breeding occurs at about 3½ years of age, and that breeding usually produces only one cub. After that, she will generally produce twins and sometimes triplets, but each set of cubs will stay with her for more than a year, and she will mate only in alternate years. The killing of young bears can reduce the birth rate drastically, forcing the suspension of hunting. Any small bear—a specimen weighing less than about 140 pounds—should be considered a cub or yearling and should not be shot. (Some states impose strong penalties for the killing of undersized bears.) And a bear accompanied by cubs should never be shot.

At present, Alaska has more black bears than any other state, and some Alaskan districts permit hunting at all times of year. Washington, which has the second-largest population, opens a season for almost two months in early fall and about three months in spring. Some other states also have spring as well as fall seasons; in some you can use dogs, and in some bait is also legal.

The best states for hunting black bears are Alaska, Washington, the Rocky Mountain states (especially Colorado), and the Lake States (especially Michigan).

At one time, record-book trophies were scored by hide measurements. There were objections to this system because a pelt can be stretched. Skull measurement is more reliable and is now used to score both black-bear and grizzly trophies. The regions with the most bears don't always produce the biggest trophies. In recent years, the most outstanding black bears have generally come out of the Rockies.

The use of bait never appealed to me much, but it does draw bears, and in some regions it can be combined with other bear-hunting methods or with hunts for other game. In states like Washington, for instance, the deer season is open during part of the bear season. After a hunter has field-dressed a deer and dragged out the carcass, he may decide to return and take a stand near the entrails. Because bears kill many fir and pine trees by girdling them to gnaw the cambium—one of their preferred foods—timber companies welcome hunters in their woods during spring and fall. Some of these timberlands are prime habitat for both deer and bears.

Bears are not true hibernators, but during periods of severe cold they den up and experience a very deep sleep during which respiration is greatly reduced. (The female gives birth while denned.) In the fall, bears are voracious because they're putting on fat for denning. In early spring, having come out of their dens only recently, they're again very hungry. So baiting works as well in the spring as in the fall. The hunter doesn't need game entrails. He can hang up a calf's head or a big chunk of cheap meat and waste from the nearest slaughterhouse. Very early morning is the time when he's most likely to see a bear approach the offering, but if no bear shows up, he just has to wait. Waiting amid swarms of spring insects near an odoriferous bait demands more bear-killing enthusiasm than I can muster.

But sometimes baiting is only a prelude to the hunt. For several days, perhaps, no bear shows up. Then one morning the hunter finds the bait has been consumed, and he spots fresh tracks along a nearby stream. (Good bait-hanging places are near lush vegetation and waterways.) He can try to follow the tracks, still-hunting along the stream, although still-hunting is the least productive method of taking black bears. He's luckier if he has hounds; he can cast them on the fresh trail, and that's an often successful technique.

Bear hunting with hounds differs from one region to another. In Washington and in parts of the Lake States, a hunter may drive a truck or other vehicle slowly along logging raids, with his hounds riding behind the cab. He usually has a couple of outstanding hounds that serve as pack leaders and "strike dogs"—the dogs that first detect fresh scent. Bears frequently cross logging roads and sometimes walk along a roadside for a short distance. When the vehicle crosses a fresh trail, a strike dog lets the hunter know by an excited yelping. The hounds are thereupon cast on the trail, and the hunt begins.

Occasionally a bear is quickly treed, but a mature bear—particularly one that has been chased before—almost always heads for a combination of thick cover and steep terrain, and the hunt can last all morning or all day. The hunter wants to arrive on the scene quickly when (and if) the dogs tree the bear, yet he can't really keep up with the chase. He follows the hounds and often tries to head them off, partly by sound and partly by simply knowing the area.

A 10-year study in Washington proved that black bears don't wander nearly as much as was once thought. The home ranges of Washington bears average about two to four square miles. Studies in Michigan, Montana, and New York showed comparable home ranges, although bears in Virginia and Wisconsin were found to roam more widely. At any rate, a bear that's pursued will sooner or later circle around (as will most game when pressed by hounds) and come back to its primary home territory, if not to the immediate area where the chase began.

By truck when possible, otherwise on foot, the hunter keeps moving in the direction the hounds take, or he gets around in front

Tennessee bear hunters rest after a successful chase. The hounds are typical of the packs used to run black bears in a number of states.

or comes back to the starting area—whichever maneuver seems likely to put him close to where the bear finally trees or is cornered.

I knew a guide in New Hampshire who ran the same half-dozen big Plott hounds for bobcats and bears, and he used no truck. He simply followed as closely as he could while his hunting clients did their best to keep up.

I knew another man in North Carolina who conducted traditional Southern hunts involving great crowds of hunters and hounds—sometimes up to about 40 of each. As I said, the regional styles are quite different. Instead of following the dogs or trying to intercept the chase, the men went on stand in advance at the likely points—on ridges, at crossings, and along trails. Sometimes a pronounced change in the chorus of hound voices proclaimed that a bear was treed. In that case, whoever was closest moved toward the sound. But the cover was thick, the terrain rugged, and the bears seldom felt sufficiently pressed to tree. More often, one of the standers would hear a swell of hound bugling and a crashing of brush, after which he might get a fast shot at a black bear bolting past him.

In a hunt of that sort, the men try their best to kill the bear unless it's a small one. But some of the Northern and Western hunters who follow small packs of hounds let a treed bear go almost as often as not. Their sport is the chase, the pride and thrill of good dog work. Not much skill is needed to shoot a treed bear from a distance of a few feet. If the hunter doesn't want the pelt or meat, he pulls his dogs away from the tree and ties them, but lets them bay at the bear for a few minutes. That seems to be sufficient reward, for they'll hunt the next bear just as eagerly. After the baying session, he pulls (or drags) the dogs away on leads.

If a treed bear is to be killed, the dogs must first be tied. Otherwise they'll attack when the bear falls. A bear that's been well hit and has only moments to live may still maul or kill a hound.

I don't think any single breed makes the best bear hound. I mentioned the New Hampshire guide who used Plotts on bobcats and bears. I also met a Tennessee guide who used several Airedales and a couple of redbones on bears as well as wild boars. Good noses, good voices, stamina, and aggression are the requisites. The difference between a fairly good bear hound and one that develops into a true strike dog is that a strike dog has an exceptional nose and a mysterious kind of "bear sense." A strike dog can be put down on a bear trail and know immediately which way the bear went, whereas another dog may follow fresh tracks in either direction and can waste hours of hunting time by doing so. A good strike dog may be valued at well over $1,000.

The black bear's preferred springtime foods include grasses, snow-lilies, willows, pine and fir cambium, skunk cabbage, starchy bulbs, roots, buds, herbs, insects, occasional rodents, and the carcasses of winter-killed animals. Later on, a bear will also gobble berries, honeycombs (and the bees that made the honey), and any vulnerable small animals or the young of large ones. Fish, too, are eaten when they can be obtained. Although black bears lack the fish-snagging abilities of coastal grizzlies, I've had shots at them along spawning streams. In the fall, the bears are strongly attracted to grapes, cherries (and other fruits when available), conifer seeds, acorns, and other nuts. As with a number of other kinds of game, an oak or beech stand is frequently a good spot to look for sign or cast bear hounds.

There's a fairly common belief that black bears are primarily nocturnal. They are not—unless unusually heavy hunting pressure has made them so locally and temporarily. But they bed in secluded thickets, and although their eyes are weak, their hearing and sense of smell are keen enough to alert them to approaching danger. This is why hunting without hounds has such a low rate of success in regions where bear hunting is common.

Bear tracks look as if they were left by a barefoot man with abnormally wide, flat feet. A foreprint left by a bear of medium size may be four inches long and slightly wider, while the hind print may be almost twice as long. The scat is roughly cylindrical unless liquified by a berry feast; it's usually an inch or more in diameter and often identifiable by animal hair, grass and root fibers, seeds, nutshells, insect husks, and similar visible matter.

"Bear trees" are of two types. One has a clawed and bitten trunk. The tooth scars are vertical and may be as high as a bear can reach when standing on its hind feet. Claw marks are frequently higher. They're longer slashes, commonly diagonal, but often vertical and sometimes horizontal. A bear may use such a tree to sharpen its claws, work out aggressive impulses, or leave a scent during breeding season (late spring to early summer in most regions) to warn away rivals and attract any passing bear of the opposite sex. The other type of bear tree is used to rub away loose hair and relieve itching when a bear is shedding in the spring. It usually has shaggy or deeply furrowed bark, and since a good one is used by more than one bear, it will show tufts of hair and be surrounded by other sign. A well-used trail may lead to such a tree. A bear trail undulates, and it may show deep depressions where heavy feet have worn away the earth.

While hunting in lower British Columbia, I discovered that most of the local hunters and guides considered bear meat almost inedible. It's possible that when bears have been feeding long and heavily on lumber-camp garbage or dead fish, their meat may be less than delectable. Moreover, bear fat is oily and rank, and bears (like some other animals) occasionally carry trichinosis. Thorough cooking does away with any danger of trichinosis, trimming does away with oily fat, and a bear that's been feeding on grasses, berries, and other vegetation in fairly high woods and meadows provides excellent meat. Well-cooked bear meat is perfectly safe and quite delicious—

When dogs are used to tree or corner a black bear, a bow-hunter can make a clean kill with a broadhead arrow. Where bait is legal, the range is sometimes comparably short and, in the author's opinion, archery makes baiting more sporting.

rather like beef. Sometimes a medium-sized bear can be dragged out on a travois; a big one has to be quartered and packed out—an arduous but worthwhile chore.

The basic field-dressing procedure for bears is the same as for antlered game (see the Whitetail Deer section). But skinning is more difficult than the peeling, cutting, and "fisting" away of a deer hide. To remove the entrails, you will have slit the animal from anus to sternum. Now slit from the chest toward one corner of the mouth and then from the rectal area out along the inner surface of each hind leg to the feet and from the sides of the chest out along the inner surface of each front leg to the feet. Skin around the pads and turn the pelt inside out to disjoin the claws, which are supposed to remain on a bear "robe." If a guide or other experienced bear hunter is present, it's best to do this job under his guidance or let him do it.

Some hunting books offer advice about the skinning of the head. I won't. This is so delicate a chore that you shouldn't attempt it unless you've at least studied a book on taxidermy and practiced on other game heads. If you're going to have the head mounted by a professional taxidermist, let him skin it. All you then have to do is sever the head at the axial joint, just as I described the procedure for trophy mule deer, and leave it in the skin, connected to the rest of the robe.

Grizzlies are even less predictable than black bears in their reactions to humans. All bears are dangerous, grizzlies particularly so. At one time they inhabitated a large part of the continent, but because of their attacks on people and also because of their occasional penchant for preying on livestock, they were exterminated in many regions. Although Montana still allows a very small number of grizzlies to be taken annually on a special-permit basis, Alaska is the only remaining state with a sizable grizzly population and good hunting for the species. Canada has good grizzly hunting in the Yukon, the Northwest Territories, and British Columbia. Controlled hunting doesn't threaten the Alaskan and Canadian grizzly populations.

Because of their great size and characteristic color, Alaskan brown bears were once regarded as a distinct species, but they're a coastal subspecies of grizzly. Our other subspecies is the interior

Outdoor writer and former guide-outfitter Les Bowman (right) and a hunting friend examine a good-sized grizzly. Note the bear's shoulder hump and somewhat concave face, which differentiate the grizzly from the black bear.

grizzly. Both are the same species as the European and Asian grizzlies. However, Alaska's brown bears are bigger than the other grizzly races—bigger, in fact, than any other land-dwelling carnivore except perhaps the polar bear. Browns are found on some of Alaska's southernmost islands (particularly Admiralty and Kodiak) and along parts of the state's lower coasts (particularly around the head of the Alaska Peninsula). The Kodiak bears are the largest. Unfortunately, having come into conflict with local ranchers, they've been substantially reduced in numbers.

A mature interior grizzly *(Ursus arctos horribilis)* may weigh 300 to 600 pounds, depending on region, habitat, and frequency of contacts with man. A brown bear *(U. a. middendorffi)* may weigh 750 or more. An eight- or nine-year-old male specimen on Kodiak Island may weigh 800 to 1,200 pounds, stand four feet high at the shoulders, and tower almost 10 feet tall when he rises on his hind legs to test the breeze. In some areas these coastal grizzlies are protected, but Alaskan guide-outfitters can take a hunter into prime legal habitat, and the season on both browns and interior grizzlies runs from September into early June.

Alaskan and Canadian guide-outfitters can also take a hunter into prime interior-grizzly country. At this writing, British Columbia no longer has a spring season but has a fall season from September through December. In the Northwest Territories, the season runs from mid-July through mid-November and in the Yukon from August through October. Most of the top record-book coastal grizzlies have come from Kodiak, most of the top record-book interior grizzlies from British Columbia.

Hunting literature is overstocked with "silvertips." Some interior grizzlies are, indeed, true silvertips—quite grizzly in color. But some are also brown or bronze. A few in Canada are almost black, and many of those in the area of Mount McKinley are blond. The surest mark of species identification is the grizzly's shoulder hump; both subspecies have this hump, which inspired the nickname "roachback"—a name more appropriate than silvertip, though no longer as common.

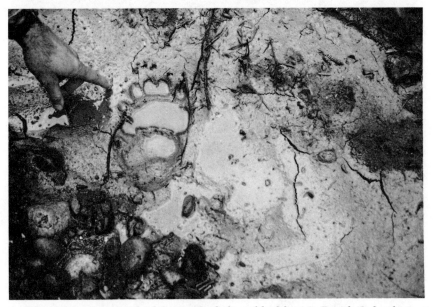

The author photographed this track of a large black bear in British Columbia. It's the print of the right front paw. Note the size of the paw in relation to the hunter's hand.

An Alaskan brown bear comes ashore from a salmon-spawning river with a 28-inch catch. The Alaskan brown is a coastal subspecies of grizzly, and it rivals the polar bear as the world's largest land-dwelling carnivore. During the salmon runs, hunting for browns is excellent near the spawning streams.

The Northwestern salmon streams and the high berry patches near them are generally the best places to scout for grizzlies. As all kinds of berries ripen in summer, grizzlies gather in high, open patches of the bushes, though not in the dense gatherings attracted to spawning rivers. Depending on the time of year, recent experi-

Claw marks on trees are a common type of bear sign. If the claw scratches on
this aspen were fresh, the bark would look torn, the wood raw and perhaps
oozing sap. Old marks like these scab over to become dark, dry welts.

ence, and the sign he notes, a guide may take a client away from the
rivers to glass open mountain meadows, slopes, bushy swales, and
tundra.

Other preferred grizzly foods include grapes, pine seeds, nuts,
acorns, alder bark, aspen leaves and twigs, spruce cambium, wild

oats, and horsetail. Your guide will know the bear habits and habitat in his locale, so trust his decisions about the kinds of places to scout.

Bears also eat carrion and animals they kill themselves, ranging from small rodents to occasional big game. When a grizzly kills a large animal, it eats what it can, then caches the remainder and returns to it later. Sometimes the bear digs a shallow depression, but it covers the carcass with a big, conspicuous heap of branches and earth. If you find a grizzly's cache, you can assume the bear is somewhere nearby.

Sometimes a hunter or guide finds a heavily used grizzly trail meandering across a meadow or open valley, as wide and clear as a human path but rutted and pitted here and there. The tracks are shaped like a black bear's but much larger, and the long claws of the forefeet print more clearly and farther ahead of the toe pads. (Though a black bear climbs trees and a mature grizzly cannot, the black's claws are considerably smaller; sometimes they leave no impression.) The hind print of a big interior grizzly may be more than 10 inches long. A reliable observer once measured tracks left by a very big Alaskan brown bear and found that the hind print was 16 inches long, 10 inches wide, and sunk 2 inches into hard sand.

Finding fresh tracks and other kinds of sign (which are mostly the same as those I described for black bears, but larger) can indicate the vicinity where a bear is feeding or bedded, but actually following the tracks can be unrewarding or downright dangerous. A grizzly swings off course now and then to sniff the wind, checking its back trail. Upon scenting or hearing a hunter, it may hide or it may circle to see what's following it. And it may stalk the man who is stalking it.

Some kinds of grizzly sign are unique. If there's sufficient snow, a bear may playfully toboggan down a slope on its haunches, thus forming a very noticeable slideway. When fruit is ripening, it may tear up a berry patch. It may also dig gaping holes to root out marmots and smaller rodent prey.

Whether or not you've found sign and whether or not you actually see a grizzly, if you hear certain sounds—grunting, coughing, jaw-popping, tooth-clicking, or a low woofing—be ready for an immediate attack. Any of those noises can be considered a final threat before a charge.

Spawning runs of one kind of salmon or another occur in some part of grizzly country from June to October. September is probably

Torn-up patches of ground like this show where a bear has been rooting. The grizzly that left this sign had been digging up and eating roots, as well as any grubs or rodents exposed in the process.

the best month to hunt the big bears. Coho salmon or other fish are running in many of the Alaskan and Canadian streams, and the coats of the grizzlies, which are thin and poor in July, are thickening again, nearly prime. Hunting along the streams at this time is an adventure often capped by the taking of an outstanding trophy.

Perhaps the most obvious, or highly visible, kind of bear sign is a meandering trail across an open meadow. The dark streak between the hunters and the distant river in this photo is a heavily used bear trail in Montana.

Wild Boars

Several varieties of wild swine are hunted in the United States. In parts of the deep South from Texas to the Atlantic, sportsmen occasionally hunt feral hogs—descendants of domestic hogs that strayed into the wild. When I was a boy, I saw bands of feral "razorback" hogs on country roads in Georgia and Florida. They were small but mean, and youngsters were urged to give them a wide berth. I'm told that the animals have become less bold, more secretive, now that they're hunted. Florida has granted them the status of game animals—good to eat and enjoyable to hunt. To maintain their numbers, the state opens a season on wild hogs only from about mid-November into early January. The relatively small feral hogs can be managed with the same arms I recommended for javelina. I have a friend in Texas who hunts them on horseback—"riding to the hounds" for hogs instead of foxes. He uses a .38 Special revolver since the range is going to be short when the hounds have run a pig to ground.

In addition to these feral hogs, there are larger swine, descendants of stray domestic hogs that interbred with wild boars imported from Europe. These are encountered in the same regions where European boars are hunted. Sometimes they weigh over 150 pounds, so they demand the same arms that are used for pure-blooded wild boars. This is just as well, because a hunter who thinks he's probably chasing a small crossbreed may find himself confronting a large, relatively pure-blooded tusker.

"Wild boar" is a term commonly reserved for the tusker, the true European wild hog—also known as the Russian or Prussian boar. The European progenitors of the wild boar now found in America sometimes weighed 600 pounds. I've read that in Poland and probably one or two other countries, occasional boars still grow that large, or nearly so. In America, a mature specimen with almost pure bloodlines is apt to weigh between 200 and 350 pounds. With so many deer and squirrels competing for mast, a boar in this country probably expends more energy to obtain less food than in Europe, so it never grows as large. However, 200 pounds of tough-hided, copiously tusked ferocity is quite enough animal to call for something more than a .38 Special or a javelina gun.

These wild hogs are almost invariably hunted with hounds and are always shot at close range. (Even with no dogs in the way, you can seldom see a hog at any substantial distance in the woods.) Hence, stopping power is important and trajectory is not. Handguns are sometimes used, the appropriate calibers being .357, .41, and .44 Magnum. Where the law requires shotguns, 12-gauge rifled slugs should be used in a repeater.

Rifles are more common. A .30-30 lever-action carbine is typical of the rifles carried by guides in the Smoky Mountains, but a guide plans to use his rifle only when necessary to back up a client, and I think his choice is influenced not only by tradition but by the comparatively low price of a lever .30-30. A better choice for the hunter is an autoloading or pump-action .30-06, an autoloading .44 Magnum carbine, or one of the black-bear rifles I suggested. Bullets weighing 180 grains or more are recommended, and you want your power coupled with speed of repeat fire.

Slug shotguns intended for deer hunting are the best smoothbores for wild hogs. Actually, any 12-gauge repeater will do, but for the best accuracy with slugs, it ought to have a fairly open choke if not a standard slug boring. It should also have rifle-type sights and, in my opinion, a carrying sling.

Neither a rifle nor a handgun should be scoped for boar hunting. When a large, furious boar is thrashing about in thick brush 10 or 15 yards from you, what you need is something that helps you aim fast. An open sight is best on a handgun. An open sight or an aperture sight with the disk removed is best on a rifle.

In America, a mature European wild boar of either sex usually stands about 30 inches high at the shoulder and measures four to five feet long. Its upper tusks (evolved from canine teeth) are sometimes fairly straight but usually curl out and up along the sides of the

A hunter smooths back the bristly fur of a wild boar's snout to show one of its upward-jutting tusks. This Tennessee boar was killed with a high-powered, Mannlicher-stocked carbine, a good choice for such hunting. Open sights are best because shooting is at close range and you often have to aim fast.

flat-nosed snout. This tusk-and-snout conformation is an adaptation for rooting, but the tusks are also formidable weapons. One slash can fatally gore a dog or man. Ordinarily, the tusks are about three to five inches long. They're negligible on some specimens that have considerable feral-swine blood in their ancestry, but I've seen out-standing head mounts with thick ivory tusks over eight inches long.

The tusks of males grow longer and have more upward curl than those of females, but in a hunting situation, you can't tell a male from a female. Either sex is legal game.

A boar with little or no feral ancestry is usually black, though sometimes dark gray or brown, and the guard hairs are often tipped with gray or white, giving the animal a somewhat grizzled appearance. Some of the hybrids are spotted tan and black. Hybrids, incidentally, are just as ferocious as the purebloods. A wild boar has a shape somewhat like that of a bison, with top-heavy shoulders and stubby legs. The short legs are deceptive; whether fleeing or charging, a boar can run 30 miles an hour.

The wild boar is native to Europe and Asia. In 1893, a sportsman named Austin Corbin stocked a hunting preserve in Blue Mountain in New Hampshire with 50 specimens from Germany's Black Forest. European hogs still exist on a few preserves in upper New England and have now been established on preserves in Pennsylvania and several other states. Beginning in 1910, another sportsman, George Gordon Moore, released Russian boars on a preserve in North Carolina's Snowbird Range, near the Tennessee border. About 10 years later, the first boar hunt took place on the preserve. Some hounds were killed, and some of the hogs escaped into the Smokies. In 1925, Moore released some more boars near Monterey, California, and since then introductions have been made on Santa Cruz Island, off California's coast.

Today, California's European boars have spread into the Santa Lucia Mountains in Monterey County and, to the south, have crossed with feral hogs in San Luis Obispo County.

Hybrids or feral hogs are now found in Arkansas, California, Florida, Georgia, Missouri, Oregon, Texas, and probably a few other states. They sometimes damage crops and have been known to kill domestic lambs and kids. As they're considered agricultural pests, only Florida regulates the hunting of them. Florida and south-central Texas (around Kerrville) probably have the best feral-hog hunting.

Much more exciting, of course, is the pursuit of pure or nearly pure European wild boars, and the two states for this unusual sport are North Carolina and Tennessee. The hunting is best in western North Carolina, near the state line. On the other side of the line, in eastern Tennessee, the boars are just as large but not quite as plentiful. North Carolina has a split season covering much of November and December; Tennessee has a split season running through parts of October, November, and December, plus an archery season late in September. Compound bows are legal, as are longbows if they're capable of propelling a standard broadhead hunting arrow at least 150 yards. It takes a powerfully propelled arrow to kill a wild boar cleanly, so bows with light pull-weights are impractical and may be dangerous.

Local hunters in North Carolina and Tennessee work as guides and provide good hound packs. In addition, the North Carolina

In addition to the true wild boar, descended from imported European game, several states are well populated with hybrids or feral hogs like this Florida pig. Feral hogs are wild swine descended from strayed domestic stock. They can be fierce fighters. The one pictured has quit running and turned on a strike dog. Florida has classified these hogs as game animals, subject to closed seasons and regulated hunting.

Wildlife Resources Commission (headquartered in Raleigh) and the Tennessee Wildlife Resources Agency (headquartered in Nashville) conduct state-managed hunts on public wildlife-management areas.

Horses, and occasionally hunting vehicles, follow the hounds that follow the hogs in parts of California, Texas, and Florida. In the Smokies of North Carolina and Tennessee, you have to go on foot, climbing steep ridges and bulling your way through swamps, laurel hills, brushy thickets, and vine-bound tangles. You should be in good physical condition when you attempt such a hunt. In other states, where wild boars are hunted on preserves, the sport isn't usually as taxing physically. Still, it's a good idea to question the preserve owner about such matters in advance.

Wild boars are more or less omnivorous, but during the fall season, the best places to cast hounds are where the hogs find their preferred foods—acorns, beechnuts, hickory nuts, or pecans. Acorn mast is best. After the acorns are about gone, the boars root about in swamps and marshes.

Both wild boars and feral hogs, but especially the wild boars, are most active in dim light. The best time to start hounds is around sunup.

Though wild boars breed somewhat irregularly, their rut peaks in December, making that a good month to hunt.

Some hounds are trained to run either boars or bears. No single breed ranks first as a boar dog. Plott hounds, Airedales, and crossbreeds are probably most common. Some of the best packs have been bred for many generations to attain keen scenting ability, strong voice, stamina, pugnacity, and the agility needed to keep a hog in place until the hunters arrive. A boar may come to bay against rocks, a hill or creek bank, or a thicket of rhododendron or other vegetation. Sometimes a boar just decides to turn and fight. The bigger a pack is, the more successfully and safely the dogs can ring the hog and hold it. Some guides use at least a dozen hounds, except where regulations limit the number to eight.

This Tennessee wild boar has been overtaken by a pair of strike dogs in typical cover, and one of the hunters has arrived to make his shot. The hunting is best in North Carolina and Tennessee for pureblooded or nearly pureblooded tuskers like this one.

Wild boars are more intelligent than most people realize. Sometimes they seem to understand that the real danger isn't from the hounds but from the men following the hounds. A boar may suddenly quit fighting the pack to charge an arriving hunter. You have to be quick but careful. It isn't easy to get a clear shot at a boar hemmed in by frenzied dogs, and the chances are better if two or more men are at hand. The very best kind of hunt involves four or five men, all capable of long-distance jogging and climbing, and all quick and accurate with their guns. Having several partners increases the probability that one or more hunters will reach the dogs while they still hold the boar, and that someone will get a clear shot.

Hunting without dogs is a poor gamble except on some preserves. Boars wander quite a bit, using no habitual trails, although they may be concentrated in rich feeding spots. They can hear or scent a man from a considerable distance. If an old boar has previously eluded

Caribou

There are several types of caribou, and several types of caribou terrain and cover. Moreover, other types of big game may be on the trophy-wanted list during a hunting trip for caribou. All of these factors influence the choice of a rifle.

Because caribou are less resistant to shock than most big game, high-powered cartridges and heavy bullets aren't needed. On open tundra where good long-range trajectory might be important, something as light and fast as a 120-grain 6.5mm Magnum or 140-grain .264 Magnum will suffice. For woodland caribou, one of the cartridges I recommended for Eastern whitetail deer will suffice.

But your caribou rifle may well be your sheep, bear, or moose rifle. Personally, I consider the .30-06 the best all-around bet. Other good selections for caribou and additional big game include the .270, .284, 7mm Magnum, any of the .300 Magnums, and the .338.

If I were to take a handgun north for caribou and other big game, I'd make it a .44 Magnum. A .357 would do just as well for caribou, but I'd have moose or bear in mind and would be more confident with the bigger Magnum. With recoil also in mind, I'd probably leave it unscoped and reserve it for reasonably close shots, using my scoped rifle for longer range.

In Eastern woodland-caribou (and moose) country, I'd use a 2½X or 4X rifle scope, and my sighting-in distance would be 100 yards; for barren-ground hunting, I'd use a 4X rifle scope, zeroed at 200 yards.

Wild as they are, American caribou belong to the same species as European and Asian reindeer. The dozen or so subspecies found in Canada, Greenland, the Arctic islands, and Alaska are grouped into three primary types: barren-ground caribou, mountain caribou, and

The late Jack Keller (left), an ardent Northwestern hunter, poses with his guide and a good barren-ground caribou. This bull's antlers, still in velvet but fully developed and hardened, show the lack of symmetry that's characteristic of the species.

woodland caribou. The three types differ somewhat in antler characteristics and size. Because crossbreeding is common where the ranges overlap, the Boone and Crockett Club's record books have established a fourth trophy classification—the Quebec-Labrador caribou—which is intermediate between barren-ground types found to the north and west of that region and woodland types found to the south and east.

Regardless of type, the scoring of antlers depends on beam length, spread, and circumference; brow-tine length; palmation; symmetry (though caribou antlers are never very symmetrical); and total number of tines (which is extremely variable). To qualify for the record book, a woodland caribou must score at least 295 points on a Boone and Crockett scoring chart; 375 is minimum for a Quebec-Labrador caribou, 390 for a mountain caribou, and 400 for a barren-ground caribou.

Through evolution, antlers become adapted to a given kind of cover. Enormously wide antlers would become entangled in bushy woodland cover, so a woodland caribou's antlers have less sideward sweep than those of barren-ground caribou. Spread is a relative concept, however; a woodland trophy can be magnificent, requiring a very large, bare wall to accommodate its main beams, which sometimes measure more than four feet around their primary curve.

Caribou cows are the only female deer that normally have antlers. Fortunately, their relatively short, spindly antlers can't be confused with a bull's enormous crown, so it's easy to distinguish the sexes. In some regions at some times, cows can be and are killed for meat, but ordinarily a hunter is searching for a trophy bull.

Among most varieties of caribou, the antlers are far more impressive than the body size. Barren-ground, woodland, and Quebec-Labrador caribou range in weight from about 150 pounds (for some cows) to 400 pounds (for some bulls). However, a bull mountain caribou of the Osborn strain, found in upper British Columbia, may weigh over 600 pounds; in other words, it may be as big as a bull elk.

Barren-ground caribou are occupants of the tundra and taiga, from upper Labrador across northern Canada and most of Alaska. Mountain caribou are found chiefly in British Columbia. Quebec-Labrador caribou are found where indicated by the name. Woodland caribou are fairly abundant in Newfoundland, parts of Labrador, Saskatchewan, and northern Alberta; there are also some in British Columbia, a few in Manitoba, and a very few in Nova Scotia and New Brunswick.

Barren-ground caribou are Alaska's most plentiful big game, and will probably continue to be if the herds aren't devastated by oil pipelines and other mineral exploitation or by the land-grabbing maneuvers of several special-interest groups. Barren-ground caribou are also fairly plentiful in the Yukon and the Northwest Territories. The best hunting for trophies of this variety is on the Alaska Peninsula and in the area between Mount McKinley and the Yukon. The best region for big mountain caribou is northwestern British Columbia. Best for Quebec-Labrador caribou is the Ungava region of Quebec. And best for trophies of the woodland type is the island of Newfoundland.

At present, Alaska's caribou season lasts from early August through March (regulations differ in some parts of the state). In the Canadian provinces and territories, the open seasons vary, but they generally begin in late summer or early fall and last into midfall. To ensure the future of barren-ground caribou, the Alaska season should be shortened. Moreover, the bulls shed their antlers in December or January, so a winter or spring hunt is for meat only.

Until late September, the bulls in many regions across the continent are still in velvet, but their antlers are fully developed and hardened, and the animals are in prime condition. Over much of the range, rutting peaks and ends in October, and by the end of the rut, the bulls are gaunt. Early autumn is therefore the best time to hunt caribou. Several other kinds of game can be taken on the same September trip, and the fishing is also excellent.

Because antler formation is so variable among caribou and because some of the important characteristics aren't sharply visible at a distance, caribou trophies are hard to judge. Several good bulls are often seen together, and comparisons can be made, but a lone bull is tougher to evaluate.

The hunter or guide first assesses the general appearance—looking for plenty of sweep and massiveness. Although some excellent racks are long but low, most trophy antlers have a height equal to about two-thirds of the bull's shoulder height, occasionally more. Good main beams extend back a substantial distance, sometimes over the shoulder, then curve up and forward in a rather pronounced bow. The spread is considerably wider than the bull's body unless the animal is a woodland caribou. Near the top of the main beams there's usually but not always some palmation, and the palms or ends branch into several tines (or sometimes many). Just above the animal's head you should be able to see a brow beam. Usually two brow beams extend over the muzzle, but you may discern only one because in most instances only one is sizable—and vertically palmated. This vertical palm is called a shovel. On the very best heads, both brow beams may be palmated. When you can make out a "double shovel," you can almost always be sure you're looking at an outstanding trophy.

Jutting forward from the main beams a little above the brow beams are two fairly long beams that look rather like an extension of the main growth. These secondary beams, called the bez formation, are usually palmated and multitined. About halfway up on each of the main beams there's often one more, fairly small tine, extending to the rear.

To see all these antler characteristics, you should have a binocular—8X35 would be my choice—and a 20X spotting scope is also needed.

Even with your optical equipment, you may not be able to make out the important antler details if you spot a very distant caribou. Color may then help determine whether the animal is worth a long stalk. A caribou is mostly tan or grayish-tan, with some darker areas on the legs and about the face and with a good deal of white on the neck, chest, underside, rump, ankles, and sometimes even on the back. The hair on the underside of the neck usually grows long enough to form a mane. As a bull matures, his neck grows progressively whiter, and the white spreads. On some prime bulls, it extends all the way back over the shoulders. A distant bull that shows plenty of white is worth stalking, although it's a gamble. For one thing, the bull may be gone before the stalk can be completed. For another, a magnificently white-maned bull may be in his prime—four or five years old—or past it. If he's old, this year's antler growth may be disappointing.

Many hunters consider caribou stupid. Perhaps they are, or perhaps evolution just hasn't programmed them to react to human intrusion as most big-game species do. Spooked by sound or scent, a caribou may run far enough to be safe, or it may retreat only a couple of hundred yards and then stop to look at what startled it. The animal may even come trotting back most of the way to investigate.

For a species that evolved in fairly open terrain, the caribou has surprisingly weak eyesight. Caribou bulls, like elk, boss harems of cows, and hunters have now and then been amused to observe a bull try to add a pack horse to his harem. Sometimes a caribou will come hesitantly closer to investigate a waved hat or handkerchief. Sometimes one will let a man come within 50 yards if he crawls slowly, for caribou habitually let wolves come that close and, if the wind doesn't betray the hunter, they can't seem to tell the difference between a crawling human and stalking wolf.

I have an acquaintance who once kept an Alaskan caribou bull entranced long enough to get a shot by walking forward with his arms raised to simulate antlers while bobbing his body from the waist like a rival bull in the rut.

The neck mane and shoulders of a mature caribou show plenty of white. When the antlers of a distant caribou can't be seen clearly enough for evaluation, a large expanse of white marks an animal worth stalking. However, it's always a gamble because a white-maned bull like this Manitoba specimen may be past his prime, with antlers no longer as impressive as those he developed in past years.

Winter food is the reason for the famous caribou migrations, which are merely shifts into the lowlands in the case of some woodland and mountain caribou but are 800-mile treks in the case of some of the huge barren-ground herds. In most regions the animals move southward in August from the tundra to the sparse edges of forest, but throughout most of their range, they continue to rely heavily on the whitish lichen called caribou moss or reindeer moss. The tundra is far from barren in the summer. This lichen sometimes grows more than two feet thick. The animals will be grazing on lichens, grasses, horsetail, and fungi, browsing on berry bushes, dwarf willow, birch, Labrador tea, and assorted other shrubs or saplings. If a hunter or guide sees no sign or animals along the migration routes that have been heavily used in past years, he looks for these kinds of vegetation.

A bit later, when frost comes, the animals are often found feeding in muskeg areas. Muskeg is always good for hunting woodland caribou. The races inhabiting more open terrain move into the forest edges at the end of summer but come out again to rut, and hunting is then good on the lower tundra and in the transitional zone, or taiga.

This is a herd of Quebec-Labrador caribou on Opiscoteo Lake in northern Quebec. Such herds migrate to find winter forage where the tundra ends and the taiga—the swampy, coniferous woodland—begins.

Early in the season there are obvious places to glass: ridges, wide saddles, and windy rises where the animals can feed in relative freedom from the clouds of flies and other insects that bother them at this time of year. Also look carefully at snow patches, where sizable bulls often seek escape from heat and insects.

Caribou are daytime feeders, grazing or browsing before the sun is far up. Late in the morning they bed randomly on gravelly ridges, hilltops, and other cool places. On warm days, check any nearby rivers or ponds in the late afternoon, and look for mountain caribou above the timber.

A caribou's hoof lobes are widely separated and the tracks are broad pairs of crescents, often five inches across—wider than they are long. Behind the crescents you may see dots left by the long dewclaws. Tracks won't necessarily lead you to waiting caribou, but fresh ones indicate the nearby presence of game.

Here's a typical caribou track on thin snow. Its width would be at least as great as its length if the long, low dewclaws had not sunk into the snow, leaving clear twin impressions behind the print of the hoof lobes.

In cold weather, a herd hidden by a rise or other terrain feature may be revealed by a much different kind of sign—vapor rising from the animals.

And sometimes caribou feet provide audible rather than visual sign. Long tendons in their ankles slide over the small bones with

A hunter and guide pose with a record-book mountain caribou. Both of this bull's brow tines, jutting over his muzzle, have developed substantial vertical palms. A bull with both brow tines palmated is a highly desirable "double-shovel" trophy.

each step they take, producing a click. Grazing animals can be heard at least 50 yards away, even if they're walking on soft ground. When they're that close, you usually see them, but once in a while they're behind brush or timber or a small hill, and when you hear them, you can easily stalk through the intervening cover.

If you spook them, they may fade back only a short distance, or they may gallop away with their antlers laid back and their high-rising legs carrying them along at 30 miles an hour. You can't overtake them, but they probably won't go very far. Note their direction of travel and the likely feeding or bedding spots in that direction; then start hiking, and you may head them off while there's still light.

Elk

A summer-fattened bull elk in the Rockies can easily weigh 700 pounds. A very large one may weigh close to 1,000. A powerful cartridge is needed for this big, shock-resistant game. You want a fairly flat-shooting cartridge, too, because shots are sometimes long. The most popular choices are probably the .30-06 and the .300 Magnums with 180-grain bullets, though you can obtain clean kills with something a little lighter or heavier.

Many hunters like a .270 or .284 with 150-grain bullets or a 7mm Magnum with 150- or 175-grain bullets. Others favor the 200-grain .338; if this seems a trifle heavy, remember that its velocity is closely comparable to that of the 175-grain 7mm Magnum at ranges all the way out to 300 yards. Personally, I like the idea of using a single versatile rifle—a rifle I'm accustomed to—for most or all big game, and I'll stay with the .30-06.

Plenty of elk have been jumped at 30 yards in timber, but they're more often killed at ranges between 150 and 300 yards. In early fall, the high, wide mountain meadows and slopes attract good bulls. For hunting at this time, I'd use a 4X scope (or a variable model set at 4X) and my sighting-in distance would be 200 yards. Later in the season, when elk come down into thicker cover, I'd just as soon have a 2½X scope on my rifle, zeroed at 100 or 150 yards.

Much as I like a .357 Magnum revolver for whitetails and mule deer, I think that anyone who can handle heavy recoil is best served by a .44 Magnum for bigger game, including elk. For some shooters, the .41 Magnum is a good compromise. I'm not a long-range hand-gunner (very few people are), and because of the .44's kick, I wouldn't scope it. However, if you're good enough with a pistol, you might consider scoping a big-bore sidearm.

You might also consider using one of the single-shot pistols, specially chambered for any of the very powerful wildcat (nonstandard) loads that are employed in long-range metallic-game-silhouette competitions. For such matches, these guns are often mounted with aperture sights of the type used on target rifles, and I think an aperture-sighted pistol might prove to be an efficient tool for long, careful shots at big game in fairly open terrain.

Elk once inhabited most of North America. Much of their grazing land was turned into farms, towns, and pasturage for cattle. Great numbers of elk were killed by market shooters, by ranchers who wanted every blade of grass for their livestock, and by farmers who wanted to stop damage to fences, crops, and winter haystacks.

Today, the several remaining races of elk chiefly inhabit the Rocky Mountain states, Canada's four westernmost provinces, and Washington and Oregon. A fully protected remnant population of a small subspecies called tule elk resides in central California.

The largest race, both in numbers and individual size, is the Rocky Mountain elk. In addition to its primary ancestral range, this subspecies is found in remnants or transplanted herds in widely scattered states, including some Eastern ones where the animals are protected. Descendants of transplanted Rocky Mountain elk are hunted in Oklahoma, Nevada, eastern Washington and Oregon, and South Dakota's Black Hills and Custer State Park (where a special annual hunt thins the herd to that particular habitat's carrying capacity).

A darker, often larger, but smaller-antlered variety called the Roosevelt, or Olympic, elk inhabits the Olympic Mountains of Washington and the Cascade Mountains and coastal forests from Vancouver down through Oregon. In Washington and Oregon, Roosevelt and Rocky Mountain elk inhabit quite separate areas, and Oregon sets separate seasons for them. Roosevelt elk can also be hunted in Alaska, which is farther north than the original range of any subspecies. A herd was established on Afognak Island (off the Alaska Peninsula, just above Kodiak) in the 1920's.

The herds in the Prairie Provinces represent one more race, the Manitoba elk. Like the Roosevelt elk, it's darker and smaller-antlered than the Rocky Mountain type. Evidently elk are rather quick to evolve adaptations to different kinds of environment. On a timbered, mountainous Vermont preserve where the forage isn't quite the same as in the West, I've seen elk descended from Rocky Mountain transplants; they resembled tule elk or mule deer in body and antler size.

The best hunting and the biggest trophies are found in Washington, Wyoming, Colorado, and Montana. However, Washington currently has a short season and tends to discourage nonresident hunters. For that matter, the Rocky Mountain states have begun to discourage outsiders by raising nonresident-license fees. A big-game hunt has become a costly enterprise in terms of equipment, transportation, licenses, and guide-outfitter fees. In planning a hunt, you may want to write to game departments and guide-outfitter associations in several states to learn all you can about mixed-bag possibilities and combination licenses.

In most regions, the elk season opens in September, and its duration depends on the game census. In some of the better elk states, the season may last two or three months, while in other states, it may last two weeks or less. Several states have early archery seasons, and at least two, Colorado and Idaho, also have special muzzleloader seasons. As a rule, the most northerly regions open the seasons earliest. This doesn't impede trophy hunting. Regally antlered bulls can be taken in September or even late August; by then, the antlers are fully developed, hardened, and, in most regions, losing their velvet if it isn't already shed. Though most non-residents hope for trophies, either sex is legal in many areas.

By the time a bull is in his fourth autumn, his antlers have their normal mature complement of six long tines (in rare instances seven) on each side. A six-pointer is called a royal bull, a rare seven-pointer is called an imperial. Since almost all trophies have six tines on each main beam, it isn't so much the number that distinguishes a splendid trophy as the length and spread of the rack and the girth of the beams. Assuming that a bull's habitat supplies adequate nutrition and minerals, each year's antlers grow bigger until he's six to eight years old. (This is true of moose, too.) His subsequent antlers will rarely grow bigger and may well diminish.

To a hunter unfamiliar with elk, the first rack seen usually looks gigantic, its rearward sweep incredible. The guide's judgment is extremely important in such matters, but the hunter himself should know what to look for. When a bull lowers his head to graze, evaluation may be easier because the antlers tip up somewhat. Their length should appear almost as great as the animal's total height. When the rack is held more or less horizontally, its length should look about as great as the distance from brisket to ham. Sometimes a good rack doesn't seem especially high when viewed from front or rear, but it will be considerably wider than the animal's body and, even from a distance, should have a massive look.

The American elk is closely related to Europe's red deer and Asia's maral, yet early settlers evidently confused it with the European moose, which was called elk. Wapiti, the more precise name for American elk, is a Shawnee word for white deer. A typical Rocky Mountain elk is brown on the head and neck and along the spine; its legs are almost black, and the thick fur on the underside of the neck is often very dark. But there's a light rump patch, and the animal's sides and flanks are pale, sometimes very pale. There's far more resemblance to a white deer than to a moose. An average Wyoming elk is about the size of a trail horse, and pale enough so that it's easy to understand why guides don't like to bring palominos into the mountains during hunting season. The rump patch and the pale slabs of the sides stand out clearly against a dark background, so watch for pale shapes when glassing the landscape.

Most elk herds, like mule deer, move to lower elevations as winter comes on. In some localities, the animals migrate up to 60 miles, but most herds don't travel far, and where the climate is mild—as in the home range of Roosevelt elk—the shift is very slight. In most parts of the Rockies, early-season hunting is best on the high meadows and mountain "parks" (high, relatively level pastures rimmed by forest and/or higher slopes). Later in the season, the hunting improves in the timber down below.

The methods of hunting change as the animals drift down. Let's discuss high-country, early-season hunting first. Until snow forces a change in their habits, elk are primarily grazers. In the Rockies, the rut peaks in late September, making that month a good time to hunt.

This bull elk, photographed in Utah, is grazing in a typical "park"—a level mountain pasture hemmed by timber. During the early part of the season, hunters should carefully glass all high meadows, as elk prefer to graze in such places until snow forces them to seek browse at lower elevations.

Just before and during the breeding period, good bulls are frequently out on the open pastures, eating grasses and the grasslike sedges. They may be alone or with cows. Typical early-season hunting consists of riding high plateaus (occasionally going on foot where a horse can't climb) and stopping to glass open vistas. The same type of binocular I recommended for caribou hunting is needed here, and a 20X spotting scope is also very helpful, although field glasses may be useless later on, when elk are hunted in thick woods.

In addition to scouting, one other method is often productive early in the season—and only then. This is "whistling," or bugling, for elk. At first the mature bulls travel alone or in small groups, while the cows, calves, and juveniles move and feed in somewhat larger herds. A bull doesn't actually gather a harem; rather, he takes command of an existing herd, keeping the cows together while driving yearlings and older males away. Even before the bulls disperse to seek cows, they begin to bugle, and their calls become louder and more frequent as rutting peaks.

Herd bulls bugle and so do unattached bulls. In fact, the bachelors sometimes seem to call more often. Hunters speak of "challenging," but the unique sound is often uttered by a bull when no other bulls are in the vicinity. Some naturalists have speculated that bugling functions merely as a tension-reliever. It may not be a challenge, but it's accepted as such by any bulls that hear it, a fact that helps the hunter.

The bugling sometimes reveals an animal's location, and this in itself is an obvious help. In addition, a hunter or guide can do his own whistling to elicit an answer. Hearing the call, a bull sometimes gives away his location by answering. And sometimes he not only answers but approaches the sound, spoiling for a fight.

Cows bugle, but mostly in the springtime and not as loudly as bulls. Any response to your bugling comes from a bull. You'll hear a loud, shrill whistle—almost a scream. Actually, the animal's call begins with a short bellow and ends with grunts, but only the whistling carries a substantial distance.

The hunter blows into an elk whistle—a tube that may be made of brass piping, rubber, plastic, or some other material—while cupping his hands over the end of the instrument to control tone and volume. It should be done sparingly. Beginners tend to whistle too much and at too low a pitch. Alien noises spook elk, so it's unwise to whistle for them unless you've been coached by an experienced whistler or have heard elk scream and have practiced before the hunt. In most cases, any bugling should be left to the guide. It works best early in the morning and late in the afternoon, and it should be done from a high point where the hunter can see an elk approaching from any direction.

When hunting the high country, you'll do a lot of glassing from promontories and ridges. As you approach a crest, take care not to skyline yourself or you may spook animals on the far side. This kind of scouting is tiring, and sometimes a rest stop can be put to good use, particularly if you've seen sign or the elk themselves in the area. You may find a trophy just by sitting on a lookout above a park, grassy slope, trail, or natural crossing.

Sometimes scouting can also be combined with still-hunting, but because elk have extraordinary hearing and scenting ability, you must first climb high and then hunt quietly downward through the rising thermal currents.

In a few regions, elk drives are conducted, either on foot or with horses. A good place for a drive is a wooded canyon or small, steep valley. The drivers push downwind through the woods, as if driving deer. The elk, hearing or scenting them, will move out ahead or to the sides. The standers take positions overlooking openings or crossings where the elk are likely to emerge.

An elk's cloven hooves leave tracks that are smaller and rounder than those of a moose, but much bigger and rounder than those of a deer. Early in the season, the droppings in the high pastures are often chips, rather like cow dung. Later, when the animals drift down and switch from grazing to browsing, the droppings look like oversized deer pellets, sometimes more than an inch long. Another kind of sign is a mangled shrub or sapling; rutting bull elk, like the smaller deer species, attack saplings and bushes as if conditioning themselves for battle with rival males. Still more promising is a wallow. Mature rutting bulls scrape out muddy wallows, then urinate and defecate copiously in the depressions. Sometimes you can smell a wallow before you see it. Sometimes, in fact, you can smell a rutting bull before you see him if he's close but hidden in cover.

Roosevelt elk leave yet another kind of sign. They gnaw away strips of tree bark and rub the raw wood with their lacyrmal glands.

This very fine bull elk is watering in a Montana stream. Behind him can be seen a grazing meadow. Good foraging areas with convenient watering places should be carefully scouted.

The purpose of these scent posts is uncertain. Whatever purpose they serve, fresh strippings mean that elk are probably nearby.

Elk like to graze early in the morning and late in the afternoon. Check the sunny slopes and meadows near timber. Throughout the rest of the day they may be bedded or feeding sporadically. They like to bed high on slopes where they have a wide view and can test the

Elk tamped this clear trail through the grasses of a high Wyoming meadow. The profuse droppings shown here are typical of elk scat found early in the season, when the animals have been grazing rather than browsing.

rising thermals, and they especially like clear spots of ground next to boulders, logs, stumps, or trees. If the weather is very warm, you may also find them bedded on river bars, and if it's windy you may find them in thickets, wooded ravines, or on lee slopes. They're most active in open meadows on cool, humid, or drizzly days.

In early or mid-October, when the rut has subsided, the bulls often drop down into such dense woods that hunting is extremely difficult because you can't see for any substantial distance and your every movement can be heard. Toward the end of that month in some regions, later in others, the animals move down still farther and begin to disperse over somewhat more openly wooded slopes. The hunter's chances then improve again. He can work through any woods that offer good browse—mountain mahogany, mountain maple, aspen, willow, sage, fir, pine, bog birch, berry bushes— whatever is reachable and edible. In the coastal rain forests, Roosevelt elk are heavy browsers during most or all of the season;

Howard Copenhaver (left), a Montana guide-outfitter, congratulates an elated client who has just taken a magnificent elk trophy. Bugling helped in locating and stalking the animal. A bull like this, with six fully developed tines on each beam, is known as a royal elk.

they feed on willow, alder, mountain ash, berry bushes, assorted conifers, devil's club, ferns, maple, and vine maple. Like caribou, they eat mosses and lichens. They even gnaw decaying logs.

One good thing about late-season elk hunting is that the snow facilitates tracking. If cows are legal where you're hunting, any and all sign may interest you. But if you want a bull, don't assume that large hoof prints are always made by males. A mature cow can leave impressive tracks. However, cows seldom travel alone, so a single set of tracks usually means you're on the trail of a bull.

Elk meander along in wide loops, occasionally turning to look back. They also watch their back trails when they bed. You don't want to give yourself away by staying right on the animal's trail. It's better to parallel the trail or make a wide circle to get above a browsing or bedded bull.

You may lose his trail when you move off, but on snow you should be able to find it again. Go slowly and keep watching and listening. You can make educated guesses about where an animal is heading, but you never know when you may overtake him. If you're careless, he'll detect you before you detect him. Light through the trees or a thinning of the cover usually tells you when you're coming to a clearing. Approach it slowly and stop before you get there. Then sneak up, looking across and around it before you step out. The bull you want may be poised at the far side, watching.

Moose

The moose is the world's largest species of deer. A bull of North America's smallest subspecies may weigh as much as 1,200 pounds, and a bull of the largest race may weigh almost 1,800. Strangely, for animals of such immense size, they're not hard to kill with a properly placed bullet. Consider the fact that where short-range hunting is possible, moose are sometimes killed with broadhead arrows; Quebec has a brief archery season in September.

Cartridges like the .30-30, .32, and .35 don't deliver many foot-pounds of energy, relatively speaking, yet all three have been used to fell a good many moose in Northeastern woods where the range is often short; and at somewhat longer ranges, light (130-grain) bullets in a .270 have taken trophies. While none of these calibers is ideal, power and bullet weight are less of a problem in some regions than variability of range.

I know an experienced big-game hunter who went to Ontario for moose twice in the 1960's and used a canoe to hunt along the Oba River. On both occasions he took two rifles—a .35 lever-action firing 200-grain bullets for short range and a 7mm Magnum bolt-action in which he used 175-grain loads for longer shots. On the first trip, he drifted around a woody point, came almost face to face with a moose feeding on lilies, and killed it with the .35. On the next trip he and his guide beached the canoe at a bend where the streamside cover opened up, and there, with his 7mm Magnum, he killed a moose almost 200 yards away.

In the West and Northwest, long shots are far more common than short ones, so your chosen hunting region will influence your decision about a rifle. East or West, my friend's 175-grain 7mm Magnum loads might be regarded as a sensible minimum. My own preference would be for 180-grain loads in a .30-06 or .300 Winchester Magnum. Either of these has good velocity and trajectory for a variety of ranges, plus the energy, penetration, and expansion for clean kills. But for a hunt in eastern Canada, I might follow my friend's example and bring along a lever-action as well—for use while still-hunting through thick woods or as a second rifle close at hand in a canoe.

For Eastern moose, a number of other calibers are also practical: the .338, .348, .358, .350 Magnum, and .444. In the West or Northwest, the 7mm Magnum, .30-06, or .300 Magnum would be a better choice and, as I've stressed elsewhere in this book, one of these would also serve well for other big game that might be taken on the same hunt.

Moose have occasionally been hunted with sidearms as well as rifles; for handgun recommendations, see the section on elk, as the same advice applies.

In the Rockies, western Canada, or Alaska, where most shots are made at over 200 yards, I'd put a 4X or variable-power scope on my rifle and would sight in at 200 yards. In eastern Canada I'd cut that zero distance in half and, if I brought only one rifle on a hunting trip, I'd probably settle for a 2½X or variable scope. If I brought two rifles, the one for short range would be aperture-sighted, and the one for longer shots would be equipped with the same sort of scope I'd use in the Northwest.

Europe and Asia have three subspecies of moose, and North America has four. Our smallest is the Shiras, or Wyoming, moose, sometimes also called Yellowstone moose. It seldom weighs more than 1,200 pounds or stands more than six feet high at the withers, although moose have long legs, adapted to wading. This subspecies is distributed through Wyoming, Montana, Utah, Idaho, and southeastern British Columbia.

Two races, the Northwestern moose and the Eastern, or Canada, moose, are so much alike that the Boone and Crockett record books make no distinction between them. A mature bull of either subspecies weighs between 1,000 and 1,400 pounds; a good one may have a five-foot antler spread. The Eastern variety is found from Newfoundland and Nova Scotia through the Maritimes into Ontario. The Northwestern moose ranges from western Ontario to

A moose of the Eastern, or Canada, subspecies leaves the shallows of Fox Lake in Ontario. A hunter would be well advised to hold his fire until this splendid bull is close to shore. A moose is too big to be dragged out of a lake, and the chore of dressing and quartering one in the water is difficult and uncomfortable.

British Columbia and up through the Northwest Territories and the eastern part of the Yukon.

The Alaskan, or Alaska-Yukon, moose is the largest. A bull may weigh almost 1,800 pounds; he may be 7½ feet high at the shoulders, with antler tips almost 10 feet above his hooves. Those antlers can weigh over 85 pounds, and many of the record-book trophies have a spread of more than six feet. This subspecies ranges through most of Alaska, the Yukon, and adjacent portions of British Columbia and the Northwest Territories.

In outlining moose distribution, I've mentioned only regions where the animals are abundant, not the bordering regions where they're present but scarce. Moose have never been as plentiful as the smaller deer species, and of course some of their habitat has been taken from them. Yet the range of the species still covers most of the North Country and has receded very little in historic times. In the lower Rockies the range has actually expanded, and moose have also become exceptionally well established in Newfoundland, where they were introduced from the mainland in 1904. Because of remote habitat and the expense of a long hunting trip, the annual moose harvest is fairly light.

At present, moose thrive and are hunted in both of the Canadian territories and all provinces except Nova Scotia and Prince Edward Island. They're also hunted in six states—Alaska, Idaho, Minnesota, Montana, Utah, and Wyoming. However, Minnesota hunting is for residents only and is severely limited. The best moose hunting is in southern Alaska (particularly on the peninsulas), the Yukon, the Mackenzie District of the Northwest Territories, northern Ontario, and western Quebec. It's also very good in Newfoundland, upper Alberta, western Wyoming, and eastern Idaho.

In any of those areas your chance of shooting a moose is good, but the most enormous antlers are likely to be found on the Kenai Peninsula and the Rainy Pass area in Alaska, and in the central part of the Yukon.

Alaska's season now opens at the beginning of September and lasts to the end of the year. In the Northwest Territories it opens in mid-July and in the Yukon at the beginning of August. Elsewhere it generally begins in September. Where the population is relatively low, it may last only until the end of the month, but in the best hunting regions, it lasts into late fall or winter. By mid-August a bull's antlers are hardening, and the best hunting months in most regions are September and October. I like early September. The rut has begun, and that helps. Rutting is at its height near the end of that month, but by then the flesh of the big bulls may have become rank and tough.

Permit systems prevent overhunting if a moose population declines, but the opposite situation—too many moose for the habitat—is more common in some regions. As with elk, overcrowding is alleviated by allowing the hunting of either sex. A hunter who makes a long trip into game country usually wants a trophy. But local residents (and quite a few nonresidents who have collected trophies in past years and then return to hunt mixed game) sometimes care little about acquiring another set of antlers. While cows and young bulls have no value as trophies, they make excellent eating.

A hunter and guide smile over a moose in the Canadian Northwest. This rack will make an excellent trophy. Note that although the antlers have considerable upsweep (as many do) they also have a substantial spread. In judging a potential trophy viewed from the front or rear, try to see whether the rack is about twice as wide as the animal's body; if so, it's probably a good one.

Where cows can be hunted, pass up any that are accompanied by young. A calf stays with its mother for almost a year, and an orphaned calf seldom survives the winter.

Even in the relatively flat woods that characterize some Northeastern areas, a 7X35 binocular and 20X spotting scope are valuable for scanning slopes and evaluating distant heads. I think I'd prefer an 8X35 binocular in the Far Northwest.

Moose antlers often look smaller than they are. The animal beneath them is so enormous that his crown may seem merely adequate. A front or rear view is helpful in sizing up a trophy, because a good rack protrudes quite far; from tip to tip it's about twice as wide as the chest. Another way to judge is by comparing antler spread with the height of the legs. A bull's legs may be over 40 inches long, but a trophy rack, if upended on the ground, would extend well above the legs, about to the middle of the body. If you have a broadside view of the animal, the antlers should shade the bull's eye and a large portion of his relatively short neck.

The smaller tines growing along the edges of the antler palms will probably be impossible to count, but if the rack is large, it usually has quite enough points, and they're only one of several factors determining trophy rank. Scoring depends heavily on spread, palm length and width, girth of beams (measured between the skull and the palms), and symmetry.

Mountain hunting—that is, most Western hunting for moose—is chiefly a matter of riding from one ridge or wide, high meadow to another, dismounting to climb when necessary, and glassing the openings before moving out of concealing timber. There may be less worry about skylining yourself than in elk hunting, because moose

Photographed in the Absarokas, north of Yellowstone National Park, this is a bull of the Shiras subspecies, America's smallest race of moose. It may be small by comparison with other American moose, but a mature bull like this one may weigh up to about 1,200 pounds and may stand six feet high at the shoulder. It is grazing in high but swampy habitat where water is plentiful.

have somewhat weak eyesight, but they're quick to detect movement, and they have very keen hearing and scenting ability.

Good lookout places are rises above meadows, waters, and the fringes of browse thickets. Moose feed in the water as well as on land, and they'll often leave a lush browsing thicket just for a drink; they're most commonly found watering late in the day. Bear in mind that they don't like to abandon a spot where the living is easy. If a bull isn't rutting, he may remain for two weeks in a single big willow thicket or similar spot that combines plenty of food and cover.

When seen at a great distance (or in woodland shadow), a moose looks black rather than brown. In timber, particularly among dark conifers, the animal can be hard to make out. In Wyoming I spotted one that I would have sworn was a shadow had he not moved.

But in open Northwestern country, especially after frost has taken the leaves from many of the deciduous shrubs, you can now and then spot a moose two miles away. It looks like a black splotch against the paler background above the timberline. At that distance, you may not be able to appraise a trophy with a 20X spotting scope, so the guide and you must decide whether to gamble on a long, arduous approach. If you decide to go ahead, line up the moose's position with a couple of landmarks. Some patches of terrain look much alike, and it's disheartening to make a long approach only to realize that you're no longer sure where you last saw the object of your efforts.

After the initial approach to a distant moose, you stalk it like an elk, from above when possible, and with much attention to the direction of the wind.

The shoulder of a big-game animal is an unfortunately tempting target for riflemen accustomed to game the size of whitetails. The heavy, massive shoulder blade of a moose can deflect a bullet. The surest aiming zone for a quick kill is the lung area, *behind* the shoulder.

A spooked moose can easily run as fast as smaller deer—which means at least 35 miles an hour. But moose prefer to walk or trot, and when they do run, they almost always pause to look back after going a short distance or reaching the edge of cover. In this respect, they're like several kinds of plains game. At moderate range, a good marksman can kill a trotting moose, but if the animal is running fast, your best bet is to restrain yourself—wait for the pause.

Hunting moose near Cochrane, Ontario, a guide uses a traditional birchbark horn as a megaphone. A bull moose doesn't bugle but will often come to a good imitation of the trumpeting call uttered by cow moose during the rut. The guide is kneeling amid streamside bushes, for calling works best near or on the water.

Moose hunters in all regions should pay particular attention to stands of willow, aspen, and birch—three favorite foods of the species. Very early in the season, a number of marsh and aquatic plants also strongly attract moose. The animals like to graze on horsetail, waterlily, watershield, pondweed, wild rice, and wild celery. Other foods that attract them, particularly after autumn weather forces them to do more browsing than grazing, are maple, dogwood, mountain ash, fir, balsam, poplar, alder, serviceberry, and assorted low-branched trees and bushes.

In the Northeast, the four primary hunting methods (often used in combination) are canoeing, calling, waiting on stand, and still-hunting. With any of these methods, it helps to know that moose don't move around much when there's a strong wind, but they become very active right after a cool, windy period.

A still-hunter will do well to work very slowly upwind along shorelines or moose trails. While doing so, he should carefully watch any nearby water or thickets. He should also scout any areas where he's found beds or wallows. It pays to stop frequently, listening and crouching down to look under low branches and into thickets. Watch for black splotches—exposed parts of an animal—or pale antlers.

A bed is just a depression marked by tracks and droppings. A wallow is a torn patch of ground, several inches deep, perhaps a yard wide and four feet long, where a rutting bull has horned and scuffed the earth, then muddied it with urine and wallowed in it. A cow will roll in it, too, and moose looking for mates are attracted to the odorous wallows.

Where moose have been grazing on succulent plants, their droppings are often chips and splatters. Where they've been browsing, their droppings are pellets, usually oblong and considerably larger than those of deer. Late in the season, they have to rely on woodier browse, and the pellets acquire a distinctively dry appearance, like compressed sawdust. Even without seeing tracks, you can usually guess whether you're looking at elk or moose sign. Moose droppings are larger and more copious.

Hunters in Ontario make a last-minute check of topographical maps before setting out to still-hunt for moose. Even in country that you know well, maps are an important hunting aid as well as a safeguard against getting lost.

Moose tracks are more pointed than elk tracks and bigger— usually over five inches long. The track of a prime bull may easily be 6 inches long, 4½ inches wide.

When tracking a moose, stay parallel to the trail rather than right on it. A suspicious bull, like most deer, will circle back to pick up scent or sound. If the trail begins to wind sharply, almost zigzagging, or if it leads into a dense thicket, you'd better stop, listen, watch, and then proceed very slowly, very alertly. The bull has gone in there to bed, and you may jump him.

Like most big game, moose leave clear trails. This one snakes through high grass toward thick cover. The best way to work such a trail through the woods is to move parallel to it. A moose that becomes suspicious will often circle back, listening and sniffing. You may get a shot when it circles toward you.

This bull moose is wading a pond in the interior of Alaska. He represents the largest subspecies, the Alaskan, or Alaska-Yukon, moose, which occasionally weighs nearly 1,800 pounds. The one pictured has such a big head and body that the antlers don't look very impressive, yet they're of trophy proportions. Throughout their range, all subspecies of moose wade to feed on aquatic plants, and a hunter can sometimes surprise one at the water's edge.

Beaver ponds, streams, muskeg, game trails, and the fringes of browse thickets are all good locations for taking a stand as well as for still-hunting.

Canoeing is the easiest Eastern method. It's simply a matter of silently paddling and drifting along, hoping to surprise a moose either in the water or within view through shoreline openings. At likely spots or where sign is observed at streamside, the canoe can be beached while a hunter scouts, still-hunts, or waits on stand. Quite often, calling is done from a canoe, and it's also done from stands.

The onset of the rut is the best time of the season for calling; early evening is the best time of day, and the best areas are in the lowlands, near food thickets and water.

A rutting bull wanders about, searching for a receptive cow. When he finds one, he stays with her (and with her calf if she has one) for a week or 10 days—while she remains in oestrus. Then he leaves to seek another mate. Nothing is more dangerous and unpredictable than a cow moose with a young calf in the spring, but a rutting bull is also very unpredictable. Sometimes an old, experienced bull will take cautious hours to approach a call, circling for scent or finally deciding against the whole enterprise. Sometimes a bull (most often a younger one) will crash right into view. They've charged men and locomotives—not, apparently, because they took these alien presences for cows or rival bulls, but because their aggression and frustration demanded release.

A bull moose doesn't bugle. The cow does. She emits a long, loud, trumpeting bawl. An interested bull replies by grunting, a sound that goes unheard by the hunter unless the animal is quite close. "Talking to the bulls"—calling—is done vocally, and a guide typically uses his cupped hands or a rolled birchbark horn as a kind of megaphone. If you haven't heard cows calling and then practiced your imitation, don't try it in the woods. It's much better to leave this to a guide who has spent years listening and practicing.

However, a hunter who has never seen a moose can help the guide with sound effects. If the bugling is done from a canoe or the water's edge, either of which is an excellent idea, the hunter can dip up a hatful of water and then dribble it back into the lake or stream. The sound carries surprisingly far on a calm evening. To a bull moose, it's the lovely tinkle of a cow urinating. And, for reasons better understood by moose than by me, a cow moose that's wailing and urinating is nearly irresistible to a lustful bull moose.

I would have liked to end the book with that last mystery of nature, but conscience squeezes out one more tip. A moose is too enormous to drag up a stream bank after the kill, and if you ever help an irascible guide to dress and quarter one in cold, thigh-deep water, you'll know enough next time to hold your fire until the moose heads for shore.

Index